High Courts and Economic Governance in Argentina and Brazil

High Courts and Economic Governance in Argentina and Brazil analyzes how high courts and elected leaders interact over neoliberal restructuring, one of the most significant socioeconomic transformations in recent decades. Courts face a critical choice when deciding cases concerning national economic policy, weighing rule of law concerns against economic imperatives. Elected leaders confront equally difficult dilemmas when courts issue decisions challenging their actions. Based on extensive fieldwork in Argentina and Brazil, this study identifies striking variation in interbranch interactions in the two countries. In Argentina, while the high court often defers to politicians in the economic realm, interbranch relations are punctuated by tense bouts of conflict. The Brazilian high court and elected officials, by contrast, routinely accommodate one another in their decisions about economic policy. Diana Kapiszewski argues that the two high courts' contrasting characters – political in Argentina and statesman-like in Brazil – shape their decisions on controversial cases and condition how elected leaders respond to their rulings, channeling interbranch interactions into persistent patterns.

Diana Kapiszewski is Assistant Professor in the Department of Political Science at the University of California, Irvine. Her PhD dissertation won the American Political Science Association's Edward S. Corwin Award for best dissertation in public law. Her articles have appeared in *Perspectives on Politics, PS: Political Science and Politics, Law & Society Review*, and *Law and Social Inquiry*.

High Courts and Economic Governance in Argentina and Brazil

DIANA KAPISZEWSKI
University of California, Irvine

CAMBRIDGE
UNIVERSITY PRESS

CAMBRIDGE UNIVERSITY PRESS
Cambridge, New York, Melbourne, Madrid, Cape Town,
Singapore, São Paulo, Delhi, Mexico City

Cambridge University Press
32 Avenue of the Americas, New York, NY 10013-2473, USA

www.cambridge.org
Information on this title: www.cambridge.org/9781107008281

First published 2012

Printed in the United States of America

A catalog record for this publication is available from the British Library.

Library of Congress Cataloging in Publication data
Kapiszewski, Diana.
High courts and economic governance in Argentina and Brazil / Diana Kapiszewski.
pages cm
Includes bibliographical references and index.
ISBN 978-1-107-00828-1
1. Courts of last resort – Brazil. 2. Courts of last resort – Argentina.
3. Brazil – Economic policy. 4. Argentina – Economic policy. 5. Political
questions and judicial power – Argentina. 6. Political questions and judicial
power – Brazil. I. Title.
KG501.K37 2012
343.8107′0269–dc23 2012015675

ISBN 978-1-107-00828-1 Hardback

Additional resources for this publication at www.cambridge.org/9781107008281

Contents

Web appendices at www.cambridge.org/9781107008281

Figures and Tables

FIGURES

TABLES

Acknowledgments

This research was carried out with funding from the National Science Foundation and the University of California, Berkeley, and under the auspices of the Fulbright Scholars program. The University of California, Irvine, provided funds for write-up support. I am very grateful to all of these institutions.

I owe a debt of gratitude to all of my interview respondents, and to all of the other individuals who helped me in so many ways, in Argentina and Brazil. Without their cooperation, candor, and generosity, this research would have been much more difficult, if not impossible. In particular, in Argentina, I would like to thank Drs. Alberto Bianchi, Roberto Gargarella, Luis Lozano, Roberto Luqui, Roberto Saba, and Alfonso Santiago, as well as the justices, past and present, of the Corte Suprema de Justicia de la Nación, and their clerks. In Brazil, I would especially like to thank Drs. Jader Brilhante, Flavio Dino, Eduardo Faria, Marcos Faro de Castro, Marcelo Siqueira, and Rafael Vasconcelos, as well as the justices, retired and sitting, of the Supremo Tribunal Federal, and their clerks (in particular, Drs. Rodrigo Kauffman and Vilmar Nery). All of these people, and many others, shared their knowledge and experience, and countless hours, to help me understand their Courts and their countries.

I am also extraordinarily grateful to my research assistants in each country for their exceptional hard work and dedication. Without their persistence, the newspaper archive associated with the project would never have been created. Without their perpetual good cheer and friendship, my experience in each country would have been far less rich. In Argentina, my immense appreciation goes to Lucas Arrimada and Claudia González. In Brazil, my heartfelt gratitude goes to Antonio Augusto Ignacio Amaral, Filipe Albernaz Pires, Giovani Menicucci (who continued to help me after I returned to the United States), Régia Grazielle Santos, and Suelen Bianca de Oliveira Sales. (Special thanks as well to Menina, who adopted me in Brasília, and has kept me company ever since.)

This book grew out of my doctoral dissertation, and thus sincere thanks are also owed to my dissertation committee, all now emeritus University of California, Berkeley, faculty: cochairs David Collier and Robert A. Kagan, and Ruth Berins Collier and Martin Shapiro. I am particularly grateful to David and Bob. David is an extraordinary person, had an extraordinary impact on my graduate career, and continues to have an extraordinary influence on my professional trajectory. I would not be where I am today without his guidance and advocacy. And there is no better dissertation advisor in the world than Bob. Bob knew just when to challenge me and just when to gently suggest that what I had produced was good enough, and he never stopped supporting and encouraging me. His intellectual guidance, kindness, and optimism were crucial to my academic development, and to the dissertation. If I am even one-quarter as effective at advising my own graduate students as David and Bob were when advising me, it is because of what I learned from them.

Special thanks also to the students of Latin American politics who were my compatriots as I completed my PhD in political science at the University of California, Berkeley: Chris Cardona, Ralph Espach, Tasha Fairfield, Maiah Jaskoski, Sally Roever, and Wendy Sinek. And very special thanks to Carla Yumatle for her sage guidance, warm encouragement, and enduring friendship.

I am also extremely grateful to the community of scholars of comparative judicial politics. These individuals – who actually do form a community – were enormously encouraging and welcoming when I first began to make my way into this field, engaging in long conversations about possible dissertation topics, sharing contacts, and orienting my thoughts and work. Many have become good friends. Very special thanks to Dan Brinks, Rebecca Bill Chavez, Jodi Finkel, Gretchen Helmke, Lisa Hilbink, Alexandra Huneeus, Druscilla Scribner, Jeff Staton, and most especially to my MAS partner Matt Taylor. I would also like to thank the two anonymous Cambridge University Press readers who reviewed the first version of the manuscript, and especially the reader who reviewed the manuscript for a second time. Their insights and guidance made this book much stronger, and I could not be more thankful for the time they spent making my work better. I also thank Eric Crahan at Cambridge for his attentiveness, perpetually prompt help, and patience.

Thanks to the good fortune of joining the political science department at the University of California, Irvine, I also owe thanks to the faculty there who have been professionally and personally supportive. I am also indebted to my graduate students, who are a constant source of inspiration, ideas, and positive energy (and who waited longer than they should have for feedback on their work while I completed revisions to this book). In particular, Katja Newman did an absolutely outstanding job compiling the book's index – remaining good-natured throughout what was an undeniably tedious process. I am immensely thankful for her assistance.

Finally, I am deeply grateful for the support of my family. Huge thanks go to my parents, Bill and Connie Brown, for their multifaceted and never-ending support and encouragement, for teaching me – by showing me – the value of hard work and tenacity, and for never ceasing to believe that their daughter can do absolutely anything. Thanks as well go to my father-in-law Andrzej Kapiszewski, who lost a battle with cancer as I finished the dissertation on which this book is based, but whose intellectual spirit remains alive on its pages, and to my mother-in-law Maria Kapiszewska, whose grace and strength are an inspiration both personally and professionally. And most of all, I extend my unending gratitude and love to my husband Kapi, without whose support, patience, and kindness I could never have done so very many things, including completing this book.

1

High Court–Elected Branch Interactions in Latin America

"Don't fool yourselves, thinking you can go to the bank and get your money."[1]
– Reaction of Argentine President Eduardo Duhalde to a Supreme Court decision in 2002 declaring unconstitutional a freeze on bank deposits

"Supreme Court decisions are not discussed, they are obeyed."[2]
– Common refrain of Brazilian presidents coined by Ulysses Guimarães

1.1. INTRODUCTION

High court justices across Latin America serve as the final arbiters of controversies crucial to society and the state. They do so in volatile contexts marked by resurgent popular participation, domineering executives, and recurrent economic crisis. Justices thus routinely face complex trade-offs between sanctioning short-term policy fixes and encouraging constitutional entrenchment, between satisfying popular and political pressures and building a commitment to the rule of law, between ensuring their survival on the bench and constructing judicial power. When high courts issue rulings that place them in conflict with elected leaders, those leaders face their own difficult choices: Should they continue to pursue important but constitutionally questionable policies, or comply with high court dictates even at the risk of political or economic turmoil? This book describes and explains the different ways in which Latin American high courts and elected authorities approach these decisions, and explores the implications of their interactions for democratic governance, the role of courts, and the rule of law.

Consider the quandary faced by Brazil's high court, the Supreme Federal Tribunal (*Supremo Tribunal Federal*, STF) in April 1990. The Court had before it a case concerning the constitutionality of a presidential decree freezing bank

[1] Original quote: "*No se dejen engañar, suponiendo que podrán ir a los bancos a buscar su dinero,*" *La Nación*, February 2, 2002, "Declaran inconstitucional el corralito."

[2] Original quote: "*Decisão do STF não se discute, cumpre-se.*"

accounts, part of a broad structural reform program introduced to address devastating hyperinflation.[3] President Fernando Collor de Mello had issued the decree just weeks after his inauguration as the first directly elected president after a 20-year period of authoritarian rule. Brought to power with a mandate to defeat inflation, Collor remained quite popular despite the bank freeze, boasting a public approval rating of over 70 percent when the high court received the case.

The STF confronted a critical choice. The legal merits of the case recommended declaring the policy unconstitutional as it blatantly violated property rights. Yet doing so would place the high court in the unenviable position of defying a very popular transitional president, and leave it vulnerable to accusations of being overly legalistic and impeding economic recovery. Moreover, President Collor might draw on his broad political support to simply ignore such a challenge. Alternatively, the STF could uphold the policy. Doing so could facilitate the success of the new economic program and could even bolster democracy, given the corrosive effects of crisis on political stability. Endorsing the policy would also obviate the need for compliance, mitigating the justices' concern that elected leaders might disregard their ruling. Yet sanctioning a seemingly unconstitutional exercise of government power would open the high court to criticism that it lacked independence and was undermining the rule of law. The STF weighed these factors for more than a year, and ultimately decided not to decide, dismissing the case on a technicality. Yet to the frustration of elected leaders, the high court emphasized that its decision in no way prevented *lower courts* from ruling the bank freeze unconstitutional. The STF's ruling thus sidestepped direct interbranch conflict but encouraged battles at the trial-court level.

High courts are not the only institution that must make challenging decisions when politics are judicialized. When Courts issue rulings to limit the exercise of government power in high-salience cases, elected leaders face their own quandary. Consider the situation in Argentina just over a decade later. In December 2001, in an effort to address dramatic economic crisis, President Fernando De la Rúa also declared a freeze on bank accounts. De la Rúa fled office shortly thereafter, and the presidency subsequently changed hands four times in less than two weeks. Under the second interim leader, Argentina defaulted on most of its US$ 141 billion debt. Yet on the first day of the judicial term in February 2002, amidst the continuing turmoil, the Supreme Court (*Corte Suprema de Justicia de la Nación*, CSJN) emphatically declared the bank freeze unconstitutional.

In deciding how to respond to the high court's ruling, President Duhalde (appointed by the Argentine Congress in early January 2002) faced a difficult dilemma. On the one hand, defying the ruling was a tempting option. Given growing animosity between the CSJN and the executive, abiding by the

[3] Inflation had reached an annualized rate of 6,821 percent by 1990 (Reinhart and Savastano 2003: 21).

decision could be seen as an embarrassing "defeat" at the hands of the high court. Also, the high court was at the time extremely unpopular, reducing the political cost of defying it. And lifting the freeze could ignite a massive run on the banks (precisely the outcome the policy had sought to prevent), resulting in economic panic that could exacerbate political instability. On the other hand, Duhalde faced strong incentives to comply with the CSJN's ruling and lift the freeze. Ignoring the decision would represent a significant affront to the rule of law and would be viewed as such by the international community and some Argentines. Disregarding the decision would also antagonize the high court, perhaps encouraging it to invalidate the policy in the thousands of identical cases that were rising through the judiciary – and to rule against the government on other crucial cases in the future. In the end, Duhalde made a choice that aggravated simmering interbranch tensions: He called on congress to accelerate impeachment hearings against every justice on the high court, and largely ignored its ruling.

These examples are hardly anomalous. Latin America's high courts and elected officials have repeatedly confronted choices similar to these as the region's courts have been called to the center of the political stage more often in the postauthoritarian period. The way in which the elected and judicial branches interact as they address such dilemmas has critical implications for Latin America's political and legal development. How they do so thus raises questions of empirical interest and normative concern. First, how have Latin American high courts and elected leaders interacted over politically crucial cases over the last twenty-five years – have those interactions tended to be collaborative and cooperative, conflictual and confrontational, or a mix of both? Second, if the nature of those interactions has differed across countries, what explains that variation?

Drawing on both rational choice and historical institutionalism, this book advances the Court character thesis to account for the tenor of interbranch relations.[4] I argue that a high court's character shapes the way it decides cases of crucial political significance and conditions the way elected leaders respond to its rulings, channeling their interactions into relatively enduring patterns. The informal institutional features that compose a Court's character can contribute to producing lasting patterns of interaction because they are comparatively stable themselves, with roots in the politics of Court crafting that political authorities have traditionally employed, public opinion, and the high court's internal culture. Of course, contextual political factors – elected leaders' attacks on the judiciary, economic crisis, political divisions, and many other dynamics – also influence how elected leaders and high courts interact. But the *way* such factors affect interbranch interactions is mediated by the character of the high court. In short, the study highlights the historical and institutional foundations of interbranch relations.

[4] The terms "high court" and "Court" (with a capital "C") are used interchangeably.

To illustrate the Court character thesis, the book examines high court–elected branch struggles over economic policy in Argentina and Brazil during the two decades following regime transition. Focusing on a single policy realm over time represents a departure from other studies of high court politics and interbranch relations in Latin America, yet doing so has significant substantive and methodological advantages. Most Latin American polities transitioned to democracy in economic disarray, and the economic policy arena was a crucial – and controversial – one for society and the state following regime change. Facing substantial international and domestic pressure for reform, elected leaders sought to adopt a more neoliberal, open-market economic model. In many countries, some elements of economic reform programs and the process that elected leaders employed to legislate and implement them seemed to violate the constitution. In these newly democratic contexts, citizens, civil society, and the political opposition were quite sensitive to elected officials' disregard for legal and constitutional constraints on their power, and they increasingly turned to the region's newly empowered courts to challenge economic policies, producing a judicialization of economic governance.[5] Indeed, although Latin American judiciaries became involved in a diverse range of politically important conflicts after regime transition, in many countries it was their involvement in economic policy making – their decisions on cases concerning privatizations, salaries, pensions, and the like – that drew them definitively into politics and the popular consciousness.

Further, high courts and elected leaders cannot be assumed to interact in the same way across policy arenas or areas of law: High courts are selectively assertive vis-à-vis national political authorities, and compliance with judicial rulings, at least in less-institutionalized settings such as those of many Latin American countries, likely exhibits similar variation.[6] Evaluating patterns of interbranch interaction in a particular issue area removes "policy arena" as a potential cause of cross-case and cross-national variation in those interactions, facilitating assessment of the effect of institutions. In addition, cases concerning economic policy were decided throughout most of the period under study in both Argentina and Brazil, and the two countries' Courts heard cases concerning very similar types of economic policies. Finally, while economic reform and policy making are often viewed as developed and managed exclusively by government technocrats and international financial institutions, showcasing the interbranch struggles that can ensue when constitutions and economic policy appear to be at odds reveals the roles that high courts have played in neoliberal restructuring – arguably the most significant socioeconomic transformation Latin American countries have undergone in recent decades.

[5] Economic governance refers to efforts to manage the economy, control economic crisis, and encourage economic growth and development.

[6] High courts probably also interact differently with different powerful actors, recommending that interactions between high courts and particular types of political actors also be studied separately.

Argentina and Brazil, two of the region's largest democracies, are good cases in which to compare and contrast interbranch interactions over economic governance for several reasons. Their contextual and institutional similarities mean that a range of factors that might affect those interactions are held constant, helping me to evaluate the effect of the dynamics and variables of theoretical interest. Both countries transitioned to democracy at approximately the same moment (and have been democracies since),[7] and both have been governed by dominant presidents. Leaders in both countries sought to carry out programs of economic stabilization and neoliberal reform that raised significant constitutional questions. Further, the two countries' high courts are similar on a range of institutional dimensions. In both contexts, the high court sits atop a federally structured judicial system, and both high courts experienced empowering reform during the period of interest. Justices are appointed using similar processes and enjoy similar formal independence protections in the two countries, each high court is charged with constitutional review (although only the Brazilian Court can perform abstract review), and both stagger under huge case loads that skyrocketed during the time period under study due to the filing of hundreds of thousands of cases regarding national economic policy.[8]

Despite these similarities – and the filing of comparable court cases – strikingly different patterns of interbranch interaction over economic policy emerged in Argentina and Brazil during the first two postauthoritarian decades. I argue that the contrasting characters of the countries' high courts helped to produce that variation. In Argentina, interbranch interactions were more erratic. The CSJN, which had long been *politicized* by the country's leaders and had consequently assumed a *political* character, generally *submitted* to elected leaders when ruling on cases concerning critical economic policies. Yet the Court's political nature also contributed to generating tense bouts of interbranch *confrontation* in which the CSJN struck down major policies and elected leaders disregarded its dictates and threatened and attacked the Court. Brazilian leaders, by contrast, had long *professionalized* the STF, creating a *statesman* Court. Interbranch interactions over economic policy were correspondingly more stable and mutually *accommodating*: The high court was more centrist and evenhanded in its rulings, and elected leaders obeyed its decisions as they could and rarely attacked the Court outright.

The book contributes to the public law and comparative politics literatures by examining and accounting for patterns in judicial decision making and elected branch responses to high court rulings *in tandem*. While the study is situated squarely in the realm of theory generation (like much of the scholarship in the young comparative judicial politics research program, e.g., Ginsburg 2003; Hilbink 2007; Trochev 2008), the argument builds on and augments

[7] Argentina was led by an authoritarian regime from 1966 to 1973 and from 1976 to 1983, and Brazil was ruled by a military dictatorship from 1964 to 1985.

[8] Web Appendices 2.1 and 2.4 contain case-load statistics for the two high courts. Web appendices at www.cambridge.org/9781107008281.

extant strategic theories of interbranch relations as well as historical institutional accounts of judicial dynamics.

The book is based on 20 months of field research in Argentina and Brazil (2004–5). Data collection entailed conducting more than 250 interviews in Spanish and Portuguese with former and current high court justices, high court clerks, economists, constitutional scholars, law professors, political scientists, government personnel, civil society organizations, and journalists. With the assistance of a team of research assistants in each country, I also created a searchable electronic archive containing more than 14,000 newspaper articles about the Argentine and Brazilian Courts and their most important decisions, and collected many primary documents concerning the Courts and cases under study.

In the remainder of this chapter, I propose an integrated analytic framework for studying patterns of interbranch interaction, and discuss each element of the framework in theoretical context. I then further develop the argument at the heart of the book, the Court character thesis, explicating its connection to several bodies of literature – on judicial empowerment, the politics of judicial appointments, informal institutions, and interbranch relations. The chapter's final section outlines the structure of the book.

1.2. PATTERNS OF HIGH COURT–ELECTED BRANCH INTERACTION

Most studies of judicial politics in Latin America analyze and seek to account for variation in high court decision making (e.g., Scribner 2004; Helmke 2005; Hilbink 2007 among many others). This is a crucial area of study. In developing democracies such as those in Latin America in which courts traditionally have shied away from ruling assertively, judicial decisions that challenge powerful actors are an important development that warrants detailed analysis. Moreover, as discussed below, judicial assertiveness lies at the heart of judicial power: courts need not challenge political actors consistently in order to be considered powerful, but we would likely not think of courts that only rarely (or only weakly) challenge such actors as powerful.

Yet if a central goal of the judicial politics literature is to understand what roles courts play in political, economic, and legal development, evaluating and explaining judicial decision making on politically important cases is only one part of the enterprise. We must *also* examine and account for how powerful actors – and elected leaders in particular – respond when courts issue rulings that do not favor their interests (Miller and Barnes 2004). How often and to what extent do elected leaders comply – and retaliate – when courts issue challenging decisions on politically crucial cases? And why do they comply and retaliate as they do?

I propose an inductively generated framework for the integrated study of high court decision making *and* elected leaders' responses – for identifying, analyzing, and helping to explain the *patterns of interaction* that emerge between the judicial and elected branches of government. Table 1.1 outlines four possible

TABLE 1.1. *Patterns of High Court–Elected Branch Interaction*

Pattern of Interaction	Tendencies in High Court Behavior				Tendencies in Elected Leaders' Behavior	
	Assertiveness			Approach to Decision Making	Compliance with High Court Rulings	Retaliation against High Court Rulings
	Direction of Rulings	Intensity of Endorsements	Intensity of Challenges			
Confrontation	Challenge	Weaker	Stronger	Various (*not* Deferential)	Non-/Partial	Frequent
Court submission	Endorse	Stronger	Weaker	Deferential	Partial	Infrequent
Accommodation	No clear tendency	No clear tendency	No clear tendency	Various (*not* Deferential)	Partial/Significant	Infrequent
Court domination	Challenge	Weaker	Stronger	Various (*not* Deferential)	Significant/Full	None

patterns of interaction: *confrontation*, *Court submission*, *accommodation*, and *Court domination*. Each pattern reflects particular tendencies in high courts' assertiveness and approaches to decision making, and in elected leaders' compliance and retaliation.[9] The typology captures the essential range of variation on all three underlying dimensions: (1) Courts are minimally assertive in the Court submission pattern (row two) and maximally assertive in the confrontation and Court domination patterns (rows one and four, respectively); (2) they take only one factor into account when ruling in the Court submission pattern (row two) and might take a range of factors into account in the other patterns; and (3) elected leaders are minimally respectful of Courts and their dictates in the confrontation pattern (row one) and maximally respectful in the Court domination pattern (row four). Combining the first and the third dimensions but leaving out the second, Courts are probably most consequential in a pattern of Court domination (row four), and least relevant in a pattern of Court submission (row two). Of course, more than one pattern might exist in any polity over time, in different policy arenas, or in distinct areas of law.

Despite Argentina and Brazil's contextual and institutional similarities – and despite the filing of court cases concerning comparable types of economic policies – high court–elected branch interactions over economic governance in the two countries were strikingly different in the postauthoritarian period. In Argentina, the dominant pattern of interbranch interaction was *Court submission*: most often adopting a *deferential* approach to decision making (in which the elected branches' preferences are the dominant consideration), the CSJN tended to endorse the exercise of government power strongly while only rarely and weakly challenging elected leaders. Those leaders, for their part, complied only partially with the Court's weak challenges but rarely retaliated. Yet *Court submission* was interrupted by episodes of interbranch *confrontation* during which the CSJN challenged the exercise of government power more often than it endorsed, issued weaker endorsements and stronger challenges, and adopted a range of approaches to decision making (in particular, a *self-protective* approach in which justices' corporate or institutional interests were the dominant consideration). During those moments of interbranch confrontation, Argentine leaders tended to ignore or comply only partially with the Court's challenging decisions, and frequently retaliated.

In Brazil by contrast, interbranch interactions over economic governance followed a more stable pattern of *accommodation* during the 20 years after regime transition. The STF was somewhat more evenhanded than its Argentine counterpart, challenging and endorsing the exercise of government power with approximately the same frequency, and issuing both strong and weak challenges and endorsements. Moreover, it adopted a variety of approaches to decision making (especially a *pragmatic* approach, in which the potential political and economic consequences of its rulings weighed heavily).

[9] The framework does not consider the juridification of legislative debates or of statute writing (see, e.g., Tate and Vallinder 1995), as these do not entail active institutional interplay.

Throughout the period, elected authorities tended to comply partially or significantly with the STF's rulings and rarely threatened or attacked it.[10] Thus, the first three patterns in the typology are illustrated in this book; the fourth might characterize contexts with a very well-established high court, for instance Germany (Kommers et al. 2004: 71), or in which a Court briefly wielded exceptional power, as in Hungary in the 1990s (Scheppele 2003: 222–3).

A number of additional points concerning the analytic framework bear noting. Although there is undoubtedly a relationship between high court assertiveness and elected branch responses, I do not mean to imply that the former is the main cause of the latter or vice versa. Courts' anticipation of elected branch compliance with their rulings may impact the direction or intensity of their decisions, but Courts balance a range of considerations when deciding politically important cases: Different considerations become salient at different moments, depending upon the case, the context, and Court character. Similarly, the way in which elected leaders respond to judicial rulings is shaped by a range of contextual and political factors – including, again, the character of the Court they are facing. The goal is simply to outline patterns that high court–elected branch interactions over a set of cases might follow. The relevant question is, why does one pattern or another emerge?

The typology also illustrates the importance of analyzing high court decision making and elected leaders' responses to high court rulings *together*. For instance, if we only examined high court assertiveness, we might see no difference between Courts that are involved in very different relationships with the elected branches: confrontation and Court domination have the same scores on the variables in the first three columns of Table 1.1. Further, we can only accurately evaluate judicial power and impact if we examine judicial and political leaders' behavior in tandem. As noted previously, whereas a Court that only rarely and weakly challenges elected leaders would seem to be weaker than a Court that challenges frequently and aggressively, learning that the second Court's rulings are rarely obeyed would change our evaluation of the Courts' relative power. Likewise, even though we might automatically assume that Courts that valiantly defend the constitution are helping to entrench the rule of law, they may be doing little to achieve that end (and may in fact be undermining progress toward it) if leaders ignore their decisions.

Similarly, if one were to examine only the frequency of elected branch compliance and retaliation, Courts involved in an accommodation pattern of interaction with elected leaders would seem quite powerful. Yet the scores on the variables in the columns describing judicial assertiveness suggest that such Courts exhibit no tendency toward challenging elected leaders, let alone toward challenging them strongly. Moreover, whereas a Court that only elicits partial

[10] The scores for the accommodation pattern are somewhat vague because, as Chapter 6 discusses, high courts' rulings and elected leaders' responses can be mutually accommodating in two different ways.

compliance with its strong challenges might seem to lack power, if its endorsements of the exercise of government power are routinely *weak* (meaning it often withholds legitimacy-granting support for leaders' policies), it might have more power than its ability to compel compliance suggests. In short, examining judicial assertiveness without simultaneously considering compliance, or vice versa, yields an incomplete and potentially misleading portrait of judicial power and of interbranch relations.[11]

Employing the analytic framework offered here has implications for case selection.[12] Most analyses of Latin American high courts are small-N[13] qualitative studies,[14] while a handful are large-N quantitative analyses of hundreds or thousands of opinions or individual votes by high court justices.[15] What we have learned through small-N analysis forms the bedrock of our knowledge about Courts in the region. Yet such studies' reliance on a small number of cases – which are infrequently systematically selected – raises questions about the internal validity of their claims; further, the complex, contingent hypotheses they often produce are difficult to test elsewhere. On the other hand, the large-N quantitative analyses have clear theoretical goals, pinpoint precise relationships among variables, and advance arguments that are falsifiable and whose generalizability can be determined. Also, most authors of large-N studies of Latin American Courts use systematic case-selection techniques. However, for practical reasons, such scholars can rarely scrutinize closely the context in which the cases they study were filed and decided, the details of the cases themselves, the content and intensity of Court rulings on those cases, or compliance with judicial dictates. Yet close analysis of these elements is often necessary to avoid misinterpretation – particularly when analyzing politically important cases, which can be complicated and can generate complex judicial rulings.

Given the multifaceted analytic framework employed here and the multiple features of high court rulings and interbranch interactions it requires studying, this book pursues a middle ground: examining an intermediate-N number of systematically selected cases.[16] Doing so allows me to capitalize on the strengths of both small-N and large-N analysis. Like scholars who engage in small-N analysis, I can closely examine multiple aspects of the cases under study including their content; the legal issues they raised; their policy and

[11] Of course, a complete assessment of judicial power would also include analysis of formal elements (for instance, jurisdiction, judicial review authority, standing). Yet particularly in institutionally insecure settings, there may be a large gap between a Court's formal power and the power it actually wields, and the latter is arguably what interests us.

[12] Political scientists have long argued the comparative advantages of small-N vs. large-N analysis; see, e.g., Lieberson (1991); Savolainen (1994); and Collier and Mahoney (1996).

[13] The size of the "N" refers to the number of court cases (not country cases) under study.

[14] For instance, Nino (1993) and Gargarella (2004) on Argentina; Uprimny (2004) on Colombia; Faro de Castro (1997a) and Arantes (2005) on Brazil; López-Ayllón and Fix-Fierro (2003) on Mexico; and Pérez Perdomo (2005) on Venezuela; see Kapiszewski and Taylor (2008).

[15] For instance, Helmke (2002, 2005); Scribner (2004).

[16] Appendix 1.1 describes the technique employed to select court cases for study.

political details and stakes; and the institutional, political, and legal context in which they were filed, considered, and resolved, helping me to identify the approaches to decision-making justices adopted. Careful examination of each ruling allows me to evaluate both their direction and their intensity (rather than coding them dichotomously endorse/challenge government power). I can also trace the power struggles that ensued after the rulings, gauge elected leaders' compliance with them, and identify their broader implications. In short, I can precisely score each variable in the framework quantitatively and qualitatively. Further, systematically selecting and analyzing a theoretically relevant number of cases gives me a stronger basis from which to make causal claims. The following subsections discuss each aspect of the analytic framework in further detail.

High Court Assertiveness

High court assertiveness refers to a Court's issuance of decisions that challenge other actors' exercise of power – that seek to nullify, restrict, or change their behavior (see the second through fourth columns of Table 1.1).[17] High courts can challenge or endorse the exercise of government power through the letter or spirit of their rulings (or both).[18] That is, they can mandate that elected leaders begin to do something, cease doing something, or change the way they do something with respect to a particular policy or more generally. Likewise, high courts can sanction government action or policy and/or support the broader exercise of government power. The letter and spirit of high court rulings can be identified through careful reading of the rulings themselves, and consultation with experts. Assessing a high court's tendency to be assertive vis-à-vis the elected branches on a particular set of cases entails assessing both the direction and intensity of its rulings on those cases. With regard to the first, if the Court challenged (endorsed) the exercise of government power in at least 66 percent of those cases, a score of "challenge" ("endorse") is assigned; otherwise a score of "no clear tendency" is assigned (see column 2 in Table 1.1).

Few comparative judicial politics studies have systematically evaluated the strength with which Courts endorse or challenge elected leaders' exercise of power, that is, the intensity of their rulings. Yet decision intensity matters: weak

[17] *Assertiveness* is different from *activism*; the latter is used, often pejoratively, to describe a perceived judicial tendency to stray (generally in a liberal direction) from established precedent and/or supposed constitutional or legislative intent (adapted from *Merriam Webster's Dictionary of Law*). Assertive rulings may or may not be activist in this sense.

[18] As used here, a ruling's letter refers to what it says about the constitutionality of a particular policy; its spirit refers to what it says or implies about the exercise of government power more broadly. The distinction is obviously reminiscent of *Marbury v. Madison*. To offer an example from the present analysis, in the *Rodríguez* case, the Argentine CSJN did not rule on the constitutionality of the questioned policy, but strongly endorsed the broader exercise of government power by indicating that evaluating a particular kind of decree power was not within its ambit.

challenges and strong challenges can imply very different types of interbranch interaction. The tendency in the intensity of a Court's endorsements of (challenges to) the exercise of government power on a certain set of cases reflects the relative frequency with which it strongly versus weakly endorsed (challenged) that exercise. Again, if at least 66 percent of its endorsements (challenges) were strong (or weak), a score of strong (or weak) is assigned; otherwise, a score of "no clear tendency" is assigned (see columns 3 and 4 in Table 1.1).[19]

Whereas most studies analyze whether judicial decisions were for or against the government, there are good reasons to examine, instead, whether they endorsed or challenged the exercise of government power. First, the latter can be easier to measure objectively.[20] Determining whether a decision concerning the constitutionality of a particular policy was for or against the government requires a clear understanding of the government's policy preferences at the moment the high court handed down its ruling – yet governments do not always have well-developed preferences on the policies questioned in high court cases, and those preferences may have changed from the time the policy was enacted (particularly if it was enacted by a different government than the one in power when the ruling is issued, see Dahl 1957b). Moreover, the national government is not a unitary actor: A ruling that seems to be "for" an executive may well be "against" an opposition-controlled congress. Finally, it makes some sense to examine courts with respect to their constitutional role – ensuring government power is exercised along constitutional lines.

High Court Approaches to Decision Making

This study posits that high court rulings on politically crucial cases vary not only in assertiveness but also with regard to the *approach* to decision making adopted (see the fifth column of Table 1.1). (Of course, the approaches Courts adopt likely influence the assertiveness of their rulings; see Kapiszewski 2011b.) The approach a high court adopts when ruling on a case (the top row of Table 1.2) depends on which (one or more) of a series of considerations impinge most significantly on its decision-making calculus (the middle row of Table 1.2). For instance, justices have assumed a *self-protective* approach to decision making when their corporate or institutional interests heavily influence their rulings, and a *deferential* approach when the elected branches' preferences are the most salient consideration.

[19] Appendices 5.2 and 5.3, and 6.2 and 6.3 outline the schemes for scoring the direction and intensity of the Argentine and Brazilian Courts' rulings on the cases under study.

[20] Of course, evaluating whether a ruling endorsed or challenged the exercise of government power is not always straightforward – and some rulings do both. For example, in 1987, the Argentine CSJN upheld a law congress had passed to limit its own power to prosecute lower-level officers from the previous military regime (the *Ley de Obediencia Debida*). The ruling *endorsed* the exercise of government power since it validated a law passed by congress but simultaneously *challenged* the exercise of government power by limiting the degree to which the state could put military personnel on trial for abuses during the previous regime.

TABLE 1.2. *Approaches to High Court Decision Making and Corresponding Considerations and Models of Judicial Behavior*

Approach to High Court Decision Making	**Principled**	**Preference-driven**	**Self-protective**	**Support-building**	**Deferential**	**Pragmatic**
Corresponding considerations impinging on decision making	Law and merits of the case	Justices' ideology	Justices' corporate/ institutional interests	Public opinion	Elected branches' preferences	Potential political/ economic consequences of decision
Corresponding Models of judicial behavior	Legal	Attitudinal		Strategic		(None)

Identifying the foundations of judicial decision making (in particular on cases in which the elected branches are a party or have an interest) is a central focus of the judicial politics literature. As Table 1.2 demonstrates, the inductively generated set of approaches to high court decision making posited here (the top row) tracks the dominant theoretical models of judicial behavior (the bottom row) – legal, attitudinal, and strategic – save the institutional model in its purest form (when it points exclusively to how formal institutions influence judicial decision making and thus diverges most from the strategic model).[21] Even though the main theoretical models of judicial behavior are not incompatible and are in fact nested within one another to some degree, scholars have often suggested or implied that courts respond primarily to *one* impulse, be it their policy preferences, the configuration and power of their political counterparts, or law and institutions. In line with other scholarship that has begun to complicate the dominant paradigms of judicial behavior,[22] I posit that *multiple* consideration(s) motivate high court decision making on politically salient cases. Put differently, justices adopt a shifting blend of approaches when deciding such cases.[23] Yet Courts tend to favor a particular approach or approaches, at least when deciding cases in a given policy arena, and those tendencies form an integral part of interbranch interactions.

Identifying the approaches to decision making that justices adopt allows us to distinguish between rulings that *look* quite similar but have distinct motivations, and thus imply different types of interbranch relations. For example, imagine two rulings strongly endorsing an arguably unconstitutional exercise of government power; the Court issuing the first ruling assumed a pragmatic approach to decision making while the Court issuing the second assumed a deferential approach. The second ruling would seem to indicate a lack of independence (which the first would not) and would suggest interbranch interactions marked by Court submission (while the first could suggest a pattern of accommodation, for instance). Likewise, consider two challenges to a seemingly unconstitutional exercise of government power, one in which a

[21] Cultural explanations (often advanced to account for courts' *lack* of assertiveness in some Latin American countries) are likewise not captured in the framework. Karst and Rosenn (1975), for instance, argue that judicial assertiveness is impeded by the formalistic nature of Latin American legal culture, and Frühling (1984) suggests that Chilean judges' reluctance to challenge the constitutionality of legislation has its roots in their traditional training.

[22] Scholars are increasingly arguing that multiple factors influence judicial decision making. For instance, Shapiro and Stone Sweet (1994) offer a combined institutional and strategic account. Baum argues that legal rules and practices *interact* with attitudes or ideology (1993) and, more broadly, that judges play to multiple audiences (2006). Iaryczower, Spiller, and Tommasi (2000) found evidence of both the attitudinal and strategic models in Argentina, and Scribner (2004) did as well in both Argentina and Chile. Geyh (2010) reviews work on the U.S. Supreme Court positing multicausality, and Klein and Mitchell (2010) gather multiple theories and models of (the psychology of) judicial behavior.

[23] For instance, public opinion might be less important in a case about a tax on certain corporations and more important in a case about a freeze on private bank accounts. Which consideration(s) matter to a certain case depends on its content and the decision-making context; see Kapiszewski 2011b.

Court assumed a self-protective approach to decision making and another in which a Court assumed a principled approach. Although we would need to carefully analyze additional dynamics around the decisions, the former would be more likely to form part of a pattern of interbranch confrontation than the latter. In short, identifying the approaches to decision making that high courts adopt allows for more accurate characterization of interbranch relations.

I used expert opinion and observations from participants in the high court cases under study to evaluate the approaches the Argentine and Brazilian Courts took when deciding those cases. Specifically, I searched four types of sources for statements or assertions regarding why each case was decided as it was: (1) the Court's written ruling;[24] (2) transcripts from the extensive set of interviews I carried out about each case and ruling; (3) a set of newspaper articles discussing the case; and (4) a set of relevant books and journal articles (Appendix 1.1 outlines data collection in more detail). I categorized each factor mentioned in those sources as relating to one of the six considerations (and corresponding approaches to decision making) mentioned in Table 1.2.[25] I interpreted the frequency with which expert sources mentioned a consideration when discussing a case to be an indicator of the likelihood that consideration was important to the Court's decision making on that case. As previously, a Court is understood to have a *tendency* to adopt a particular approach to decision making (and the corresponding score is assigned) if it adopted that approach when deciding at least 66 percent of a set of politically important cases; otherwise, a score of "various" is assigned (see column 5 in Table 1.1).

Each approach to high court decision making deserves elaboration. First, law and legal considerations – the strength and development of a legal case, whether a policy blatantly violates the constitution, the existence (or absence) of settled legal doctrine – may impinge on a high court's decisions, leading it to assume a *principled* approach to decision making. Relatively few contemporary legal scholars (and even fewer political scientists) argue that law determines legal outcomes, at least in the mechanical sense in which the legal model has been (mis)represented in the literature.[26] Indeed, even though Latin American countries follow the civil law tradition (which emphasizes the role of judges as *la bouche de la loi*) and a strictly legal approach to decision making is taught in most Latin American law schools, few scholars have adopted

[24] After all, even if we sometimes question the correspondence between Courts' written rulings and their actual reasoning, Courts generally offer logical explanations for their decisions and justify any departure from previous jurisprudence.

[25] For instance, if a newspaper article asserted that a high court's decision was influenced by a visit from the Minister of Justice, I categorized that "consideration" as "elected branch preferences." Appendices 5.4 and 6.4 outline how statements and assertions were scored.

[26] A pure legal approach was more popular in the United States up to the mid-twentieth century; one example of work in this vein might be Wechsler (1959). And of course, some legal scholars continue to promote a legal approach to judicial decision making in a prescriptive sense (e.g., Dworkin). On the purely legal theory side, L. A. Hart may be the paradigmatic positivist.

the legal model as an explanation for judicial decision making in the region.[27] Yet scholars continue to believe that law matters (Friedman 2006). Gauri and Brinks (2008: 17), for instance, suggest that examining the legal framework is a good starting point for understanding variation in judicial support for social and economic rights. Other scholars seek to identify subtler ways in which law affects judicial behavior. For instance, a spate of studies since the mid-1990s have understood law as a professional "norm of reasoning" that obligates judges to forsake outcomes that cannot be justified by professionally constructed references to authoritative legal rules or procedures (e.g., Knight and Epstein 1996; Tamanaha 1996; Gillman 2001). Richards and Kritzer (2002) have explored the effect of "jurisprudential regimes" on the U.S. Supreme Court,[28] and Whittington (2000) considers the impact law may have as a discursive practice.[29] New institutionalist approaches that suggest that rules and legal precedent influence and constrain judicial decision making also overlap with the rendition of the legal approach offered here.

Justices adopt a *preference-driven* approach when their policy preferences and ideological leanings prove important in their decision making. This, of course, is the notion at the core of the attitudinal model of judicial behavior, central in the U.S. judicial politics literature. Perhaps the earliest manifestation of this model was Pritchett's work on the U.S. Supreme Court (1948); it was subsequently developed by Schubert (1965) and Rohde and Spaeth (1976) and is now most forcefully advocated by Segal and Spaeth (1993, 1999).[30] More recently, the model has also been applied in Canada (e.g., Ostberg and Wetstein 1998, 2002, 2007; Alarie and Green 2007; Ostberg et al. 2009).

Alternatively, justices might adopt a *self-protective* approach to decision making, in which their corporate or institutional interests (those of the judiciary as an institution, or of public sector workers more generally) are relevant to their rulings. For instance, a Court might use decisions on politically crucial cases to strike back after elected leaders tacitly or overtly threatened them or the Court. Justices' corporate interests may also motivate them to rule in a particular way on cases concerning public sector salaries or pensions or to decide (or duck) a case in order to demonstrate that disputes of its ilk fall within (or outside) their purview. The idea that Courts' institutional interests affect their decision making is different from the argument in some institutional accounts that particular formal characteristics or institutions (either external or internal to Courts, for instance inquisitorial proceedings, case-by-case decision making, or lack of coercive or financial resources) impinge on judicial decision

[27] Barros's (2003) study of Chile weaves in more law than most analyses of the region's courts.

[28] These have proven controversial; see the exchange between Lax and Rader (2010a and 2010b) and Kritzer and Richards (2010).

[29] Another example might be Luhmann's (e.g., 1988) autopoietic theory of law, which suggests that social (or legal) systems function according to their own "code."

[30] Hilbink (2007) points to *judicial* ideology to explain the persistently illiberal behavior of Chilean judges, highlighting how the judiciary's traditional apoliticism combined with the incentives established by its institutional structure produced that outcome.

making.[31] Instead, the insight here is akin to the somewhat more strategic arguments scholars have made to explain Chilean courts' traditional *lack* of assertiveness. Couso (2002), for instance, argues that Chilean courts tempered their decision making in the constitutional realm in an effort to preserve their power to freely decide less-contentious struggles in the legal realm. And Huneeus's (2010) account of some Chilean judges' assertiveness over human rights cases highlights their need for "institutional atonement" for their jurisprudence during the dictatorship.[32]

Fourth, justices assume a *support-building* approach when public views about a case are important to their decision making. The notion here is similar to that advanced by Friedman (2009) and Staton (2004, 2006). Concerning Mexico, Staton suggests that Courts may be more likely to challenge elected leaders in a politically crucial case when the case is well-publicized – and when a segment of the public or media can be expected to support and defend an assertive ruling. That argument differs from accounts of judicial decision making that suggest that justices may feel freer to challenge elected leaders in high-stakes cases if strong societal support for the *Court* raises the political cost for the elected branches of retaliating against its rulings – that is, if "basic social support structures" are in place. Such arguments have been made concerning Mexico (e.g., Staton 2002; López-Ayllón and Fix-Fierro 2003), Argentina (Smulovitz and Peruzzotti 2003), and Egypt (Moustafa 2003); Epp (1998) offers a related argument – that courts' assertiveness increases as more societal organizations use litigation as a strategy for social change.

Justices might also adopt a *deferential* approach to decision making. This occurs when elected leaders' preferences about a ruling influence a Court's decision making. The elected branches often have strong preferences regarding high court rulings on politically crucial cases and may exert considerable pressure on Courts to defer to their desires. Many explanations within the strategic actor framework allude to how elected leaders' preferences affect judicial decision making, although they tend to highlighting the conditions under which those preferences will influence courts *less*, for instance, (a) when the existence of a multiparty system makes legislative repeal of judicial rulings more cumbersome and less likely (Cooter and Ginsburg 1996; Ríos-Figueroa 2003); (b) when parties alternate in power more often (Ramseyer 1994); (c) when there is greater political competition, in particular, divided government (Chavez 2004a; Scribner 2004); or (d) when courts have issued decisions within elected leaders' "tolerance intervals" and incrementally expanded them

[31] For example, Kagan et al. (1978), analyzing U.S. State Supreme Courts, suggest that courts are more assertive when they can control their case loads (and thus elect to focus on important cases); Ginsburg (2002) alludes to a similar control mechanism in some Asian cases. Also, Clayton and Gillman (1999) and Gillman and Clayton (1999) gather work analyzing the decision making of the U.S. Supreme Court from a new institutionalist perspective.

[32] Huneeus's account highlights that Chilean judges were better able to actuate the institutional preference for penance when the strict hierarchy that normally constrains decision making temporarily ceased to bind.

(Epstein, Knight, and Shvetsova 2001). In an interesting twist, Helmke (2005) found that in Argentina's uncertain institutional environment, high court justices ruled against the sitting government more often toward the end of its tenure, in hopes of gaining favor with the incoming administration. The idea advanced here is simply that elected leaders' policy preferences can figure into (and even dominate) high court deliberations on politically important cases.

Finally, a Court has adopted a *pragmatic* approach to decision making when the potential repercussions of its rulings – for the institutional system, for governability, or for economic or political stability – influence its decision making. Gargarella (2003) and Nino (1996), for example, writing about judicial decision making in Argentina in the late 1980s, suggest the high court proceeded cautiously in the human rights realm (among others) due to concerns about military rebellion; Smulovitz (2005) posits something similar about judicial rulings in the early 2000s. Indeed, few scholars would likely deny that justices consider the consequences of their decisions. Yet the idea that high courts are guided by political and economic concerns – that their rulings reflect a desire to facilitate governance and an orientation toward the common (political) good – is not captured in the core theories of judicial decision making. This approach is thus introduced into the analysis mainly on an inductive basis. To be clear, the idea is *not* that Courts shy away from issuing rulings that would induce or exacerbate economic or political crisis for fear leaders will disregard their decisions (implicit in certain versions of the separation-of-powers model); Courts ruling on that basis would be understood to have adopted a deferential or self-protective approach to decision-making in the present framework. Likewise, the idea is not that Courts hesitate to make rulings that could complicate governance because they do not want to be blamed for any resulting mayhem; Courts so-motivated would be understood here to have adopted a self-protective approach. The idea, instead, is that Courts consider the consequences of their decisions because they feel some responsibility for governing.

The idea that Courts adopt a variety of approaches when resolving crucial conflicts reemphasizes the political nature of constitutional review and Constitutional Courts and demonstrates how much the judicialization of politics – with the multiple competing pressures it applies on judicial decision making – requires of Courts. It suggests that installing a high court with a particular ideological composition may not guarantee judicial outcomes of a particular type. Likewise, dynamics such as political fragmentation will not necessarily produce unbridled assertiveness as Courts attend to considerations beyond the strategic. More broadly, Courts' adoption (and rejection) of these approaches reflects their assumption (and avoidance) of the different roles they can play in democracy – from serving as a venue for (or thwarting) political representation, to holding elected leaders constitutionally accountable, to facilitating (or obstructing) governance. The approaches to decision making that Courts adopt, in other words, are a critical feature not only of interbranch relations but of the political landscape more generally.

Elected Branch Compliance

Compliance with judicial decisions concerns how quickly and completely those against whom courts rule obey the letter and spirit of their decisions. Measuring compliance presents a range of challenges (see the sixth column of Table 1.1).[33] To name just a few, it is not always obvious from judicial opinions what compliance with them would entail, as they can be (intentionally or unintentionally) vague. Also, those against whom courts rule may have strong incentives to conceal whether they fully complied with challenging decisions. It may be difficult to identify compliance if it occurs in ways that are different from (though have the same effect as) the behavior called for by a court. Finally, it may not be obvious whether action taken following a judicial ruling is actually a response to it (which it must be in order to consider the behavior compliance) if, for instance, it was taken long after the ruling.

This study evaluates the difficulty, speed, and completeness of elected leaders' compliance with the letter *and* spirit of Argentine and Brazilian high court rulings on the cases under study in which the Courts challenged the exercise of government power.[34] I gathered data to evaluate compliance through expert interviews with actors on all sides of each case, and from newspaper articles discussing their aftermath.[35] The tendency in elected branch compliance with a particular set of challenging rulings reflects the relative frequency with which elected leaders failed to comply, or complied partially, significantly, or fully; that is, the score assigned corresponds to the level of compliance in which elected leaders engaged in response to at least 66 percent of a Court's challenging rulings on a certain set of cases (see column 6 in Table 1.1).

What difference courts can make to law, society, and politics – the question at the heart of most comparative judicial studies – relates closely to their power. If we adopt a Dahlian (1957a) notion of power (that is, if we understand it as the ability to compel an actor to do something he or she would prefer not to do), it follows that judicial power is inextricably linked to how quickly and fully those against whom courts rule comply with their rulings. Yet while judicial power has long been a central concept in comparative judicial politics, scholars have only recently begun to offer theoretical accounts of elected leaders' compliance with challenging judicial decisions.[36] While using the term

[33] See Kapiszewski and Taylor (forthcoming) for a detailed discussion of the pitfalls and promise of studying compliance with judicial decisions.

[34] As most judicial decisions in civil law systems (except Constitutional Courts' rulings on abstract review cases) hold only for the case at hand, gauging elected leaders' compliance with the general spirit of Court rulings means holding leaders – and Courts – to a very high standard.

[35] Appendices 5.5 and 6.5 outline the scheme for scoring compliance with the Argentine and Brazilian Courts' rulings on the cases under study.

[36] Some scholars include compliance in their definitions of judicial power even though they do not empirically evaluate it. Finkel (2003: 779–80), for instance, defines judicial power as comprising independence, authority (the idea of compliance with judicial decisions by losing parties), and jurisdiction. For Tate and Vallinder (1995: 2), judicial power is measured by the formal strength of the judicial branches of government, the degree of judicial involvement in crafting

"judicial power," scholars have often focused primarily on judicial assertiveness (e.g., Finkel 2005 and Wilson and Rodríguez Cordero 2006 among others), labeling courts that frequently or strongly challenged the exercise of government power "powerful" without confirming whether their decisions were obeyed. Others who did consider compliance did not address the question of *why* a court's decisions were obeyed (e.g., Uprimny 2004; Cepeda Espinosa 2005; Faundez 2005 on the Colombian Constitutional Court). Still others, for instance Wilson (2005) and Santiso (2004), explored the broad effects on policy making and democracy of high court rulings (examining the Costa Rican Supreme Court's constitutional chamber and the Brazilian high court respectively), but did not investigate whether their specific rulings were obeyed.

Four lines of explanation for variation in compliance with judicial decisions are emerging in the comparative judicial politics literature (see again Kapiszewski and Taylor forthcoming).[37] Legitimacy theory (e.g., Caldeira and Gibson 1995; Gibson, Caldeira, and Baird 1998; Vanberg 2001; Carrubba 2003; Staton 2004) posits that a court's "diffuse" support (support for the court or the judiciary in general), or its "specific" support (support for its rulings) affects compliance. Another set of studies highlights the role that external actors – such as interest groups or societal or political power brokers – can play in ensuring that compliance is monitored and that noncompliance results in legal action (Spriggs 1997; Epp 1998; Trochev 2008; see also Brinks and Botero 2010). Of course, the parties to a particular case can also monitor and encourage compliance with a judicial ruling (Gauri and Brinks 2008: 4).

A third set of studies highlights the contribution that courts make to compliance with their own rulings. Communications theory (e.g., Wasby 1970; Dolbeare and Hammond 1971; Baum 1976; Spriggs 1997; Staton and Vanberg 2008), for example, suggests that courts' framing and articulation of their rulings influence compliance. Others posit that courts' engagement in "dialogic activism" – broadly framing public policy recommendations in their decisions but leaving the specifics of implementation to public authorities and directly calling on them to engage in dialogue – encourages compliance (Dixon 2007; Gargarella 2011; Rodríguez-Garavito 2011). Staton (2010) argues that the Mexican Court's "public relations campaigns" (engagement with the media) encouraged compliance. Finally, some scholars offer more normative accounts, suggesting that the strength of the rule of law or judicial independence in countries that form part of the European Union helps to account for their leaders' compliance with the rulings of the European Court of Justice (Burley and Mattli 1993; Mattli and Slaughter 1995), for instance, or that a desire to bolster the legitimacy of the legal system inspires compliance (Pollack 1997; Mattli and Slaughter 1998).

public policies, and the extent to which nonjudicial decision-making forums are dominated by legalistic rules and procedures.

[37] Canon and Johnson 1999 assess earlier literature, much of it United States based.

The Court character account of interbranch interactions offered here draws on the first and third lines of explanation. High court legitimacy is an integral part of Court character. And the idea that particular informal institutional features of Courts influence interbranch interactions aligns with arguments that courts themselves can encourage (or discourage) compliance (although high courts do not have control over all aspects of their character). Fittingly, given that the phenomenon of interbranch interactions combines high court decision making and compliance, both the first and third lines of argumentation have analogues in the judicial decision-making literature – legitimacy theory in strategic accounts of judicial behavior, and judicial influence on compliance in the attitudinal and institutional models of judicial behavior.

Elected Branch Retaliation

Elected leaders' compliance with a court's decisions is an incomplete indicator of how those leaders interact with the court. Particularly in contexts where high courts are only beginning to accumulate power, elected leaders may retaliate against judicial decisions that challenge their power in politically important cases. Such retaliation, the final element of interbranch interactions as conceptualized here (see Table 1.1, last column), might be of two types. One type represents an attack on a judicial ruling ("policy retaliation"). A legislature might actively override a decision or otherwise seek to weaken or negate it or dilute its future effects; alternatively, legislators might amend the constitution or pass new laws with the goal of modifying the legal foundation for future judicial rulings. The second type of retaliation represents an attack on the Court itself ("institutional retaliation"). In the wake of an unfavorable ruling or series of rulings, elected leaders may narrow a Court's jurisdiction or decrease its budget, for instance, or target specific justices, perhaps seeking to impeach them or pressuring them to resign (see again Kapiszewski and Taylor forthcoming).

While some scholars include retaliation in their definitions of compliance (e.g., Trochev 2008: 188), the two are distinct actions that can combine in different ways and reflect different types of interbranch interactions. They are therefore considered separately in this study. Data to evaluate the frequency with which and degree to which elected leaders retaliated against the CSJN and STF rulings under study were gathered through expert interviews and from newspaper accounts of the repercussions of each high court challenge.[38] The tendency in elected branch retaliation against a certain set of challenging rulings issued by a Court reflects elected leaders' degree of retaliation (in any of the ways just mentioned) in response to at least 66 percent of those challenging decisions (see column 7 in Table 1.1).

[38] Problems similar to those involved in measuring compliance also afflict measuring retaliation. Appendices 5.5 and 6.5 outline the scheme for scoring elected branch retaliation.

The comparative judicial politics literature has mainly examined elected leaders' retaliation against high court rulings implicitly, in studies of judicial independence. Some studies focus on the formal institutional trappings of de jure independence (independent budgetary or salary control, for instance – see Smithey and Ishiyama 2000; Ríos-Figueroa 2006). Others enter the messy terrain of de facto judicial independence, exploring the informal strategies elected leaders use to influence judicial rulings (see Larkins 1996; Ferejohn, Rosenbluth, and Shipan 2007 among many others). This study falls in line with the latter set of work, examining Latin American leaders' choices about when and how much to retaliate against challenging high court decisions.

1.3. EXPLAINING INTERBRANCH INTERACTIONS: THE COURT CHARACTER THESIS

Why do particular patterns of interaction emerge between high courts and elected leaders? This study offers an institutional account of interbranch relations: the Court character thesis. The thesis posits that Latin American leaders, due to historical institutional forces and contemporary political contingencies, adopted a particular politics of Court crafting in the postauthoritarian era. Their Court-crafting strategies shaped the *character* of their high courts – understood as a syndrome of interdependent and relatively stable informal institutional features. In turn, the Courts' character conditioned how they decided politically crucial legal disputes and how elected leaders reacted to their challenging decisions – that is, high court character shaped interbranch interactions. Taken together and repeated over time, those interactions formed identifiable patterns. Figure 1.1 depicts the thesis.

The Court character thesis was developed via analytic induction – through analysis of cross-national variation in interbranch interactions around a systematically selected sample of the most politically important cases (in a range of substantive areas) that the Argentine and Brazilian high courts considered during the first two postauthoritarian decades (N = 122; see Appendix 1.1) – although it is illustrated here using the subset of those cases that concern economic policy (N = 44).[39] The dozens of visits I made to each high court and interviews I conducted with Court personnel demonstrated that the two Courts are dramatically different institutions. I hypothesized that the institutional contrast was linked to cross-national variation in interbranch interactions over politically salient cases. A comparative analysis of the two Courts' institutional features paired with process tracing revealed how a subset of those features (the Courts' character) introduced incentives to and imposed constraints on the Courts and on elected leaders as they struggled over critical cases, leading them to interact in particular – and persistent – patterns in the postauthoritarian period. The intermediate-N number of cases examined here and their focus on a specific

[39] Since the analysis is based on a subset of the cases used to develop the thesis, the study is not a test of the thesis, but rather an *illustration* of how it accounts for interbranch interactions.

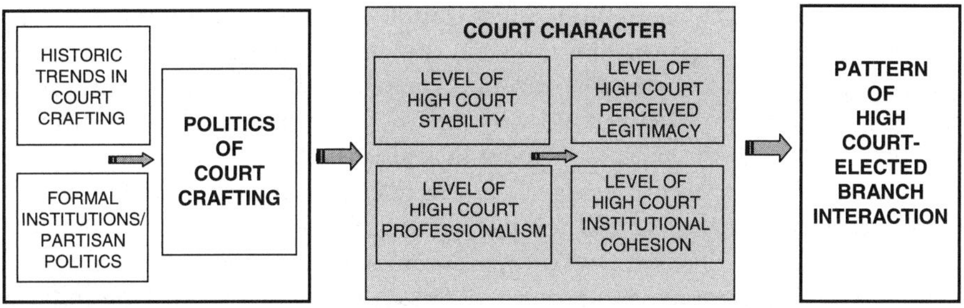

FIGURE 1.1. Explaining patterns of high court–elected branch interaction: The Court character thesis.

issue area put generalizing these findings and argument on somewhat shaky inferential ground. Nonetheless, the fact that the cases are a subset of a systematically selected sample of the most politically important cases the two Courts decided in the posttransition era offers some assurance of external validity, suggesting that the Court character thesis may help explain interbranch interactions over crucial political issues regardless of their substantive content.[40]

The Court character account of interbranch interactions raises three questions: Why do elected leaders adopt a particular politics of Court crafting? What is Court character and how is it produced? And how does Court character affect interbranch interactions? That is, what is the argument and mechanism behind each arrow in Figure 1.1? I address each question in turn.

An Institutional Account of Court Crafting

Over the last twenty-five years, leaders around the world have formally empowered courts (and high courts in particular), expanding their jurisdiction and augmenting their review powers, and established safeguards for their independence.[41] An impressive literature has developed to help us understand these choices.[42] When courts with augmented formal powers and autonomy become more involved in politics, their composition is of critical concern to citizens and elected leaders alike (Malleson 2007: 4). If the account advanced here is correct and Court *character* conditions interbranch relations, then who sits on newly empowered high courts should likewise be of critical concern to scholars

[40] The book's insights are likely not generalizable to interbranch interactions around the less-salient, less-important cases that dominate the work of high courts with little docket control, however.

[41] This is not to ignore the multiple tools that elected leaders often have at their disposal to informally compromise judicial power and independence – failing to release money budgeted for the judiciary or pressuring for particular decisions through the media, for instance.

[42] Chapters 3 and 4 of this study discuss high court empowerment in Argentina and Brazil showing how leaders in each country engaged in *judicial centralization* – increasing each high court's control over the rest of the judiciary and facilitating its receipt of politically salient cases – and Chapter 3 briefly reviews the main theoretical propositions that seek to explain judicial empowerment.

of judicial politics. Concern with Court composition in turn implies increased analytic attention to the formal rules and procedures guiding high court size and the appointment of justices – for instance, whether there is a judicial career that reaches to the apex court and what actors participate in the appointment process.[43] Yet it *also* implies examining the informal politics of Court crafting those charged with that task employ – the frequency with which (and means by which) they change the size and composition of the Court, and the professional profiles and ties to themselves their appointees possess.[44]

Whereas a large body of literature addresses the politics of federal judicial appointments in the United States,[45] there is less systematic study of the formal rules and procedures guiding high court appointments, or of informal Court-crafting practices, in developing democracies. Moreover, scholars have tended to focus more on the *effects* of institutional design than on why particular formal judicial selection mechanisms are established in the first place (Epstein, Knight, and Shvetsova 2002: 194).[46] Nonetheless, some important accounts have appeared. Concerning formal rules, most discussions are embedded in country case studies (e.g., Hilbink 2007 on the Chilean judiciary; Trochev 2008 on the Russian Constitutional Court; Linares 2010 on the Salvadoran Supreme Court; and the contributions to Malleson and Russell 2007).[47] Malleson (2007: 5) posits that political culture plays a role in the formation of judicial selection systems. Russell (2007: 423–4) highlights how "awareness ... of the social and political significance of judicial power" led to the development of particular constitutional provisions guiding the appointment of judges in Namibia and South Africa. And Epstein et al (2002: 195), in their excellent comparative analysis of formal rules of judicial selection, argue that the development and evolution of judicial selection rules result from bargaining processes among relevant

[43] In some countries such as France, for instance, appointments to the highest courts are managed completely within the judiciary and shielded from political influence (Russell 2007: 423).

[44] Throughout the book I use the term "informal" to describe practices and institutional features that are not mandated by or formalized in written rules, laws, or the constitution (yet may not be formally forbidden) that become entrenched through repeated behaviors (definition adapted from Helmke and Levitsky's definition of informal institutions [2006: 1]).

[45] For instance, Davis (2005); Epstein and Segal (2005); Wittes (2006); Greenburg (2007); and Stone (2010), to name some of the most recent work. Many studies highlight the increasing politicization of appointment processes in the United States since the 1980s and, accordingly, adopt a strategic approach to explain those processes (e.g., Epstein and Segal 2005). Other scholars offer multicausal accounts (e.g., Stras 2008) or demonstrate how broader social, political, and historical factors have driven evolution in appointment processes (e.g., Gerhardt 2000).

[46] For example, various chapters in Malleson and Russell (2007) consider the implications of different selection systems for judicial independence and accountability as well as for courts' quality, diversity, and representativeness; Linares (2010) considers selection systems as one aspect of the different models of "judicial governance" whose performance he evaluates.

[47] This nineteen-chapter book includes country case studies from Europe, Asia, the Middle East, and Africa (plus Canada, the United States, New Zealand, and Australia); it includes only a few countries that might be classified as developing democracies and does not examine Latin America.

political actors, and also posit that political uncertainty affects the adoption of judicial selection mechanisms (with greater uncertainty leading to the adoption of mechanisms designed to enhance judicial independence).

In terms of informal Court-crafting practices, most explanations tend toward the strategic, demonstrating how appointment practices respond to formal institutions and conjunctural political factors. Country case studies, for instance, often illuminate the politics behind high court appointments by exploring particularly contentious moments in high courts' history. In the post-communist area, Trochev (2008: 65–72, 80–5) discusses the battles that surrounded appointments to the Russian Constitutional Court from 1991 to 1995, noting their connection with political struggles around federalism. Sadurski (2010: 109–10) and Druker (2008: 189–206) address such battles in the Czech Republic in the mid-to late 2000s. And Scheppele recounts the "wing-clipping" of the Hungarian Constitutional Court in the late 1990s (2003: 227). In Latin America, Finkel (2008: 53–5) discusses the controversial replacement of several Argentine justices in the mid-1990s, highlighting its roots in negotiations surrounding constitutional reform. And Castagnola and Pérez-Liñán (2011) identify three causes for the dismemberment of Bolivia's Constitutional Tribunal in the mid-2000s: the Court's weak legitimacy, its activism, and legislative gridlock preventing the confirmation of justices. A bit more broadly, Voeten (2007) suggests that European leaders who favor integration seek to appoint activist judges to the European Court of Human Rights.

A few studies have examined broader and more persistent patterns in Court crafting. O'Brien (2007) highlights variation in the degree to which judicial appointments in Japan and South and Southeast Asian democracies are, overall, politicized. Llanos and Figueroa-Schibber (2007) find that the Argentine Senate's ability to effectively oversee presidents' Court-crafting practices between 1983 and 2007 depended on executive resources in the senate, the level of the appointment, and presidents' broader goals and ambitions – as well as formal rules guiding selection. Castagnola and Pérez-Liñán (2011: 303) outline three "paths to judicial submission" (dismantling, packing, and reshuffling). Pérez-Liñán (2011) reviews 250 examples of high court reshuffling in Latin America between 1900 and 2010, revealing Latin American leaders' penchant for "judicial takeover" (appointing a majority of high court justices in a single year) and suggesting the phenomenon has its roots in Courts' formal institutional features (i.e., judicial term limits) and political instability.[48] Indeed, several scholars have highlighted the ubiquity of high court politicization in Latin America, understood as elected leaders' manipulation of Courts for political gain and/or staffing of Courts with partisan appointments (e.g., Domingo 2004; Scribner 2004), and some have linked that dynamic to judicialization

[48] In a related piece, Pérez-Liñán and Castagnola (2009) seek to explain turnover on high courts in eleven Latin American countries from 1904 to 2006; they highlight the importance of "'natural' (legal and biological) factors," as well as political conditions empowering, and institutional incentives promoting, executive manipulation.

(e.g., Domingo 2004; Ferejohn 2002: 63–5 posits the same connection well beyond Latin America). On the whole however, scholars tend to focus on specific appointment strategies adopted at particular moments, rather than identifying or seeking to account for broader politics of Court crafting that persist over time.

Perhaps a theoretical gap has existed with regard to informal Court crafting because there is assumed to be little variation, and thus no puzzle. Around the globe – or at least where political leaders are involved in making judicial appointments – it is obviously the norm for them to try to craft high courts that will help them realize their policy objectives. Postauthoritarian Latin American leaders were particularly motivated to do so given the judicialization of politics (and, especially, of economic governance). And leaders in Argentina and Brazil were perfectly poised (institutionally) to do so: while in many Latin American countries high courts themselves, judicial councils, and/or other organs all participate in making high court appointments, in Argentina and Brazil executive influence on the process is maximized, and the legislature plays the only other significant role.

Yet the previously mentioned work – and the country cases examined here – demonstrate that informal Court crafting is quite heterogeneous and does not necessarily entail compromising judicial integrity. As Castagnola and Pérez-Liñán (2011) recount, Bolivian leaders tacitly *dismembered* the Constitutional Tribunal. In Argentina, leaders *politicized* the CSJN, manipulating its size and composition and often appointing justices with strong ties to the executive (even if their qualifications were somewhat weaker). And in Brazil, leaders *professionalized* the STF: they held the number of justices constant, allowed the Court's composition to evolve naturally, and appointed justices with strong experience in the federal judiciary, prosecutors' office, or legislature (or some combination), to whom they generally had weak ties (if they had ties at all).[49] Leaders in other Latin American countries have undoubtedly adopted other practices. Why do we observe this heterogeneity – what drives Court crafting?

Complementing strategic explanations that focus on how the political dynamics of the moment affect judicial appointments, I offer an account of Court crafting that blends elements of historical and rational choice institutionalism. Historical trends in Court crafting, entrenched over time in a path-dependent process,[50] in combination with the formal rules guiding Court composition and contemporary partisan politics, shape leaders' Court-crafting preferences and their latitude to pursue them. In Argentina, historic high court

[49] I gathered information to evaluate Court crafting from secondary sources (previous analyses of the Argentine and Brazilian high courts), from interviews of experts on both judiciaries, and from the curriculum vitae of past and present justices on both Courts; see Chapters 3 and 4.

[50] For a similar historical institutional analysis of how virtuous and vicious cycles of government enforcement/social adherence and enforcement failure/noncompliance emerge in the area of tax collection in Latin America, see Bergman (2009).

politicization had produced a Court that was, far more often than not, docile and subservient, incentivizing leaders to continue to politicize the Court. Yet partisan politics (the dominance of and divisions within Peronism) constrained elected leaders to some degree, sometimes complicating high court politicization and leading to less-consistent Court crafting. In Brazil, a very different politics of Court crafting had become the norm and expected practice over time: high court professionalization. Elected leaders were incentivized to professionalize the STF because doing so had historically produced a predictable Court that was more likely to take mainstream legal positions and to lend legitimacy to laws that it upheld – and because veering from tradition would have cost them the support of the influential legal community and antagonized a Court that they needed on their side. Partisan politics (dramatic party system fragmentation and weak party loyalty) further encouraged professionalization as they required presidents to rally broad-based coalitions to support high court appointments – coalitions that would have been difficult to assemble for unqualified or personalistic nominees. Elected leaders' Court-crafting choices, I thus suggest, are ultimately shaped by historical pressures and contemporary institutional and political constraints.

Court Character

This study employs an original conceptualization of Court character comprising an interacting set of informal institutional features: a Court's stability, professional profile, perceived legitimacy, and institutional cohesion. Court-crafting practices have a direct and immediate effect on the first two aspects of Court character. A Court's level of stability reflects how often its configuration, and the actual and mandated number of justices, change due to normal attrition or to irregular, illegal, or unconstitutional actions by those who appoint justices. The information necessary to evaluate the Argentine CSJN and Brazilian STF's stability was drawn from accounts of their institutional history available on their Web pages and in scholarly sources.[51] The second feature of a Court's character, its professional profile, reflects choices regarding the backgrounds of appointees (whether those appointees have experience in the federal executive, legislature, prosecutorial organ, or judiciary prior to appointment), their legal specialization, and their connections to those who appointed them. The Argentine and Brazilian high courts' professional profiles were assessed using information drawn from sitting and retired justices' curriculum vitae, from interviews with justices and experts on the judiciary, and from scholarly examinations of the Courts.[52]

These two features contribute to the formation of the third and fourth features of Court character – perceived legitimacy and institutional cohesion. Perceived legitimacy concerns both public support for the Court and

[51] Web Appendices 3.1 and 4.1 contain the relevant data; scoring is discussed in Chapters 3 and 4.

[52] Web Appendices 3.2, 4.2, and 4.3 contain the relevant data; Chapters 3 and 4 discuss scoring.

professional support for it within the legal community. The perceived legitimacy of the Argentine and Brazilian high courts was evaluated using information gained through a systematic review of coverage of the Court in a major national newspaper in each country, and data gathered via the Latinobarómetro public opinion survey.[53] We would expect (and in fact I find) that a more stable Court including justices with stronger professional profiles has stronger perceived legitimacy. Of course, a Court's stability and professional profile do not *determine* its perceived legitimacy; its decisions affect its legitimacy (as Hoekstra [2003] has shown for the United States Supreme Court), and the degree to which its rulings appear to be obeyed by powerful actors likely does as well. Yet as Chapters 3 and 4 discuss, interviews carried out in connection with this project suggested that the Argentine and Brazilian Courts' stability and their justices' profiles strongly influenced popular and professional opinion about the Courts.

The final feature of Court character, institutional cohesion, has four facets. The first is the degree of consensus among justices regarding the role the Court should play.[54] Second is the presence of recognized leadership on the Court, either formal (an elected or appointed Court "president" or chief justice) or informal; the relevant question in either case is whether the other justices respect the individuals in these positions. Third is collegiality – both of the deliberation and decision-making process and of justices' overall interactions. Finally, procedural continuity reflects how often the Court (or other actors) change (or disregard) fundamental rules such as those guiding standing, how cases arrive to the Court, its jurisdiction, and so on. Each of these features was assessed in Argentina and Brazil through multiple interviews with sitting and retired high court justices and clerks, as well as by reading the Courts' rulings and local scholars' accounts of their decision making. The first two elements of Court character (stability and professional profile) also contribute to institutional cohesion. The more stable a high court and the stronger and more homogeneous the professional backgrounds of its members, the more experience working together justices acquire, the more mutual respect can grow among them, the more easily a consensual notion of the Court's role can emerge, and the more sense it makes to establish and follow consistent procedures – in other words – the more naturally and easily institutional cohesion will develop.

The Court Character Account of Interbranch Interactions

In contexts where courts have long wielded power, scholars have developed several approaches to explaining high court–elected branch relations.[55] In

[53] Web Appendices 3.4 and 4.5 contain the relevant data; Chapters 3 and 4 discuss scoring.

[54] Of course, even on the well-institutionalized United States Supreme Court, not all justices agree on the Court's role. The lack of agreement is more troublesome in weakly institutionalized settings where political leaders can more easily exploit (or address – through expansion and packing) a lack of role consensus.

[55] Barnes (2007: 28–34) reviews three "modes of interbranch analysis" in the United States: separation-of-powers games, regime politics studies, and microinstitutional analysis.

polities where judicial power has begun to expand more recently, explaining interbranch interactions is a newer enterprise.[56] In line with what has been referred to as the "strategic revolution in judicial politics" (Epstein and Knight 2000), most accounts fall in the strategic camp. One set of studies argues that political divisions afford courts space to hand down assertive decisions, and make it harder for the government to ignore or coordinate to overturn such rulings. For instance, Ginsburg's study of Asian courts posits the existence of two models of judicial review, "low equilibrium" (in which courts issue relatively few challenging decisions, which are generally of little importance) and "high equilibrium" (in which courts issue many important decisions and elected leaders generally obey them). Ginsburg argues that where a consistently dominant party can constrain courts, low-equilibrium judicial review is likely, while in contexts of party system fragmentation high equilibrium judicial review emerges (2003: 251–2).[57]

Epstein et al. (2001), in their study of the Russian Constitutional Court, posit that in young democracies, Courts will only rule on cases in policy areas on which all elected leaders (the president and both houses of parliament) see eye-to-eye (in their parlance, when their "tolerance intervals" overlap) and will generally weakly endorse the exercise of government power. In contrast to Ginsburg's account and others based on the fragmentation of political power, in Epstein et al.'s model, elected leaders do not need to coordinate to attack a Court: one branch of government alone – and either the upper or lower chamber of parliament by itself – can threaten high courts. Correspondingly, young Courts are more likely to *avoid* deciding crucial cases when there are pronounced political divisions (i.e., when the three branches of government's tolerance intervals overlap very little). Yet if Courts do not miscalculate when weakly endorsing the exercise of government power under conditions of unified government, their legitimacy grows, and they should eventually be able to issue more rulings on important cases in a growing spectrum of policy arenas regardless of political divisions (and with compliance).

A second set of explanations broadens the strategic map to examine the effect the relationship between courts and *society* has on interbranch relations.[58] Vanberg (1998, 2001) and Carrubba and Van Winkle (2000) posit that high courts are more likely to be assertive, and government authorities more

[56] As with judicial power, some studies of "Court-executive relations" only examine judicial decision making rather than also exploring how elected leaders respond to Courts' politically challenging decisions. I discuss here work examining mutual interbranch interactions.

[57] Such arguments might seem to suffer a logical lapse: If the elected branches cannot coordinate sufficiently to overturn judicial rulings, how can they coordinate sufficiently to comply with them? Yet, in fact, it might be harder for political leaders to coordinate to develop and pass a constitutional amendment that serves to overturn a judicial decision than to coordinate to amend a statute in order to comply with a Court's dictates. Complying with a ruling that vetoes a statute, for instance, could require elected leaders to do nothing at all. Indeed, judicial power is constructed, in part, out of this asymmetry. I thank an anonymous reviewer for this insight.

[58] Note that Epstein et al.'s (2001) account also implicates society, as the evolution of interbranch relations rests in part on high courts' increasing popular legitimacy.

likely to comply with their challenging rulings, when Courts have a loyal constituent base ready to defend them. Staton's (2004) argument follows a similar logic: He posits that Mexican courts are more likely to challenge elected leaders in a certain case – and those leaders more likely to comply – when they anticipate public support for that challenging ruling, an outcome more likely to obtain when courts "go public" in concerted attempts to rally popular support for their decisions (Staton 2006, 2010).

Like explanations of Court crafting, then, most theories of high court–elected branch relations suggest that Courts' willingness to challenge the exercise of government power and elected leaders' willingness to comply with those challenges are strategic choices based on momentary calculations about factors in the political environment – in particular the configuration of political power and societal support. The political context is certainly replete with cues and dynamics that guide and influence interbranch interactions – from political divisions and societal pressures to economic crisis and democratic stability. This book does not dispute that. Rather, I aim to broaden our analytic focus to consider how historical-institutional legacies of judicial development and Courts' resulting characters *also* affect interbranch interactions and help to explain the relatively persistent patterns in which they emerge. We can better understand interbranch relations and the way justices' and elected leaders' strategic behavior varies across time and space, I submit, if we consider the political, historical, and institutional foundations of their behavior.

To add some nuance, the Court character thesis argues that the congeries of informal institutional features that comprise a Court's character shapes the way it decides cases of crucial political significance and conditions the way elected leaders respond to its challenging decisions, leading to the emergence of identifiable patterns of interbranch interaction. Court character serves to channel interbranch interactions into enduring patterns because it tends to remain fairly stable. Why? First, Court-crafting practices (that is, choices about populating high courts, reflected in the stability and professional profile aspects of Court character) tend to become locked-in as the resulting Courts serve appointers' purposes (at least for a time) and expectations form in society and the political and legal communities about how high courts are constituted. This legacy quality demonstrates why it is not counterintuitive to account for the nature of *mutual* interbranch relations by pointing to the character of just one involved entity (Courts): At least in polities where elected leaders carry out Court crafting, Court character embodies historic elected branch preferences and choices. Second, public opinion (reflected in the legitimacy dimension of Court character) tends to evolve slowly. And finally, Courts' institutional cohesion depends on informal norms and practices justices develop (for instance, to what degree leadership emerges and is respected, how justices treat each other in and out of conference, and whether procedures exist and are followed), which become part of institutional culture and thus difficult to alter. In other words, each aspect of Court character is sticky.

A brief description of how Court character shaped interbranch relations in Argentina and Brazil should clarify how the argument works. Table 1.3 outlines the causal framework. In Argentina, more often than not since mid-century, leaders sought to *politicize* the CSJN, frequently trying to resize and repopulate it and to appoint allies even if their professional backgrounds were weaker. The result was a *political* Court: less stable, with a weaker professional profile, less legitimate, and less institutionally cohesive. The Court's instability and insecurity, and the weaker qualifications of some of its justices, encouraged it to defer to elected leaders, endorsing the exercise of government power in the crucial economic realm (*Court submission*). The CSJN's weaker legitimacy and institutional cohesion likewise facilitated this outcome: The Court had few exogenous or endogenous sources of strength to support rulings challenging elected leaders. Yet the Court's political character was a double-edged sword. When an executive who had not yet managed to align the Court with his administration (or who had lost his loyal majority) threatened the CSJN, those threats served as a rallying point that helped the Court to overcome its weak cohesion and issue strong challenges on highly salient cases. Indeed, the Court was liberated to do so by the fact that even noncompliance by elected leaders would do little to tarnish its already dull institutional image. In fact, elected leaders generally complied only partially or even ignored such strong challenges, given the established expectation that they would eventually be able to replace the Court with one that *would* defer to them, and the relatively low political cost of disobeying the unpopular institution. In this way, the CSJN's political character encouraged *Court submission* interrupted by bouts of interbranch *confrontation* over economic governance.

The character of Brazil's high court, which contrasts sharply with that of its Argentine counterpart, shaped very different interbranch interactions there. Brazilian authorities had traditionally *professionalized* the high court – keeping its size and composition stable and appointing justices with strong, varied professional backgrounds regardless of their political or personal allegiances – and they continued these practices in the postauthoritarian era. This produced a *statesman* court – a more stable, professional institution with more perceived legitimacy and cohesion. The STF' s character contributed to producing a pattern of interbranch interaction marked by *accommodation* in the realm of economic governance. The STF's particular mix of justices (those with more political experience who tended to worry about the consequences of their rulings, and those with more judicial experience who tended toward a literal defense of the constitution) required intracourt compromise (possible due to the Court's collegiality). On some occasions, the STF issued "middle-of-the-road" rulings – weaker endorsements and challenges – that accommodated elected leaders who had introduced constitutionally questionable policies. On other occasions, one "camp" of justices or the other moved to the decision-making forefront. When justices with more judicial experience did so, the STF issued strong challenges to elected leaders (helping the Court to retain its legitimacy with the influential legal community). Yet such decisions were often followed

TABLE 1.3. *Patterns of Interbranch Interaction over Economic Governance in Argentina and Brazil, and Corresponding Court Character and Politics of Court Crafting*

	Argentina	Brazil
Patterns of interbranch interaction	**Court submission** (Tendency for high court to endorse the exercise of government power, issue stronger endorsements and weaker challenges, and adopt a deferential approach to decision making; tendency for elected leaders to comply partially and retaliate infrequently) **Confrontation** (Tendency for high court to challenge the exercise of government power, issue weaker endorsements and stronger challenges, and reject a deferential approach to decision-making; Tendency for elected leaders to comply partially or not at all and retaliate frequently)	**Accommodation** (No clear tendency in direction or intensity of high court rulings, but tendency to reject a deferential approach to decision-making; tendency for elected leaders to comply partially or significantly and retaliate infrequently)
Court character	**Political**	**Statesman**
Stability	Less stable	More stable
Justices' professional backgrounds	Justices with less experience in federal judiciary, executive, or legislature; some justices with stronger ties to appointers	Justices with more experience in federal judiciary, executive, legislature, or prosecutor's office; weaker ties to appointers
Legitimacy (support among public & legal community)	Weaker	Stronger
Institutional cohesion	Weaker (Weaker consensus on role; weaker leadership; less collegiality; less procedural continuity)	Stronger (Stronger consensus on role; stronger leadership; more collegiality; more procedural continuity)
Politics of Court crafting	**Politicization** (Manipulation of the size and composition of the high court and appointment of justices with somewhat weaker qualifications and stronger ties to elected leaders)	**Professionalization** (Maintenance of the high courts' size and allowance for natural evolution in its composition; appointment of justices with stronger professional profiles and few ties to elected leaders)

by rulings in which justices with more political experience had a stronger hand; their influence facilitated interbranch negotiation and resulted in pragmatic rulings (often endorsements) that helped the STF to retain its support among political elites. This alternation was another way in which the Court's rulings accommodated elected leaders. Threatening or ignoring the statesman Court could have been politically (and financially) costly for elected leaders. Given the judicialization of politics, they could expect to continue to face off with the STF – a Court whose multifaceted support and institutional cohesiveness lent it the potential to be a formidable enemy if antagonized by political authorities (rather than backing down, as strategic approaches would predict and as a Court of a different character might do). Brazilian leaders thus accommodated the Court, complying with its rulings as they could.

In short, facets of the Argentine and Brazilian high courts' distinct characters contributed to producing very different patterns of interbranch interaction over economic governance in the postauthoritarian period. This argument builds on and extends strategic accounts of interbranch relations, blending rational choice and historical institutionalism. The Court character thesis takes as a given that political and judicial leaders are goal-oriented, although I argue that rather than having exogenously bestowed and stable preferences, Courts establish multiple substantive and institutional goals internally and reprioritize them as they decide different cases. Likewise, I understand the choices that justices and politicians make as they pursue those goals to be, in part, reactions to the opportunities and constraints in their environment; indeed, I show how partisan politics affect the Court crafting that shapes Court character.

Yet I take issue with two basic tenets of the strategic approach. First, arguments in the strategic vein often implicitly assume that courts *want* to challenge elected leaders and focus on identifying the factors that limit their ability to do so (that lead them to rule *strategically*). The Court character thesis, by contrast, suggests that Courts are not necessarily, and certainly not exclusively, predisposed to challenge political authorities; statesman Courts such as Brazil's are a case in point. Second, strategic approaches to explaining relations between high courts and elected leaders often seem to understand each interbranch interaction as an independent event in which judges and politicians decide how to act based on the current political environment and their expectations about how other actors might act. This study posits that we can understand interbranch interactions better by examining them over time, considering the connections among different interactions. Doing so reveals how comparatively stable informal high court features condition the strategic choices that justices and elected leaders make as they tangle over politically crucial cases, producing relatively persistent patterns of interaction. Historical institutional trajectories influence strategic behavior even in politically unstable settings such as those of Latin America.

The present account thus also contributes to the emerging line of inquiry on informal institutions in Latin America. Scholars of judicial dynamics in the region have examined how formal judicial institutions (rules and procedures formalized in law or enforced through official channels) affect judicial behavior (e.g., Arantes 2005; Cepeda Espinosa 2005; Wilson 2005; Ríos-Figueroa and Taylor 2006). Yet cognizant that focusing exclusively on formal rules when studying political dynamics "can yield an incomplete – if not wholly inaccurate – picture of how politics works" (O'Donnell 2006: 287; see also Helmke and Levitsky 2004), some students of Latin American courts have also begun to consider how a range of *informal* institutions affect judicial behavior (e.g., Brinks 2003; Chavez 2004a; Couso 2005; Hilbink 2007). I build on that foundation to highlight how elected leaders' informal Court-crafting *practices* and the informal institutional *features* that compose Court character – practices and features that are created and reinforced through the repetition of elected and judicial actors' behaviors over time rather than being mandated in written form – shape political and judicial outcomes.

1.4. STRUCTURE OF THE BOOK

Chapter 2 offers background information that sets the stage for the remainder of the analysis. It first describes the legal transition that Argentina and Brazil – like countries across Latin America – have been undergoing since their transitions to democracy. This transition comprises the placement of issues relating to the rule of law and legal accountability on the political/electoral agenda, growing concern about rights within civil society, constitutional renewal or reform, as well as judicial reform and judicialization. The chapter then offers a brief review of the central aspects of neoliberal reform in each country. Finally, it describes how the simultaneity of legal and economic transition generated a judicialization of economic governance in each context.

Given the judicialization of economic governance, Latin American policy makers could anticipate judicial challenges to their crucial economic initiatives. For elected leaders who had championed constitutional renewal, rule of law entrenchment, and judicial reform, ignoring such challenges would seem incoherent. They thus devised a different solution – a two-pronged judicial strategy that would enlist their high court's help in setting their economic policies firmly in place, discussed in Chapters 3 and 4. On the one hand, Argentine and Brazilian leaders engaged in *judicial centralization*, empowering and hastening the arrival of cases to their high courts, drawing them irrevocably into the political game. Second, in an effort to create high courts that would facilitate governance, elected leaders adopted a particular politics of Court crafting. Court-crafting practices in the two countries were quite distinct, the chapters demonstrate, guided as they were by history (the Court-crafting politics that had become locked in since the mid-twentieth century in each context through a path-dependent process) *and* by partisan politics and formal institutions. Argentine and Brazilian leaders' very different politics of Court crafting produced Courts of contrasting characters.

Chapters 5 and 6 examine and account for the divergent patterns of interbranch interaction over economic governance that emerged in Argentina and

Brazil in the postauthoritarian period, analyzing high court rulings and elected leaders' responses on a systematically selected intermediate-N set of cases (N = 18 in Argentina; N = 26 in Brazil). The chapters use qualitative analysis, including rich case studies, and draw on rational choice and historical institutionalism, to develop and advance the Court character thesis – arguing that the Argentine and Brazilian high courts' very different characters contribute to explaining the contrasting patterns of interbranch interaction in the two contexts.

Finally, the book's conclusion summarizes its findings and their implications and discusses the study's contributions to broader debates in comparative politics and public law – concerning the institutional approach to accounting for political phenomena, and the relationship between entrenching the rule of law and economic development. It also suggests that the connections the book draws among Court crafting, judicial decision making, and elected branch compliance and retaliation imply the existence of broader judicial cycles that nest into larger political processes in different ways, leading Courts to be both causes and effects of crucial political outcomes.

2

Setting the Scene: Latin America's Triple Transition and the Judicialization of Economic Governance

"*We need a way to avoid being exposed to the risks of the New Deal.*"
– An aid to Argentine President Menem, referring to United States Supreme Court rulings against President Roosevelt's economic program in the 1930s (Prillaman 2000: 123)

"*With that constitution, the country will become ungovernable.*"
– Brazilian President José Sarney's public reaction to the 1988 Constitution (mentioned in EC-11)

2.1. INTRODUCTION

The regime transitions that occurred in Latin America through the 1980s, part of the "third wave" of democracy that rolled across much of the developing world from the mid-1970s to the early 1990s, have received extensive attention from scholars of the region (O'Donnell, Schmitter, and Whitehead 1986; Huntington 1991; Linz and Stepan 1996; and Collier 1999 among many others). Likewise, political scientists have thoroughly analyzed the economic transition (the abandonment of inward-looking state-led economic development and adoption of market-based reforms) that many Latin American polities underwent in the postauthoritarian period to address the dramatic economic crises of the 1980s and put their countries on more solid economic footing (see, e.g., Haggard and Kaufman 1992, 1995; Oxhorn and Ducatenzeiler 1998; and Stokes 2001). Scholars have also highlighted the negative implications – for democratic quality and stability, and for economic development – of the escalating public discontent, socioeconomic conflict, and other dynamics associated with the simultaneity or rapid succession of these two transitions (e.g., Smith 1991; Kingstone 2006).[1]

[1] Of course, neither regime nor economic transition was unidirectional: Events in Venezuela and Honduras early in the twenty-first century showed the fragility of democracy, as those in Ecuador and Bolivia suggested significant regional heterogeneity with respect to the acceptance of neoliberalism and market-based economics.

This book showcases the challenges created by the simultaneity of economic restructuring and a *third* transition that began as Latin American countries emerged from authoritarian rule: a halting, nonlinear, and multifaceted process of legal and judicial change that we can label a *legal transition*.[2] This transition, which proceeded unevenly – in different ways, in different directions, at different paces, and to different degrees – across Latin America, is marked by five interacting elements.[3] First, the rule of law and legal accountability have been increasingly emphasized in public discourse and on political and electoral agendas. Second, political and social actors have become more concerned about the fulfillment of constitutional rights (see, e.g., Sikkink 2005). A third element is constitutional renewal and reform, which have raised the profile of the region's constitutions and increased the likelihood that they would form the basis for individual and collective policy contestation. Fourth, judicial reform programs aimed at enhancing courts' efficiency and independence from elected leaders and augmenting access to justice have been introduced in most countries (see, e.g., Prillaman 2000: 15; Finkel 2001; and Brinks 2005). Finally, politics were judicialized: citizens and civil society groups with unmet expectations regarding representation and government accountability, and members of the political opposition whose policy objectives were thwarted in congress, increasingly turned to newly empowered and formally independent courts to vindicate rights and contest policy.[4] In short, the judicial arena became a locus of politics, drawing Latin American courts into political conflicts to a greater degree than ever before.

The significance of these changes cannot be overstated. A legal transition alters political dynamics by raising the constitutional and judicial stakes. Whereas not long ago the conventional wisdom held that constitutions are of little importance in Latin America (e.g., Rosenn 1990b), following salient processes of rewriting and reform, constitutions now often serve as the basis for crucial judicial cases and rulings, making them – and the degree to which

[2] Scholars have suggested that Central and Eastern European polities underwent triple or quadruple transitions, considering the establishment of state institutions, and in some cases completion of the nation-building process, the third or fourth transitions (see, for instance, Kuzio 2001). Analysts have also posited that African countries experienced a triple transition, with the third transformation being the emergence from colonial rule (e.g., Mattes and Bratton 2001). Zakaria (1997) suggests something similar to the third (legal) transition posited here, referring to the rise of constitutionalism and liberalism. My conceptualization builds on a series of dynamics mentioned by Domingo (2004: 105).

[3] As with multifaceted economic transition, the separate elements of the legal transition have also progressed at different speeds over time in the *same* context.

[4] Judicialization has received a great deal of scholarly attention in Latin America (e.g., Domingo 2004; Gargarella 2004; Sieder, Schjolden, and Angell 2005; Taylor 2008; Couso, Huneeus, and Sieder 2010) and around the world (see, among many others, Tate and Vallinder 1995; Ferejohn 2002; Shapiro and Stone Sweet 2002; Stone Sweet 2002; and Hirschl 2004). Nonetheless, the concept remains contested. Following Hirschl 2008, I define judicialization as an increasing use of courts by political and social actors to hold leaders accountable, influence policymaking, and resolve political conflict.

policy attends to them – increasingly critical. The way in which a legal transition evolves also has implications for whether and how courts can contribute to establishing binding institutional constraints on the exercise of state power. And as courts are drawn further into the policy process, who judges are and how they rule become more and more important.

The dramatic neoliberal economic restructuring that began as (or soon after) Latin American countries transitioned from authoritarianism – and that placed economic policy making at the top of the political agenda and at the center of political conflict in the postauthoritarian period – is more familiar. Facing substantial international and domestic pressure for reform, the region's elected leaders – again, to differing degrees and at different paces – sought to move their economies away from statist, import-substitution industrialization toward a neoliberal, open-market model. The initial steps focused on economic stabilization (via shock therapy to control inflation, wage and price freezes, and the introduction of new currencies) and structural adjustment (including selling state enterprises; scaling back the state's role as investor and regulator; cutting government programs and services; reforming the civil service, tax and social security systems; and opening the economy through trade, capital, and financial market liberalization). In many countries, some elements of the chaotic policy mix through which stabilization and structural adjustment programs were introduced, and some aspects of the processes that elected leaders employed to legislate and implement them, seemed to entail constitutional infringements and faced strong opposition from certain citizens, civil society groups, politicians, and political parties. For instance, policy responses to economic crisis such as freezes on bank accounts, devaluations, and salary cuts or pension reductions arguably impinged on property rights and other constitutional guarantees. Likewise, when presidents who wished to carry out reforms expeditiously introduced policies by decree rather than using legislative channels, they sometimes crossed boundaries of executive authority.

Had governments implemented their constitutionally questionable and unpopular reform and crisis-management policies in democratizing contexts that were *not* in legal transformation, less constitutional controversy might have erupted.[5] Yet the legal transition that many Latin American countries were undergoing heightened the sensitivity of citizens, civil society organizations, and the political opposition to elected officials' bending of legal and constitutional rules. It also raised awareness of judicial options to redress grievances. As a result, civil society organizations, interest groups, policy entrepreneurs, and politicians who opposed elected leaders' flouting of rights and institutional boundaries increasingly framed their frustrations – or political battles lost in congress – in legal or constitutional terms, and turned to newly

[5] Consider Chile, where neoliberal reform was implemented under dictatorship, that is, in a context that was decidedly not undergoing a legal transition: reform was neither vigorously opposed (at least publicly), nor judicialized.

empowered courts to challenge economic policies. In other words, the depth and simultaneity of Latin America's legal and economic transformations led to the judicialization of economic governance.

Thus while economic reform and economic governance are generally viewed as managed exclusively by government technocrats and international financial institutions (IFIs), in many contexts societal actors and opposition politicians have also sought to participate in the management of the economy. At times they did so by invoking courts, constitutionalism, and the rule of law, drawing courts into economic debate and battle as well. This chapter briefly examines Argentina's and Brazil's legal and economic transitions, describing how their simultaneity led to a judicialization of economic governance in each country.

2.2. ARGENTINA'S LEGAL TRANSITION

The brutality of the military regime that ruled Argentina from 1976 to 1983 (see Guest 1990; Nino 1996), and its relatively rapid collapse following Argentina's defeat in the Falkland Islands War in 1982, placed issues of the rule of law and rights concerns at the top of the political agenda as the country transitioned to democracy in 1983. In 1994, Argentina significantly revised its constitution, reforming the judiciary in the process. In part due to these aspects of the country's legal transition, politics became judicialized in the posttransition period, and remain so thirty years later.

Inclusion on the Political/Electoral Agenda of Rule of Law Issues

Argentina's first postauthoritarian president, Raúl Alfonsín (1983–9), had run for office on a platform that emphasized bringing to justice those who had committed illegal acts under the previous military regime, and institutionalizing legal changes to ensure the protection of human rights (Nino 1996: 61–2). Just days after his inauguration, Alfonsín signed a decree creating the National Commission on Disappeared Persons (CONADEP), with a mandate to determine the fate and whereabouts of those who had disappeared during the dictatorship (Nino 1996: 68–70). With the eventual cooperation of myriad human rights organizations, CONADEP amassed 50,000 pages of files, which it summarized into a report in September 1984.[6] And in 1985 and 1986, Argentina placed on trial, convicted, sentenced, and jailed officials of the military *juntas* of the previous authoritarian period. The trials, in combination with the subsequent filing of countless cases involving lower-ranking military and security officers accused of repression, engendered considerable discontent within the

[6] The report identified approximately 9,000 people who had died or disappeared during the "dirty war" carried out under the seven-year dictatorship, but some human rights groups estimate that at least 30,000 died or disappeared (*BBC News*, August 21, 2002, "Argentina's 'Dirty War' Files Released"). The report was subsequently published under the name *Nunca Más* (Never Again), and sold more copies than any other book in Argentine history (Nino 1996: 80).

military, which successfully pressured to end them.[7] Nonetheless, issues relating to the rule of law had been placed irrevocably on the political agenda.

The political focus shifted to dealing with the devastating economic legacy of authoritarian rule in the later 1980s and 1990s. However, Peronist President Carlos Menem (1989–99) retained rule of law issues on the political agenda through his discourse (for instance, repeated references to "rule of law construction"), perhaps convinced by the IFIs overseeing market-based reforms that legal reform and juridical security would augment investor confidence (and, by association, economic growth), or perhaps to garner popular support. Yet the Menem administration's periodic *disregard* for the rule of law and alleged alarming levels of corruption were at least as important for keeping issues of the rule of law (and legal accountability in particular) on the electoral and popular agenda (Domingo 2004: 104, 115, 119).

In late 2001, economic collapse propelled Argentina into unprecedented crisis. Following President Fernando De la Rúa's (1999–2001) resignation in late December 2001, three interim leaders held office briefly before congress appointed Peronist Eduardo Duhalde president for a two-year period on January 1, 2002. Spiraling crime and public insecurity made the state's ability to maintain law and order central political concerns and key issues in the next presidential contest, held in April 2003.[8] A salient example of the degeneration of the rule of law with the 2001 crisis, one that brought legal and security issues very much to the fore, were the increasingly disruptive activities of the *piqueteros*, a social movement of the unemployed.[9] Néstor Kirchner (2003–7), the Peronist and then protégé of Duhalde who was ultimately victorious in the 2003 presidential contest,[10] reignited rule of law concerns linked to the previous dictatorship as soon as he assumed office in May 2003, encouraging congress to declare null and void the late 1980s laws that had ended the trials of officials involved in the previous military regime.[11] In addition, the president sought to purge the country's military and police leadership in an effort to address corruption and public concern about the state's capacity to provide law-bound public security (Freedom House 2006: 3). In all, throughout

[7] Moreover, in October 1989 and December 1990 President Carlos Menem (1989–1999) officially pardoned nearly 300 civilians and military officers accused or convicted of engaging in terrorism or state-sponsored violence.

[8] President Duhalde announced in July 2002 that the presidential election would be held in April 2003 rather than December 2003 as initially planned (*New York Times*, July 3, 2002, "Argentine Leader Moves Elections Forward").

[9] The death of two *piqueteros* during protests in Buenos Aires in June 2002, which judicial investigations and the press blamed on the state intelligence agency, further augmented the issue's salience (*New York Times*, July 3, 2002, "Argentine Leader Moves Elections Forward").

[10] Former President Menem won the largest plurality but bowed out of the race before a run-off scheduled for mid-May was held.

[11] Even though congress is empowered to repeal laws (rendering them void into the future), it cannot annul them retroactively, as it sought to do here. The Supreme Court overturned the amnesty laws in June 2005, and military officers were again placed on trial later that decade.

the postauthoritarian period, issues related to the rule of law were constant fixtures on the political agenda.

Civil Society's Increasing Concern with Rights

Countries across Latin America experienced enormous upsurges in civil society activity around the issue of human rights as their countries moved toward democratic transition (O'Donnell and Schmitter 1986). The resurgence of civil society in Argentina was a particularly vigorous one.[12] Myriad human rights organizations sprung up in the late 1970s and early 1980s, and individual rights-related activity also increased. The CONADEP report and the trials of former military officials kept Argentines' attention riveted on human rights after regime change, and important rights-focused nongovernmental organizations (NGOs) continued to form thereafter. Rights groups persisted in pushing human rights issues well into the 1990s, engaging in regional and international cooperation in their attempts to circumvent the laws halting military trials (Sikkink 2005: 273, 278). The integration into the constitution (through its 1994 reform) of a series of international human rights treaties and agreements (Article 75, clause 22) again focused attention on rights.

A broader discourse of rights extending to social and economic rights also developed in the postauthoritarian era as legal mobilization emerged as a tool to claim existing rights *and* to develop new rights (for instance in the area of interpersonal relations), and actors used the new discourse to call public attention to rights-related demands and conflicts (Smulovitz 2005: 169). Finally, the Kirchner administration's emphasis in the first decade of the 2000s on reopening trials against those who had perpetrated rights abuses under the military regime further strengthened the resolve of human rights activists and groups.

Constitutional Reform

In a region in which rewriting the constitution has been referred to as the "favorite indoor sport" (Rosenn 1990b: 7), Argentina exhibits unusual constitutional stability. The country is still ruled under its first national charter (the 1853 Constitution). The constitution has been reformed on only six occasions since promulgation,[13] perhaps due to relatively high barriers to amendment.[14] Consequently, the extensive reform carried out in 1994 was a significant

[12] Sikkink (2005: 272) suggests that Argentina's was a "society-led" transition to democracy.

[13] The charter was reformed or amended in 1860, 1866, 1898, 1949, 1957, and 1994 (just once in the postauthoritarian period) and remains relatively brief (approximately 12,600 words in 2012).

[14] Per Article 30, a vote of at least two-thirds of congress is necessary to initiate a process of constitutional reform or rewriting, and changing the charter requires the election and operation of a constitutional convention.

political event.[15] The reform was based on a bargain between the country's two major political parties, the Peronists and the Radical Party (*Unión Cívica Radical*, UCR): strengthening institutional constraints on the presidency (the Radical Party's priority) in exchange for the possibility of consecutive presidential reelection (the Peronists' main goal).[16] The reform served to establish some important controls on executive authority,[17] but their implementation ultimately did little to rein in the president (Finkel 2001: 85–98); moreover, certain elements of the reform worked to *expand* presidential power.[18] Argentina would continue to be characterized by hyper-presidentialism (or "delegative democracy," O'Donnell 1994).

Two facets of the constitution of particular import to this study are its inclusion of rights (and economic and social rights in particular) and mechanisms to enforce them, and its stipulations regarding government involvement in the economic realm. The 1853 Constitution (as reformed over time) provides a broad range of individual and some collective social and economic rights. Workers' rights were added to the constitution in 1957, and the charter offers other special protections to labor (Carrió 1996: 178). Citizens' right to file *amparo* claims was constitutionalized through the 1994 reform,[19] and the position of national Ombudsman (*Defensor del Pueblo*), charged with ensuring the protection of constitutional rights, was also created (Finkel 2001: 98). Further, several international treaties and agreements regarding human rights were integrated into the charter through the 1994 reform, most with constitutional status (Article 75, clause 22), meaning that Argentina's charter formally contains as many rights and guarantees as do some social constitutions such as Mexico's 1917 charter and Colombia's 1991 Constitution. By contrast, even after its 1994 reform, the Argentine Constitution does not include guidelines concerning the economic model under which the country should operate or to what degree the government should intervene in the economy. The charter does, however, include a few clauses concerning customs and duties, discuss the economic activities congress is empowered to carry out, and outline a few

[15] The 1994 reform did not produce a "new" constitution. The first article of the Declaratory Law calling for the formation of a constitutional assembly (December 1993) expressly noted the need to "partially reform" the 1853 charter (Finkel 2001: 92, Helmke 2000: 190).

[16] See Finkel (2001: 85–124) for an in-depth examination of the Peronist-UCR bargain and the general political dynamics underpinning the 1994 reform.

[17] For instance, the presidential term was decreased from six to four years; judicial independence was increased (mainly through changing the appointment procedures for high court justices and the creation of a National Judicial Council); the number of senators was increased (to provide the opposition additional legislative representation); and the Office of Auditor General (led by a major opposition party) was created (see Finkel 2001).

[18] For instance, the constitutional provision barring immediate presidential reelection was removed, Decrees of Necessity and Urgency (DNUs) were constitutionalized (although their use was limited to particular areas and exceptional conditions), and a partial presidential veto was established (see Finkel 2001).

[19] An *amparo* is a type of remedy entailing accelerated judicial decision making on cases in which plaintiffs allege that the government has violated their constitutional rights through arbitrary or illegal action (Helmke 2000: 272).

of congress's general responsibilities in the economic realm.[20] The 1994 reform also assigned several commercial treaties a status "higher than laws."[21]

Judicial Reform[22]

As in many Latin American countries in the postauthoritarian era, Argentina's judicial reform was encouraged and supported by IFIs, which viewed it as critical for entrenching the rule of law and strengthening democracy.[23] Nonetheless, national-level reform in Argentina was narrow and incremental (Prillaman 2000: 111). Under Alfonsín, efforts focused on the replacement of the Supreme Court and the modernization of criminal and penal laws. Menem's reforms in the 1990s centered on judicial efficiency and access. The 1991 penal code reform doubled the number of federal judges sitting on criminal courts, and eventually oral argumentation was introduced into the federal criminal justice system.[24] The National Judicial Council created via the 1994 constitutional reform was charged with selecting all judges (except for Supreme Court justices) through a reformed process, overseeing lower-court judges, and administering the judiciary.[25] Also, the judicial records system was computerized to facilitate case tracking and management and hasten case flow. Finally, Menem established a national judicial studies center to analyze reform, introduced an impressive program of alternative dispute resolution and mediation, increased access to free legal aid, and expanded the use of public defenders and prosecutors (Prillaman 2000: 113–21; Ungar 2002: 10–11, 145–8). Menem's perceived manipulation of courts and judges dampened the reforms' potential positive effects on judicial legitimacy, however (Prillaman 2000: 121).

Judicialization of Politics

Courts emerged as a venue in which individuals and civil society could press rights claims and the opposition could engage in political contestation in

[20] The activities concern, specifically, customs, taxes, allocations and subsidies to the provinces, debt and credit, management of national lands, the Central Bank, and the regulation of trade and integration. The general responsibilities include, for instance, "providing for the prosperity of the country" (Section 75, clause 18), and "providing everything relevant to human development, economic progress" (Section 75, clause 19).

[21] Although the Argentine legal system does not officially provide for an intermediary position between laws and the constitution, per the charter, such treaties trump domestic law (following congressional approval) (Section 75, clause 24).

[22] For a more detailed description of judicial reform in Argentina, see Prillaman (2000), Ungar (2002), and Finkel (2004).

[23] The Inter-American Development Bank's project in Argentina was one of the largest judicial reform initiatives planned by an IFI (Ungar 2002: 10–11).

[24] Finkel (2001: 84–5) suggests that the president picked judges to fill the newly created posts whom he believed would serve as a "filter" to terminate inconvenient cases.

[25] The Council's members were not sworn in until November 1998, and the Council did not begin to operate until early 1999 (Finkel 2004: 72; 99).

postauthoritarian Argentina. As a result, the judiciary – including the high court – has been overrun with cases since the mid 1990s (Web Appendix 2.1 provides the CSJN's case-load statistics).[26] Throughout the decade, newspaper articles repeatedly referred to the judicial "crisis" caused by the judiciary's overload (in tandem with its other deficiencies), outlined governmental plans to address that crisis, and cautioned of a growing "judicial emergency."[27]

Of course, the dramatic increase in courts' case loads could simply be the result of increased litigiousness around nonpolitical issues. Yet there is evidence that the judicial explosion resulted from the judicialization of politics. First, on average, almost half of the cases filed with the high court each year between 1995 and 2001 were filed by plaintiffs questioning pension laws passed during the 1980s and early 1990s (see again Web Appendix 2.1). Other types of "repeat cases" worth millions of dollars to the government – in particular regarding the constitutionality of currency adjustments associated with economic crisis – were also filed with the Court in the 1990s and early 2000s (Santiago 1998: 352–4).[28] Moreover, scholars often allude to a judicialization of politics in Argentina,[29] and several experts I interviewed described the opposition's use of courts as a political strategy (EC-14, EC-23); discussed the "*industria del juicio*" (lawyers' encouragement of plaintiffs to sue the state, EC-30, EC-35); and suggested that the dismantlement of most limits on executive power meant that control of the state was essentially carried out through *amparos* in the 1990s (E-18). These accounts point to a judicialization of politics in Argentina.

2.3. ARGENTINA'S ECONOMIC TRANSITION AND THE JUDICIALIZATION OF ECONOMIC GOVERNANCE

This section briefly describes Argentina's postauthoritarian (1984–2003) economic context. It then discusses the central aspects of the reforms the country's new leaders introduced to address the economic disaster military leaders had bequeathed them (Acuña 1994: 64), and the key policies they put in place to combat the economic crisis that rocked the nation beginning in 2001.[30] Courts were called on to consider each element of the economic transition resulting in a judicialization of economic governance.

[26] Because the high court's original jurisdiction is quite limited, most cases reach it on appeal. Thus, a dramatic increase in the filing of cases in lower courts is the only way that the high court's case load could have exploded as it did.

[27] NP 01-R-631; NP 01-R-632; NP 01-R-253; NP 02-R-464; NP 02-R-537; NP 02-R-539; NP 02-R-542; NP 02-R-553; NP 02-R-1038; NP 01-R-855; NP 01-R-869; among many others.

[28] All were concrete review cases; unlike its Brazilian counterpart, the CSJN cannot carry out abstract review. See Web Appendices 2.2 and 2.3.

[29] For instance, Domingo suggests that in the early 2000s, "courts ... remained pivotal to political and economic outcomes" and that judges were "dictating political outcomes" (2004: 115); Smulovitz describes how "courts are redefining public policies" (2005: 161).

[30] This chapter offers an extremely abbreviated and selective review of Argentina's economic history from 1984 to 2003. For a complete analysis, see, for example, Gerchunoff and Llach (2003).

Economic Context

The Alfonsín government initially sought to address the country's indebtedness, low rates of investment, salary lags, and stagflation by resuscitating the Radical Party's traditional "economic nationalism."[31] Despite positive short-term results, the government's efforts ultimately proved insufficient (Acuña 1995: 32–3). By the end of 1988, inflation, high interest rates, decreasing investment, recession, and increasing external debt combined to create a crisis of unprecedented proportions. Food riots broke out in several provinces, and between August 1988 and July 1989 retail prices rose 3,610 percent, while wholesale prices climbed 5,061 percent (Acuña 1995: 36–7). The Peronist Party's victories in the May 1989 elections surprised few, and after Alfonsín relinquished office in July (five months early), Menem assumed the reins of power in a country on the brink of economic collapse.

Under Menem, economic transition began in earnest. Even though his campaign proposals regarding the economy were unclear in 1989, Menem's policies once in office were decidedly neoliberal, prompting scholars to label his program "neoliberalism by surprise" (Stokes 2001). Opposition to reform and to the "bait and switch" tactics used to introduce it encouraged Menem and his allies to cut constitutional corners. Nonetheless, their reforms helped to eradicate inflation, decrease poverty, and ignite growth: on average, the economy grew by more than 6 percent annually through the 1990s (although growth was stronger earlier in the decade). These advances helped Menem defeat a broad field of rivals in the 1995 presidential contest. Yet unemployment remained above its 1989 level for much of the decade, exports rose and fell, and service on the external debt lagged until 1995 (Díaz 2002: 43–64; Acuña 1995: 39–40).

By 1999, in part as a result of several economic shocks,[32] the Argentine economy had begun to weaken, and the country had slipped into recession. In search of new leadership, Argentines elected Fernando De la Rúa in October 1999.[33] Despite his efforts and an early December promise by the International Monetary Fund (IMF) and private banks of an economic infusion of as much as $39.7 billion, labor unrest grew, the economy and exports stagnated, budget deficits persisted, foreign investment and consumer spending flagged, and

[31] That is, increasing real wages and augmenting public spending and investment while implementing price controls, increasing taxes on exports, and decreasing payments on the country's external debt to levels significantly below what creditor banks and the International Monetary Fund (IMF) expected.

[32] These included a flattening of prices for Argentine commodities, higher costs for capital for emerging economies, an appreciation of the dollar against other currencies, the Asian crisis, and currency devaluation in Argentina's main trading partner, Brazil (*New York Times*, February 3, 2002).

[33] De la Rúa, a member of the Radical Party, was running as the candidate of the center-left *Alianza* coalition, which included the Radical Party and the National Solidarity Front (*Frente País Solidario*, FREPASO). He defeated both Eduardo Duhalde (a Peronist, yet arch-rival of Menem), and Domingo Cavallo (chief architect of Menem's economic reforms).

unemployment continued to rise.[34] Even after De la Rúa's desperate reinstatement of Domingo Cavallo as Minister of the Economy in March 2001, and dramatic policies such as freezing bank accounts in early December 2001 (the *corralito*), the country soon descended into the deepest financial and social crisis in its history. Cavallo resigned as Minister of Economy on December 15, 2001, and five days later De la Rúa stepped down as president, fleeing the *Casa Rosada* by helicopter amid pot-banging public demonstrations. In the last days of the year, Argentina defaulted on most of its US$ 141 billion debt, the most comprehensive and complicated sovereign debt default in world history.[35]

Throughout 2002 the Duhalde (2002–3) government implemented an extraordinary array of short-term economic measures in hopes of preventing complete financial collapse, stabilizing the economy, and qualifying for IMF assistance.[36] There were signs of hope by the end of the year,[37] and in January 2003, Argentina and the IMF finally reached an eight-month $6.7 million stand-by agreement on a loan package. The subsequent Kirchner administration (2003–7) employed a mixed approach to facilitating economic growth. Kirchner immediately took a tough stance against big business and was persistently reluctant to risk Argentina's precarious social stability by honoring international obligations.[38] However, he renegotiated defaulted debt with private investors, implementing a program that led to the conversion of more than three-quarters of the country's privately held debt to several types of bonds by March 2005.

Stabilization Plans and Monetary Policy

This subsection and the subsequent four outline some of the main aspects of economic reform in Argentina, many of which generated intense constitutional controversy. Argentina's first posttransition economic stabilization plan, Alfonsín's *Austral* Plan, was introduced in June 1985. The heterodox initiative sought to contain inflation by establishing a new currency (the *austral*), deindexing contracts, freezing salaries, and controlling prices and public

[34] *New York Times*, August 16, 2000, "Former Argentine President Warns of Economic Peril."

[35] *The Economist*, September 11, 2003.

[36] These included repeated interventions to support the *peso*, controls on foreign exchange, taxes on exports, bank holidays, various exchange offers (*canjes*) through which depositors could swap frozen bank deposits for low-interest bonds, and several measures to loosen the *corralito* (*New York Times*, March 26, 2002, "Peso Down Steeply, Argentines Strengthen Currency Curbs"; *New York Times*, March 5, 2002, "Hard Pressed Argentina to Tax all Exports"; *New York Times*, April 22, 2002, "Bank Holiday and Creditors Add to Crisis in Argentina"; *New York Times*, April 26, 2002, "Argentine Congress Tightens Rules on Bank Withdrawals"; *New York Times*, December 3, 2002, "Argentina Lifts its Freeze on Most Bank Accounts").

[37] *New York Times*, December 16, 2002, "Amid Financial Despair, Argentina Sees a Little Summer"; *New York Times*, February 25, 2003, "Signs of Life in Argentina."

[38] For instance, Kirchner failed to repay the $2.9 million Argentina owed the IMF on the basis of the January 2003 agreement (the largest default in the institution's history) (http://www.europaworld.com/pub/entry/ar.is.57, retrieved September 30, 2008).

tariffs. The plan temporarily helped the country to avoid a downward spiral into hyperinflation and to regain public, investor, and international confidence. However, by the end of 1986, inflation was again on the rise. Two broad strategies implemented in July 1987 and August 1988 had short-lived or minimal results (Acuña 1995: 35).

In September 1989, just two months after taking office, Menem established the institutional framework for his economic reform program: the extensive Law of Economic Emergency (Law 23.697).[39] The law aimed to stop the transfer of public funds to private firms; eliminate subsidies and promotional regimes; increase the independence of the Central Bank; halt the printing of money; liberalize commerce, foreign investment, and capital markets; and adjust public contracts and facilitate privatization. Moreover, following the failure of several piecemeal attempts,[40] the Menem administration succeeded in controlling inflation. The cornerstone of that success was the Convertibility Plan (Law 23.928, passed March 1991), brain-child of Minister of Economy Domingo Cavallo. Convertibility created a new currency (the *peso*) and stabilized it by pegging it to the U.S. dollar and requiring that 100 percent of the monetary base be backed by Central Bank reserves. The plan forbid the indexing of contracts and included measures aimed at improving fiscal accounts and controlling prices and the costs of production. However, it also required the government to renounce both exchange-rate and monetary policy, leaving it with few tools to respond to external economic shocks. Some believe the plan's longevity ultimately led to the extreme overvaluation of the *peso* as the 1990s progressed (*New York Times,* February 3, 2002; Smulovitz 1997: 11).

Fearing a massive run on banks as Argentina plunged into crisis in late 2001, the executive imposed a bank freeze (subsequently dubbed the "*corralito*") in early December (Decree 1570). A month later, congress promulgated the Law of Public Emergency (Law 25.561), which, among other changes, abolished convertibility: The *peso* would no longer be pegged to the dollar. And in early February 2002, the Duhalde administration issued a decree (DNU 214)[41] instituting several adjustments to monetary strategy including forcibly converting all debts and deposits from dollars to *pesos* (*pesificación*). A dizzying array of decrees and legislation followed as leaders groped to stabilize the financial system. These hasty changes to Argentina's already unstable legal framework led to an acceleration of constitutional challenges to economic policy in the courts.

[39] The law contained twenty-eight proposals in thirty chapters and was followed by a series of decrees and an additional law modifying the charter (*Carta Orgánica*) of the Central Bank.

[40] One such attempt was Plan Bonex (imposed via Decree 36/90 issued in January 1990), which included a series of measures such as freezing private savings accounts above the sum of one million *australes* and converting the frozen funds into ten-year government bonds.

[41] Argentine presidents can issue various types of decrees. DNUs, which did not officially form part of the legal system until they were written into the Constitution and softly regulated in the 1994 reform, are in theory reserved for urgent situations in which quick executive action is necessary; see footnote 18 (this chapter).

Opening the Economy and Privatization

By the late 1980s, Argentina's gigantic and inefficient public sector was contributing substantially to the country's fiscal deficit: more than 300 public enterprises engaged in a wide variety of economic activities including natural resource exploitation, services, infrastructure, industry, and banking. For the Menem government, ending the era of economic nationalism – privatizing state-run firms, deregulating, and debureaucratizing – was a crucial step toward opening the Argentine economy to the opportunities of globalization and increasing fiscal rectitude. The basis of the government's privatization program was the Law of State Reform (Law 23.696, passed August 1989), which authorized the partial or total privatization of all state firms. Even though the idea of privatization – particularly of disastrously inefficient public services – was initially supported by many Argentines, only certain factions of Peronism backed the initiative. Opposition from the other factions complicated the passage of legislation and encouraged privatization by decree (EC-21), inducing court cases questioning the manner in which privatizations were carried out. Nonetheless, 200 state firms were privatized during Menem's first term, and 50 more were privatized by 1997 (Díaz 2002: 65–93).

Social Security Reform

Argentina's pension system had entered into deficit in the 1970s and pervasive inflation through the 1980s worsened financial disequilibrium.[42] The government found it increasingly difficult to pay pensions, encouraging court cases against the state. As a result, the Menem administration passed various laws aimed at setting new rules for the system between 1991 and 1995.[43] Two were particularly important. The Integrated Pension System Law (Law 24.241, published October 1993 and effective April 1994) overhauled the national pension system, establishing a mixed system (including both public and private schemes), and requiring that pension increases be tied to growth in pension system revenue rather than to pensioners' pre-retirement income and increases in the salaries of active workers (as had been the case). The Pension Solidarity Law (Law 24.463, published March 1995) sought to minimize the immense costs of the new system by, among other things, explicitly derogating previous adjustment rules and stipulating that future increases would be determined in the annual budget law (Santiago 1998: 352–3). Both laws were controversial, and pension policy remained at the center of legal battles throughout the 1990s.

[42] As in other Latin American countries, the roots of the pension crisis were relaxed entitlement conditions, a brief period of wage averaging to calculate benefits, high payroll taxes that encouraged evasion, and easy access to the system (Arenas de Mesa and Betranou 1997: 331).

[43] The Convertibility Law mentioned previously, for instance, prohibited all indexation, tacitly invalidating all existing mechanisms of pension adjustment.

Fiscal and Tax Reform

The Menem government had little success with fiscal reform. Significant resistance from the business community and opposition parties watered down attempts to reform or establish new fiscal instruments (for instance, Law 24.073, passed April 1992), and the government's subsequent focus on collecting existing taxes did little to help revenue match public spending. The Menem government ran a deficit throughout the 1990s (save 1992 and 1993, the years in which the most significant privatizations occurred) and even the Law of Fiscal Responsibility (Law 25.152, passed September 1999), a direct attack on public spending, failed to bridge the gap (Díaz 2002: 115–39). Despite $1.4 billion in budget cuts, the introduction of another austerity package, a $2 billion tax increase, and the Law of Zero Deficit (Law 25.453, passed July 2001) instituted under De la Rúa, dramatic fiscal imbalances remained into the early 2000s (Gerchunoff and Llach 2003: 452).

Civil Service and Labor Reform

Due in part to the employment security and good salaries traditionally associated with working for the state, Argentina's civil service was extremely bloated by the end of the 1980s. Shrinking and professionalizing the civil service was thus a priority through the 1990s. A new civil service system introduced in May 1991 (*Sistema Nacional de Profesión Administrativa,* SINAPA, Decree 993) recategorized government workers; implemented new selection, evaluation, and training systems; reregulated collective negotiation (via the Law of Collective Negotiation in the Public Sector, Law 24.185, passed March 1993); imposed a new Collective Labor Agreement (implemented December 1998); and reregulated public employment (via the Regulatory Framework for Public Employment, Law 25.164, passed October 1999) (Díaz 2002: 259–76). By 1997, the national-level civil service had shrunk in size considerably, and progress had been made toward professionalization.

Broader labor reform and the flexibilization of the labor market ignited strong opposition from Argentina's politically powerful unions. The Alfonsín administration largely excluded business leaders from policy discussions and sought to neutralize labor's resistance by reforming union organizations. These initiatives were ultimately unsuccessful, and helped to prompt thirteen general strikes between 1983 and 1989. Reform accelerated under Menem.[44] He issued a decree to guide collective bargaining processes (Decree 1334) in July 1991, and four months later congress passed an extensive National Employment Law (Law 24.013) introducing strategies for regularizing informal workers and new forms of contracting, and reforming unemployment benefits. The law was

[44] From its birth in the 1940s through the mid 1980s Peronism was essentially a labor-based party with strong ties to "old guard industrial unions." However, following the transition to democracy, the party transformed itself into a "machine party" less dominated by labor. See Levitsky (2001) concerning the complicated relationship between Peronism and unions.

amended several times through the 1990s, but the large follow-up phase of the program was abandoned (Díaz 2002: 167–203). A little less than a decade later, in April 2000 under De la Rúa, congress passed a controversial new labor code including measures aimed at cutting labor costs to address unemployment and augment business productivity.[45] Like pensions, salaries and labor agreements were at the center of judicial controversy through the period under study.

The Judicialization of Economic Governance

Argentine leaders' attempts to respond to economic crisis and carry out market-based reform produced a complicated mix of measures. Some policies seemed to violate the constitution in form, content, or both, and many engendered significant societal opposition and political controversy (Pellet Lastra 2001: 472). For example, taxes imposed by executive decree appeared to trample constitutional restraints on executive power, bank freezes were unpopular and seemed an obvious infringement on property rights, and retirees considered social security reform to be fundamentally unjust and a violation of their constitutional right to an adjustable pension. Argentina's advancing legal transition heightened the sensitivity of the political opposition, citizens, and civil society to these apparent constitutional violations, and heightened their awareness that a judicial option existed for voicing their disagreement and questioning government action. Accordingly, these actors increasingly turned to the courts to challenge the constitutionality of the decrees and laws used to enact economic reform, producing a judicialization of economic governance.[46]

2.4. BRAZIL'S LEGAL TRANSITION

After twenty years of military rule (1964–85), democracy returned to Brazil in January 1985. As in Argentina, rule of law issues were an important item on the electoral and political agenda in the postauthoritarian period. The complete rewriting of the 1967/1969 constitution – resulting in an extended and detailed charter – contributed significantly to that outcome. Civil society's concern with rights did not increase as much as might have been expected given the strong rights orientation of the new charter, however. Also, comprehensive judicial reform did not occur until 2004. Nonetheless, the judicialization of politics accelerated shortly after regime transition, continued throughout the first two posttransition decades, and continues today.

[45] *New York Times*, June 10, 2000, "One-Day National Strike Freezes Much of Argentina."

[46] Congressional dynamics further encouraged the judicialization of political battles. The Peronists dominated both houses of congress through much of the 1990s, making it difficult for dissident Peronists or opposition congressmen to prevail in the legislature. Political obstacles and the ongoing legal transition encouraged the opposition to dress their ideological disagreement with particular policies in constitutional clothing and question them in the courts.

Inclusion on the Political/Electoral Agenda of Rule of Law Issues

Riordan Roett, a specialist on Brazil, has suggested that "a strong and palpable sense of the importance of laws and legality has marked Brazilian history for two centuries" (quoted in Rosenn 1990a: 774). Brazilian statesmen in particular have had strong faith in law's potential to resolve problems (Ballard 1999: 240–5; Konder Comparato 1990: 769; Passos 2002: 4; Rosenn 1984: 19; JG-05); indeed, even the country's military rulers sought to confer an air of formal legitimacy on their regime by "unleashing a deluge of legislation" (Taylor 2004a: 108; Skidmore 1988; Ballard 1999; Rosenn 1984: 32). Consequently, Brazil has laws and decrees regulating every aspect of life with great specificity, creating a veritable legal labyrinth. Yet paradoxically, illegality is rampant.[47] The result is a "profound tension" between formal rules (constitutional and legal) and actual practice (Pereira 2000: 220), with state agents having a particularly ambivalent relationship with legality.[48] Rule of law issues have thus long been on the electoral and political agenda in Brazil. What was new in the postauthoritarian era was an emphasis on closing the gap between law and practice and making the country's "myth of constitutionalism" a reality (Rosenn 1990a: 774).

Rewriting the constitution was a central issue in the campaign preceding the country's first postauthoritarian presidential election in 1985, in which the wildly popular Tancredo Neves was indirectly elected by the Electoral College. When Brazilians went to the polls in November 1989 to participate in the first direct presidential elections in almost three decades, they chose populist Fernando Collor de Mello, whose presidential platform emphasized ending corruption (Rosenn 1990a: 773).[49] And as a perennial presidential candidate through the 1990s and in his fourth (and finally successful) bid for office in 2002, Luiz Inácio "Lula" da Silva, the head of the PT (the Workers' Party, *Partido dos Trabalhadores*), Brazil's most coherent political party, emphasized its high ethical and moral standards (Vidal Luna and Klein 2006: 30, 35).

Civil Society's Concern with Rights

Rights groups and other civil society organizations participated in the constitution-writing process, and the 1988 charter contains an extended series of new rights and remedies that "practically invite civil society to challenge government acts and policy" (Ballard 1999: 247). However, legal scholars and

[47] In many areas of life (and law), employing the "*jeito*" (finding a way around a rule or legal obstacle) is the norm and conforming with formal legal rules the exception (Rosenn 1984: 2). For a study of the disjuncture between labor law and practice in an earlier era, see French (2004).

[48] For instance, unchecked state agents (generally police) regularly trample constitutional guarantees of the poor, nonwhite, and socially marginalized (Pereira 2000: 218).

[49] Ironically, Collor repeatedly abused presidential authority (Power 2000: 23) and allegedly engaged in corruption himself, leading to his impeachment, conviction, and removal from office in 1992; these events arguably brought rule of law issues even further to the fore.

other experts interviewed in connection with this project suggested that concern with rights grew more incrementally, a broad discourse around new social and economic guarantees emerged more gradually, and new rights-focused NGOs formed more slowly than one might have expected given the content of the charter (e.g., CSE-15; EG-04; EG-07; EG-10; I-5). More frequent filing of far-reaching rights cases involving or extending to many individuals began only later in the posttransition period (EG-10),[50] and the STF had resolved relatively few such cases by the mid 2000s (I-13).[51] The persistent lack of clarity about the level at which human rights treaties were integrated into the legal system also evidences the weaker focus on rights (CSE-15).[52] In sum, whereas Brazilians were beginning to recognize their established rights and their potential to pursue rights claims by the mid 2000s (EG-04),[53] rights served as a basis for the judicialization of politics to a lesser degree in Brazil than in Argentina through much of the postauthoritarian period.

Constitutional Reform

When it was revealed in March 1985 on the eve of president-elect Tancredo Neves's inauguration that he was suffering from a serious ailment, his running mate, José Sarney, was sworn in as acting president. Sarney, a conservative politician with ties to the previous military regime, officially became Brazil's first posttransition president shortly before Tancredo's death in April 1985. These dynamics – combined with judicial continuity[54] and the military's ability to retain much of its legitimacy during regime transition (Vilhena Vieira: 2002: 125) – meant that no officials from the previous military regime were tried in the postauthoritarian period (as occurred in Argentina).[55] Instead, Brazil's strategy for dealing with the legacy of authoritarian rule was a simultaneously cathartic and divisive process of constitutional renewal (1986–8) that dramatically altered the country's institutional context. The new constitution, the country's

50 Of course, a growing concern with rights may emerge in the absence of a greater propensity to seek their enforcement in court, and this may have occurred in Brazil (Kapiszewski 2011a); see also Hoffman and Bentes (2008).

51 Only three such rights cases appear in the sample on which this book is based – fifty-five systematically selected politically important cases received by the STF between 1985 and 2004. Justices I interviewed did emphasize that individual rights (in particular criminal rights) had been an important focus of the Court, however (JG-01; JG-02; JG-03; JG-06).

52 Brazil only began to ratify the main human rights treaties in the 1990s. Some treaties were ratified by a simple majority in the legislature and thus entered the legal landscape on the level of laws, whereas others were approved via the procedure used to approve constitutional amendments and so are understood to be at the same level as such amendments in the legal hierarchy.

53 By the late 2000s, the STF's docket included a number of key rights cases, for instance, regarding affirmative action/quotas, stem cell research, anencephaly, gun control, and reduced prison time for heinous crimes (EG-10).

54 Unlike in Argentina, Brazilian leaders replaced no justices or judges at regime transition; the entire (arguably conservative) judiciary remained in place.

55 Regarding Brazil's transition and military politics, see Stepan (1989), Hagopian (1996), and Hunter (1997).

seventh[56] and one of the longest and most detailed in the world (Pereira 2000: 220),[57] was perhaps the core facet of Brazil's legal transition.

The constitution-writing process was at once inclusive and conflictive.[58] The sitting congress drafted the document in a mobilized context, and pressure groups representing multiple facets of Brazil's pluralist and corporatist culture had direct input into the new charter (Taylor 2004a: 8). As a result, the constitution regulates myriad policy areas (Rosenn 1990a: 777; Arantes 1997: 198). Many preferences and claims were included in the text in a vague or general way, and it is replete with non-self-executing provisions requiring complementary legislation to become effective. At the same time, certain sections contain detailed clauses that resemble public policy more than constitutional provisions (Couto and Arantes 2008). Various clauses conflict with each other, and others embody objectively counterproductive or unrealistic economic principles, increasing the likelihood that public policies will collide with the constitution.[59] These qualities contributed to considerable litigation by citizens and groups asking courts to fill in the charter's gaps or prioritize conflicting clauses (Kerche 1999: 66; Vilhena Vieira 2002: 39–40).

Perhaps as a result of the inclusivity of the constitution drafting process, the charter reflects dueling economic philosophies (Konder Comparato 1990). In many senses, it is *dirigiste*. It has strong statist and nationalist overtones and prescribes a program intended to produce political, economic, and social transformation through multifaceted government involvement in the economy and society (Ballard 1999: 247; Vilhena Vieira 2002: 38, 129–130).[60] President Cardoso (1995–2003) pushed through a series of constitutional amendments in the mid-1990s that were somewhat successful in defusing constitutional conflicts around neoliberal reform, for instance, easing restrictions on privatization and the operation of foreign companies in Brazil (Negretto 2004: 550; Couto and Arantes 2003: 149–50).[61] Nonetheless, the charter

[56] If the 1969 Constitution is considered a new charter, rather than an amendment of the 1967 Constitution, the 1988 Constitution is Brazil's eighth.

[57] In 2012, the Constitution contained 250 articles (all with multiple clauses and many with dozens), 95 transitory articles, and 74 amendments – and topped 70,000 words.

[58] The constitutional process and product have attracted great scholarly attention; see Konder Comparato (1990); Rosenn (1990a, 2000); Martínez-Lara (1996); Souza (1997); Reich (1998).

[59] Justices in particular expressed frustration with the charter, commenting that its detail in multiple areas of law implied that legal change often required constitutional amendment, which "generates immense difficulties that tie up the country" (JG-01). Couto and Arantes also suggest that the Constitution's inclusion of sundry public policy provisions mean that "lawmaking" must often be done through constitutional reform (2008: 1).

[60] Articles 22, 23, 24, 48, and 52 outline a range of economic activities on which the state can legislate, and the charter also strongly encourages government involvement in private business. It proclaimed the state to be the "normative and regulatory agent of economic activity" (Article 174), discriminated against the participation of foreign companies, and authorized a federal monopoly in a variety of spheres in the original writing (Articles 176 and 177).

[61] Constitutional amendments may be proposed by the executive, by at least one-third of the chamber of deputies or senate, or by more than half of the state legislatures. Proposed amendments are debated and voted on in the chamber and the senate, in two rounds, and are approved

retained great potential to complicate the implementation of market-based economic reform and invited the filing of cases requiring courts to adjudicate between reform and the charter's statist and nationalist tendencies. Yet the charter also *limits* state intervention. It curbs the state's ability to tax (e.g., Articles 150–3)[62] and emphasizes free enterprise and competition (e.g., Article 170; JG-06), encouraging the formation of small and micro-enterprises in particular (Article 179). In short, no matter politicians' economic ideology, there was some constitutional basis to question policies based on the opposing ideology in the courts.

Finally, as noted previously, the charter includes an extensive and detailed list of rights and was in fact dubbed the "Citizen Constitution" (*Constituição Cidadã*) (Zaverucha 1998: 105). Part II enumerates an extraordinarily broad range of individual and collective rights and duties (Chapter I) and an extensive series of social rights (Chapter II). Part III describes additional rights granted to civil servants (Section II), and Part VIII explains how the state is to fulfill and guarantee certain rights awarded to citizens. Scholars have commented that constitutional designers appeared to pay little attention to the potential cost or plausibility of enforcing the multitude of rights in the constitution (Taylor 2004b), a concern made graver by the charter's enhancement of access to courts, discussed next. The limits to taxation mentioned earlier and the charter's embodiment of fiscal federalism[63] exacerbated fiscal imbalances and compromised the central government's ability to amass the money needed to carry through on the document's statist intentions and rights guarantees (Lamounier 1999: 176), triggering constitutional litigation. Constitutional reform was thus central to Brazil's legal transition and the foundation for the judicialization of economic policy.

Judicial Reform

Some judicial reform occurred via the 1988 Constitution. The charter established new mechanisms to access the courts and broadened the use of and standing to employ others, and introduced small claims courts to handle less complex civil suits and less serious criminal offenses.[64] It also created the

if they obtain three-fifths of the votes of members of each house in both rounds (Article 60, 1988 Constitution). Certain provisions (*cláusulas pétreas*) cannot be amended; these include the federal system of government; direct, secret, universal, and periodic suffrage; the separation of powers; and some individual rights.

[62] Expressing frustration with the Constitution's regulation of taxation, one justice suggested, "What we need is constitutional liposuction" (EC-47).

[63] Fiscal federalism refers to the diversion of federal revenues to states and municipalities – often with little corresponding shift in spending responsibilities.

[64] The charter also empowered and increased the autonomy of the Office of the Federal Prosecutor (the *Ministério Público*, MP) (Articles 127–13), whose prosecutors (*procuradores*) often bring cases to the courts in the public interest. See Kerche (1999); Porto Macedo Junior (1995); and McAllister (2008).

Superior Tribunal of Justice (*Superior Tribunal de Justiça*, STJ) to hear appeals of nonconstitutional cases,[65] and introduced formal mechanisms to augment judicial independence from the other branches of government. IFIs did not carry out a broad judicial reform project in Brazil as they did in Argentina (Ballard 1999: 234, 267), however, and only narrow and halting reform occurred between 1988 and 2004 – perhaps because the government (as defendant in many cases) benefited from the system's inefficiency and ineffectiveness (I-2; Taylor 2004a: 137–45). Yet lower-court judges also opposed some aspects of reform, and a major reform program introduced in 1992 stalled in congress for more than a decade due to their opposition. What little reform did occur mainly focused on increasing access to courts and judicial efficiency (Prillaman 2000; Taylor 2004a: 139–42).

Three changes of relevance to the high court were introduced in 1993 and 1999, however. Constitutional Amendment No. 3 (1993) created the Declaratory Action of Constitutionality (*Ação Declaratória de Constitucionalidade*, ADC), a type of abstract review case. Also, Law 9.868 and Law 9.882 (both of 1999) regulated the process for filing and deciding two additional types of abstract review cases, the Direct Action of Unconstitutionality (*Ação Direta de Inconstitucionalidade*, ADIn) and the Argumentation of Failure to Comply with a Fundamental Precept (*Argüição de Descumprimento de Preceito Fundamental*, ADPF), respectively (Rocha and Paulo 2003: 91).[66]

Judicial reform finally occurred via Constitutional Amendment No. 45, passed by congress in December 2004. While the reform did not affect the STF during the time period of study (1985–2004), it is instructive to understand two elements that sought to address one of the STF's most significant challenges during the first twenty posttransition years: its immense case load. First, the reform requires a party seeking to file a case with the STF using either of the two most-often used mechanisms of concrete review (an extraordinary appeal, *recurso extraordinário*, or a direct appeal, *agravo de instrumento*) to justify the appeal by identifying the case's relevance to society (*repercussão geral*); with a vote of two-thirds of the justices, the STF can refuse to hear the appeal despite the justification (SS-02, JG-03, JG-04).[67] Second, the reform mandates that the STF can, with the vote of two-thirds of its members, establish its summary jurisprudence (referred to as a *súmula*) as binding (*vinculante*)

[65] The thirty-three-member STJ is an institutional innovation: Instead of creating a new Constitutional Court as many countries did since World War II, Brazil created an "everything-but-constitutional" court that serves as the guardian of federal legislation (with the exception of labor, military, and electoral legislation, which are protected by separate court systems). The objective was to relieve the STF's jurisdictional burden.

[66] Web Appendix 2.3 lists the mechanisms used most often to access the STF.

[67] Thus, the Court can dismiss technically perfect but irrelevant cases, and accept technically flawed but important cases (JG-02, JG-03). The *repercussão geral* mechanism closely resembles the Argentine *gravedad institucional* mechanism, the abuse of which, according to constitutional scholars and justices, contributed to the gross *inflation* of the CSJN's case load.

regarding a particular legal theme or issue. Lower courts are to refuse to hear cases challenging the understandings in the STF's established summary jurisprudence, and the STF must adhere to it in future rulings (EG-03).

Judicialization of Politics

As noted previously, various aspects of the Brazilian Constitution practically invite litigation, and many mechanisms exist to bring cases to the judiciary. Consequently, societal actors and the political opposition increasingly turned to courts to resolve political and social conflict in the postauthoritarian period. Case load statistics serve as partial evidence of this phenomenon. A study carried out by Khair (2004) found that most Brazilian courts experienced at least a tripling of their case load between 1990 and 2003 (with the case load of first instance federal courts increasing almost tenfold). Further, as Web Appendix 2.4 shows, the number of cases filed with the high court (the vast majority on appeal) doubled from 1990 to 1997, had tripled by 1999, had quadrupled by 2000, and had increased almost ninefold by 2002. There is also strong evidence that the source of the increase in litigation was a judicialization of politics.

Scholars of the Brazilian judiciary have suggested that courts' case loads increasingly comprise policy-related cases.[68] Justices also highlight the judicialization of politics. One justice, referring to the multifaceted instability and crisis that marked the postauthoritarian period, commented that "there is no issue related to a crisis that fails to go, eventually, to the courts" (JG-01). Another justice estimated that between 70 and 80 percent of the STF's cases during that era involved the state's early 1990s efforts to address inflation (JG-05). Moreover, ADIns (abstract review cases emblematic of judicialization, see again Web Appendix 2.3) have been filed with increasing frequency since regime transition – in particular by opposition political parties (Taylor 2004a: 166–9). Indeed, several STF justices indicated that it was not uncommon for opposition legislators or advocates of special interests to file ADIns in which political or ideological opposition to certain laws or policies was thinly coated in constitutional discourse – thereby continuing in the STF political battles lost in congress (JG-02, JG-04, JG-06, JG-07).[69] In sum, there is good evidence that Brazilian politics have been judicialized.

[68] Khair (2004: 11) asserts a direct relationship between superior courts' increased case loads and the federal government's implementation of economic and tax policy. Faro de Castro notes the increasing use of litigation to challenge official policy (1997a: 242). And Ballard chronicles greater antagonism between the executive and federal courts during the 1990s due to judges' increasing involvement in controversial political arenas, estimating that at least half of the cases clogging the courts questioned public sector action (1999: 232, 252, 269).

[69] As one oft-quoted anecdote goes, when opposition congressman Jamil Haddad was asked by a justice why he was always filing cases with the STF, he responded, "I can influence politics more by activating the STF than I can through congress" (Teixeira 1997: 60; CSM-05).

2.5. BRAZIL'S ECONOMIC TRANSITION AND THE JUDICIALIZATION OF ECONOMIC GOVERNANCE

Brazil, like Argentina, underwent significant economic reform in parallel with its legal transition. This section offers a brief overview of the Brazilian economic context between 1985 and 2004. It then outlines key tenets of the economic stabilization plans and reform initiatives implemented during that period illustrating how they encouraged constitutional conflict. Due to the constitution's detailed nature and economic orientation, several economic reforms had to be introduced via constitutional amendment, requiring congressional supermajorities that were difficult to rally in Brazil's fragmented political context. Consequently, the country's economic transition, like its legal transition, occurred unevenly with more change in some areas than others.

Economic Context

The presidential term of Brazil's first posttransition leader, José Sarney (1985–90), began with a set of democratizing reforms but was ultimately dominated by constitutional rewriting and economic turmoil. By the late 1980s, Brazil had fallen into the worst inflationary crisis of its history (Rosenn 1990a: 775). The broad economic reform program President Collor (1990–2) launched immediately following his inauguration soon failed, and by 1991 Brazil settled into brutal recession. Gross domestic product (GDP) contracted between 1990 and 1992, and investment, employment, and real wages all fell (Kingstone 2000: 192). Itamar Franco (1992–4), who assumed the presidency following Collor's impeachment, did not immediately impose a stabilization plan, and practically halted privatizations. Inflation steadily rose. In May 1993, Franco appointed Fernando Henrique Cardoso finance minister, and in many respects relinquished power to him. Cardoso focused on resolving the country's fiscal problems through constitutional reform and the development of an innovative and ultimately successful stabilization program, the *Real* Plan.

Cardoso stepped down as finance minister in April 1994 to run for president, and his victory in the October 1994 contest was based in good measure on the success of the *Real* Plan. While his careful strategizing and skilled negotiation facilitated adoption of some of his economic initiatives (such as privatization) during his first presidential administration (1995–1999), marshaling congressional support for other priorities (such as reform of the civil service, tax, and social welfare systems) was more difficult. By the late 1990s, crisis was brewing. Brazil's domestic public debt had skyrocketed, the currency was increasingly overvalued, and the economic downturn induced by financial collapse in Southeast Asia in 1997 was exacerbated by the Russian collapse in August 1998 (Lamounier 1999: 180).

Cardoso's reelection in October 1998 – despite poor economic prospects – was likely due to a popular perception that only he could contain the crisis.[70] Intransigent congressional politics and constitutional obstacles hamstrung his efforts in his second administration, however. Cardoso had indicated that social justice would be a priority in his second term, but he refocused on enacting policies to sustain the *Real* Plan as crisis deepened. Despite his efforts, in mid-January 1999 the Central Bank was forced to float the currency, which immediately lost 10 percent of its value against the dollar. Yet even given popular fears, in a testament to the strength of the plan, high inflation did not recur. Even as Cardoso's electoral coalition began to splinter by early 2000 and economic crisis continued to threaten, restructuring continued apace.

The value of the currency declined by more than 50 percent during 2002, however, due to jitters generated by Argentina's 2001 financial crisis and concern that the PT's Lula, who had spent much of the 1990s (and his 2002 presidential campaign) railing against neoliberal reform, would win the October 2002 presidential election (Taylor 2004a: 39–45). Win he did, and following his victory, the PT partnered with other left and center parties to build a majority legislative coalition. Further, Lula's campaign platform had presaged strong investment in sectors such as education and health care, and his government established some important social welfare policies in its first two years, such as the "Zero Hunger" (*Fome Zero*) program. Yet his administration remained engaged with the international financial community, and in the main followed and built upon the Cardoso government's fiscal discipline and the groundwork it had laid for market reform and augmenting global competitiveness (Hunter and Power 2005: 130). Despite continuing economic challenges, relative economic stability marked the first two years of Lula's term, and continued thereafter.

Stabilization Plans

This subsection and the next four review important aspects of the complex and multifaceted processes of stabilization and state reform carried out in Brazil during the first two posttransition decades. Each facet of reform induced extensive constitutional controversy. To begin, starting in the late 1980s, elected leaders introduced a series of economic stabilization programs in an effort to control inflation (a prerequisite for deeper structural reforms). Most plans involved a new currency, wage and price freezes, and new indexes to correct for inflation. The latter two aspects disrupted the price and wage indexation schemes (or "monetary adjustment," *correção monetária*) that were written into most contracts in the late 1980s and early 1990s to compensate for inflation,

[70] In June 1997, the constitution was amended (with encouragement from Cardoso) to allow executives at all levels of government to run for one consecutive reelection, opening the way for him to compete for the presidency in 1998.

and Brazil's enterprising lawyers capitalized on these contractual violations, generating mountains of litigation.

The first stabilization plan, the heterodox *Cruzado* Plan, was implemented in February 1986 (Lamounier 1999: 171). The plan created the illusion of monetary stability but failed to address inflation's underlying causes, and had collapsed by late 1986 as inflation surged (Rosenn 1990a: 775). Two further attempts by Sarney to stabilize the economy, the Bresser Plan (July 1987) and the Summer Plan (*Plano Verão*, January 1989) enjoyed only temporary success (Negretto 2004: 549). Just two weeks after his inauguration, Collor issued a package of provisional measures (*medidas provisórias*, MPs)[71] that together comprised the Collor Plan, "the most interventionist and draconian stabilization plan in Brazil's history" (Kingstone 2000: 191). The heterodox plan, which sought to address the structural foundations of economic instability, introduced wage and price controls and a new currency, banned price indexation, implemented a series of measures to streamline administration and quash government spending, and imposed a bank freeze (Kingstone 2000: 191). The bank freeze induced waves of court cases alleging that it violated property rights, and produced weak short-term results, dampening political support for structural adjustment (Negretto 2004: 549). A second stabilization plan in 1991 (Collor Plan II) also failed rapidly, and no further plans were introduced for more than two years (Ballard 1999: 255; Taylor 2004a: 26).

Brazil's most technically sophisticated and successful adjustment plan was the Fiscal Stabilization Program (the *Real* Plan), introduced in congress in December 1993 and implemented in stages between March and July 1994 under President Cardoso (Skidmore 2000: xiii–xiv). The plan was based on a commitment to fiscal austerity (it included fiscal adjustments and increased federal control over the subnational financial system) (Montero 2000: 68) and was anchored by the introduction of a new currency (the *real*) and a gradually sliding pegged exchange rate (Kingstone 2000: 194; Weyland 2000: 48).[72] The plan required fiscal sacrifices up-front, helping to prevent the boom-and-bust cycles that had plagued previous plans. Following its introduction, inflation fell, GDP increased, and capital began to flow back into the significantly

[71] This type of executive decree, established in the 1988 Constitution, can be issued only under conditions of "relevancy (importance) and urgency." MPs are similar to Decrees of Necessity and Urgency in Argentina but are subject to greater congressional scrutiny. The 1988 Constitution initially included few procedural or substantive limitations on MPs, but Constitutional Amendment No. 32 of 2001 defined areas in which the president was prohibited from issuing MPs; extended the time limit for congress to convert MPs into law; stipulated that presidents could only reissue MPs once; and prohibited presidents from reproposing or reissuing, in the same legislative session, MPs that were rejected or that expired in that session.

[72] While pegging the *real* to the dollar controlled inflation initially, it also led to the *real's* overvaluation, which increased imports and created a current-account deficit. To finance the deficit and maintain the *real*'s value (and thus continue to control inflation), attracting investment became a priority, thus domestic interest rates had to be kept high. Yet to attract foreign direct investment, fulfill IMF obligations, and achieve economic stability, reducing the public debt was key – implying fiscal austerity at all government levels (Samuels 2003: 551–2).

liberalized economy. Waves of broken contracts and other disputes also followed in its wake, however, many of which were brought to the courts for resolution (Taylor 2004a: 213).

Opening the Economy and Privatization

The *Real* plan would only continue to control inflation and engender economic stability if broader public finance reform, deeper structural reform, and liberalization were carried out, and an important element of those initiatives was opening the economy and privatizing state companies. Under Collor, nontariff barriers were dissolved, and average tariffs were cut in half between 1990 and 1994 (Amann and Baer 2002: 947–8). These changes subjected domestic firms to serious foreign competition for the first time in decades, and the administration encouraged internal competition with antimonopoly initiatives. Collor also initiated the National Program of De-Statization/Privatization (MP 155 of March 1990, converted into Law 8.031 of April 1990), which set privatization targets (Power 2000: 191).

Franco did little to expand Collor's privatization program, but Cardoso capitalized on the success of the *Real* Plan in 1995 and 1996 to push through a series of amendments to the relatively statist and nationalist "economic order" articles of the 1988 Constitution in hopes of facilitating private investment (and foreign direct investment in particular). In part as a result, privatization of large state-owned firms accelerated under Cardoso: receipts totaled approximately US$ 105.3 billion by 2002 (Amann and Baer 2005: 424).[73] Privatizations were questioned in courts around the country and repeatedly declared unconstitutional. However, judicial action only slowed and suspended privatization processes, never preventing a final sale (Fishlow 2000: 354).[74]

Social Security Reform

Social security reform, considered crucial for reducing the budget deficit, mainly focused on the public sector pension system. As the 1988 Constitution guaranteed retired public sector workers a particular pension level, reform entailed challenging constitutional rights, strong vested interests (including those of senior bureaucrats), and powerful public sector unions (Samuels 2003: 569). Cardoso submitted a major social security reform to congress in March 1995 via a constitutional amendment,[75] but progress stalled. As crisis brewed

[73] As in Argentina, privatization mainly occurred through granting concessions rather than permanent transfers of assets (for example, the Telebrás monopoly, auctioned in 1998 for US $19 billion). However, some sales were permanent: Company Vale do Rio Doce (CVRD), a large mining concern, was permanently privatized in 1997.

[74] Elected leaders generally found a way to "batch" cases against privatizations in a court that had supported the sale, or to raise such cases to the high court (which tended to support the government's privatization efforts) (JG-02; EC-25).

[75] The reform called for the establishment of a minimum retirement age; a sliding benefit scale dependent upon a worker's age at retirement; caps on pension benefits in *both* the private and

in 1998 the chamber passed a diluted version of the reform, and the senate finally approved Constitutional Amendment No. 20 in December 1998 (Taylor 2004a: 41). The constitutionality of several aspects of the amendment was challenged in and by the judiciary, as were some of the additional reforms subsequently introduced through a series of laws.[76] Constitutional Amendment No. 41 (passed at the end of 2003 under Lula) aimed in part to reinstate the portions of these reforms that judges had invalidated,[77] and pensioners again turned to the courts to question features of the amendment they believed violated their vested rights. As in Argentina, then, pension reform created significant constitutional controversy.

Fiscal and Tax Reform

Brazil has long suffered from fiscal imbalance (EC-34, EC-41). While high inflation helped *resolve* fiscal conflicts through the early 1990s,[78] once inflation had been tamed, Brazil's fiscal problems were laid bare, and the need to devise schemes to augment extraction and decrease state spending (also necessary to underpin the success of the *Real* plan) became more acute than ever. Yet the constitution impeded progress toward this goal as it prioritized just the opposite – limiting the state's ability to tax and laying the groundwork for a generous welfare state – placing the law and fiscal discipline at odds. This fundamental conflict, combined with Brazil's already-high tax burden, haunted elected leaders as they sought to tighten fiscal policy and increase tax revenues,[79] encouraging judicialization.[80]

A substantial tax increase and one-time tax levy on all financial transactions were introduced in mid-1990. A Provisional Tax on Financial Transactions (the *Imposto Provisório sobre Movimentação Financeira*, IPMF) and a tax to help fund the social security system (*Contribuição para Financiamento da*

public sectors; a tax on public sector retirees' pensions; and modification of the formula used to calculate pension benefits (Panizza 2003: 80).

76 For instance, Law 9.783 (January 1999) imposed a tax on monthly civil service pension payments over R$ 1,200, and Law 9.876 (November 1999) set a formula for calculating retirement benefits, raised the minimum number of years civil servants had to work before retiring, and increased fines for late payment (Taylor 2004a: 209).

77 The amendment increased the minimum retirement age, tightened ceilings on pension benefits, reduced benefits awarded to pensioners' survivors when pensioners passed away, and imposed taxes on the pensions of better-off Brazilians (Hunter and Power 2005: 131).

78 For instance, high inflation immediately corroded the value of any salary increase the government awarded, meaning that it would not actually have to pay workers more in real terms.

79 Maintaining fiscal restraint was further complicated by fiscal skeletons (*esqueletos*) – debts originating in previous administrations that new administrations inherited, at times unknowingly. Sometimes that debt took the form of judicial cases that had yet to be decided (JG-04).

80 A justice insisted on the veracity of the following story: When the government was preparing a certain tax law, the minister of finance asked an aide what portion of the law he thought was unconstitutional. The aide responded that he thought the law was about 40 percent unconstitutional. When asked how he arrived at that figure, he clarified that he estimated that 40 percent of the citizens whose rights the law violated would question it in the judiciary (JG-05).

Seguridade Social, COFINS) were established via Constitutional Amendment No. 3 in March 1993; each was considered by the courts. The Emergency Social Fund (*Fundo Social de Emergência*, FSE), introduced via constitutional amendment in March 1994, raised taxes for two years, placed limits on transfers of public funds to states and municipalities, and reduced constitutional earmarking of revenues (Taylor 2004a: 30–1).[81] The program, along with Cardoso's subsequent efforts to restrict subnational spending and indebtedness and restructure state and municipal financial systems, aimed to limit subnational governments' capacity to jeopardize macroeconomic stability and augment the executive's control over fiscal management (Samuels 2003: 553; Lamounier 1999: 171).

Cardoso introduced piecemeal changes rather than pursuing broad fiscal reform (Samuels 2003: 563, 566). In part in response to judicial challenges to the IPMF, Constitutional Amendment No. 12 (August 1996) imposed a different sort of levy on financial transactions (Provisional Contribution on Financial Transactions, *Contribuição Provisória sobre Movimentação Financeira*, CPMF), and in 1996 and 1997 congress passed several laws modifying the country's fiscal structure incrementally (Montero 2000: 70).[82] Following the Asian and Russian financial crises of the late 1990s, however, the government doubled real interest rates and launched a drastic fiscal austerity plan with the goal of cutting the public sector deficit by US$ 18 billion (2.3 percent of GDP) (Panizza 2003: 83). In addition, the Law of Fiscal Responsibility (Complementary Law 101, passed May 2000) offered the government several tools for fiscal management (including mechanisms to control subnational debt and finances).

By the first quarter of 2003 the combined federal, state, and municipal tax burden had reached almost 36 percent of GDP. Consequently, calls for tax reduction were widespread when Lula took office. The new president quickly introduced a reform that simplified and unified states' value-added tax; decreased the business tax burden; abolished systems that induced wasteful competition among states; and extended the CPMF. Yet Lula did not make comprehensive progress on fiscal reform during his first two years in office (Montero 2005: 144).

Civil Service Reform

The inclusion of civil servants' tenure rights in the constitution and the strength of public sector unions combined to severely complicate civil service reform. Cardoso was unable to rally congressional support for substantial reform and

[81] The measure was reestablished in a slightly different form via three Constitutional Amendments: No. 10 (March 1996), No. 17 (November 1997), and No. 37 (March 2000).

[82] For instance, the Kandir Law (November 1996) sought to reduce mounting trade- and current-account deficits, and reworked the states' value-added tax on exports (introducing the *Imposto sobre a Circulação de Mercadoria e Serviços*, ICMS).

initially made only limited inroads through incremental measures passed as ordinary laws. When the Asian financial crisis hit Brazil in October 1997 however, incentive structures shifted: Significant reform passed both houses of congress in June 1998 enshrined as Constitutional Amendment No. 19 (Taylor 2004a: 30).[83] Lula made no significant reforms during his first two years in office however (Costin ND: 5).

The Judicialization of Economic Governance

In Brazil, as in Argentina, the simultaneity of economic and legal transition in the postauthoritarian period induced the judicialization of economic governance. Initiatives to reform the state were fundamentally at odds with the spirit of existing state-led development policy, and many were unpopular with the public and the opposition. The new constitution's statist and nationalist bent, its inclusion of myriad rights, and its limits on taxation were also in tension with elected leaders' economic reform policies. Consequently, reform was opposed through traditional interest group politics and the legislative process. Nonetheless, Cardoso (the leading reformer of the period) was able to cobble together majorities and supermajorities in congress to pass reform measures (Taylor 2004a: 205). With the legislative route to opposing policies essentially blocked and with legal transformation in progress, opponents turned to the courts to contest economic policy.

Expressing opposition to economic policy through the courts was relatively easy in Brazil. First, the 1988 Constitution provided an excellent vehicle (even given reforms to its "economic order" articles in the 1990s). Further, plans to combat inflation and stabilize the economy were often made by administration *técnicos* who prioritized technical requisites over legality, opening the door to constitutional contestation of economic policy (JG-05). Reform's opponents became quite adept at repainting ideological opposition to reform policies in constitutional colors (Taylor 2004a). And constitutional reform had broadened and facilitated access to the judiciary, welcoming a wider range of actors to challenge economic policy in the courts.[84] The result was an accelerating judicialization of economic governance.

2.6. CONCLUSIONS AND COMPARISONS

During their first two postauthoritarian decades, Argentina and Brazil experienced a dual transition different from the one to which the literature on

[83] The bill, among other provisions, allowed for the firing of public sector employees due to poor performance or when their jobs were redundant, set a maximum salary level, and revoked a provision that granted all civil servants the same employment status (Costin ND: 5).

[84] Constitutional reform had awarded two constituencies bound to contest the reforms – organized corporate actors and political parties – special standing in the courts and especially before the high court (Taylor 2004a: 219).

third-wave democracies points: simultaneous legal and economic change. With regard to the former, rule of law issues were almost immediately on the electoral and political agenda in both countries. While a broad rights consciousness developed more quickly and fully in Argentina, citizens, civil society groups, and the political opposition in both contexts filed cases with the courts regarding rights violations connected with central government economic policy. Brazil's 1988 Constitution includes far more social and economic rights than does Argentina's 1853 charter and presents a series of additional complications for economic governance; nonetheless, the integration of international human rights treaties into the Argentine charter and Brazilian President Cardoso's "economic amendments" to the 1988 charter (which loosened constitutional constraints on economic policy making) served to bridge these gaps. Judicial reform occurred earlier in Argentina than in Brazil, but a significant judicialization of politics occurred in each context.

Concerning economic change, both countries rejoined the ranks of the world's democracies in the mid-1980s in deep economic crisis. Urged on by the international financial community, Argentine and Brazilian leaders implemented market-oriented reforms to halt galloping inflation and engaged in structural adjustment and state reform more generally. They introduced stabilization plans, sought to open the economy and privatize state-run businesses, and moved toward implementing social security, fiscal, and civil service reform. Nonetheless, both countries continued to be vulnerable to economic distress throughout the first two postauthoritarian decades.

Had Argentina and Brazil not been experiencing legal transformation at the same time elected leaders sought to implement policies to address economic crisis and reform the state, conflicts between those policies and national constitutions may not have bubbled to the surface. But both countries *were* in the throes of a legal transition, and latent constitutional conflicts became manifest and judicialized. No matter what strategy elected leaders in either country adopted to collect more, spend less, and advance their economic initiatives, judicial challenges sprung from all sides. In short, both countries experienced a judicialization of politics in general and a judicialization of economic governance in particular in the postauthoritarian period, significantly raising the stakes of economic reform for high courts and elected leaders.

Two implications and sets of questions follow. First, leaders in both countries had incentives to appeal politically important cases up the judicial hierarchy and to craft high courts that would facilitate governance. To what degree were elected leaders able to craft such Courts, what factors affected their ability to do so, and what did those Courts look like? Second, crucial cases concerning economic policy generated critical choices for judicial and elected leaders. High courts, no matter how crafted, faced a difficult choice each time they received a case questioning the constitutionality of an economic initiative elected leaders viewed as crucial to economic stabilization: Should they endorse the initiative (that is, prioritize economic stability) or challenge it (that is, prioritize the rule of law)? For their part elected leaders faced a parallel quandary when Courts struck down their policies – deciding whether to comply with the ruling, and whether to retaliate against the Court.[85] How did justices rule, how did elected leaders react, and why did the two interact as they did over economic governance? The rest of this book takes on those questions.

[85] Economic reform involved efforts to open the economies of Latin American countries and involve them in globalization more generally. This implied a concomitant opening to international legal pressures, for instance, to sign onto and enforce international rights treaties. Thus another way to think of the quandary courts and elected leaders faced when deciding cases or reacting to judicial decisions in which economic policies were deemed to have violated fundamental rights is as a decision between economic (neo)-liberalism and social (or legal) liberalism.

3

Politicization and the Political Court in Argentina

"It is impossible to govern if the Supreme Court is against all of the executive's political initiatives and might declare all the laws implemented by it unconstitutional."

– Raúl Granillo Ocampo, a top official in the administration of Carlos Menem, rationalizing the government's 1990 enlargement of the Supreme Court[1]

3.1. INTRODUCTION

This book argues that a Court's character – its institutional stability, the professional qualifications of its justices, its perceived legitimacy, and its institutional cohesion – shapes the way the Court and elected leaders interact over politically crucial legal cases. High court character springs from the politics of Court crafting adopted by those responsible for appointing justices. Chapters 3 and 4 explain why Argentine and Brazilian elected leaders adopted different politics of Court crafting during the first two postauthoritarian decades and describe the result: Courts of very different characters.

As Chapter 2 suggested, soon after their transitions from authoritarian rule, countries across Latin America experienced a judicialization of politics – and, of particular import to this study, a judicialization of economic governance. Citizens, civil society, and the political opposition increasingly turned to courts to challenge policies they opposed, or considered illegal or unconstitutional. Given advancing judicial reform, it was possible that courts with new formal powers and independence safeguards would rule for those challengers. Were judicial tides to turn that way, even Supreme Court rulings favoring elected leaders' policies would not necessarily stem them, given Latin America's civil law tradition and the absence of the doctrine of *stare decisis*. To complicate matters further, ignoring inconvenient judicial decisions could make elected leaders look inconsistent, as many new democratic leaders had placed or kept

[1] International Commission of Jurists (1990: 1, cited in Helmke 2000: 140).

rule of law issues on the political agenda, reformed their countries' constitutions, and broadened courts' formal powers. Moreover, ignoring challenging judicial decisions would compromise the legitimacy that judicial *endorsement* of their questioned policies could lend (Domingo 2005).

Elected leaders thus needed a way to encourage judicial support for their economic reforms. Some leaders – and certainly those in Argentina and Brazil – adopted a two-pronged approach. First, they awarded new powers, and hastened the arrival of cases, to high courts. In other words, they centralized judicial power in the institution with the last judicial word on judicialized political conflicts. Second, they adopted a particular politics of Court crafting with the goal of shaping a Court that would facilitate governance – ideally legitimating their policies in the process (or at least cementing them firmly in place). The utility to elected leaders of the first prong of their approach was thus predicated on their success with the second.

With regard to the first prong, centralizing judicial power, Argentine and Brazilian leaders employed relatively similar strategies. They routinely appealed politically important cases they lost in lower courts and developed mechanisms to expedite and ensure their arrival to the top of the judicial hierarchy, awarded high courts new powers, and enhanced high courts' vertical control over the rest of the judiciary. These actions empowered high courts and hastened their introduction into politics.

An impressive literature has developed over the last twenty-five years addressing why leaders formally empower courts and increase their formal independence. To mention just a few of the most prominent accounts, some scholars suggest that elected leaders empower courts because they anticipate courts can be partners in governance (e.g., Whittington 2005: Magaloni 2008; Nunes 2010). For instance, courts can help leaders monitor the bureaucracy to ensure that their policy preferences are being implemented (McCubbins, Noll, and Weingast 1987); in particular, appeals of lower court rulings convey information concerning street-level bureaucrats' compliance up the judicial hierarchy (Shapiro 1981). Other analysts hold that leaders empower courts in an effort to "credibly commit" their regimes to the rule of law, thereby hoping to entice foreign investment (e.g., North and Weingast 1989; Moustafa 2003, 2007).[2] Ginsburg (2003) advances an alternate credible commitments account – that elected leaders seeking to facilitate constitutional reform empower courts to convince the political opposition that they will abide by new constitutional commitments. Other scholars argue that bargaining among old and new political elites around the time of regime transition leads to the particular levels of power and independence awarded to courts (e.g., Magalhães 1999; Schiemann 2001).

Other work advances an "insurance" argument, highlighting the importance of political competition to (or positing an "electoral market logic" behind)

[2] Related accounts, mainly of authoritarian regimes, suggest that leaders empower courts in order to present an image of limited power in a bid to augment their legitimacy (e.g., Gandhi 2008).

judicial empowerment (e.g., Ramseyer 1994; Ginsburg 2003; Finkel 2004, 2005, 2008). According to these accounts, elected leaders who expect to leave office empower courts as a form of political insurance to help prevent incoming leaders from disassembling their programs and to sustain an even electoral playing field. Hirschl (2004) advances a similar account, positing that "hegemonic elites" who feel politically threatened grant review powers to judiciaries composed of judges whose ideological preferences match theirs with the expectation that judicial elites will help political elites to cement their policy program in place and retain their hegemonic status. Several studies however – for instance, Trochev (2004) on Russia and VonDoepp and Ellett (2011) on new African democracies – argue that leaders in politically *stronger* positions empower courts and politically weaker leaders compromise judicial power. Rebolledo and Rosenbluth (2010), analyzing Mexico, also suggest that elected leaders tend to manipulate courts, rather than formally empower them, when there is more political competition. And in a recent minisymposium (Hilbink and Woods 2009), scholars of courts in multiple world regions offered a series of accounts questioning the tenets of insurance theory and emphasizing how ideas and social and historical forces influence judicial empowerment. Ingram (2009) also takes the insurance argument to task, teasing out the multiple causal pathways that might underpin it.[3]

The account advanced here – that elected leaders engaged in judicial centralization in order to make high courts partners in governance – is most consistent with those offered by Whittington (2005), Magaloni (2008), and Nunes (2010). Yet it is not inconsistent with credible commitments arguments that suggest leaders grant courts new powers to persuade potential foreign investors that the law rules, and that their money will not be expropriated should they invest in those leaders' countries.[4] It is less consistent, however, with Hirschl's (2004) hegemonic preservation thesis, as neither Argentine nor Brazilian leaders ever quite reached a hegemonic status during the time period under study, and their empowerment of courts was more an effort to push through a program they were developing than to lock an existing program in place. Further, Argentine and Brazilian dynamics did not follow an "insurance policy" logic: Argentine President Menem (1989–99) and Brazilian President Cardoso (1995–2003) appealed cases to their high courts continuously and increased their formal powers on a number of occasions, yet for much of their time in office, neither feared losing power.

[3] Of course, a country's legal tradition (i.e., civil law vs. common law) also influences what roles it is considered appropriate for courts to play, thereby affecting to what degree they are empowered and granted independence.

[4] Ginsburg's alternate "credible commitments" argument, however, does not seem to explain Argentine and Brazilian leaders' judicial empowerment choices. Even though Argentina did reform its constitution in 1994, judicial empowerment continued thereafter; likewise, most judicial empowerment occurred in Brazil after the constitution was rewritten between 1986 and 1988.

Argentine and Brazilian leaders thus carried out the first prong of their approach to enhancing judicial support for governance, judicial centralization, in somewhat similar ways. This was not the case with the second prong. The politics of Court crafting that leaders in the two countries adopted – the frequency with which and means by which they changed Court size and composition, and the professional profiles of their appointees – differed dramatically. In Argentina, more often than not, elected leaders sought to proactively shape the Supreme Court into a judicial ally by *politicizing* it. They repeatedly attempted to manipulate the CSJN's size and composition (constitutionally or otherwise), and executives often sought to appoint justices who, beyond being ideologically compatible, were close allies or party affiliates (even if some had relatively weak qualifications). This practice produced an unstable, insecure Court with a relatively weak professional profile, less perceived legitimacy, and weak institutional cohesion – a Court easily swayed by the political winds. In other words, high court politicization produced a *political* Court in Argentina. Brazilian leaders, by contrast, engaged in high court *professionalization* creating a *statesman* Court.

Cross-national variation in leaders' Court crafting practices presents something of a puzzle. Around the world, those responsible for crafting high courts have strong incentives to appoint justices with views as close to their own as possible. Argentine and Brazilian leaders were particularly motivated to do so in light of the judicialization of politics and their own efforts toward judicial centralization, which hastened the arrival of politically crucial cases to their high courts. Moreover, Argentine and Brazilian leaders were formally *able* to craft Courts that would facilitate governance: In both countries, presidents appoint high court justices and the senate confirms those appointments. Why, then, do we observe this variation in Court crafting and, consequently, in Court character? What factors shaped Argentine and Brazilian leaders' Court-crafting preferences in the postauthoritarian era, and what forces facilitated and constrained their ability to pursue them?.

Offering a contribution to the emerging theoretical debate around this question, I argue that institutional and political factors combine to influence Court crafting. In Argentina and Brazil, the politics of Court crafting that had become entrenched since mid-century through a path-dependent process shaped leaders' Court-crafting preferences and practices in the postauthoritarian era – yet formal judicial selection rules in interaction with partisan politics also influenced their preferences and latitude to pursue them. In short, elected leaders reacted strategically to formal rules and contemporary contingencies – but their choices were anchored in history.

In Argentina, Court crafting (while not fully consistent) had tended toward politicization since mid-century, particularly during democratic periods. This historic trend made seeking to politicize the Court the natural (indeed, expected) choice for the country's new democratic leaders. And even when partisan politics (the domination of and divisions with Peronism) inhibited leaders from crafting their preferred Court, resulting in political "misalignments" between the president and high court, leaders' *efforts* at politicization antagonized the Court, exacerbating interbranch conflict and motivating continued attempts at politicization. As a result, the historic trend toward high court politicization continued in Argentina in the posttransition period, reproducing a political Court. In Brazil by contrast, leaders' historic professionalization of the high court, multiparty politics, and more cooperative interbranch relations worked together to perpetuate high court professionalization through the postauthoritarian era, producing a more stable statesman Court.

3.2. JUDICIAL CENTRALIZATION: HIGH COURTS IN THE HOT SEAT

The judicialization of key policies – such as those aimed at addressing the legacy of authoritarian rule, introducing economic reform, and attending to the multifaceted crisis that struck Argentina at the turn of the twenty-first century – presented elected leaders with a formidable challenge. The institution of formal precedent (and underlying principle of *stare decisis*) do not exist in the country's civil law system: High court decisions are not formally binding on other courts hearing identical cases. Despite the CSJN's efforts to impose a weak form of precedent,[5] lower courts remained relatively free to rule against leaders' crucial policies (EC-03; EC-20). When they did so, elected leaders had three options: comply (perhaps reversing important policy initiatives and generating fiscal losses); ignore judicial challenges (signaling weak adherence to the rule of law they themselves had promoted and antagonizing courts that were likely to continue to receive cases questioning crucial policies, given the judicialization of politics); and appeal.

In view of Argentine leaders' expectation that they could craft a high court that would help them realize their policy goals, the least risky option was appeal, in tandem with other strategies to expedite the CSJN's receipt of politically important cases – in other words – judicial centralization. This section describes that process. Elected leaders and the CSJN had taken steps toward effecting judicial centralization before the period under study, but had done so inconsistently;[6] it would thus be misleading to suggest that posttransition attempts at judicial centralization were an extension of an earlier process, as was the case with high court crafting.

[5] The CSJN has long insisted that lower court judges have a "moral obligation" to follow its jurisprudence, and it considers baseless lower court rulings that stray from its precedents without bringing new arguments to justify that departure (Ferreyra 2004: 15, 21). The degree to which lower courts adhere to this informal norm is unclear, however, as they are infrequently studied.

[6] For example, following President Juan Perón's 1949 reformulation of the constitution, Article 95 required all lower courts to follow Supreme Court jurisprudence in federal and nonfederal matters. This reform and other Peronist innovations were annulled in 1955, however, and efforts to constrain the use of the high court followed. For instance, in 1958 (via Article 24, clause 6 of Decree-Law 1285), military rulers limited the circumstances under which an ordinary appeal to the high court could be filed (personal correspondence, Alberto Bianchi, May 3, 2007).

The Elected Branches as Agents of Judicial Centralization

One tactic of judicial centralization that elected leaders pursued was persistent appeal to the high court of cases lost in lower courts. A number of institutional features facilitated escalating politically crucial conflicts up the judicial hierarchy. First, it is relatively easy to gain access to the high court. While it has limited original jurisdiction, its appellate jurisdiction is quite broad and several mechanisms exist to appeal federal appeals court or state Supreme Court decisions to the CSJN (see Web Appendix 2.2). Moreover, beyond the Court's long-standing ability to dismiss technically defective cases without full consideration, it has little formal control over its docket. All properly constructed cases in its original and appellate jurisdiction require the full consideration of the entire Court. While Law 23.774 (passed in April 1990) modified Article 280 of the Civil and Commercial Procedural Code, empowering the Court to use an expedited process to review extraordinary appeals and direct appeals (the majority of its cases), and to dismiss those that are not "sufficiently important," it is unusual for crucial cases appealed by the government to be so dismissed. In short, elected leaders could appeal most politically important cases to the Court, knowing it had few formal means to reject those cases.

The government's appeals had several functions. First, since federal appeals court and state Supreme Court rulings are suspended when certain types of appeals are filed (see Web Appendix 2.2), appeal could delay the opposition's ability to capitalize on lower court rulings in its favor. Second, appeal significantly overloaded the Court (particularly when the government appealed thousands of repeat cases regarding pension policy and policies implemented to address the 2001–3 economic crisis), slowing its decision making on all cases, including the most controversial.[7] Third, the overwhelmed Court's slowness sometimes resulted in questioned policies being in place long enough to serve the purpose elected leaders had in mind when they introduced them,[8] or to allow leaders to develop an alternative policy or present the questioned policy as a fait accompli, making further challenges seem futile.[9] Yet the main goal of persistent appeal was to escalate politically crucial cases to a Court elected leaders would craft (and, later in the posttransition period, effectively had crafted) to lean toward endorsing the exercise of government power. Such endorsements helped to set their policies firmly in place throughout the period (as the CSJN's rulings cannot be appealed), and were of some symbolic value early on before the Court's legitimacy quickly evaporated.

7 Similarly, the Court's immense case load allowed it to stall.

8 The CSJN's decisions are always prospective: when it declares a law unconstitutional, the law is considered unconstitutional only from that moment forward, rather than from the law's inception.

9 Toward the same end, in some instances, the Court used the doctrinal device of ruling that a questioned policy had "become" constitutional (or unconstitutional) due to ensuing events or policy. This doctrine resembles a Spanish doctrine, although in Spain it is only invoked after a constitutional change, not when circumstances have changed but the constitutional text has remained the same (EC-34). The case studies in Chapter 5 provide some examples.

Executives also took additional measures to facilitate the arrival of politically important cases to the high court and to augment its control over judicial outcomes. For example, the Law of Pension Solidarity (*Ley de solidaridad previsional*, Law 24.463, Article 19, passed 1995) broadened access to the Court, allowing the Social Security Administration (*Administración Nacional de Seguridad Social*, ANSES) to use an ordinary appeal to raise all cases lost in a special social security appeals court to the CSJN.[10] The law also freed the Court to review all aspects of the appealed decision (not just constitutional issues) and required lower courts to follow its rulings in analogous cases (SC-03; private correspondence from constitutional scholar, April 3, 2007). Further, in November 2001, the executive introduced a new clause to the Civil and Commercial Procedural Code (Article 195 bis) that allowed direct appeal to the CSJN of first-instance court injunctions affecting fundamental activities of state entities (Article 50, Delegated Decree 1387/01).[11] This special appeal remained in place through April 2002 and was often employed by banks to contest lower court injunctions releasing frozen bank deposits following the imposition of the *corralito* in December 2001.[12] In its stead, in April 2002, congress enacted temporary legislation (an "antileakage" law) that prevented bank account holders from accessing their frozen funds on the basis of a lower court decision; access was blocked until all judicial appeals had been exhausted and the CSJN rendered a conclusive decision in favor of the account holder.[13] All of these legal and legislative innovations hastened the arrival of politically important cases to the CSJN.

The High Court as Participant in Judicial Centralization

To some degree, high court justices also participated in the process of judicial centralization. For instance, until early in the first decade of the 2000s, the Court continued to employ the doctrine of "institutional importance" (*gravedad institucional*), which allows it to consider cases with significant technical flaws that it deems to be of great "transcendence."[14] The Court also continued to use – and in fact expanded the use of – a doctrinal device known as

[10] As Web Appendix 2.1 shows, most CSJN rulings between 1997 and 2005 dealt with pension policy. Prior to Law 24.463, the amount of money involved in a case had to exceed some minimum in order for the losing party to use an ordinary appeal to reach the high court; the new law abolished that minimum. The high court declared the relevant article of the pension law unconstitutional in *Itzcovich v. ANSES* (decided March 2005, *La Nación*, March 30, 2005, "La Corte falló a favor de los jubilados"), and it was declared void by Law 26.025 of April 2005.

[11] This language is obviously quite vague and the decree gives no further information; certainly the lack of clarity facilitated judicial centralization.

[12] *La Nación*, December 29, 2001, "La Corte impide que los jueces ordenen devolver los ahorros;" Gelli (2003c).

[13] *New York Times*, April 26, 2002, "Argentine Congress Tightens Rules on Bank Withdrawals."

[14] The Court established the practice in the early twentieth century and admitted more cases on the basis of the doctrine after 1960 (personal correspondence, constitutional scholar, May 3, 2007).

"arbitrary ruling" (*sentencia arbitraria*) in order to accept cases that did not concern federal or constitutional issues (and thus could not be appealed using an ordinary or extraordinary appeal) when it deemed the decision of a federal appeals court or state Supreme Court to be so legally or constitutionally aberrant (or so at odds with a ruling the CSJN had issued on a similar case) as to require reconsideration. The doctrine has become essentially a back door to the Court, enlarging its jurisdiction and case load considerably.[15] In addition, the high court facilitated judicial centralization on a more piecemeal basis through the 1990s by accepting important cases via *per saltum* – that is – accepting cases on appeal directly from lower instance courts before they were heard by an appellate court or state Supreme Court; while the mechanism exists in other legal systems, it lacks any constitutional or statutory basis in Argentina (see Bianchi 2002a II: 331–4). In sum, elected leaders and the high court itself worked to increase the number of cases – and the number of politically crucial cases in particular – that reached the CSJN.

3.3. COURT CRAFTING ARGENTINE STYLE: POLITICIZATION

In the context of multifaceted legal transition, an accelerating judicialization of politics (and especially of economic governance), and ongoing judicial centralization, Argentine leaders needed a Court that would help them govern. Although not perfectly consistent, their Court-crafting politics centered on *politicization* in the posttransition period: they repeatedly attempted to manipulate the Court's size, rid it of unsympathetic members, and appoint justices who would support their policy initiatives (despite some justices' dubious qualifications). This section describes high court politicization in Argentina, and the next explains its origins, arguing that history combined with contemporary contingencies to shape elected leaders' Court-crafting preferences and practices.

Repeated Attempts to Manipulate the Court's Size and Membership

The Argentine high court was repeatedly resized and reconfigured during the period under study (1984–2003) and beyond.[16] The Court consisted of five members upon Argentina's transition to democracy in 1983. In November 1987, President Alfonsín (1983–9) sent a bill to congress proposing various changes in the organization and function of the Court including an increase in

[15] The original logic of the doctrine, created by the Court in the early twentieth century, was that such aberrant lower court rulings had violated the parties' constitutional right to due process, an interpretation that converted such cases into constitutional ones thus placing them in the CSJN's jurisdiction (Bianchi 2002a II: 315). The Court began to admit more cases on the basis of the doctrine in the 1960s, and its use expanded progressively through the 1970s and 1980s until cases admitted via the doctrine constituted 70 percent of the Court's case load (personal correspondence, constitutional scholar, May 3, 2007).

[16] Web Appendix 3.1 lists all of the justices who sat on the CSJN from 1984 to 2011.

the number of justices. However, due to resistance from the political opposition, the Court, and the public bar association (*Colegio Público de Abogados*), and considerable criticism in the press, the plan was shelved by April 1988 (Pellet Lastra 2001: 449–50). However, two years later at the behest of President Menem (1989–99), congress passed Law 23.744 (published April 1990), which increased the size of the Court to nine justices.[17] From 1990 to 2003, the official number of justices was nine.[18]

Regarding the Court's composition, the CSJN sat in thirteen different configurations between 1984 and 2003; particularly given that it included only five members from 1984 to 1990, a new configuration every year and a half (on average) suggests substantial institutional instability. The repudiation of the justices of the military era and the need to strengthen democratic institutions (as well as the force of tradition, as discussed in the next section) encouraged President Alfonsín's complete replacement of the Court upon transition from authoritarian rule in 1983. Further, as Table 3.1 outlines,[19] groups of congressional deputies repeatedly called for the impeachment of various Alfonsín appointees throughout his administration, generating significant uncertainty on the Court and undermining institutional stability.

The expansion of the Court from five to nine justices in 1990 only created four new seats. Nonetheless, Menem appointed six justices (two-thirds of the expanded Court) within eleven months of assuming office due to the resignation of one sitting justice prior to, and another in response to, the expansion. Later, as part of the political bargain struck to facilitate constitutional reform in 1994, three Menem appointees resigned (at Menem's request) and were replaced between February 1994 and December 1995. The justices' willingness to step down under such circumstances highlights the Court's political nature. As Table 3.1 demonstrates, congressional impeachment battles continued throughout Menem's presidency, culminating with a chamber of deputies commission approving the impeachment of five members of the Court in August 1998 (an initiative that failed to prosper in the full chamber). These salient battles – which suggest the Court was more of a pawn than a participant in the political process – contributed to a threatened judicial atmosphere and exacerbated the institutional insecurity that successful manipulation initiatives engendered.

Impeachment battles were attenuated during De la Rúa's presidency (1999–2001), however, and remained a threat rather than a reality during the Duhalde administration (2002–3). In late 2001, congress established a committee to

[17] The politics of this episode have been discussed in detail elsewhere (see Larkins 1998; Helmke 2000; Chavez 2001 and 2004b: 456; Finkel 2001: 81; Ungar 2002).

[18] In December 2006 congress passed Law 26.183, which reduced the number of justices to five "*La Nación*, June 30, 2006, Ya es ley: la Corte Suprema tendrá menos miembros." The Court officially consisted of nine justices at the time the law was passed, but two spots were vacant; the law stipulated that the next two justices to retire from the Court would not be replaced.

[19] Although not exhaustive, Table 3.1 gives an idea of the frequency with which successful and unsuccessful attempts to change the size or composition of the Court have occurred.

TABLE 3.1. *Changes in CSJN Size and Composition and Selected Initiatives to Impeach Justices*

- High court membership completely replaced with transition to democracy in 1983;
- Request for impeachment of Justice Belluscio presented to the Chamber of Deputies in August 1987 (*La Nación*, August 8, 1987, "Piden el juicio político para el Dr. Augusto Belluscio");
- Three ex-members of San Juan Supreme Court presented a request for impeachment of Justices Caballero, Belluscio, and Fayt in 1988, and a month later their request was repeated by a group of deputies (*La Nación*, July 26, 1988, "Pedido de juicio político" and August 27, 1988, "Piden el juicio político a miembros de la Corte");
- A group of deputies called for impeachment of Justices Fayt, Petracchi, and Bacqué in May 1989 (*La Nación*, May 23, 1989, "Pedido de juicio político para tres ministros de la Corte");
- Head of Peronist block in Chamber of Deputies called for impeachment of Justices Caballero and Fayt in 1989 (Verbitsky 1993: 20);
- Request for impeachment of Justice Belluscio presented to Chamber of Deputies in September 1989 (*La Nación*, September 29, 1989, "Desorden por el pedido político de Belluscio") and again in May 1990 (*La Nación*, May 24, 1990, "Impulsan en diputados el juicio político a Belluscio");
- High court membership was expanded to nine justices in 1990;
- Political opposition presented a request for the impeachment of Justice Barra in August 1991 (*La Nación*, August 21, 1991, "Piden juicio político para Arslanian y Barra");
- Various deputies called for impeachment of Justice Belluscio in 1992 (*La Nación*, April 14, 1992, "El proyecto a juicio político a Belluscio");
- Senator called for impeachment of six members of Court in December 1992 (*La Nación*, December 3, 1992, "Piden el juicio político para seis jueces de la Corte");
- Opposition deputies called for impeachment of entire Court in October 1993 (*La Nación*, October 13, 1993, "Impulsan el juicio político de la Corte");
- Peronist Party block in Chamber of Deputies called for impeachment of Justice Boggiano in December 1993 (*La Nación*, December 1, 1993, "Habrá juicio político a Boggiano");
- Three justices were forced to retire from Court and were replaced between 1994 and 1995;
- Group of deputies called for impeachment of Justices López and Vázquez in September 1997 (*La Nación*, September 24, 1997, "Piden el juicio político de dos ministros de la Corte");
- Various opposition deputies called for impeachment of Justice Boggiano in October 1997 (*La Nación*, October 7, 1997, "Piden el juicio político a Boggiano");
- Bar Association presented a request for impeachment of Justice Vázquez in Chamber of Deputies in February 1998 (*La Nación*, February 24, 1998, "Juicio político a Vázquez");
- Chamber of Deputies commission approved impeachment of five members of Court in August 1998 (*La Nación*, August 6, 1998, "Avanza el juicio político a la Corte");
- Five justices were removed from Court and four were replaced between 2003 and 2005;
- Membership on the Court was officially reduced to five justices in 2006.

evaluate dozens of complaints against various justices, in early February 2002 legislators vowed to accelerate the impeachment of the entire Court, and in late 2002 Duhalde resurrected calls for the impeachment of several justices – all to no avail.[20] Duhalde's justice minister sought to establish better relations with the Court in early 2003 and succeeded to some degree (EC-21), but irreparable damage had already been done. As soon as President Kirchner (2003–7) assumed office in May 2003, various strategies to "clean out" the Court began to be publicly debated,[21] and in early June 2003, at Kirchner's request, congress reinitiated impeachment proceedings against five of the nine sitting justices, generating a cascade of judicial instability. One justice quickly resigned, another resigned soon after the impeachment process against him opened, a third was impeached and dismissed by congress in December 2003, a fourth resigned when impeachment was imminent in September 2004, a fifth was impeached and suspended by congress in June 2005 and dismissed in September 2005, and a sixth retired in September 2005.

President Kirchner filled the first four vacancies by December 2004. However, he delayed in filling (and in fact never filled) the two seats that were vacated in 2005 – thereby violating stipulations of his own decree regulating the appointment process (Decree 222, published June 2003, described in the next section) – while simultaneously insisting that he would maintain the Court's size at nine members. Kirchner's actions are perfectly in keeping with the tradition of high court politicization. By maintaining the Court's number officially at nine, Kirchner could deny that he had appointed a majority of the CSJN, keep it in institutional limbo, make it difficult for the Court to reach majority decisions (which, as long as its official size was nine justices, required five votes in the same direction), and compromise its will to hand down crucial rulings (JG-04).[22] In sum, most postauthoritarian leaders sought to manipulate the CSJN, and even their unsuccessful attempts served to politicize the Court.

Appointing Justices with Weaker Professional Profiles and Stronger Ties to Elected Leaders

An equally important aspect of elected leaders' Court crafting relates to the profile of the justices they appoint. Politicizing a high court entails appointing justices with relatively strong ties to the executive or his party (suggesting they will be supportive of the administration's policy initiatives) even if they have somewhat weaker qualifications. Of course, not every justice appointed to the CSJN in the postauthoritarian period matched this profile (for reasons offered later in this chapter) – yet the pattern existed and escalated dramatically during the Menem years.

Web Appendix 3.2 describes the professional profile of each of the twenty-one justices appointed to the Court between regime change and 2011, and

[20] *La Nación*, December 22, 2002, "El plan de Duhalde para frenar la Corte."

[21] *La Nación*, June 4, 2003, "Se ahonda el conflicto con la Corte."

[22] Footnote 18 (this chapter) describes the legislative resolution of the issue in December 2006.

outlines their ties to the sitting president or his party. I focus here on the eighteen justices appointed during the time period under study (1984–2003). Even though judicial review is widely considered to be the Court's most important task, only Justices Carrió, Fayt, Oyhanarte, and to a lesser degree Maqueda and Petracchi had a background in public law generally or constitutional law specifically (although Justices Barra and Vázquez had a background in administrative law). Several constitutional scholars interviewed in connection with this project suggested that justices' lack of familiarity with constitutional law could inhibit their ability to carry out judicial review functions effectively, efficiently, and consistently (E-11, E-14). Further, few justices appointed during the period of interest had significant political experience, which could aid in understanding and adjudicating politically important cases:[23] only two had held a high-ranking position in the executive,[24] and one was serving as a federal senator when he was appointed (Justice Maqueda). In terms of judicial experience, twelve justices had served on a federal trial or appeals court or been a state Supreme Court justice. Yet even judges who ascended to the CSJN on this path were not necessarily the country's best legal minds, as federal judges are appointed by the president (rather than gaining their posts through public competitions as in Brazil), and the process can also be politicized. Moreover, among justices who had not previously held a significant judicial post, only one had held an important political post.[25]

Concerning justices' ties to the sitting president or his party, one Alfonsín appointee was a close friend of the president, another was considered his "man on the Court," and most were strong anti-Peronists. Moreover, renowned Argentine legal scholar Carlos Nino has suggested that all were "close friends of the administration" (Nino 1996: 72).[26] With the important exception of Justice Bossert and perhaps Justice López, every Menem appointee in the early 1990s had relatively strong ties to the president, his party, or both. Several justices (with the most outstanding examples being Justices Moliné O'Connor and Nazareno) were close allies of the president, and others made it clear that they would staunchly support the president's policies. For instance, Justice Barra proclaimed upon appointment, "my only two bosses are Perón and Menem" (Verbitsky 1993: 56), and Justice Vázquez articulated his vision of the separation of powers in this way: "the functions are three, but the power is one" (quoted in Miller 2000: 398).

[23] Of course, appointing justices who were serving in government at the time of their appointment could also politicize the Court.

[24] Justice Oyhanarte was serving as Menem's minister of justice, and Justice Barra was serving in his second cabinet position under Menem, when Menem appointed them to the Court. Six other justices had served in a lower-ranking position in the federal executive prior to their appointment.

[25] Justices Petracchi, Bacqué, Moliné O'Connor, Barra, Nazareno, and Maqueda had never held a significant position in the judiciary; of these, only Maqueda had significant political experience.

[26] Argentine journalist Horacio Verbitsky (1993: 20) likewise observed that with the resignation of Justice Carrió in April 1985, Alfonsín's lost his "loyal majority" on the Court.

Allies of President Alfonsín or Menem dominated the Court until the wave of replacements organized by the Kirchner administration beginning in 2003. President De la Rúa made no high court appointments, and President Duhalde's only appointment was certainly a Peronist but was not associated with Duhalde's wing of the party. While three of President Kirchner's four appointees were ideologically aligned with him, only one had strong ties to the president or his party (Justice Lorenzetti). In fact, their appointments marked the first time since Argentina's transition to democracy that justices were not consistently referred to in partisan terms (as potential nominees, as nominees, or following their appointment) (E-11). Yet Kirchner did put his own spin on the CSJN. Even prior to assuming office, he had vowed to put in place a Court that would support his mission to void the laws passed in the late 1980s ending the trials against former military regime officials, and he selected his nominees accordingly. His first two appointments both had a background in criminal law (which some legal scholars suggested was unnecessary given how infrequently the high court deals with that area of law). Justice Zaffaroni had a strong human rights orientation, and Justice Argibay was serving on the International Criminal Tribunal for the Former Yugoslavia when she was appointed – causing a completely predictable and decidedly disruptive seven-month delay in her joining the Court.

In sum, in hopes of crafting a high court whose decisions would tend to promote their policy initiatives, Argentine leaders sought to politicize the CSJN in the postauthoritarian era: They repeatedly attempted to change the Court's size and composition and to appoint justices with ties to the executive or his party, even if their qualifications were weaker. Some leaders were more successful than others in their politicization initiatives, but even unsuccessful attempts served to politicize the Court. Of course, presidents in many countries seek to appoint ideologically compatible justices. What is different – and more dangerous – about high court politicization is that it involves significant, frequent, and sometimes illegal or unconstitutional manipulation of a Court and can entail appointers prioritizing political expediency over judicial qualifications.

3.4. WHY POLITICIZE? AN INSTITUTIONAL ACCOUNT

Given the political scenario they faced and the ongoing judicialization of politics – as well as their own efforts toward judicial centralization – Argentine leaders needed a Court that would facilitate governance. The CSJN's significant procedural and decisional discretion only heightened leaders' desire to carefully craft their Court. But why did most leaders seek, specifically, to *politicize* the Court – certainly not the only Court-crafting politics they might have adopted, and one with important downsides? And why was there some inconsistency over time in high court politicization – why were some leaders more successful at politicizing the Court than others?

Most explanations of Court crafting fall within the strategic camp, focusing on high court appointers' calculated responses to formal institutions and conjunctural political factors (see, e.g., Ferejohn 2002; Domingo 2004; Trochev 2008; Castagnola and Pérez-Liñán 2011). Argentine leaders certainly acted strategically: their preference for, and latitude to engage in, high court politicization were in part a reaction to formal rules concerning judicial selection and removal as they mixed with partisan politics. Yet their politics of Court crafting were also significantly shaped by tradition: Particular Court-crafting practices had become routinized – and expected – as a result of their repetition over time in each country. Institutional history, formal institutions, and political contingencies, I submit, all guided Argentine leaders' informal Court-crafting practices.

The Need for Careful Court Crafting

As noted previously, Argentina's posttransition political context – and the judicialization of politics in particular – meant that elected leaders could expect conflicts in multiple controversial areas to reach the courts. The first prong of their judicial strategy – judicial centralization – somewhat mitigated the risks of judicialization. However, appealing cases up the judicial hierarchy to the CSJN and expanding its control over the rest of the judiciary were not without risk: The Court had significant discretion in terms of which cases to consider, when to rule, and how to rule (Bohmer 2000; Gargarella 2003), and leaders possessed few tools to hold it accountable for its rulings.

Concerning discretion, the CSJN traditionally has had little formal docket control (it must accept practically every case filed with it). However, vague rules of standing allow it great freedom to determine who may file particular types of cases.[27] The Court has also taken advantage of the latitude afforded by the 1990 law that granted the Court the power to use an expedited review process to dismiss certain types of appeals (mentioned earlier in this chapter).[28] In addition, the Court has developed a political questions doctrine that it applies in what one constitutional scholar described as an arbitrary manner (Bianchi ND: 924).

Further, the Court has a good deal of discretion in terms of *when* it rules on the cases it holds, and there is startling variation in the speed with which it decides politically crucial cases.[29] No guidelines or rules exist regarding the order in which or speed with which the CSJN must hand down decisions. Instead, the Court president generally establishes which themes (and therefore

[27] For instance, the standing stipulations in the 1994 constitutional reform instituting a form of class action suit were unclear, and the Court initially interpreted them quite restrictively.

[28] In 2001 for instance, the Court used the mechanism provided by the 1990 law to reject 34 percent (372 of 807) of the extraordinary appeals and 80 percent (3,060 of 3,787) of the direct appeals it dismissed; the rest were rejected on technical grounds (Legarre 2004: 1267–80; figures exclude cases regarding social security and pensions).

[29] Just in terms of the cases concerning economic policy considered here, the Court decided some cases in as little as a day (*Kiper*) but delayed ruling on others for more than three years (*Guida*).

what cases) will be treated in the Court's weekly meetings, and the justices together decide which opinions are actually signed. The Court has also adopted several practices that facilitate delaying decision making, including sending cases to the attorney general for consideration (or to the criminal court of cassation in criminal cases). This discretion grants the Court some control over when and how to involve itself in conflict: It can rule in the midst of a political storm, or delay a decision in order to stay out of a heated controversy.[30]

The Court also has considerable discretion in terms of *how* it rules on cases. First, Argentina's confusing legal landscape, an artifact of the country's tumultuous regime history, significantly augments the Court's decision-making discretion. Over the years governments have produced a sea of laws, decrees, and other legal norms, making it difficult to ascertain which laws are actually in force. Conflicts among laws are a constant challenge (as well as source of opportunity) for the judiciary, since it falls to the courts to decide which prevails when two (or more) laws conflict. Moreover, the Court has long insisted on a "dynamic" interpretation of the constitution making "essentially anything ... theoretically possible as a matter of constitutional interpretation" (Miller 2000: 430). And in the absence of *stare decisis*, the Court is not compelled to respect (and at times has overtly disrespected) its own precedent.[31]

In short, the CSJN's ability to grab, delay ruling upon, and duck cases, in combination with its decision-making latitude, meant that judicial centralization only partly addressed the hazards of judicialization. Further complicating matters was elected leaders' lack of formal mechanisms to hold the Court accountable for its rulings. For instance, the formal institution of legislative override of Supreme Court rulings does not exist (as it does in Canada, for instance). Also, although justices' salaries are determined by law, no justice's compensation can be reduced during his or her tenure on the Court (Constitution, Article 110). The Court also enjoys relative budgetary autonomy[32] and establishes the judiciary's annual priorities (*Plan de Obras*). The barriers to constitutional reform (necessary to formally amend the Court's jurisdiction) are high. And the Court's decisions cannot be appealed (except supra-nationally). In view of these dynamics, elected leaders needed to craft a Court that would be predisposed to use its discretion to help them realize their policy initiatives.

[30] The Court's discretion in terms of when it decides cases also affords it latitude in terms of *how* it decided cases. Footnote 9 (this chapter) discusses the doctrinal device the Court uses to rule that questioned norms have "become" constitutional (or unconstitutional).

[31] Also, in several majority opinions, justices have noted that the ruling represented the thinking of the Court "in its current configuration" – emphasizing that a differently composed Court could have and likely would have made a different decision.

[32] Per the Permanent Budget Complementary Law (*Ley Complementaria Permanente del Presupuesto*, 11.672/1933) and the Law of Judicial Autarchy (*Ley de Autarquía Judicial*, 23.853/1990), the Court prepares the judicial budget (*Presupuesto de Gastos y Recursos del Poder Judicial*) but the executive can amend the proposal prior to its incorporation into the national budget (*Presupuesto de la Administración Nacional*).

A Preference for Politicization: Historical Institutional Influences

Given that many Court-crafting practices exist, why did Argentine leaders generally seek to politicize the CSJN? After all, doing so in a freshly democratic context in which rule of law issues were high on the political agenda and reforms aimed at strengthening the judiciary were planned or in motion could have weakened support for the government (or at least made it appear inconsistent on the question of the rule of law). Moreover, politicizing the Court could have alienated it, as well as compromised its legitimacy, thereby decreasing the potential for its favorable rulings to legitimate leaders' policies.

Most fundamentally, this politics of Court crafting was rooted in Argentine history. The Argentine high court was a relatively stable institution from its founding through the mid-twentieth century.[33] This changed dramatically with President Juan Perón's judicial witch-hunt in 1946 and 1947, involving the impeachment of five justices, removal of three, and resignation of a fourth. The number of justices on the Court was reduced from eight to five in 1950. Following a military coup in 1955, the high court was entirely replaced. Three members were replaced with the return to democracy in 1958, and the number of justices increased from five to seven (by law) in 1960. Following a military coup in 1966, the number of justices was again reduced to five and all members were replaced. Finally, the entire Court was replaced with the short-lived return to democracy in 1973, and again following the 1976 military coup (Pellet Lastra 2001: 477–90; see also Larkins 1998; Helmke 2000; Chavez 2001; Finkel 2001; Ungar 2002). In sum, the Court was remade with each change of regime or government from 1947 to 1983.

With regard to the profile of justices appointed to the Court, between 1862 and 1946, most justices had followed prestigious careers in the judiciary (Chavez 2004b: 456 drawing on Molinelli et al. 1999: 686). And although justices appointed to the Court between 1930 and 1947 generally had some political experience, they were loyal to the *regime* in place when they were appointed, rather than to the particular government in power. These dynamics also changed with Perón's rise to power. During the politically chaotic decades that followed, military leaders tended to appoint justices with stronger professional backgrounds while leaders elected during Argentina's democratic interludes appointed justices with less experience – but all justices were strong advocates of the *administration* that had appointed them.

The Perón appointees who sat on the Court from 1947 to 1955 had some political experience and were close allies of Perón and deeply loyal to his government. The justices appointed by the military regime that took power in 1955 had stronger judicial backgrounds but were staunchly conservative anti-Peronists with significant links to the armed forces (Molinelli et al. 1999: 677–8; Pellet Lastra 2001: 174–5). When President Frondizi remade the Court

[33] The high court was established by law in 1860 and first configured in 1863 with five members. The number of justices was increased to eight in 1869, where it stayed through 1950.

shortly after his election in 1958, he replaced three of its five members with "close friends" (friends of his, and of each other) with strong ties to his Radical Party, while leaving on the Court two justices friendly to military leaders (Pellet Lastra 2001: 210–11). The expansion of the Court to seven members in 1960 brought to the bench two justices with connections both to the former military regime and to the sitting government; one had a weak professional profile while the other had held a post in the previous military regime (Pellet Lastra 2001: 236–7).

The military retook the reins of power in 1966, again appointing stronger jurists who opposed Perón and were linked to the armed forces (Chavez 2004b: 456–7). Following his election in 1973, Peronist President Cámpora purged the Court, appointing justices with less prestige (none had followed a judicial career with honors) who were closely aligned with Perón's doctrine and thinking (Pellet Lastra 2001: 321). Finally, following the coup of 1976, military leaders again appointed justices who had been active in the judiciary or in politics during previous periods of military rule; in fact, several of the justices had already served on the Court in one of its previous configurations. While military leaders hoped to give the Court an air of neutrality by removing Peronist justices, the new members' close ties to the armed forces defeated that purpose (Pellet Lastra 2001: 361).

In short, Argentine leaders had tended to politicize the Court between mid-century and regime transition in 1983: they manipulated it relentlessly, and though justices' experience and qualifications varied, political authorities sought to maximize high court loyalty through their appointments. Yet how did this institutional history affect elected leaders' politics of Court crafting beginning in 1983?

First, the Court's history of politicization and its traditional instability made continuing to politicize it easier to justify. As Pellet Lastra's (2001) exhaustive account of the CSJN's "political history" from 1930 through 1990 details, new leaders generally replaced the Court quickly and with little ceremony between 1947 and 1983. Menem's famous response to the query of a reporter concerning his 1990 expansion of the Court from five to nine members – "why should I be the only president in 50 years who hasn't had his own court?"[34] – demonstrates how ingrained high court replacement had become. Further, Menem often publicly insisted that it was normal for presidents to appoint their friends or friends of government functionaries to the Court.[35] Likewise, the practice of replacing the Court with each change in regime or government for almost forty years produced a widespread expectation – among political and legal elites alike – that political and judicial turmoil were ineluctably linked, further facilitating the politicization of the Court.

Furthermore, given the frequency with which the Court was replaced during the second half of the twentieth century, justices and political leaders were

[34] Grondona (1994: 136) quoted in Prillaman (2000: 111).

[35] E.g., *La Nación*, December 1995, "Para Menem es normal que designen amigos a la Corte."

generally "aligned" with respect to politics and ideology, and the Court's rulings reflected its members' ties and loyalty to their appointers. Beyond periodic but quite brief episodes of assertiveness (even during authoritarian periods, see e.g., Helmke 2002; Iaryczower, Spiller, and Tommasi 2002), the CSJN tended to consistently endorse the exercise of power by those who had appointed it. History thus repeatedly demonstrated that having one's "own Court" was politically expedient, whereas retaining a Court crafted by a predecessor (i.e., contending with "someone else's Court") could be risky and complicate governance. Thus Argentine leaders sought to perpetuate politicization.

To put the dynamics in path-dependent terms (see, e.g., Mahoney 2000; Pierson 2000), the politics of Court crafting adopted by Perón at mid-century became locked in over time with leaders' periodic proactive readjustments of the Court serving as the mechanism of reproduction. Politicizing the Court created a positive feedback dynamic in which preceding politicization produced further politicization: Each step down the politicization path increased the probability of further steps along the same path because the relative benefits of politicization compared with other Court-crafting options increased over time and the costs of exit rose (Pierson 2000). In short, as long as elected leaders needed to craft a high court that would facilitate governance (as they did to an unprecedented degree through the postauthoritarian period), tradition facilitated – indeed, encouraged – politicization, contributing to the Court-crafting trend we observe in Argentina.

Limits on Court Crafting: Formal Rules and Partisan Politics

Despite these historical inducements, there was some inconsistency in Court crafting across presidential administrations in the postauthoritarian period. This inconsistency, I argue, emerged because of the way that formal rules concerning judicial selection and removal interacted with partisan politics to constrain some leaders' Court-crafting practices.[36] Contemporary institutional and political factors, in other words, sometimes limited leaders' latitude to pursue the traditional politics of Court crafting.

Concerning formal rules of appointment and removal, the number of CSJN justices is regulated by legislation rather than by the constitution, facilitating adjustment of the Court's size. Further, there are few formal requirements to be a justice.[37] However, Decree 222 (published June 2003) further regulated the nomination process and enhanced its transparency, mandating that the government publish the names and backgrounds of potential nominees, requiring those individuals to provide additional information to the public, allowing civil

[36] For more on how past practices do not fully dictate current behavior and cogent critiques of path dependence, see Thelen (1999) and Schwartz (2002).

[37] Justices must be at least 30 years old and must have been Argentine citizens for at least six years prior to appointment; further, they must be lawyers with at least eight years of service and an annual income of at least 2,000 *pesos* or the equivalent (Constitution, Articles 55 and 111). No judicial career exits: lateral entry to the Supreme Court is possible and often occurs.

society to submit written endorsements of and objections to their candidacy, and requiring the president to consider those submissions when deciding whom to nominate. Presidents' high court nominations must be approved by the senate. Although approval has typically been a formality, rule changes during the time period of study made official senate confirmation more difficult: from 1983 to 1994 a *majority* of the senators present (with quorum) had to vote in favor of a high court appointment for it to be approved (Molinelli et al. 1999: 656), but that percentage was increased to two-thirds of the senators present (with quorum) via the 1994 constitutional reform (Constitution, Article 99). Also, since the passage of Decree 222, senate confirmation has included a hearing in which nominees must respond to questions posed by civil society.

Finally, both the 1853 Constitution and its 1994 reform (Article 110) indicate that justices have life tenure until age 75 (and likely beyond that)[38] as long as they exhibit "good conduct" – an admittedly vague notion left undefined in the constitution. The constitutional triggers for impeachment and removal (the only formal process to dismiss a justice from the Court) are also vague: Impeachment may be initiated if a justice engages in "bad performance or carries out an offense connected with the exercise of his functions or commits a common crime" (Constitution, Articles 53 and 59). Throughout the time period under study, impeaching a justice required a vote of two-thirds of the members present in the chamber of deputies at the time of the vote, and subsequent removal required the assent of two-thirds of the members of the senate present at the time of the vote (Constitution, Articles 53 and 59).

Formal rules guiding judicial selection and removal certainly tempered Argentine leaders' ability to politicize the CSJN. Nonetheless, through employing certain informal Court-crafting practices – for instance, encouraging justices to leave the Court, manipulating it to such a degree that they resigned, or "fixing" senate confirmation[39] – leaders were able to circumvent some rules. Moreover, *threats* to change the size of the Court or impeach justices (e.g., statements by the president, calls by members of congress, and formal congressional proceedings) served to politicize the CSJN even when they did not result in personnel change. And ultimately, the degree to which formal rules prevented high court politicization was conditioned by partisan politics: Executives who assumed office with a strong mandate and began with and retained strong congressional backing (and those congressional majorities themselves) could more easily politicize the CSJN.

As Web Appendix 3.3 shows, Alfonsín garnered 52 percent of the popular vote in the October 1983 election (coming to office with a stronger mandate than any other president in the posttransition period). However, his Radical

[38] Article 99 of the post-1994 Constitution requires justices who reach the age of 75 to be reappointed by the senate every five years. In August 1999, the Court declared that article unconstitutional in the *Fayt* case.

[39] Footnote 17 (this chapter) lists work that describes the shenanigans in which President Menem engaged to dodge congressional opposition to his Court expansion plan in 1990.

contrast, came to power with a weak mandate,[43] and immediately challenged the Menem-appointed Court (as Menem had, by that point, become his arch rival) and was likewise challenged by it. However, while the Peronists and the Radicals together had enough representation in the chamber to impeach justices, a significant subset of Peronist deputies remained aligned with Menem.[44] Consequently, Duhalde's serial calls for impeachment ultimately led nowhere – serving only to further threaten, antagonize, and politicize the Court. In fact, Duhalde's only chance to make an appointment came with Justice Bossert's resignation in 2002. Despite the Peronists' hold on the senate, divisions within the party meant that Duhalde could not count on senate backing for a weakly qualified nominee closely tied to him. This, combined with his own weak mandate (and his loud criticism of the Court's quality), led to the appointment of Justice Maqueda – who had significant political experience and ties to Peronism, but not to Duhalde.

When Menem bowed out of the 2003 presidential race prior to the second round of voting and Kirchner was declared the victor (despite winning just 22 percent of the vote in the first round), the new president immediately picked up the impeachment mantle. Given the Court's challenges to Duhalde, and anticipating that the Radicals would join with Peronists (even Menemistas) in the chamber and senate to impeach and remove the Court's most delegitimated justices, Kirchner moved forward with a series of impeachments, leading ultimately to the resignation or dismissal of five justices. This cascade of departures produced opportunities for appointments – but due to Kirchner's weak mandate early in his first term and his personal divisiveness (including his status as a disciple of Duhalde), and to fissures within Peronism, he lacked the senate backing to appoint weak justices intimately linked to him. Moreover, it was in his interest to rehabilitate the Court and make amends with it,[45] given his publicly stated intention to reinitiate trials of the country's former military leaders (a goal he needed a sympathetic high court to achieve).[46] As a result, Kirchner followed a mixed strategy. He passed Decree 222 which modified the nomination process (described previously) and nominated respected justices – most unambiguously sympathetic to his planned initiatives – but never filled the two CSJN vacancies produced in 2005 (keeping the Court in limbo and violating his own decree). Further, in a new congressional cycle, he changed the size of the Court yet again.

43 Duhalde was chosen by congress in early 2002 to assume the presidency in the wake of De la Rúa's resignation in December 2001.

44 The Peronist party was by this time divided into several wings; see Seawright (forthcoming) for an account of Peronist politics during this period.

45 Just as military leaders often appointed more professional justices in a bid to increase their institutional legitimacy, presidents elected with weaker mandates – Duhalde and Kirchner – did the same. Decree 222 further evidences Kirchner's desire to rehabilitate the CSJN.

46 In other words, Kirchner's Court-crafting motivations were different from those of his predecessors, who had needed a high court to facilitate economic reform and help address economic crisis – both fast-moving processes requiring an immediately and assuredly supportive Court – and he consequently felt less urgency to fully and completely politicize the Court.

Party did not hold a majority in the senate (although it did capture a majority of the chamber),[40] preventing Alfonsín from appointing a full complement of justices intimately linked to him or his party (even if his first set of justices was thoroughly anti-Peronist).[41] Likewise, following the resignation of Justice Carrió in 1985, Alfonsín had to settle for an intellectually similar but politically independent replacement. And his efforts to realign the Court by proposing legislation to resize it in 1987 also proved unsuccessful. Partisan dynamics likewise prevented Peronist-driven impeachment attempts from prospering (as the Peronists controlled far less than two-thirds of the chamber). Although ultimately unsuccessful in changing Court composition, these attempts at manipulation certainly politicized the Court.

President Menem assumed office with a slightly weaker formal electoral mandate. Nonetheless, he had Argentines' support to address the tumultuous crisis into which the country had descended and strong backing in the senate (Peronists held 54 percent of senate seats as well as 47 percent of the chamber). These factors, together with the Court's challenges to Alfonsín toward the end of his term (see, e.g., Helmke 2005: 100–1), encouraged Menem to recraft the CSJN during his first administration (1989–95), and his appointments flew through the senate. As noted earlier, the composition of the Court was also an important facet of the negotiations surrounding constitutional reform in the mid-1990s. Because constitutional reform requires a two-thirds vote in both houses of congress (Constitution, Article 30), Peronists needed the support of the Radical Party to approve reform, and the latter conditioned that support on the resignation of two *Menemista* justices and their replacement by justices less attached to Menem.[42] Further, as neither party had the two-thirds chamber representation required to impeach justices during Menem's first term, pitched impeachment battles further politicized and threatened the Court but led to no personnel change. Menem did not need to further manipulate the deferential Court during his second administration – but his continuing senate majority enabled him to appoint one last justice who epitomized Court politicization (with regard to his connections to Menem and Peronism) in 1995.

De la Rúa's (Radical Party) and Duhalde's ability to politicize the Court was again constrained by partisan dynamics, although in different ways. De la Rúa came to power with a relatively strong mandate, but the Peronists retained control of the senate, hamstringing appointments, while the Radicals held less than half of the chamber, making impeachment of Menem appointees all but impossible. As De la Rúa did not threaten the CSJN, the Court did not significantly challenge De la Rúa, making politicization less urgent. President Duhalde, by

[40] Note that the Peronists did not hold a majority either, but rather only 46 percent of the seats.

[41] Of course, Alfonsín's latitude was also limited by the political moment: He was the first democratically elected president after a seven-year stint of brutal authoritarianism (in a country prone to regime shifts), and Argentines expected him to build legitimate political institutions, making politicization temporarily less available.

[42] See Finkel (2004) on the politics of constitutional reform in Argentina.

In sum, Argentina's history of high court politicization impinged on all postauthoritarian leaders. Yet formal institutions and partisan realities – domination by and divisions within Peronism – liberated some presidents to follow those impulses and limited the ability of others to do so. In the latter cases, the resulting president-Court misalignment meant that interbranch relations could turn sour, an outcome that only enhanced elected leaders' desire to politicize the Court. Thus leaders' informal Court-crafting practices certainly represented strategic choices, shaped by formal institutions and contemporary political dynamics, but they had crucial roots in history.

3.5. A POLITICAL COURT

Argentine elected leaders' attempts to politicize the CSJN, I argue, produced a Court of a particular character – a *political* Court. Four informal (that is, ingrained through repeated behaviors rather than mandated by or formalized in written rules, laws, or the constitution) yet enduring interacting features compose Court character, as conceptualized in this study. The first two, institutional stability and justices' professional qualifications, are a direct product of elected leaders' politics of Court crafting. These two features, together with a Court's decision making and other aspects of its behavior, help to produce the other two features comprising Court character: perceived legitimacy (among both the general population and the legal community) and institutional cohesion. The Argentine Court's character remained relatively stable throughout the postauthoritarian period despite the many institutional and political changes of the era – and despite being composed of *informal* institutional features – because those interacting institutional features are rooted in slow-to-evolve dynamics: historical trajectories in Court crafting, inertial public opinion, and internal Court practices that become part of institutional culture and thus difficult to alter.

Institutional Instability and Weaker Professional Profile

Continued attempts to manipulate the CSJN's size and membership produced an unstable and insecure Court. They also generated a Court with a less-professional profile. As noted previously, few justices had a background in constitutional law and an important minority had not held posts in the federal judiciary prior to being appointed to the Court; moreover, even justices who *had* formed part of the federal judiciary were not necessarily the country's finest jurists as the process for appointing federal judges was also politicized, and they did not necessarily represent the elite of the legal profession (Dezalay and Garth 2002). Finally, few justices had held important national-level government posts, and many had partisan and/or personal ties to their appointer.

Lower Perceived Legitimacy

A Court's perceived legitimacy reflects its public and professional support. The Argentine Court's instability and insecurity and the relatively weak professional profile and strong political loyalties of certain justices, together with the "Menem Court's" high-profile endorsements of constitutionally questionable policies and indiscretions on the part of several of its justices[47] – all dynamics upon which the press seized – weakened the Court's legitimacy. Data from public opinion surveys and from newspaper headlines, editorials, and articles, as well as empirical examples from the time period of interest, reveal the evolution in public and professional support for the high court (see Web Appendix 3.4).[48]

The CSJN was relatively popular at the beginning of the posttransition era – because it replaced a Court put in place by the leaders of the brutal military regime that ruled Argentina from 1976 to 1983, and because it courageously confirmed guilty verdicts handed down by appeals courts in trials of military officials from that regime. However, the Court's image soon worsened. While editorials and public opinion polls had already begun to criticize access to justice and judicial inefficiency by 1987,[49] support for the Court weakened much more – and more precipitously – through the 1990s. For instance, in a poll taken as discussions about the expansion of the Court were occurring in 1990, only 20 percent of those surveyed believed that the expanded Court would act according to law, and 56 percent believed that the executive had a great deal of influence over the Court.[50] In a poll taken two years later, 63 percent of respondents (residents of Buenos Aires) indicated that they doubted the Court was independent of the executive,[51] and a 1993 poll found that the Court was the institution that most frustrated the public in comparison with congress, the police, the Catholic Church, and other cultural and political institutions.[52]

Popular disdain for the Court is further demonstrated by the increasing tendency on the part of Argentines, through the 1990s, to refer to evolving combinations of Menem-appointed justices as the "*mayoría automática*" ("automatic majority") – that is, justices who could be counted upon to vote en bloc to "automatically" support Menem's interests and his government's policies.[53]

47 Justices' periodic lack of decorum through the 1990s has been well-documented elsewhere (see, e.g., Larkins 1998; Chavez 2004a). Two episodes are illustrative. In 1989, the presumed mistress of Justice Belluscio (a specialist in family law) committed suicide by throwing herself from the window of the Paris hotel room she and the justice were sharing (Pellet Lastra 2001: 407, 463, 468). And in 1993, Justice Boggiano allegedly removed one of the Court's signed opinions and replaced it with one more favorable to the government (Larkins 1998: 430).

48 The public's view of the judiciary as a whole is an imperfect indicator of its view of the high court: The former likely reflects people's opinion of the courts with which they are familiar or that they have used, and few Argentines have been involved in cases before the CSJN. Nonetheless, it is the closest available proxy, and some of the criticisms of the judiciary (for instance, its slowness and political nature) doubtless apply to the CSJN as well.

49 *La Nación*, September 27, 1987, "Justicia para todos."

50 *La Nación*, March 26, 1992, "Situación de la justicia nacional."

51 *La Nación*, October 26, 1992, "La gente no cree que la Corte Suprema Sea Independiente."

52 *La Nación*, November 17, 1996, "Sigue en baja la confianza de la sociedad en la justicia."

53 Although this perception was almost certainly overblown, the nickname clearly reflects the Court's weak perceived legitimacy, the phenomenon being discussed here. Only Menem appointees considered least qualified and/or most strongly tied to the president or his party were

The hoards of Argentines who gathered repeatedly in the plaza in front of the CSJN in 2002 banging pots and chanting for the resignation of the entire Court evidenced its weak legitimacy in the early 2000s. Moreover, in a survey conducted in 2003, 68 percent of those polled supported holding a plebiscite on replacing the whole Court.[54]

Professional support for the Court among the legal community was also quite weak. In 1992, for instance, the Buenos Aires bar association published an article referencing the high court's "adhesion to the executive,"[55] and in a survey of law students and lawyers in 1997, 93 percent of those polled regarded the CSJN as "completely or largely lacking in independence," whereas just 2 percent regarded it as largely independent.[56] Moreover, one day in a week-long series of articles appearing in *La Nación* in June 2000 featuring proposals submitted by lawyers, judges, and journalists for improving the judiciary focused specifically on the Supreme Court's flaws.[57] And throughout my expert interviews, constitutional scholars, lawyers – and even some former justices – repeatedly used terms such as "completely lacking in independence" (E-22) and "political opportunists" (E-11) to describe the high court and its justices; "juridical disasters" (E-12) and "grave errors" (E-01) to describe the Court's decisions; and "lamentable" (E-12) and "a horror" (E-01) to describe its performance in general.

Weaker Institutional Cohesion

The CSJN's continual changes in composition and the weaker qualifications of many of its members made it more difficult for the Court to develop institutional cohesion. Indicators of a Court's institutional cohesion include the degree of consensus among justices on the role it should play, whether there is recognized leadership on the Court, whether justices function as a unit (collegiality), and how much continuity marks the Court's procedures and operation.

A shared understanding of an institution's goals is crucial to its cohesion. Even though few Courts feature judicial unanimity around role conception, this lack of consensus is more worrisome in weakly institutionalized settings such as Argentina's where Courts are more easily blown by the political winds and used as pawns by elected leaders. My interviews suggested little agreement among Argentine justices regarding the Court's role. Many justices automatically responded "defending the constitution" when I inquired about the Court's main role (e.g., JG-01; JG-03). However, others suggested that the CSJN should work to maintain the institutional system more generally

considered to form part of these evolving automatic majorities; Justices Oyhanarte and Bossert were generally not included.

[54] *La Nación*, June 5, 2003, "Kirchner piclió remociones en la Corte."

[55] *La Nación*, November 11, 1992, "Preocupación por la seguridad jurídica."

[56] *La Nación* [Revista], September 21, 1997, "Justicia, un reclamo de muchos años," quoted in Miller (2000: fn 15).

[57] *La Nación*, June 18, 2000, "Qué hacer para que mejore la Justicia" and "Hay que rescatar la Justicia."

(JG-04), and others asserted that its role was variable, but that under certain circumstances its function was to support the administration (J-03; EC-30). Several experts on the Court also held that its role is not clear (e.g., Santiago 1998). Composition changes, partisan appointments, and the presence of some justices with weaker qualifications all inhibited the development of consensus around the Court's role.

The second aspect of institutional cohesion is recognized leadership. CSJN presidents (as the chief justice is titled) are elected by their colleagues to renewable three-year terms. Even though CSJN presidents carry out some important functions,[58] my interviews with justices suggested no special deference or respect for the position. Further, the president was not the official public spokesperson for the Court; other justices appeared in the media with frequency (Santiago 1998: 254). In sharp contrast with the Brazilian Court, in only a few interviews did constitutional scholars make reference to the presence of any intellectual leadership on the Court. Finally and perhaps most revealing of weak leadership, the Court often assumed the name of the president who appointed its justices (e.g., the "Alfonsín Court" and the "Menem Court").[59]

Collegiality – the degree to which justices engage with each other and deliberate – comprises the third aspect of institutional cohesion. The CSJN was designed as a collegial institution, but did not function as one. All case review procedures were written and individual in style (see Web Appendix 3.5). The justices seldom communicated outside the CSJN's weekly meetings, in which they did little more than sign decisions. Conversation and deliberation about cases were the exception rather than the norm due in part to the Court's gigantic case load (see Web Appendix 2.1), and justices often abstained from voting.[60] And significant internal divisions wracked the Court through the postauthoritarian era, with the most public rift being that mentioned previously between the *mayoría automática* and the rest of the Court. Collegiality, then, was also weak on the CSJN.

Finally, the Court exhibited weak procedural continuity. Even though clerks explained case review procedures relatively consistently in my interviews, they rarely referred to written rules. Further, in a full third of the cases regarding economic governance under study, the high court's consideration of, or ruling

[58] The president sets the Court's agenda, presides over its meetings, supervises its operation, carries out protocol functions, has disciplinary powers, and serves as president of the judicial council (*Consejo de la Magistratura*, an extrajudicial administrative body created with the 1994 constitutional reform).

[59] The practice contrasts with that in the United States, where the Supreme Court comes to be known by the name of the chief justice of the era (the "Marshall Court," the "Rehnquist Court").

[60] In twenty-five of the sixty-seven cases in the Argentine sample of politically important cases considered here – more than a third of the time – at least one justice abstained from ruling. This tendency was especially marked in the Menem and post-Menem eras, during which at least one justice abstained in just short of half, and just over half (respectively) of the crucial cases the Court decided.

on, the case either followed temporary procedures elected leaders established to facilitate judicial centralization (arguably compromising procedural continuity) or violated existing procedures.[61] Also, as noted earlier, there were no limitations on the time that the high court could take to decide cases, and decision time varied widely. In fact, beyond the limited procedural guidelines outlined in the constitution and established in the Court's pronouncements (*acordadas* and *resoluciones*), there appeared to be little written record of high court procedure (in contrast with the Internal Manual [*Regimento Interno*] to which Brazilian high court justices and clerks repeatedly turned to answer my questions regarding procedure). In short, procedural continuity did not mark the CSJN in the postauthoritarian period.

In sum, while not all elected leaders were able to overtly politicize the high court following Argentina's 1983 transition to democracy, their successful and failed attempts to do so produced a political Court. Despite the presence of some justices without intimate ties to their appointers and with strong qualifications, overall the postauthoritarian Court was marked by instability, a weaker professional profile, lower legitimacy, and procedural discontinuity.

3.6. CONCLUSIONS

Posttransition leaders in Argentina had to address a series of challenges – keeping democracy on track, reforming the economy, and reacting to crisis – in a context in which politics were increasingly judicialized. Lower courts could not be counted on to support all of their policies, encouraging leaders to adopt a two-pronged approach to generating judicial support for governance. First, they engaged in judicial centralization, continually appealing politically crucial cases to the high court, and sometimes bending the rules regarding its jurisdiction and the mechanisms and pathways available to access it. Their efforts – with the complicity and participation of the CSJN, especially in the 1990s – placed the high court at the center of many political controversies.

Given the CSJN's formal procedural and decisional autonomy, this first prong required a second prong – carefully crafting the high court. Argentine leaders adopted a preemptive, proactive politics of Court crafting: politicization. They attempted to maximize the alignment between themselves and the Court through frequent reformulation of its size and composition and the appointment of justices with stronger ties to their appointers and, sometimes, weaker qualifications. In part, those practices grew out of historic dynamics. Juan Perón initially politicized the high court in the 1940s, and his Court-crafting practices became locked in over time as politicizing the Court created

[61] To give just two examples, *Dromi/Aerolíneas* and *Rodríguez* were filed directly with the CSJN by a senior administration official after the government had lost the case in a first instance court (roughly equivalent to district courts in the United States federal judiciary), thus skipping over the relevant appeals court; the Court accepted the cases via *per saltum*, which, as noted previously, has no constitutional or statutory basis in Argentina (see Bianchi 2002a II: 331–4).

a positive feedback loop that encouraged further politicization. Indeed, while few students of Argentina would question that Perón's rise to power was a critical juncture in the country's history, most scholars have overlooked the immense consequences – for Argentine judicial institutions, judicial politics, and interbranch relations – of the politics of Court crafting he pioneered (although see Larkins 1998 and Chavez 2004a, 2004b).[62] Yet formal rules guiding the appointment and removal of justices and the size of the Court, as they interacted with partisan politics, also influenced Court crafting. In short, Court crafting was rooted in history but shaped by formal institutions and political contingencies.

The result of high court politicization was a political Court. Throughout much of the postauthoritarian period, the CSJN was an unstable institution including a subset of justices with weak professional profiles and marked by low perceived legitimacy and weak institutional cohesion. The way in which the Court's character shaped its rulings on politically crucial cases and conditioned elected leaders' responses thereto – that is, the way it influenced interbranch relations – is examined in Chapter 5.

[62] Of course, Perón's Court-crafting practices were consonant with another major dynamic of the time, the incorporation of labor (Collier and Collier 1991); with both actions, leaders sought to disarm potential sources of opposition, deactivating judicial contestation in the former case and defusing working-class contestation in the latter.

4

Professionalization and the Statesman Court in Brazil

"The Supreme Court has the privilege of being the last to make a mistake."[1]

– Justice Sepúlveda Pertence (quoted in various interviews conducted by the author)

4.1. INTRODUCTION

Argentine and Brazilian leaders faced many analogous challenges during the first two decades after their transitions from authoritarian rule (in 1983 and 1985, respectively). In both federal systems, presidential democracy faced – and withstood – significant threats. Following the economically traumatic 1980s, elected leaders in both contexts undertook efforts to implement significant economic reform. Both countries were also experiencing a multifaceted legal transition marked by increasingly judicialized politics – yet in neither context could elected leaders count on lower courts to endorse the exercise of government power consistently. As in Argentina, then, postauthoritarian political and institutional realities encouraged Brazilian leaders to adopt a two-pronged approach to dealing with the judiciary: They sought to centralize judicial power and to craft a high court that would facilitate governance.

The strategies Brazilian leaders used to centralize judicial power were generally similar to those of their Argentine counterparts: They appealed politically important cases to the STF and introduced mechanisms to hasten its receipt of such cases. The latter process was more formal in Brazil however. Leaders introduced permanent procedures rather than using temporary, emergency measures of the type Argentine leaders more often employed. Moreover, they increased the Court's control over lower judicial ranks to a greater degree through an expansion of the STF's abstract review powers and a broadening of standing to file abstract review cases.

However, the politics of Court crafting that Brazilian leaders employed in the postauthoritarian period – that is, the frequency with which (and means by

[1] Original quote: "*O Supremo tem o privilégio de errar por último.*"

which) they changed the size and composition of the high court and the professional backgrounds of their appointees – differed significantly from those of Argentina's political authorities. Whereas Argentine leaders proactively *politicized* the CSJN, Brazilian authorities reactively *professionalized* the STF: They refrained from changing its size or composition in irregular ways, instead waiting for vacancies to arise and appointing justices with experience in the judiciary, federal executive or legislature, or as public prosecutors, with weak (if any) party ties. This politics of Court crafting produced a stable, secure Court populated by justices with strong professional credentials that congealed as an institution and garnered support from society, the legal community, and politicians alike – in short, a *statesman* Court.

Why did Brazilian leaders adopt Court-crafting practices that differed so dramatically from those of their Argentine counterparts in the postauthoritarian era, given the similarity in the political, legal, and economic challenges the two countries' leaders faced, and in the formal institutions guiding high court appointments and removals? I argue that, like Argentine leaders, Brazilian leaders' Court-crafting preferences and latitude were influenced by historic Court-crafting traditions (which had become ingrained over time in a path-dependent process), and by the way that formal judicial selection rules interacted with partisan politics. Yet these dynamics played out differently in the two contexts. As Chapter 3 showed, in Argentina the two sets of forces placed cross-pressures on some elected leaders, with formal rules and partisan politics sometimes limiting their ability to engage in the high court politicization that history encouraged, leading to somewhat less consistent high court politicization. In Brazil, both sets of factors motivated elected leaders to professionalize the high court, generating steadier Court crafting.

Most fundamentally, high court professionalization has roots in Brazilian history. Following Getúlio Vargas's alteration of the size and composition of the Court upon gaining power in the Revolution of 1930, throughout the rest of the twentieth century, leaders (including Vargas himself) perpetually professionalized the Court. This continuity in high court crafting – despite significant and repeated changes in regime and economic model – produced a range of benefits, augmenting the Court's predictability and its ability to lend legitimacy to policies it endorsed. It also created expectations of judicial integrity (among the population, legal community, and the powerful Court itself) that made ceasing to professionalize the Court politically dangerous. Partisan politics – Brazil's extraordinarily fragmented party system – likewise encouraged high court professionalization in the postauthoritarian era by complicating senate confirmation of new appointees (thus encouraging leaders to nominate justices whose qualifications could not be questioned) and making the achievement of the congressional supermajorities needed to resize the Court and impeach justices more difficult. The resulting cooperative interbranch interactions further encouraged more consistent Court crafting centered on professionalization.

4.2. JUDICIAL CENTRALIZATION

Brazil's posttransition leaders, like their counterparts in Argentina, faced multifaceted challenges to their key programs in a context in which politics were significantly judicialized. Yet lower courts – all of which can engage in judicial review[2] – could not be counted on to support the exercise of government power. Most lower court judges were selected on the basis of their performance on rigorous and competitive public exams (rather than being appointed by politicians), and particularly at the beginning of their careers, were often quite committed to defending the legal order and/or using the law as a tool to reform government and society (in a manner some deemed "idealistic," e.g., JG-06).[3] Moreover, lower courts were relatively unaccountable to elected leaders. Building on customary respect for judicial autonomy in Brazil, the 1988 Constitution granted the judiciary unprecedented financial and administrative independence from the political branches (Articles 96 and 99): courts can elaborate their own budgets (within limits determined by the elected branches) and organize internally as they choose. The constitution also ensured all judges life tenure to the age of 70, irremovability, and irreducible salaries (1988 Constitution, Article 95).

Moreover, despite the judiciary's hierarchical nature, "judicial discipline" was weak, and the STF had few levers to keep lower courts in line. With the exception of high court rulings on abstract review cases (which are few, if often consequential – see Web Appendices 2.3 and 2.4), STF rulings do not have *erga omnes* effects. Further, until 2004 there was no explicit, informal, or tacit principle of *stare decisis* (AS-02).[4] Consequently, an array of decisions can be found on most policy issues in the lower courts (Taylor 2004a: 140; 376; AS-02).[5] Whereas the broad law regulating the judiciary's promotion system,[6] pensions and salaries, decisions, and the creation of new courts (*Estatuto da Magistratura*) was written by the STF (within limits established in the 1988 Constitution, Article 93), it enshrined lower court autonomy from the upper judicial echelons (as well as from elected leaders). Theoretically, then, courts all

[2] All state and federal courts were granted the power of concrete constitutional review in the 1891 Constitution (Dolinger 1990: 812; Sadek 1995: 10), and in most subsequent constitutions (including the 1988 charter, Article 97). Courts can evaluate the constitutionality of constitutional amendments, complementary laws, ordinary laws, delegated laws, provisional measures (MPs), legislative decrees, and legislative resolutions (Barros 2000: 1).

[3] The progressive Judges for Democracy movement in Rio Grande do Sul is an extreme example.

[4] The next subsection discusses the changes that occurred in 2004.

[5] A clerk suggested that some lower court judges who considered themselves "closer" to the people than the "eleven old folks" in the capital (a reference to the STF), had come to wear disregarding the STF's jurisprudence as a badge of honor (AS-02). As in Argentina however, the degree to which lower courts follow the STF's jurisprudence has not been systematically studied and is unclear (Vilhena Vieira 2002: 218).

[6] A judicial career has existed within the federal judiciary since 1934, and the federal judiciary's promotions are based mainly on time of service, seniority, and merit (Ballard 1999: 246).

over the country could challenge a government policy even after the high court had declared it constitutional (in its concrete review competency).

In view of the problems lower courts could cause for elected leaders, Brazilian authorities engaged in judicial centralization. Their strategy was similar (though not identical) to that of their Argentine counterparts: They appealed cases to the STF, established permanent procedures to expedite the arrival of important cases to the Court, and augmented its vertical control over the rest of the judiciary via an expansion of its abstract review competency and the broadening of standing to file abstract review cases. The insight that Brazil's leaders intentionally centralized power in the STF in the postauthoritarian era is not a novel one. Arantes (1997) has highlighted one aspect of this dynamic, suggesting that elected leaders concentrated authority in the high court in order to avoid an avalanche of cases in the lower instances that could impede the effective and stable implementation of government policies. Several of my expert respondents (e.g., EG-10) also noted that judicial centralization had occurred.[7] Building on their analyses and impressions, I review the various tactics elected leaders employed to centralize power in the STF, and consider the Court's ambivalent participation in the process.

Appealing to the STF

Elected leaders sought to have cases concerning important presidential decrees or legislation decided by the high court. In fact, according to one justice, government lawyers understood it to be their *responsibility* to appeal judicial decisions against the state, fearing they would be accused of having been co-opted by the party challenging the law or governmental action (or even held legally liable) if they did not do so (JG-03). This facet of elected leaders' judicial centralization strategy was facilitated by the STF's lack of docket control, its broad jurisdiction,[8] and the availability of many mechanisms to petition the Court to carry out concrete or abstract judicial review. Even though elected leaders' main goal in appealing cases to the STF was to increase the chances of judicial victory, doing so had other advantages. Given that the slowness of the Brazilian judiciary made appeal a lengthy process, appealing allowed the government to continue to follow a particular policy path despite losing court cases. Further, even when thousands of repeat cases concerning a particular policy were filed, the cost of appealing those the government lost was often small compared with the sum the government would have to pay if those cases were not resolved

[7] See also Brinks 2005 and Taylor 2008 on judicial centralization in Brazil.

[8] The STF has original and appellate jurisdictions. The latter can be subdivided between ordinary and extraordinary (1988 Constitution, Article 102). Whereas the Court's most important cases (those on which it rules in the abstract on the constitutionality of federal, state, or local laws or government action) often fall within its original jurisdiction, the vast majority of its cases are extraordinary appeals or direct appeals (*recursos extraordinários* [REs] or *agravos de instrumento* [AGs]; see again Web Appendix 2.3).

in its favor. The inflation that haunted the Brazilian economy through the late 1990s also encouraged appeal.[9]

Given these advantages, elected leaders, administrative agencies, state-owned companies, and the Central Bank all systematically appealed cases to the STF (Taylor 2004a: 132; JG-03; JG-04; I-10). Taylor estimates that federal, state, and municipal governments and enterprises were the plaintiff in almost 80 percent of the STF's cases between 1999 and 2003; federal government entities were the plaintiff in more than 65 percent of those cases (most of which were appeals of lower court rulings against economic stabilization plans) (Taylor 2004a: 132). More broadly, justices and experts on the high court suggested that cases appealed to the STF by the state have dominated the Court's case load since the early 1990s (JG-04; JG-05; EG-03).

To be fair, elected leaders also sometimes directed government lawyers or public entities *not* to appeal, or to desist in certain types of cases on which the STF had a track record of ruling against elected leaders. In 1995 for instance, President Cardoso decreed that the Treasury Department would no longer appeal cases in eight areas, removing some 120,000 cases from the judicial system (Ballard 1999: 269). Further, as attorney general (2000–2), Gilmar Mendes (appointed to the STF in 2002) repeatedly instructed his office to stop appealing cases it was clear the government would lose, significantly reducing the number of federal appeals. And in 2001, the government directed the *Caixa Econômica Federal*, a large federal bank, to file motions in the STF withdrawing from most cases concerning inflation indices in which it was defendant; by 2003, the *Caixa* had filed more than 50,000 such motions (Taylor 2004a: 134, 155). Nonetheless, these examples are the exception, rather than the rule, in terms of the government's handling of significant cases lost in the judiciary.

The STF did not strongly support this aspect of Brazilian leaders' judicial centralization efforts. All of the justices whom I interviewed expressed deep dismay at the Court's gigantic case load and the number of repeat cases it receives,[10] and several voiced concern at how often the *state* appealed cases to the Court (e.g., JG-04; JG-05). Indeed, elected leaders' persistent appeal contributed significantly to the ballooning of the STF's case load after the transition to democracy (see Web Appendix 2.4), with more than *one million* cases being filed with the Court between January 2000 and December 2009. Despite the STF's misgivings, persistent appeal remained an important aspect of elected leaders' strategy for judicial centralization.

9 For those who owed money (which the government often did, for instance, to pension beneficiaries), repeatedly appealing (and thereby postponing final payment of claims) was good business: Inflation caused money to lose more and more value over time, meaning that as time wore on, those who owed money owed less (JG-04).

10 The STF receives thousands (and sometimes tens of thousands) of cases about the very same issue (often questions of economic policy): Ballard (1999: 259–60) suggests that by the 1990s, between 85 percent and 90 percent of the cases before the STF involved questions it had already adjudicated.

Concentration of Authority in the STF

A second facet of judicial centralization involved concentrating judicial authority (and constitutional review power in particular) in the high court relative to the rest of the judiciary. Elected leaders' core tactics were broadening access to the Court (mainly by expanding its abstract review competency and increasing the number of abstract review mechanisms),[11] as well as increasing its control over the rest of the judiciary. The elected branches effected this concentration of authority through particular clauses of and amendments to the 1988 Constitution, two laws passed in 1999, and judicial reform in 2004.[12]

The 1988 Constitution retained innovations from the previous military regime (1964–85) that had concentrated constitutional review power in the high court (Arantes 1997: 103–15).[13] It also introduced three new abstract review mechanisms – the Direct Action of Unconstitutionality (*Ação Direta de Inconstitucionalidade*, ADIn), the Direct Action of Unconstitutionality by Omission (*Ação Direta de Inconstitucionalidade por Omissão*, ADIn *por Omissão*), and the Argumentation of Failure to Comply with a Fundamental Precept (*Argüição de Descumprimento de Preceito Fundamental*, ADPF)[14] – and broadened standing to file abstract review cases to a variety of political actors.[15] Cases filed using these new mechanisms – widely considered to be among the most important the Court receives – arrive directly to the STF rather than passing through other judicial instances. As these mechanisms were initially designed, STF rulings on cases filed using them were automatically retrospective.[16] However, Laws 9.868 and 9.882 (both of 1999) empowered the STF (with the agreement of two-thirds of its members) to set an alternate date for the efficacy of its decisions; the laws also imbued the Court's ruling on such cases with *erga omnes* effects and made them binding on its future

[11] These tactics also served to locate more public sector litigation at the high court.

[12] The 1988 Constitution's inclusion of many and diverse themes may in itself have indirectly augmented the STF's sphere of influence, and thus its power (Vilhena Vieira 2002: 21–2).

[13] A constitutional amendment in 1965, the 1967 Constitution, and an amendment in 1969 concentrated practically all constitutional control at the STF; a 1977 amendment further concentrated power in the STF, introducing measures designed to free the Court from deciding less important cases and to reinforce its role as chief constitutional guardian.

[14] See again Web Appendix 2.3. The ADPF in particular offered the STF an opportunity to interfere in the work of lower courts: An STF injunction in an ADPF can instruct lower courts to suspend their proceedings, the effects of their decisions, or almost any other measure related to the object of the ADPF (Vilhena Vieira 2002: 131–4).

[15] As one justice observed critically, even political parties holding just one seat in congress are able to contest public policy by filing abstract review cases with the STF (JG-02).

[16] That is, when a law or action (or part thereof) was declared unconstitutional in a case filed using an abstract review mechanism, the law or action was effectively (though may not actually have been) struck from the books or record as of the day it was created or carried out. This may have encouraged justices to endorse the exercise of government power in such cases, anticipating the difficulty of undoing everything that had been done on the basis of the questioned law or in the wake of the questioned action (Taylor 2004a: 132); at least one justice acknowledged his discomfort with this dynamic in interviews carried out in connection with this project (JG-05).

jurisprudence and on all other courts, further enhancing the STF's influence over the rest of the judiciary.

In addition, Constitutional Amendment No. 3 in March 1993 created the Declaratory Action of Constitutionality (*Ação Declaratória de Constitucionalidade*, ADC), which allows certain political actors to petition the Court to *confirm* the constitutionality of federal norms (see again Web Appendix 2.3).[17] In essence, the ADC allows the government to hasten a final evaluation of the constitutionality of particular norms and to prevent or attenuate scrutiny and contestation of federal policy in the lower courts (Faro de Castro1997a: 242; Rocha and Paulo 2003: 65–9).[18] From 1993, the STF's rulings on ADCs had *erga omnes* effects and set precedent, further augmenting the authority of the high court relative to the rest of the judiciary.[19] Further, a 1994 reform of Article 557 of the civil code allowed individual justices to resolve cases on which the jurisprudence of the Court was settled – thereby creating an escape valve as the STF's case load skyrocketed; an alternative solution, reducing the Court's jurisdiction, would have flown in the face of judicial centralization.[20]

Finally, judicial reform (carried out via Constitutional Amendment No. 45 in 2004) concentrated authority in the STF in three ways. As noted in Chapter 2, reform stipulated that the STF could, with the vote of two-thirds of its members, establish its summary jurisprudence regarding a particular legal theme or issue as binding for itself and judges at all levels (the *súmula vinculante*). It also mandated direct submission to the STF (rather than first to the infra-constitutional court, the *Superior Tribunal de Justiça*, STJ) of cases involving contradictions between state and federal law. Finally, the reform's creation of the National Judicial Council (*Conselho Nacional de Justiça*, CNJ)[21] reinforced the STF's position as head of Brazil's judiciary (JG-03): The CNJ ultimately answers to the STF, the STF president serves as the CNJ president, and questions regarding illegality or abuse of authority by the CNJ are heard by the STF.

[17] Constitutional Amendment No. 3 also imposed two new taxes. Favetti (2003: 89, 127–48) offers a nuanced analysis of the ADC's creation, arguing that it was established to reduce transaction costs in fiscal policy making and facilitate the "mini fiscal reform" introduced by the amendment.

[18] The mechanism may also have offered the STF a way to limit the number of extraordinary appeals and direct appeals (REs and AGs) it would accept, since its pronouncement of a law's constitutionality implied that it would dismiss subsequent cases in which the law's constitutionality was questioned (Vilhena Vieira 2002: 157, 222).

[19] Of course, using the ADC can be dangerous for elected leaders: Filing an ADC is unnecessary if the constitutionality of a law is clear, and if it is not, petitioning the Court to evaluate it entails some risk. The mechanism has been used sparingly (only thirty-two times by March 2012).

[20] Individual justices had long been able to dismiss cases with technical flaws.

[21] The fifteen-member CNJ is charged with administering the judiciary; handling discipline around the administration of the common, special, and state judiciaries at the first and second instances; and elaborating judicial policy.

The STF was more complicit with this aspect of judicial centralization. This is not surprising, since concentrating judicial authority in the STF entailed shifting ultimate (and often immediate) responsibility for decision making on important issues to the Court without a gross expansion of its case load. To give a few examples, the STF confirmed the constitutionality of the ADC mechanism when it was questioned in a series of cases in 1993, although it delayed in issuing final rulings regarding the constitutionality of the ADPF. Moreover, and revealing how judicial centralization could be a double-edged sword for elected leaders, beginning in 1993, the Court repeatedly asserted its ability to evaluate the constitutionality of – and declare unconstitutional – constitutional amendments.[22] Further, in 2002 the STF ruled Article 28 of Law 9.868 (1999) constitutional, thereby confirming that its decisions on ADIns would be binding on itself and all other courts. And early in the first decade of the 2000s, Justice Gilmar Mendes sought to introduce procedures to further augment the Court's abstract review competency (and thus its control over lower courts)[23] – although the STF also interpreted civil society groups' standing to file ADIns and other types of abstract review cases in a restrictive manner,[24] likely discouraging use of the mechanism (Rocha and Paulo 2003). Finally, the Court took several steps to try to rebalance the use of its abstract and concrete review competencies toward the former. For instance, it sought to limit how much it could legislate in concrete review cases in which plaintiffs alleged a legislative omission.[25] Also, Justice Mendes in particular sought to decrease the STF's use of "defensive jurisprudence" in its abstract review competency (AS-03).[26] Overall, through the efforts of both political and judicial leaders, judicial centralization enhanced the prominence and power of the STF.

4.3. BRAZIL'S POLITICS OF COURT CRAFTING: PROFESSIONALIZATION

Elected leaders in posttransition Brazil sought to create a high court that would help them to achieve their policy objectives for political and institutional

[22] The STF first declared an amendment unconstitutional in 1993 in ADIn 939, concerning Constitutional Amendment No. 3.

[23] For instance, he proposed a change in procedure such that the STF could decide ADIns concerning laws that had already been revoked (since revocation only removes the law from the legal order prospectively, whereas STF decisions can nullify laws from the date they were promulgated, AS-03).

[24] Even though Article 103 of the 1988 Constitution stipulates the types of groups that have standing to file ADIns, the description of the types of civil society groups that may file such cases does not correspond to a category in the juridical world; the STF consequently elaborated its own criteria.

[25] Injunctive writs (*Mandados de Injunção*, MIs, described in Web Appendix 2.3) practically call on the STF to fill legislative voids. In MI 107, the STF indicated that it would limit its rulings on MIs to notifying congress or the executive that it had engaged in unacceptable and unlawful delay in not passing the legislation or regulation in question. In subsequent rulings on MIs, however, the STF went further, indicating how the legislative void could be filled if the responsible organ were not to do so (MI 232, MI 283).

[26] This term refers to the STF drawing lines in the sand regarding the types of appeals it will take, or issuing rulings to discourage the filing of certain types of cases (AS-02).

reasons similar to those that motivated Argentine leaders to do so. Yet Brazilian leaders engaged in a very different politics of Court crafting: professionalization. Reactive rather than proactive, they kept the size of the Court steady, replaced justices only when vacancies occurred naturally (i.e., they did not pressure justices to leave the Court or remove them), and most often appointed individuals with significant experience as federal judges or prosecutors, and/or in the federal executive or legislature. This section describes high court professionalization in more detail, and the next section highlights the institutional and political factors that combined to encourage elected leaders' adoption of that politics of Court crafting.

Maintaining High Court Size and Composition

Brazilian authorities held the size and composition of the STF steady. The Court included eleven justices throughout the postauthoritarian era.[27] Further, the justices who sat on the Court when Brazil transitioned to democracy in 1985 were not replaced. In all, the Court sat in eighteen different configurations between 1985 and 2004 – a relatively small number considering the size of the Court and the fact that the initial crop of justices had already served for years during the military era.[28] Even more importantly – and it is on this point that the Argentine and Brazilian Courts differ most – no justice was induced to resign, impeached, or removed from the Court for political reasons since regime transition. As Web Appendix 4.1 indicates, between 1985 and 2004, fifteen justices retired upon reaching the mandatory retirement age (seventy years), one left to join an international tribunal, and one resigned to assume a political post. Such smooth institutional renovation continued subsequently: Of the six justices who left the STF between 2005 and 2011, three retired, one passed away, one left to assume a political post, and one resigned to pursue a position on an international tribunal. Most presidents thus appointed just a handful of justices. President Lula (2003–10) had the opportunity to nominate eight justices (filling seven seats – a majority of the high court)[29] only because seven justices happened to reach the retirement age (and one passed away) during his presidency.

Appointing Well-Qualified Justices with Weaker Political Ties

High court professionalization entailed placing justices with strong professional backgrounds on the STF. Web Appendix 4.2 lists the credentials of the

[27] Web Appendix 4.1 lists all of the justices who sat on the Court from 1985 to 2011.

[28] Compare with thirteen different configurations in Argentina (during the comparable period), where a fresh complement of justices was appointed at regime transition, where the Court was less than half the size of Brazil's from 1983 to 1990 and continued to be smaller (nine justices versus eleven) through the rest of the period, and where justices in effect have life tenure.

[29] Lula appointed three justices in 2003, one justice in 2004, two justices in 2006, and one justice in 2007; when the latter passed away in 2009, Lula nominated an eighth justice. While a ninth justice resigned in August 2010 (Eros Grau), Lula left this appointment to his successor (whom he hoped would be, and who turned out to be, his protégé Dilma Rousseff).

twenty-two justices appointed to the STF since regime change. Concerning the seventeen members appointed during the time period of interest (1985 to 2004), nine (53 percent) had served on a lower or superior federal court, and/or been a state Supreme Court justice. While this percentage is lower than the corresponding percentage in Argentina (twelve of eighteen justices appointed, or 67 percent), as noted earlier, an important qualitative difference exists: since the federal judiciary contains the elite of the legal profession in Brazil, a background in the judiciary is strong evidence of judicial preparedness and training (Rosenn 1984: 29–30). In addition, seven of the seventeen justices appointed between 1985 and 2004 previously had held posts in the newly empowered and independent federal prosecutorial organ. And eleven justices (65 percent) specialized in constitutional law (compared with only five of eighteen, or 28 percent, in Argentina). The professional background of the five justices appointed to the Court between 2005 and 2011 suggests that high court professionalization continued beyond the twenty years studied here: three of the five appointees had held important posts in the federal judiciary (two had served on the STJ), and three specialized in constitutional law.

Concerning justices' political background, six of the seventeen justices appointed during the first two postauthoritarian decades (35 percent) had previously held one or more important posts in the federal executive and/or legislature (served in a presidential cabinet and/or as federal deputy or senator),[30] compared with three of eighteen appointees (17 percent) in Argentina. All six were serving in the executive branch when they were appointed to the Court. Of the five justices appointed between 2005 and 2011, one held an important post in the federal government at the time of appointment.[31] Some justices' political experience prior and subsequent to their time on the Court is emblematic of a broader dynamic this book highlights: The STF forms a critical part of the political process.

Justices who held a post in the administration at the time of appointment obviously had ties to the president who appointed them. A few additional president-justice connections can also be identified: Justice Madeira knew his appointer (President Sarney) for two decades before his appointment (CSE-14); Justice Marco Aurélio Mello is the cousin of his appointer (President Collor); and some considered Justice Corrêa's appointment by President Franco a reward for the appointee's political loyalty (CSE-12). Some have also suggested that political orientation, judicial ideology, and party affiliation were more important appointment criteria for President Lula than for his postauthoritarian predecessors (JG-06). Indeed, at least three of Lula's nominees had

30 Five of the six had served either as minister of justice or attorney general, whereas the sixth (Célio Borja) had headed the Special Assistant Body to the President of the Republic from 1985 to 1986; four of the six had also been a federal deputy or senator. An additional four justices had served in some other high-ranking post in the federal executive.

31 Of the justices appointed between 1985 and 2011, only Gilmar Mendes and, to a lesser degree, José Francisco Rezek had significant legal *and* political experience.

connections to the PT,[32] prompting some to refer to a subset of his appointees as the PT's "delegates" in the STF ("*a bancada do PT no STF*") during the early years of his administration (CSM-02). Yet on all other occasions, justices barely knew the president who appointed them (CSM-01). Further, few justices were popularly identified with any political party – and there was little expectation among the general public or the political elite that justices would consistently support the interests of the president who appointed them, or those of his or her party.[33] Indeed, little debate has surrounded the appointment of justices to the prestigious and powerful STF – and most nominees were approved by broad senate majorities.[34]

In short, Brazilian leaders professionalized (rather than politicized) the STF during the first two postauthoritarian decades and, arguably, beyond. They maintained its size, and filled vacancies when they arose naturally with justices with strong professional profiles who generally had few ties to the president who appointed them or to his party.

4.4. EXPLAINING HIGH COURT PROFESSIONALIZATION: AN INSTITUTIONAL ACCOUNT

The ongoing judicialization of politics, elected leaders' efforts at judicial centralization, and the STF's formal autonomy, meant that political authorities needed to craft a Court that would facilitate governance. Yet why did they choose to professionalize the high court – and what conditions allowed (or encouraged) them to employ that politics of Court crafting relatively consistently through the postauthoritarian period? Indeed, appointing justices to whom they were not connected politically and who had experience in the federal judiciary – crucial aspects of professionalization – could backfire on elected leaders. As noted earlier, federal judges are often strong jurists (given the rigorous tests required to enter and ascend within the federal judiciary), and the federal judiciary has a certain mystique and corporate culture (CSE-18). Drawing justices from such a pool could produce a legalistic Court oriented toward striking down laws whose constitutionality had been questioned.

[32] Justice Peluso had ties to the PT; Justice Ayres Britto had long been a member of the party; and Justice Toffoli had served as an aide for the PT leadership in the chamber of deputies (1995–2000), as a lawyer for the PT during Lula's presidential campaigns in 1998, 2002, and 2006, and was serving as his attorney general when he was appointed.

[33] Even Lula's "PT justices" did not do so (CSE-23). To give another example, Minister Jobim became known as the "leader of the *government* in the Court" because he often supported the views of the president who appointed him (Cardoso) *as well as* those of his successor (Lula), who were from different political parties (I-7).

[34] Even the senate vote on Lula's eighth and most controversial appointment, Justice Toffoli, was 58 in favor, 9 against (with 3 abstaining and 10 not present) (*Brazil Focus Weekly Report*, October 2, 2009); to give one other example, the senate vote on Justice Lewandowski was 63 in favor, 4 against (with no abstentions and 14 not present) (http://jornal.jurid.com.br/materias/noticias/senado-aprova-indicacao-enrique-ricardo-lewandowski-para-stf).

I argue that as in Argentina, elected leaders' politics of Court crafting were significantly shaped by history. Brazilian leaders had consistently professionalized the STF since shortly after the Revolution of 1930, and that practice was reproduced, via a path-dependent dynamic, through the contemporary period. Formal institutions guiding high court size and the appointment and removal of justices – in interaction with partisan politics – *also* encouraged professionalization in Brazil, producing interbranch cooperation that further promoted that Court-crafting practice. This marks a contrast with Argentina, where the historical Court-crafting legacy was politicization, and where formal rules and partisan politics sometimes facilitated but at other times *inhibited* elected leaders' employment of the traditional politics of Court crafting. In short, distinct institutional histories and political contingencies led to different Court-crafting choices in Argentina and Brazil – and thus Courts of contrasting characters. This account builds on existing strategic explanations of Court crafting, highlighting how history shapes political authorities' responses to formal institutions and contemporary political factors.

The Need for Careful Court Crafting

Brazilian leaders faced a complex scenario in the early posttransition period. Democracy remained fragile, and the country experienced prolonged economic crisis. Further, the advancing judicialization of politics meant that – more often than ever before – courts would be called upon to evaluate the constitutionality of the laws undergirding leaders' key policies and political and economic reforms, and that elected leaders would need the judicial seal of approval.[35] Yet judges' strong commitment to the 1988 Constitution (which had, after all, increased their independence and empowered them) meant that lower courts could not be counted on to endorse elected leaders' policies consistently. Thus, leaders' best strategy was to appeal cases lost in lower courts to the STF (a strategy facilitated by the country's permissive appeals structure) and to enhance that Court's control over the rest of the judiciary.

Appealing cases to the STF was not a panacea, however. First, the Court has great decision-making discretion. Whereas it traditionally has had little formal control over its docket (no political questions doctrine exists, for instance), it has long been able to dismiss technically flawed appeals without hearing. Further, as noted previously, the STF has been known to engage in defensive jurisprudence, ruling in a way that discourages the filing of certain types of cases.[36] The Court also has discretion with respect to the timing of its decisions.

[35] Because courts can evaluate the constitutionality of constitutional amendments, carrying out economic reform via constitutional amendment, to which some leaders likely anticipated resorting (and ultimately did), or passing amendments to ease the constitutional way for their policies, would not exempt leaders' actions from judicial review.

[36] Judicial reform in 2004 empowered the STF to dismiss extraordinary appeals and direct appeals (REs and AGs) if the parties failed to identify the case's relevance to society (*repercussão geral*) (see Chapter 2).

The STF president decides when the full Court will hear (and rule on) cases it considers (those deemed most important), and sequencing need not coincide with how long cases have been in the Court.[37] Individual justices – who have issued most of the Court's rulings since the early 2000s – have analogous discretion (see Web Appendix 4.6). Further, the judicial system does not set a statute of limitations on declaring laws invalid: A law can be declared unconstitutional at any point – even decades – after it went into effect (Rocha and Paulo 2003: 58). The Court's astronomical case load affords it additional latitude to ignore or delay deciding certain cases. And any time before the final votes on a case are cast, justices may request time to study the case in greater detail ("*pedir vista*"), thereby suspending deliberations.[38] Finally, while most justices emphasized that the Court's slow decision making resulted from the number and complexity of the cases on its docket, some justices and clerks (and experts) acknowledged that the STF president sometimes chose the "most opportune" moment to hand down rulings (e.g., JG-04; AS-02; CSE-02).[39]

The Court has significant latitude in terms of *how* it decides cases as well. The country's legal landscape is replete with ambiguity and contradictions.[40] As noted previously, the 1988 Constitution is also vague and, in places, internally inconsistent, thus providing ample constitutional support for a ruling in either direction on many cases. Further, the constitution awards the STF significant procedural autonomy, and the Court itself has established most of the rules that guide its decision-making process (Laws 9.868 and 9.882 notwithstanding). Moreover, the Court decides how much time will pass between its issuance of an injunction in a certain case (a provisional/summary ruling which, when challenging the exercise of government power, generally suspends all or part of the questioned law or decree until the Court rules on the merits) and its final ruling on the merits; in addition, there is no requirement that the final ruling employ the same criteria or be in the same direction as the injunction (JG-01, JG-02).[41] And as noted earlier, since 1999 the STF can decide whether

37 Just in the sample of politically crucial cases under study here (N = 55), the STF decided some cases on the merits in as few as twelve days, and also took as long as eleven years to do so.

38 One clerk explained that even though rules exist concerning when justices should return certain abstract review cases (ADIns) they requested to review, they can often (formally or tacitly) extend the period of time for which they hold cases (AS-02).

39 A justice suggested that at times the Court waits to hand down rulings until society has had time to discuss and become familiar with the issue addressed in the case so the rulings are not misunderstood and are better accepted (JG-04). An expert on the Court noted that it sometimes lets cases regarding contentious issues "mature" before deciding them (CSE-02). And a clerk observed that the STF has accelerated rulings on "more important cases" (AS-03).

40 Legal contradictions stem from the immense number of laws in force (a result, in part, of the country's various regime changes and the legal refurbishing that often accompanies them) and the poor quality of many laws and regulations (Rosenn 1984: 19); moreover, it is often difficult to determine which statutes are in force as new legislation is often introduced with the phrase, "All provisions to the contrary are hereby revoked" (Passos 2002: 4).

41 The Court's discretion in terms of the timing of its injunctions and rulings on the merits allows it to test the waters or signal its discontent with certain policies before making a final ruling.

its rulings on certain abstract review cases will be prospective or retrospective (and can set the exact point from which a law declared unconstitutional in such cases will lose effect, see Web Appendix 2.3). One constitutional scholar commented that this ability frees the STF to make more radical decisions since it can limit the effects of those decisions by making them prospective (EG-10).

Second, appealing to the STF was not a certain solution for elected leaders as they have few formal tools to hold the STF accountable (Sadek 1995: 11; Taylor 2004a: 338). Although certain STF decisions can be appealed, the Court tends not to dramatically transform its rulings,[42] and formal legislative override does not exist. Moreover, as with lower courts, constitutional guarantees of judicial autonomy limited elected leaders' control over the high court. Even though constitutional reform is easier in Brazil than in Argentina, as explained later in this chapter, reform still requires congressional supermajorities. In short, executives' desire to appeal lower court challenges to their laws and actions up the judicial hierarchy – in combination with the high court's significant discretion and leaders' lack of formal levers to heel the Court ex post – made creating a Court that would tend toward facilitating governance politically expedient.

A Preference for Professionalization: Historical Institutional Influences

Given the various Court-crafting practices Brazilian leaders might have adopted, why did they choose to *professionalize* the STF? This politics of Court crafting had roots in Brazilian history. While the size of the Court changed on three occasions between mid-century and the 1985 transition to democracy (just as often as in Argentina), these changes (and attendant modifications in composition) were the *only* instances of high court manipulation between 1930 and 1985.[43] Shortly after Getúlio Vargas's military-led regime rose to power in the Revolution of 1930, the number of justices on the Court was reduced from fifteen to eleven (Decree 19.656 of 1931), and six justices were forced to retire (Decree 19.711 of 1931). Between that episode and 1985, however, the Court's composition changed irregularly (not through natural attrition) on only three occasions, all under military rule (1964 to 1985). Institutional Act (*Ato Institucional*, AI) No. 2 (1965) expanded the number of justices to sixteen; AI No. 5 (1969) forced three justices to retire and two more subsequently petitioned for retirement in solidarity; and AI No. 6 (1969) reduced the number of justices to eleven (Sadek 1995: 11). Thus the STF's composition was kept relatively stable compared to the Argentine Court's during the second half of the twentieth century, with manipulation occurring only under military rule.

42 Any decision made by a single justice can be appealed (either to one of the Court's five-member chambers or to the full Court), and decisions of the chambers and of the Court sitting *en banc* can also be appealed under certain circumstances; such appeals are often used as a delaying tactic by the government. Final rulings on the merits made by the full Court in abstract review cases cannot be appealed by any means.

43 The STF was created in 1890 (Decree 510) with seventeen justices. The 1891 Constitution reduced the number of justices to fifteen, where it stayed through 1931.

Regarding the professional profile of STF justices since the mid-twentieth century, Web Appendix 4.3 outlines the legal specialty for most justices,[44] and the preappointment professional background of each justice, who sat on the Court from 1931 to the mid-1980s. The data demonstrate that under both dictatorship and democracy, Brazilian leaders appointed justices with strong professional qualifications. Of the sixty-seven justices appointed to the Court between 1931 and 1984, forty had significant experience in the federal executive or legislature (60 percent), thirty-six had played an important role in the public prosecutorial organ (54 percent), and forty-two had held significant positions in the federal judiciary (63 percent). Moreover, forty-three justices had experience in two or three of those categories (64 percent), and only one justice had no experience in any of the three. As a contemporary member of the Court explained to me, military leaders in particular were careful to appoint justices with strong professional backgrounds in hopes of avoiding criticism that they were simply appointing flunkies (JG-06).

Few data regarding justices' party affiliations or ties to appointing executives before the transition to democracy are available. Nonetheless, no respondent interviewed or written work consulted in connection with this project indicated that justices' weak party identification since 1985 represented a change from the past.[45] Although inconclusive, this could suggest that political ties between Brazilian leaders and their Court appointees were also weak during the second half of the twentieth century – and in any event, likely weaker than such ties in Argentina.[46]

In short, high court professionalization beginning in the 1930s produced a Court populated by justices who were secure in their posts, with relatively strong professional credentials, who likely possessed weaker political ties to their appointers. Yet how did a tradition of high court professionalization influence elected leaders' Court-crafting choices in the postauthoritarian era? Historic high court professionalization both incentivized elected leaders to continue professionalizing the Court *and* imposed constraints on their ability to adopt a different politics of Court crafting.

On the one hand, although professionalizing the Court had not guaranteed that it would consistently support government policies, the STF had proven

[44] Data on legal specialty were only available for forty-seven of the sixty-seven justices; fourteen had a background in public law, administrative law, or constitutional law. However, since the STF's jurisdiction has only been limited to constitutional matters since 1988, it was less critical that justices have a well-developed background in constitutional law from 1931 to 1985, and more important that the Court include justices with a healthy mix of law backgrounds, as appears to have been the case.

[45] For instance, none of the passages concerning the composition of the Court between 1930 and 1985 in Viotti da Costa's (2001) well-known history of the STF (69–71, 128–9, 150–5, 180–1) mentions justices' partisan connections.

[46] As the rest of this book makes clear, the lack of ties does not imply that political leaders and justices never worked in concert. For example, as Pereira (2005: 12) suggests, there was a good deal of judicial-military cooperation in Brazil during its authoritarian periods between 1930 and 1985, in particular with regard to addressing what were seen as "political crimes."

to be a predictable governing partner (rather than periodically acting as a loose cannon as its Argentine counterpart could do). It had generally taken mainstream legal positions and was able to lend legitimacy to the government actions and policies that it upheld. And its inclusion of justices with political experience (whose appointment formed part of high court professionalization as defined here) meant that at any point some subset of its members believed that the STF had a role to play in governance and appreciated the difficulty of governing in Brazil's crisis-prone, idiosyncratic institutional context. All of these dynamics motivated elected leaders to continue pursuing high court professionalization.

On the other hand, historic professionalization obviated the need to manipulate the Court as Argentine leaders had done. While Argentine justices' close alignment with and ties to their appointers could make retaining a Court created by a predecessor ("someone else's Court" as Menem put it) potentially hazardous, new leaders in Brazil inherited a more professional Court that was not automatically predisposed to oppose them and thus did not pose an immediate risk. Further, historic professionalization made it more difficult for new democratic leaders to justify manipulating the Court, had they wished to do so. Because the only changes in the Court's size and only irregular changes in its composition had occurred under military rule, removing or replacing justices rather than waiting for vacancies to appear would have been an aberration and raised serious questions about the new leaders' intentions. Appointing less-qualified justices would likely have had the same effect. Moreover, democratic leaders' historic tendency to keep the Court's composition stable had clearly demonstrated to the justices and broader legal community that regime (or political) change did not *have* to induce judicial turmoil (as has become the norm in Argentina). Had a leader sought to manipulate the STF, justifying his actions by pointing to regime change (in 1985) or government change (thereafter), he might have expected a backlash from the judiciary, and especially from the Court, given its interest in protecting its image.[47] Moreover, manipulation would have delegitimized and antagonized an institution that elected leaders needed to be legitimate (so its endorsements of their policies carried weight, facilitating governance), and on their side. In short, elected leaders would have found it very difficult to deviate from high court professionalization had they desired to do so.

To highlight the path-dependent nature of the Court-crafting process, during the second half of the twentieth century, Brazil's leaders followed the example set by Vargas in the 1930s of iterated replacement of STF justices. Waiting to appoint new justices until vacancies appeared on the Court (rather than engaging in proactive manipulation of the high court as in Argentina) served

[47] Three observations suggest the STF cares about its institutional image: the frequency with which it employed a mode of decision making that could be labeled "self protective" when ruling on important economic cases (see Chapter 6); its sessions are public and televised; and it has a busy press office (EG-04).

as the mechanism of reproduction, perpetuating high court professionalization – and generally cooperative interbranch relations, further encouraging high court professionalization – from the 1930s forward. In short, as long as elected leaders needed a Court that would facilitate governance, as they did in particular during the most intense periods of neoliberal reform, history encouraged leaders to professionalize the high court.

Further Motivation for Professionalization: Formal Rules and Party-System Fragmentation

If institutional history encouraged high court professionalization in Brazil, formal rules concerning the size of the STF and the appointment and removal of justices, combined with partisan dynamics, encouraged the same. Taken as a set and considered out of context, formal procedural rules (e.g., nomination requirements, congressional confirmation) constrained Brazilian and Argentine leaders' Court-crafting choices to approximately the same degree. Yet two aspects of the Brazilian context meant that, de facto, formal rules set more significant limits on Brazilian leaders' Court-crafting choices. First, given the history of high court professionalization and the mystique that had come to surround the Court at least in some legal and political circles, bending or departing from formal rules through informal processes (such as those Argentine President Menem used to facilitate senate confirmation of his nominees) was more politically costly. Second, party-system fragmentation in Brazil meant that the majorities needed to appoint justices and the supermajorities needed to change the size of the Court and remove justices were more difficult to achieve than they were in Argentina, implying a need to appoint justices palatable to multiple parties with myriad interests, and complicating shrinking or enlarging the STF or impeaching its justices.

With regard to changing the size of the STF in particular, Brazilian leaders had less discretion than their Argentine counterparts. Both the 1967 and 1988 constitutions set the number of justices on the Court (Article 113 and Article 101, respectively) rather than the number being established via ordinary law. Consequently, altering the Court's size required a constitutional amendment throughout the time period under study. Further, promulgating such amendments increased in difficulty during the period: from 1985 to 1988, the approval of an absolute majority of congress (in two rounds of voting) was required to promulgate any constitutional amendment (1967 Constitution, Articles 50–1), but after 1988, three-fifths congressional approval (again offered in two rounds of voting) was required (1988 Constitution, Article 60).[48]

As in Argentina, presidents nominate high court justices, and the senate confirms those nominations. There are likewise few requirements to be a justice:

[48] Until 1988, amendments could be proposed by the president, or by a petition signed by at least a quarter of the senate or the chamber, or by at least half of the country's state assemblies. After 1988, signatures of a third of the senate or chamber were necessary to propose an amendment; the rules for presidential or state assembly proposal remained the same.

Presidents can nominate any native Brazilian (changed to "citizen" in the 1988 charter) older than 35 years of age when appointed (changed to between the ages of 36 and 64 in the 1988 charter) with outstanding judicial knowledge and an impeccable reputation (1967 Constitution, Article 113; 1988 Constitution, Article 101).[49] As to senate confirmation, whereas the 1967 constitution did not indicate what portion of the senate needed to vote in favor of a nominee to confirm him or her (Article 113), the 1988 constitution clarified that confirmation requires the positive vote of an absolute majority of the senate (Article 101). Brazil's confirmation rules are thus slightly stricter than were Argentina's from 1984 to 1994 (majority vote of senators present with quorum) but looser than Argentina's after the 1994 constitutional reform (two-thirds senate vote). Further, senate deliberations on Supreme Court nominees are required to be public in Brazil (1988 Constitution, Article 52). Nonetheless, as noted earlier and as in Argentina, legislative confirmation has traditionally been a formality (Ballard 1999: fn 216) and there is generally little public discussion of STF appointments (EG-10).

Finally, both the 1967 and 1988 Constitutions are vague with respect to the triggers for and process of impeachment and dismissal, affording elected leaders significant latitude in this area. Neither charter stipulates the process of accusing an STF justice of misconduct (*crimes de responsabilidade*). However, both indicate that the senate is responsible for trying and deciding such cases against justices, with a vote of two-thirds of the senate necessary to remove (1967 Constitution, Article 43; 1988 Constitution, Article 52). Justices removed from the STF may not hold public office for five years (changed to eight in the 1988 charter), with their impeachment and removal not replacing or preventing any required criminal process.

In Brazil, partisan politics – the extreme fragmentation of the party system (Hunter and Power 2005: 133) and politicians' weak party ties – interacted with these formal rules to encourage (and allow) high court professionalization, reinforcing the influences springing from institutional history. Web Appendix 4.4 outlines the percentage of the popular vote with which presidents were elected between 1985 and 2011 and also lists the distribution of seats in the Brazilian Senate and Chamber with which parties *began* each legislative period. Since party switching is rampant in Brazil, the figures likely reflect the actual distribution of seats in the legislature only briefly (before switching began).[50] Yet there seems to be no overall logic to party switching (congressmen do not

[49] The STF generally includes at least one former state Supreme Court justice from São Paulo, and a balanced geographic representation. Given President Cardoso's appointment of the first woman to the Court (Justice Ellen Gracie Northfleet, in 2000) and President Lula's appointment of the second (Justice Cármen Lúcia Antunes Rocha, in 2006), as well as Lula's appointment of the first Afro-Brazilian (Justice Joaquím Barbosa, in 2003), the Court will likely continue to include at least one female and at least one Afro-Brazilian. None of these practices directly affects Court crafting as conceptualized here.

[50] The rate of party switching in Brazil is among the highest in the world. Upwards of one-third of federal deputies switch parties during their terms, and may switch repeatedly (Desposato 2006: 68, 63), while on average a fifth of Senators do so (Desposato 2004: 5). See Amorím Neto, Cox, and McCubbins (2003) for more on party switching.

switch overwhelmingly to the party of the president, for instance), and there is thus no reason to believe that any one party was likely to have many more or many fewer seats later in the legislative period.

Despite being an "accidental president," Sarney (1985–90) and his economic policies were relatively popular early in his term.[51] Nonetheless, the president began to lose legitimacy as economic crisis spiraled and his efforts to combat it failed.[52] Likewise, Collor (1990–2) took office with a reasonable mandate (even though he was a political outsider) but would become engulfed in scandal just over a year later. Franco (1992–4), Collor's vice-president, assumed the presidency when Collor was removed and was thus somewhat tainted by his association with the disgraced president. These presidents' weak or diminishing mandates compromised their ability to appoint justices in their own political mould, had they wished to do so.[53] Presidents Cardoso (1995–2002), Lula (2003–10), and Rousseff (2011–), by contrast, were all elected with relatively strong mandates. However, congressional representation evolved in a way that would limit those presidents' appointment latitude. While the Brazilian Democratic Movement Party (*Partido do Movimento Democrático Brasileiro*, PMDB) held strong majorities in the senate from 1986 to 1995 and in the chamber from 1986 to 1990, no party held more than one-third of the senate after 1995 (and by 2007 no party held more than one-quarter). The chamber was even more divided, with no party holding more than one-quarter since 1990.

These party-system dynamics promoted the appointment of well-qualified justices without strong political ties and inhibited elected leaders from resizing the Court or impeaching justices in at least three ways. The first relates to party ties. In a country in which even career politicians are not necessarily loyal to a particular political party, it is unsurprising that most high court nominees were not closely connected to one.[54] Second, the PMDB's domination of the senate between 1986 and 1995 prevented the three presidents of the era – none of whom was a member of that party – from appointing justices closely tied to them politically (or from trying to resize the Court or impeach its members). Subsequently, increasing party-system fragmentation meant that presidents had to construct coalitions around their nominees to gain sufficient senate backing to confirm them, again encouraging the nomination of well-qualified justices not closely tied to any party or tendency.[55] Moreover, such

[51] As Chapter 2 outlined, Sarney was Tancredo Neves's running mate in the presidential contest of January 1985; after Neves won the election, it was revealed that he was gravely ill, and Sarney became acting president, assuming the presidency when Tancredo died.

[52] *New York Times,* May 17, 1987, "Friends Deserting Sarney as Brazilian Economy Worsens."

[53] Sarney had been affiliated with the government party during the dictatorship (though he left it shortly before regime transition) and was likely not unhappy with the composition of the STF at the moment of transition.

[54] Likewise, senators were unlikely to vote against politically neutral nominees but might have balked if the president tried to bolster his own party's political clout by stocking the Court with appointees from that party.

[55] Cardoso was most successful in forming legislative coalitions; Sarney's coalitions were weaker than Cardoso's, and Collor's were weaker still (see Amorim Neto et al. 2003). Although Lula's

coalitions were tenuous (in particular given rampant party switching) and had to be periodically rebuilt (Amorim Neto et al. 2003; Taylor 2006: 205). It thus made little sense to choose a nominee with a particular political background in order to please a coalition that could disintegrate before the question of the nominee's confirmation even came before the senate. Finally, divisions in the senate and chamber also made it more difficult to gather the supermajorities needed to change the size of the Court (which must be done via constitutional amendment) or impeach justices.

In sum, Brazil's history of high court professionalization, the formal rules concerning changing the Court's size and composition, and partisan realities encouraged postauthoritarian leaders to continue to professionalize the STF – to allow its composition to change naturally, and to appoint well-qualified justices without strong political ties. In other words, as in Argentina, Brazilian leaders' politics of Court crafting was a strategic reaction to formal institutions and political realities but was grounded in history.

4.5. A STATESMAN COURT

A Court's character refers to its institutional stability, its justices' professional qualifications, its perceived legitimacy (among the general population and the legal community), and its institutional cohesion. These qualities interact: A Court's stability and its justices' professional profiles (both direct results of elected leaders' Court crafting practices) affect its level of legitimacy and cohesion. Brazilian leaders' efforts to professionalize the STF produced a Court with a statesman character: a stable institution populated by justices with strong legal or political backgrounds, with relatively high perceived legitimacy, and strong institutional cohesion. This section considers each feature of the Court's character in turn.

Institutional Stability and Justices' Professional Qualifications

Brazilian leaders' professionalization of the STF produced a stable Court. Crucial to the Court's view of itself and to its behavior and interactions, justices were secure in their posts: They did not fear that elected leaders would change the Court's size suddenly for political reasons or pressure them to step down because of their rulings. High court professionalization also produced a Court that included some justices with strong judicial backgrounds and some justices with strong political backgrounds: Justices' professional profiles were consistently solid but varied. Justices with more political experience, who had a greater appreciation of the challenges governing Brazil

ability to form coalitions was uneven, his very strong mandate and increasing popularity through his second term (he left office in 2010 with an 83 percent approval rating per a Datafolha poll reported in the *Jornal do Brasil*, October 27, 2010) facilitated his appointment of the relatively controversial Justice Toffoli in 2009 (*Brazil Focus Weekly Report*, September 18, 2009).

entailed, tended to be more concerned with the political consequences of their rulings and were thus sometimes referred to as "consequentialists." Justices with more experience in the judiciary tended to pay stricter attention to legal and constitutional considerations and were sometimes described as "legalists." Due to the Court's collegiality, this internal heterogeneity – a salient feature of the STF's character – did not produce insurmountable divisions among the justices (as discussed later in this chapter). Further, most justices were trained in constitutional law – precisely the area with which their cases by definition dealt – and relatively few had strong partisan or personal connections to their appointer.

Greater Perceived Legitimacy

As Web Appendix 4.5 outlines, the STF enjoyed relatively high levels of perceived legitimacy (support among the public and within the legal community) in the early posttransition era.[56] The only data in the appendix for the first postauthoritarian decade are drawn from twenty-five newspaper editorials. Seventeen of those editorials were wholly supportive of the Court and the judiciary, and three were partially positive. Thirteen Brazilian public opinion surveys regarding the STF or the judiciary were identified for the 1995–2005 period: Five were wholly positive, and one was partially positive. Whereas these data would suggest a dip in the Court's legitimacy during the second postauthoritarian decade, cross-national studies carried out between 1995 and 2005 add perspective. Data from the annual Latinobarómetro survey of seventeen Latin American countries (as well as from other international polls) indicate that support for the Brazilian judiciary is exceptionally strong by regional standards. It ranked first or second in the region in terms of the percentage of respondents who indicated having "a lot of trust" in the judiciary in seven out of ten years between 1995 and 2005, and never ranked lower than fourth. In comparison, Argentine courts consistently ranked tenth or lower. Finally (and again in contrast to Argentina), while it is not unknown for groups with a strong interest in a particular case to organize a rally outside the Court, there have been no large-scale protests *against* the STF.

Trends in the data regarding professional support for the judiciary and the high court among legal scholars, judges, justices, and legal organizations reflect those in the public opinion data. Ten of the seventeen entries in Web Appendix 4.5 that assess professional opinion in the posttransition era were positive (particularly earlier in the period). Further, in stark contrast with Argentina,

[56] Until recently, it was unusual for public opinion organizations or newspapers to poll Brazilians regarding their views on the courts, and polls that were taken generally asked only about the judiciary in general. The appendix thus mainly includes public opinion data on the judiciary as a whole – an imperfect indicator of public opinion about the STF specifically, but the closest available proxy. However, the appendix also offers quotes from newspaper headlines, articles, and editorials concerning the STF. Despite the spotty nature of the data, certain trends are clearly visible.

most legal scholars I interviewed praised STF justices and the Court's work.[57] They highlighted justices' strong qualifications, emphasized the Court's credibility, and insisted that its decisions were always obeyed (EG-02; EG-05; CSE-02; CSE-03; CSE-04; CSE-07; CSE-12, and many others). Across the opinion spectrum, then, the picture that emerges is one of relatively strong support for the high court in Brazil in comparison with Argentina and other Latin American countries.

A few pieces of evidence support the claim that the high court's perceived legitimacy is associated with the first two features of its character (its stability and the professional profiles of its justices). First, as Chapter 6 shows, the STF has handed down some unpopular decisions and has only just begun to decide major cases regarding rights issues. If public opinion were based solely only the STF's rulings, it would likely be more negative. Further, given the Court's penchant for issuing "pragmatic" rulings, the STF no doubt defended the constitution less rigorously than some jurists and legal scholars might have preferred. This again suggests that the legal community's relatively positive views of the Court must be based on something in addition to its rulings. Moreover, several interview respondents referred to the aura of legitimacy and respect that historically has surrounded the institution (e.g., CSE-03; CSE-19; EG-05). All of this suggests that the STF's positive image stems in good part from its venerable institutional history and the fine jurists who have been its members.

Stronger Institutional Cohesion

The STF's stability and composition allowed it to develop relatively strong institutional cohesion (i.e., consensus among justices on the role the Court should play, recognized leadership, collegiality, and procedural continuity). Concerning role perception, practically every justice I interviewed answered "to defend the constitution" when asked to specify the STF's primary function. Follow-up questions, however, revealed two distinct visions of how to accomplish that goal. As discussed previously, justices with more experience in politics tended to believe they served (and could preserve) the institutional system best when they considered the political or economic consequences of their decisions (hence their nickname, "consequentialists") (e.g., CSM-01; JG-03), whereas justices with backgrounds in the judiciary more often understood constitutional defense to entail close attention to legal considerations (hence their label, "legalists") (e.g., CSE-04; EC-33).[58] Despite these differences, greater clarity and consensus on role conception marked the Brazilian Court than the Argentine – perhaps because the latter includes justices drawn from neither the judicial nor political elite.

[57] Of course, opinions were not uniformly positive. For example, two respondents suggested that the Court simply follows the pretensions of the elected branches (EG-12; EC-07), and one asserted that justices now think more politically (clearly meant to be a criticism) (CSE-15).

[58] This distinction was also clear from reading the individual votes in high court rulings.

The STF's stability over time and its inclusion of strong jurists allowed it to develop two distinct types of leadership. The STF has a formal presidency that rotates among the justices, falling every two years to the justice who has sat on the Court the longest but not yet served as president.[59] While STF presidents are not nearly as influential as the chief justice in the United States (due in part to the post's short term in Brazil), interview data suggest that the *role* of president is recognized (and respected) by justices, legal scholars, and politicians alike. The STF president represents the Court in official functions, and is more likely to speak with the press than are other justices. Also, the power to decide certain types of important cases is reserved for the president of the Court.[60] The Court president also chooses exactly which cases will be heard (and defines the order in which they will be heard) in each session in which the Court sits *en banc*, manages those sessions, and interprets the direction of each justice's vote.[61] This agenda-setting and, ultimately, decision-making power affords the president significant (and recognized) authority. Some interview respondents even suggested a link between the presidency of particular justices and certain STF decisions (e.g., CSE-23). Simultaneously, the STF has an intellectual leader (a *decano*, generally the justice who has sat on the Court the longest) to whom the other justices turn for direction. Justices and legal scholars were generally consistent in identifying who these intellectual leaders had been over time (frequently mentioning Justices Moreira Alves and Sepúlveda Pertence). In short, unlike in Argentina where neither justices nor scholars highlighted the importance of either formal or intellectual leadership on the CSJN, two types of meaningful leadership peacefully coexist on the STF.

We might expect weak collegiality on the STF given the increasing proportion of rulings issued by just one justice since the mid-1990s, and the contrasting judicial philosophies on the Court (consequentialists vs. legalists). Yet interview data (e.g., CSM-03; JG-03) and personal observation of the Court in action suggest a collegial atmosphere in which justices function as a unit to a greater degree than in Argentina.[62] Several factors mitigated against institutional fragmentation. First, the STF sits *en banc* to deliberate and resolve the most important cases it receives, meaning that the justices are constantly interacting.[63] (This differs from Argentina where case resolution is carried out

[59] Whereas justices vote for the STF president, doing so is a formality. Clerks and justices emphasized that the automatically rotating presidency allowed the Court to avoid internal campaigning, "deal-making," and conflicts among the justices over elections (AS-01, AS-04, JG-03).

[60] For example, one justice recalled a situation in which judges all over the country were awarding pension adjustments to retirees, and he, in his capacity as STF president, issued an injunction suspending all such decisions until the STF had decided a case on the merits (JG-01).

[61] Justices' votes are proffered orally when the Court rules *en banc*, and their direction is not always clear. Defining votes, particularly in close and important cases, is a critical function.

[62] I attended many Court sessions between February and November 2005 and watched many more on *TV Justiça*, the judiciary's dedicated television channel.

[63] In addition, for most of the time period under study, summaries of the cases to be heard in the STF's sessions were not distributed prior to the session; consequently, justices had to rely on

through the exchange of written draft opinions among the justices, who gather only to sign rulings rather than to deliberate.) Moreover, and again in contrast with Argentina, clerks assured me that all Brazilian justices attended the Court's sessions and voted on all cases it decided *en banc* (unless they were officially excused from doing one or the other) (AS-01; SS-02; AS-03). These sessions are often quite spirited (particularly given the theater atmosphere that their live broadcast on *TV Justiça* can create), generating real debate. And while at times strong disagreements emerged among the justices (especially on cases that drive a wedge between consequentialist and legalist justices), they appeared to have no lasting negative effects on collegiality. The Court's stability likely contributed to this outcome. The stakes of any interjustice arguments were lower in Brazil than in Argentina because the threat of replacement did not loom; moreover, justices' confidence that they would continue to interact with each other for the foreseeable future encouraged civility and compromise. Most justices' strong professional backgrounds likely also fed the mutual respect that seemed to mark most of their interactions.

More anecdotally, collegiality is apparent from the moment one enters the building that houses the Court. Inside the STF's bright, modern "annexes" built in the early 1960s, judicial functionaries whiz by on mini-forklifts used to transport cases, people nod and exchange greetings in the hallways, and upon entering a justice's chambers, visitors are immediately exposed to the cheerful hubbub of the young administrative staff who sits at the front. By contrast, inside the "Judicial Palace" in Buenos Aires, constructed a century ago, bedraggled Court workers lug carts of haphazardly placed cases around the battered (though distinguished) halls of the perpetually darkened and silent fourth floor, and one must pass through several tall, heavy wooden doors to enter a justice's hushed chambers.[64]

The final aspect of Court character is procedural continuity. Like the broader federal judiciary (see Taylor 2004a: 7), a consensual set of procedures and norms guide the Court's operations – the distribution of cases it receives and its deliberations and decisions on the cases it hears *en banc* (arguably its most important).[65] I conducted an extensive set of interviews regarding the Court's internal procedures with the clerks of five sitting justices, and their responses to my questions regarding review and resolution procedures followed for cases the full Court decides were remarkably consistent. Moreover, whenever clerks were not sure of a particular procedural detail, they turned either to the STF's internal manual (*Regimento Interno*), to the text of Laws 9.868 and 9.882 (which regulate certain abstract review mechanisms), or to the constitution

each other to explain cases and to offer reasonable interpretations and solutions. Such reliance would likely have been impossible without, and probably enhanced, collegiality.

[64] The fourth floor is silent, that is, unless a protest is in progress involving the beating of drums and burning of items inside the Judicial Palace, as occurred during more than one of my visits to the Court in 2004.

[65] Each case the Court receives is distributed to a single justice for initial review. Web Appendix 4.6 outlines the Court's structure and its case review and resolution procedures.

itself (a copy of which every clerk had at hand). To be clear, my interviews suggested that the procedures for processing cases that justices decide individually (developed by each justice and his or her staff) can differ; indeed, clerks and justices alike referred to different justices' chambers as "islands" with regard to those procedures (e.g., AS-04; JG-03). Yet this variation is less consequential as justices are only able to decide cases on their own when the STF's jurisprudence on the issue or policy in question is set. When the Court decides major cases and sets jurisprudence, procedural continuity is the norm. Further evidence is offered by the fact that very few of the decisions under study here exhibited procedural irregularities. Again, the contrast with the Argentine Court's weak procedural continuity is striking.

To sum up, Brazilian leaders by and large perpetuated high court professionalization in the postauthoritarian period, thereby crafting a *statesman* Court. The STF's statesman character – like its Argentine counterpart's political character – persisted relatively steadily throughout the period because, despite being mainly informal (not mandated by or formalized in written rules, laws, or the constitution), the institutional features that compose Court character stem from dynamics that tend to evolve slowly. Elected leaders' politics of Court crafting are rooted in history and are reproduced and locked in through repetition over time. High court legitimacy reflects public opinion, which tends to be slow to change as well. And Court cohesion is based in large part on the informal practices that justices develop, which tend to become part of a Court's institutional culture and thus difficult to modify. Moreover, those features are interacting, such that the stickiness of each tends to reinforce the stickiness of the others.

4.6. CONCLUSIONS AND COMPARISONS

The multiple political and economic challenges that Argentine and Brazilian leaders faced in the postauthoritarian period, the advancing legal transition, and their anticipation that lower courts could challenge critical policies encouraged leaders in both countries to adopt a two-pronged approach to dealing with the judiciary. On the one hand, they hastened or enhanced the involvement of high courts in the political game via judicial centralization. That is, elected leaders appealed cases lost in lower courts and established a series of legal and constitutional mechanisms to facilitate the arrival of politically important cases to the high courts. Also, especially in Brazil, they enhanced the high court's control over the lower judicial echelons.

On the other hand, leaders sought to craft a high court that would be a partner in governance. In Brazil, elected leaders did so by professionalizing the Court. They allowed its size and composition to evolve naturally and appointed justices with significant professional experience who rarely had strong links to them or their party (although many shared their general ideological orientation). This process produced a stable Court including justices with strong and varied professional profiles, which enjoyed a relatively high degree of perceived legitimacy among the general public and legal community, and possessed institutional cohesion – that is – a statesman Court. As Chapter 3 discussed, while Court crafting in Argentina was somewhat less consistent, leaders most often sought to politicize the CSJN (and even their unsuccessful attempts often had that effect), producing a political Court.

Judicial centralization is important, given its relationship to Court crafting, but does not represent much of a theoretical puzzle. In view of the judicialization of politics, elected leaders in both countries needed a way to fend off judicial challenges to their policies and set their initiatives firmly in place. Given lower courts' unreliability and the overall inefficiency of the judiciary in each context, the optimal strategy was to hasten the arrival of politically important cases to the high court. Cross-national differences in the politics of Court crafting that elected leaders employed *is* puzzling, however, and I propose that historical institutional influences, together with contemporary formal institutions and political realities, explain that variation.

The politics of Court crafting that emerged in each country had its roots in history. Brazilian leaders had professionalized the STF through the second half of the twentieth century, and a series of governing benefits had accrued as a result. Moreover, ceasing to professionalize the Court would have frustrated expectations built on decades of experience (especially in the influential legal community) and antagonized a Court that elected leaders needed on their side. Indeed, as with Argentina, Brazilian scholars have tended to overlook the long-term importance of the Court-crafting practices that settled into place after the 1930 Revolution – despite seeing that moment as a critical juncture in other ways (i.e., the end of the republican period and the founding of the modern political system, Lamounier 1999: 132, 150). In Argentina by contrast, authorities had politicized the CSJN since mid-century, and the example and weight of that historical trajectory encouraged a continuation of that politics of Court crafting in the postauthoritarian period.

Yet formal institutions and partisan politics also shaped elected leaders' politics of Court crafting. In Brazil, these dynamics further encouraged high court professionalization. Given the formal rules guiding judicial selection, the removal of justices, and establishing the size of the high court, in tandem with dramatic party-system fragmentation and weak party loyalty, presidents had to rally broad-based coalitions to change the size or composition of the Court – coalitions that would have been difficult to assemble for unqualified or partisan nominees. In Argentina, by contrast, partisan politics – the dominance of and divisions within Peronism – had different effects over time, sometimes encouraging and sometimes complicating high court politicization. In sum, while elected leaders' Court-crafting practices are in part strategic reactions to formal institutions and party-system dynamics, they are also strongly influenced by history.

Explaining when and why elected leaders formally empower courts and establish formal safeguards for judicial autonomy are crucial undertakings. This analysis suggests that identifying and explicating the *informal* yet persistent practices that elected leaders employ to craft their Courts are equally important. This is so because those practices by and large determine a high court's *character*, an attribute that – together with a Court's power and independence – is fundamental for understanding its behavior and interactions. Moreover, the congeries of informal institutional features that compose Court character tend to be enduring, suggesting that even in politically unstable settings such as those of many Latin American countries, Courts can have recognizable – and consequential – institutional trajectories.

As a result of Argentine and Brazilian leaders' efforts to centralize judicial power, both the CSJN and the STF were called upon repeatedly to rule on politically crucial cases during the first twenty posttransition years. Due to the judicialization of economic governance, cases dealing with the constitutionality of economic reform policies were among both Courts' most important. Ruling on such cases often placed the Courts in the complicated position of choosing between defending policies that elected leaders viewed as crucial, and defending the constitution. When high courts challenged the constitutionality of their policies, elected leaders faced an analogous quandary: continue with those policies (perhaps flouting the rule of law) or comply (perhaps endangering economic recovery)? How did high courts and elected leaders interact over economic policy in the two countries, and what explains the patterns that marked their interactions? The rest of the study addresses these questions, arguing that those patterns were significantly shaped by high court character.

5

The Political Court, and High Court Submission and Interbranch Confrontation in Argentina

"My only two bosses are Perón and Menem."[1]

– Reaction of Justice Antonio Barra upon receiving word of his appointment to the Supreme Court in 1990

"There will be no changes in the economic model or with regard to monetary policy. From a practical point of view, the financial system will continue to function exactly as it has been."[2]

– Reaction of Minister of Economy Roberto Lavagna to a Supreme Court decision in 2003 declaring unconstitutional a law fundamental to the government's economic program

5.1. INTRODUCTION

To summarize the main points thus far, both Argentina and Brazil underwent a dual transition in the wake of regime change. On the one hand, they experienced a legal transition entailing an increase in the salience of rule of law issues, growing rights consciousness among citizens, constitutional and judicial reform, and a judicialization of politics that drew courts ineluctably into the political game. On the other hand, an economic transition involving a rejection of state-led economic development and the introduction of market-based reforms began in the 1990s. Argentina also experienced devastating economic crisis again around the turn of the twenty-first century. Due to the nature of economic adjustment and the advancing judicialization of politics, courts were increasingly called upon to evaluate the constitutionality of national economic policy: The simultaneity of legal and economic transformation produced a judicialization of economic governance. Anticipating judicial challenges to their

[1] Quoted in Verbitsky (1993: 56).

[2] Original quote: "*No habrá cambios en el modelo económico ni en el programa monetario. Desde el punto de vista práctico no hay ninguna modificación del funcionamiento del sistema financiero*" (NP 02–83).

major policies, leaders in both countries developed a two-pronged approach to dealing with the courts: centralizing judicial power and crafting a high court that would facilitate governance.

Economic policy and reform were of critical importance to elected authorities. Consequently, when crucial cases questioning the constitutionality of economic policy reached the high courts, as they inevitably did, justices faced significant and controversial trade-offs between endorsing the exercise of government power in the economic realm, and upholding the constitution. Elected leaders found themselves in a similar situation when high courts struck down all or part of key economic policies. In polities in which the rule of law is relatively established, elected leaders may see few alternatives to compliance when Courts strongly challenge their interests. In countries with a weaker rule of law, however – and in particular those simultaneously undergoing economic and legal transitions championed by elected leaders – leaders faced a critical choice when high courts challenged their crucial economic policies. Should they continue to pursue policies that they considered essential but that Courts at the apex of newly empowered judiciaries deemed unconstitutional? Or should they comply with such rulings, helping to entrench the rule of law but perhaps risking political or economic instability? In short, when facing high court challenges to their economic policies, Argentine and Brazilian elected leaders stood at the same crossroads at which justices had stood when they ruled on such cases: adjudicating between advancing economic governance and bolstering constitutionalism.

As high courts repeatedly make choices about how to rule on cases in which elected leaders' interests are at play, and as those leaders repeatedly make choices about how to respond to Courts' challenging decisions – that is, as justices and politicians interact over politically vital issues – patterns of interbranch interaction emerge. This study proposes an integrated analytic framework for identifying and analyzing these patterns (see Chapter 1, especially Table 1.1). Employing the framework to study a given set of legal cases entails examining the Court in question's assertiveness vis-à-vis elected leaders (the frequency and intensity with which it challenged them or their interests in its rulings) and the approaches to decision making it adopted – as well as how often and to what degree the elected branches complied with and retaliated against the Court's rulings when it challenged the exercise of government power.

This chapter and the next employ that analytic framework to examine the contrasting patterns of interbranch interaction over economic policy in Argentina and Brazil in the posttransition period. This chapter analyzes interbranch interactions around eighteen important economic policy cases decided by the Argentine CSJN between 1984 and 2003. Table 5.1 outlines the two patterns of interbranch interaction that emerged over those cases in Argentina: *confrontation* and *Court submission*.

As Table 5.1 demonstrates, the CSJN was selectively assertive vis-à-vis elected leaders in the realm of economic governance. Through most of the

TABLE 5.1. *Patterns of High Court–Elected Branch Interaction over Economic Governance in Argentina*

Pattern of Interaction	Tendencies in CSJN's Behavior				Tendencies in Elected Leaders' Behavior	
	Assertiveness			Approach to Decision Making	Compliance with CSJN Rulings	Retaliation against CSJN Rulings
	Direction of Rulings	Intensity of Endorsements	Intensity of Challenges			
Confrontation	Challenge	Weaker	Stronger	Various (*not* Deferential)	Non-/Partial	Frequent
Court submission	Endorse	Stronger	Weaker	Deferential	Partial	Infrequent

period under study, as we will see, it tended to strongly endorse the exercise of government power (following the Court submission pattern). Yet at critical moments, it tended to strongly challenge the exercise of government power (following the Confrontation pattern). While no particular approach to decision making dominated during periods of interbranch confrontation, the Court tended to adopt a deferential approach during periods of Court submission. For their part, elected leaders tended to comply incompletely with the Court's challenging decisions – and tended to comply even less during moments of interbranch confrontation. Elected leaders also tended to retaliate against the Court's challenging decisions, though to differing degrees (more in the confrontation pattern, less in the Court submission pattern). In contrast to this cycle of Court submission interrupted by periodic episodes of interbranch confrontation in Argentina, a more stable pattern of interbranch *accommodation* emerged in Brazil.

My explanation for this cross-national variation in patterns of interbranch interaction draws on both rational choice and historical institutionalism. The Court character thesis posits that a Court's character, a discrete set of *informal* institutional features, leads the Court and elected leaders to interact in certain ways when crucial policy objectives clash with the rule of law. Because the institutional features that compose Court character reflect elected leaders' historic choices, inertial public and professional opinion, and norms and practices ingrained in Court culture, Court character tends to be enduring, leading to relatively persistent patterns of interbranch interaction. In Argentina, the high court's *political* character – its instability, and its weaker professional profile, legitimacy, and institutional cohesion – led to interbranch interactions that vacillated between Court submission to elected leaders and interbranch confrontation. In Brazil, the Court's *statesman* character encouraged interbranch accommodation. The chapter's final section offers several case studies illustrating the argument.

5.2. INTERBRANCH INTERACTIONS OVER ECONOMIC GOVERNANCE IN ARGENTINA: COURT SUBMISSION AND CONFRONTATION

Two patterns (or a combined pattern) of interbranch interaction over economic governance emerged in Argentina in the postauthoritarian period: Court submission and confrontation. Table 5.2 lists (in chronological order) the systematically selected set of Argentine high court cases that were evaluated to arrive at this characterization: eighteen of the most crucial cases regarding economic policy to come before the CSJN between 1984 and 2003.[3] As noted previously, the framework for analyzing patterns of interbranch interaction employed in this study takes into consideration a high court's assertiveness and approach to decision making (columns three and four), as well as the degree to which elected leaders complied with and retaliated against its challenging decisions (column five). Scores on these parameters are aggregated to discern the overall patterns of interbranch interaction (column six). This section describes the eighteen Argentine Supreme Court cases under study, discusses each aspect of high court–elected branch interaction in turn, and evaluates the overall combined pattern of interbranch interaction in the economic policy realm in Argentina in the posttransition period.

The Cases

Appendix 5.1 describes the 18 CSJN cases under study, outlining case name and type; parties; issue area, target policy, and claim; decision timeline; and ruling. Most of the cases (thirteen of eighteen) were filed using the appeals mechanisms employed most frequently in cases that arrive to the Court: the extraordinary appeal (*recurso extraordinario*) and direct appeal (*recurso de queja*). Concerning the types of actors who turned to the high court, individuals brought eleven of the cases under study, opposition parties brought two, companies brought three cases, and civil society organizations and provinces each brought one. These proportions are quite different from the proportions in Brazil, where political parties were far more active questioning economic policy before the high court, likely due to the different mechanisms available to challenge the constitutionality of government policy in the two countries.[4]

The cases track the main policies Argentine leaders implemented to stabilize the economy and reform the state after 1984, falling into five issue areas. Several cases concern monetary policy, in particular, bank freezes and other measures to combat financial crisis (*Peralta*, *Kiper*, *Smith*, *San Luís*). The largest number

[3] Appendix 1.1 explains the case selection technique employed.

[4] See Web Appendices 2.2 and 2.3 and corresponding discussions in Chapter 2. Further, the CSJN has generally denied collective standing to legislators, instead only allowing the leader of congress to represent congress before the Court (Miller 2000: 18).

TABLE 5.2. *Patterns of High Court–Elected Branch Interaction over Economic Governance in Argentina (eighteen cases decided 1984–2003, in chronological order)*

President	Case (year of decision)	CSJN Assertiveness: Direction and Intensity of Ruling[a]	CSJN Approach to Decision Making[b]	Elected Branch Compliance with/Retaliation against Challenging Decisions[c]	Pattern of Interbranch Interaction
Alfonsín	*Rolón Zappa* (1986)	**Stronger challenge** (13.5)	Principled/ *Protective*	**Noncompliance/some retaliation** (14)	Confrontation
Menem I	*Soengas* (1990)	Stronger endorsement* (–8)	*Deferential*	(Not applic.)	
	Aerolíneas (1990)	Stronger endorsement** (–8)	*Deferential*	(Not applic.)	
	Peralta (1990)	Stronger endorsement** (–9)	*Deferential*/ Pragmatic	(Not applic.)	
	Arenera (1991)	Stronger endorsement* (–8)	Pragmatic	(Not applic.)	
	Cocchia (1993)	Stronger endorsement** (–7.5)	*Deferential*	(Not applic.)	Court submission
	Cafés la Virginia (1994)	Weaker challenge (7.5)	*Deferential*/ Pragmatic	Partial compliance/ no retaliation (7.5)	
	Benito (1994)	Weaker endorsement* (–5)	*Deferential*	(Not applic.)	
	Video Club Dreams (1995)	Weaker challenge (8.5)	Principled	Partial compliance/ no retaliation (7)	
Menem II	*Chocobar* (1996)	Weaker challenge** (8)	*Deferential*/ Pragmatic	Partial compliance/ no retaliation (5.5)	
	Rodríguez (1997)	Stronger endorsement** (–7)	*Deferential*	(Not applic.)	
	Prodelco (1998)	Stronger endorsement* (–6.5)	Principled/ *Deferential*	(Not applic.)	

	Verrocchi (1999)	Weaker challenge (8)	Principled/ *Protective*	Partial compliance/ no retaliation (7.5)	
De la Rúa	*Guida* (2000)	Stronger endorsement* (−7.5)	*Deferential*	(Not applic.)	
Power vacuum	*Kiper* (2001)	Weaker endorsement* (−4)	Principled	(Not applic.)	
Duhalde	*Smith* (2002)	**Stronger challenge*** (14)	*Protective*	**Noncompliance/ significant retaliation** (20)	**Confrontation**
	Tobar (2002)	**Stronger challenge** (12)	*Protective*	Partial compliance/ **some retaliation** (11.75)	
	San Luis (2003)	**Stronger challenge** (13)	Principled/ *Pragmatic*	Partial compliance/ **some retaliation** (12)	

Notes: * Indicates that the justices alleged to form part of President Menem's "automatic majority" (*mayoría automática*) all voted in one direction together; ** indicates that this occurred *and* all of the judges appointed by another president voted in the opposite direction.

[a] Numeric scores are based on data in Appendices 5.2 and 5.3: −11 (strongest endorsement) to −1 (weakest endorsement) and 1 (weakest challenge) to 17.5 (strongest challenge). Font darkness likewise reflects judicial assertiveness: rulings in grey font are least assertive and rulings in bold font are most assertive.

[b] Approaches in italic font are strategic. See Appendix 5.4 for data supporting these scores.

[c] Numeric scores are the sum of the "compliance" and "retaliation" scores for each case (see Appendix 5.5) and indicate the overall degree to which elected leaders' response challenged the Court: 1 to 8.25 (weakest challenge); 8.25 to 15.5 (moderate challenge); 15.5 to 23 (strongest challenge). Font darkness likewise reflects how much elected leaders' response challenged the Court: responses in bold font are the most challenging and responses in grey font the least challenging.

of cases concern salaries (especially public sector salaries) and pensions, the levels of which several administrations sought to adjust in pursuit of fiscal rectitude (*Guida, Benito, Chocobar, Verrocchi, Tobar, Rolón Zappa*). Three cases address the government's privatization initiatives or subsequent regulation (*Aerolíneas, Rodríguez, Prodelco*), and another set concern governmental efforts to bridge budget deficits by taxing more (*Arenera, Cafés la Virginia, Video Club Dreams*). Finally, two cases concern labor relations (*Soengas* and *Cocchia*).

With respect to the *form* of the policies questioned before the Court in these cases (e.g., decrees, laws), my findings both support and challenge conventional wisdom about Argentine politics. Scholars and news sources often assert that Argentine Presidents – and President Menem in particular – "ruled by decree" especially in the economic policy realm, and consistently overstepped institutional boundaries in employing decree power.[5] My data support this understanding. A presidential decree was questioned in twelve of the eighteen cases considered here (two-thirds of the sample): seven Decrees of Necessity and Urgency (DNUs) and five ordinary decrees.[6] However, we might have expected that it would be the *form* rather than the *content* of those decrees that would be questioned most often, as the Argentine Constitution clearly outlines the separation of powers and contours of executive policy making (vis-à-vis congress) but establishes few limits or requirements regarding the substance of government intervention in the economy and until the mid-1990s included relatively few rights. Yet plaintiffs more often challenged the content than the form of decrees (for instance, claiming that they violated rights rather than questioning the introduction of a policy via decree rather than legislation). One way to interpret this finding is as suggesting that Argentine presidents did not tread upon legislators' toes when decreeing economic policy as often as is commonly thought.

Two-thirds of the cases in the sample (twelve of eighteen) were resolved in the 1990s, the period during which most neoliberal reform was carried out. However, cases regarding economic policy continued to dominate the high court's docket in the early 2000s, as the controversial nature of the policies introduced to address the dramatic economic crisis into which the country descended in 2001 perpetuated the judicialization of economic governance. As Chapter 3 explained, the Court has considerable discretion in terms of when it rules on cases, and the amount of time that elapsed between the Court's receipt of and rulings on cases varied significantly (from as little as a day to more than three years). In fact, the Court took more than a year to solve half of the cases under study, a finding that is both surprising (given the political importance of these cases) and alarming (since most of the cases had risen through the notoriously inefficient Argentine judiciary and thus likely had already been in the justice system for at least a year before arriving to the CSJN). The case studies

[5] See, e.g., O'Donnell (1994) and Zakaria (1997).

[6] Chapter 2 describes Decrees of Necessity and Urgency.

at the end of this chapter reveal the strategic nature of some of the Court's accelerated and delayed decision making.

Evaluating Interbranch Interactions

This subsection describes the CSJN's behavior with regard to the eighteen cases under study (its assertiveness and approach to decision making) and elected leaders' reactions (compliance and retaliation) in turn (see again Table 5.2).

High Court Selective Assertiveness

The Argentine CSJN was selectively assertive when deciding the eighteen cases under study: it endorsed the exercise of government power in the economic realm in ten cases and challenged that exercise in eight. Overall, the Court's endorsements tended to be stronger while it was equally likely to challenge the exercise of government power weakly and strongly (on which more below).[7] The scoring takes into consideration the direction and intensity of both the letter and the spirit of the high court's rulings, a distinction that can prove important. For example, the CSJN threw out the *Aerolíneas* case against the government thus only weakly endorsing the questioned policy – yet its reasoning (that the case involved a political question that the executive and legislature should battle out without judicial supervision) freed a swath of policy making from judicial scrutiny, strongly endorsing the exercise of government power (Verbitsky 1993: 137–8; Santiago 1998: 286–7).

The finding that the CSJN was selectively assertive in the economic policy realm again contradicts some of the received wisdom on the high court. Argentine constitutional scholars hold as a truism that the Court does not challenge elected leaders – in particular President Menem – over economic governance. Indeed, it seems logical that in that complicated, controversial, and consequential policy arena, the Court would consistently defer to the elected branches. However, as Table 5.2 shows, the Court challenged at least one important economic policy during practically each presidential administration between 1984 and 2003 (with the exception of the De la Rúa administration, which lasted only two years, and the Kirchner administration, which held power for just seven months during that period). To be sure, the Court's four challenges to President Menem's policies were weak: They either accorded with elected branch preferences (as in *Cafés la Virginia*, *Video Club Dreams*, and *Chocobar*) and/or struck laws that were no longer in effect (as in *Cafés la Virginia*, *Video Club Dreams*, and *Verrocchi*) (EC-05; EC-26). Nonetheless,

[7] Appendices 5.2 and 5.3 contain the data used to score the direction and intensity of the Court's endorsements and challenges, respectively. Scoring took into consideration to what degree the Court declared the policy in question unconstitutional; what the ruling said or implied about the broader exercise of government power; whether the timing of the decision was strategic; the relationship of the decision to the next lowest court's ruling; whether the case was decided on the merits; and whether any procedural irregularities marked the decision-making process.

the Court's challenges in the pre- and post-Menem eras could be quite strong. Thus, while it would certainly be an exaggeration to assert that the CSJN consistently sought to ensure that economic policy stayed within constitutional boundaries, it challenged the constitutionality of economic policy more frequently than is generally believed.

A final note concerns the voting patterns of Menem's so-called "automatic majority."[8] Members of this group did vote together on twelve of the seventeen cases regarding economic policy decided while they sat on the Court from 1990 to 2003 (approximately 70 percent of the time), suggesting that their support for the government was dependable, if not automatic. Yet in only five of those twelve cases did the automatic majority vote *en bloc* against all of the justices appointed by another president: More often than not, the "automatic majority" justices were joined by at least one (and on several occasions, by all) of the other justices who ruled on the case. These findings suggest that the justices composing the automatic majority were not necessarily deprioritizing legal or constitutional constraints when they voted together, and cast doubt on the notion that high court decision making in Argentina is purely partisan.

High Court Approach to Decision Making

The approach to decision making a high court adopts in a particular case (or series of cases) is a reflection of the considerations that were most important to its rulings. This axis of judicial decision making is important to evaluate and understand: Judicial rulings in the same direction and of the same intensity might be rooted in different approaches to decision making and may consequently serve different political functions and reflect different things about the Courts that issued them. Of course, most studies of high courts seek to explain why justices decide cases as they do. Yet until recently, many studies sought to identify a single factor driving judicial rulings (e.g., the fragmentation of the party system or popular opinion). I suggest that over time an identifiable *congeries* of factors influences high courts' decisions on the most politically critical cases to come before them.

Specifically, this study identifies six approaches a high court might adopt when ruling on politically crucial cases, depending upon what type or types of considerations dominated its decision-making process.[9] When the merits of the case or legal factors predominated in the Court's decision making, its approach could be characterized as *principled*. When justices' policy preferences or ideology were tantamount, the Court can be said to have adopted a *preference-driven* approach to decision making. When institutional or

[8] The common perception (enthusiastically perpetuated by the Argentine media) of voting practices on the high court in the 1990s was that an evolving "automatic majority" (*mayoría automática*) of Menem appointees always voted *en bloc* to support the government's interests; see Chapter 3.

[9] Chapter 1 discusses these six approaches to decision making and their correspondence with the main theoretical models of judicial behavior (legal, attitudinal, and strategic); see in particular Table 1.2.

corporate considerations were important in a Court's decision-making calculus, it has adopted a *self-protective* approach. When public opinion regarding a case weighed heavily on the justices, their approach to decision making can be said to have been *support-building*, whereas when the elected branches' preferences strongly influenced the ruling, the justices' approach to decision making can be characterized as *deferential*. Finally, when the economic or political situation or the potential economic or political repercussions of a decision were crucial to a Court's calculations, it has adopted a *pragmatic* approach to decision making.

As the fourth column in Table 5.2 demonstrates, according to expert opinion, the CSJN adopted four approaches when deciding the eighteen economic policy cases under study: principled, deferential and protective (two strategic approaches, in italics), and pragmatic.[10] While patterns in the Court's adoption of these approaches are discussed in the next subsection, one point about each approach bears noting here. First, the Court frequently engaged in strategic decision making (far more often than its Brazilian counterpart), a finding that aligns with conventional wisdom about the CSJN (e.g., Iaryczower et al. 2000; Scribner 2004; and Helmke 2005). In particular, the Court adopted a deferential approach to decision making more often than any other (in ten of the eighteen cases or 56 percent of the time).[11] However, experts suggested that the Court assumed an approach to decision making *other* than deferential – or in additional to a deferential approach – in twelve of the eighteen cases under study (that is, two-thirds of the time), challenging theories that point *only* to strategic deference to explain the CSJN's decision making.

The approach to decision making that the Court adopted second most often – in a third of the rulings considered here (six of eighteen) – was a principled approach.[12] Obviously the implication is not that the Court *ignored* the law or the constitution in two-thirds of the cases it decided. Rather, expert opinion simply implied that the law was not the justices' primary consideration when issuing its ruling on those cases (in line with the notion that justices often

[10] Appendix 5.4 offers the data used to characterize the Court's approach to decision making on each case, and tallies the number of times the consideration corresponding to each approach to decision making was mentioned in the high court's written decision on the case, or suggested to have been important to the Court's rulings in interviews I conducted with justices and experts, in newspaper articles focusing on the case, and in scholarly sources. The Court's approach or approaches to decision making on a case correspond to the consideration(s) mentioned by at least 33 percent of the sources that provided information on that case.

[11] Particularly given the ideological alignment between Menem and the justices he appointed to the CSJN in the 1990s, it may seem difficult to distinguish between the Court's adoption of a preference-driven approach to decision making (motivated by justices' ideology) and a deferential approach (motivated by loyalty to elected leaders). Nonetheless, the sources that I consulted were consistently confident that the Court's approach was deferential rather than preference-driven on the relevant cases.

[12] This approach may have received a boost in my scoring scheme since the CSJN's written opinions (one data source) invariably mentioned legal reasoning; nonetheless a tendency toward highlighting strategic motivations in newspapers and some expert interviews likely balanced out that bias.

decide how they will rule on a case and then look for legal, constitutional, or doctrinal justification for that decision). This finding again contradicts the conventional wisdom that the CSJN pays little attention to the law. Instead, not infrequently, the CSJN assumed an approach to decision making that diverse experts interpreted as at least in part principled when ruling on politically crucial conflicts.

The CSJN adopted a pragmatic approach to decision making in just over a quarter of the cases considered here (five of eighteen rulings), according to experts. Given Argentina's economic landscape during the years under study, we might have expected the Court to adopt this approach more often when ruling on cases regarding economic policy (as its Brazilian counterpart did). Indeed, the legal infrastructure facilitated the justices' consideration of the political and economic context or the possible ramifications of their decisions on the economy. Between 1989 and 2003 (and beyond), Argentine governments periodically passed laws declaring short-term "economic emergencies."[13] In effect, these laws temporarily amended the constitution granting the executive enormous power and discretion to address the emergency situation recognized in the law. Presidents, in turn, used their emergency powers to issue policies that appeared to violate constitutional provisions, sparking constitutional controversy and court cases. Indeed, almost two-thirds of the cases under study (eleven of eighteen) concerned policies instituted under some sort of economic or financial emergency[14] – yet experts suggested that the Court's rulings were motivated by economic concerns far less often. Finally, the CSJN adopted a self-protective approach when deciding just over a fifth of the cases (four of eighteen) – mainly during bouts of interbranch confrontation at the beginning and end of the time period.

Elected Branch Compliance and Retaliation

Finally, the analytic framework for studying patterns of interbranch interaction employed here considers the degree to which elected leaders complied with and retaliated against challenging high court rulings.[15] As Table 5.2 outlines, Argentine elected leaders most often complied partially with the CSJN's

[13] For example, the Law of State Reform (Law 23.696, published August 1989) authorized the executive to "intervene" in public sector entities, thus facilitating privatization, and the Delegation of Legislative Faculties Law (Law 25.414, published March 2001) declared a public emergency and awarded the executive legislative powers. (All laws accessed at http://www.infoleg.gov.ar on July 25, 2007.)

[14] Namely *Aerolíneas*, *Chocobar*, *Guida*, *Kiper*, *Peralta*, *Rolón Zappa*, *San Luís*, *Smith*, *Soengas*, *Tobar*, and *Verrocchi*.

[15] Appendix 5.5 outlines how elected branch compliance with and retaliation against each ruling were evaluated. Evaluating compliance entailed considering to what degree and how quickly elected leaders obeyed the letter and spirit of rulings, and how difficult those rulings were to obey. Assessing retaliation involved investigating whether elected leaders passed a decree or law that undermined the Court's decision, and/or threatened the institution in the wake of the ruling.

rulings – and twice failed to comply at all. Moreover, leaders retaliated against half of the challenging decisions the Court issued during the time period under study – at the beginning and end of that period.

Patterns of Interaction

Aggregating the scores on all eighteen cases reveals that two patterns (or a combined pattern) of interaction emerged between the high court and elected leaders in the economic policy arena in posttransition Argentina (identified in the last column of Table 5.2): Court submission and confrontation.[16] From 1990 through 2000, under presidents Menem and De la Rúa, interbranch interactions followed a pattern of Court submission. Through that decade, the high court tended to endorse the exercise of government power in the economic realm, doing so in nine of the thirteen crucial cases (69 percent of the time) it decided. Eight of its nine endorsements were stronger and all four of its challenges were weaker. Moreover, expert evaluation suggested that the Court adopted a *deferential* approach to decision making far more than any other – in nine out of the thirteen cases (again, 69 percent of the time). For their part, elected leaders complied only partially when the Court challenged the exercise of government power, but never retaliated.

The period from 2001 to 2003, by contrast, was marked by high court–elected branch confrontation (note the bold font in Table 5.2, indicating greater interbranch challenges). During that period, the Court strongly challenged the exercise of government power on three of the four crucial economic policy cases it decided (75 percent of the time) and its only endorsement was a weak one. The CSJN never adopted a deferential approach to decision making, instead adopting principled, pragmatic, or self-protective approaches (or a combination). For their part, elected leaders complied partially – or not at all – with the Court's challenging rulings and retaliated against each one. While these actions undoubtedly exacerbated confrontation, it bears noting that interbranch confrontation as conceptualized here does not necessarily entail one branch deliberately antagonizing the other. Instead, the idea is that the branches were placed into conflict when the high court challenged elected leaders – and they failed to obey and/or retaliated.

It is more difficult to characterize high-court–elected branch interactions over economic policy during the Alfonsín era (E-19), in part because state reform had not yet begun in earnest and there were thus relatively few crucial high court cases concerning economic policy. Indeed, the sample under study here includes only one case decided during Alfonsín's presidency (*Rolón Zappa*). Whereas the interaction between the high court and elected leaders over that case was decidedly confrontational, interbranch interactions over

[16] See again Table 5.1 for the tendencies in high court and elected branch behavior that make up the two patterns.

another arguably important case from the Alfonsín era, concerning the constitutionality of the *Austral* Plan,[17] serve as a counterexample.

The *Austral* Plan, a heterodox and quite drastic economic stabilization program, was launched suddenly in mid-June 1985 – yet it was not until April 1989 that the CSJN ruled on the first case concerning its constitutionality.[18] In *Porcelli*, the petitioner questioned the constitutionality of a decree associated with the *Austral* Plan (Decree 1096/85), which established a new currency (the *austral*) and required contracts denominated in the previously existing currency (*pesos*) be redenominated in *australes*. Her main claim was that the decree had not been ratified by the legislature, and was thus inapplicable to her deposit with the state-owned *Banco de la Nación* (Fayt 2004: 370). The CSJN rejected her claim, arguing that congress had implicitly ratified the decree in the budget law it promulgated in October 1986, making the question of its constitutionality moot (Miller 2000: 7). Analysts questioned the Court's assertion that congressional budget laws can (tacitly) approve preexisting executive-imposed currency rules. Beyond that, they suggested that by not deciding the case (or others like it) until it had a justification for deeming questions about the policies moot, the Court had implicitly supported the practice of decreeing economic policy.[19] The CSJN's endorsement of government power in its ruling was relatively strong, and its approach to decision making likely *deferential*. Interbranch interactions over *Porcelli*, then, followed the Court submission pattern.

The *Porcelli* case suggests that high court–elected branch interactions over economic governance were not exclusively confrontational in the later Alfonsín period. Nonetheless, they certainly *were* confrontational over the most important case decided during the era, *Rolón Zappa*. Further, we know that high court rulings against the government on a broader array of politically salient CSJN cases increased by 10 percent toward the end of Alfonsín's tenure (Helmke 2005: 100–1). Although we do not know the subject matter of those cases, it seems safe to assume that some dealt with economic policy – and that any rulings striking down significant economic policies would have received grudging compliance given the accelerating economic crisis of the late 1980s. Miller (2000: 10–11) also suggests that the CSJN confronted elected leaders in the economic realm in many cases in the early posttransition period (although usually in relatively less important ones). In short, there is good evidence of high court assertiveness and reluctant elected-branch compliance

[17] The case, *Porcelli, Luis A. contra Banco de la Nación Argentina s/ cobro de pesos* (decided April 20, 1989), was the second most important case regarding economic policy that the CSJN decided during the Alfonsín era, according to my case selection criteria.

[18] It is unclear whether the delay occurred because the CSJN received no cases questioning the validity of the plan (or the specific decree that introduced it) or because the Court was stalling deciding cases it held.

[19] For example, Emilio Ibarlucia and Maria Angélica Gelli both made this argument at the conference, "Diez Años Después de la Reforma Constitucional, Un Balance," Fundación Ricardo Rojas, May 4, 2004.

in the economic policy realm in the late Alfonsín period, recommending evaluating the period as one marked, overall, by interbranch confrontation over economic governance.

A final specification of interbranch confrontation in Argentina bears mentioning. In each instance under study, the Court held thousands or tens of thousands of cases – in addition to the one at the heart of the confrontation – concerning the same policy questioned in that case. And each time, the Court adopted a similar strategy: Following its initial challenge to the exercise of government power in one or a relatively small tranche of cases, it delayed ruling on more cases for at least a year (and sometimes indefinitely). That is, the Court would neither challenge the exercise of government power further nor afford the elected branches the policy legitimation they sought. The CSJN employed this strategy even though its initial ruling held only for the case or cases decided – and even when elected leaders neither extended the compensation the Court mandated in its initial ruling to others in similar circumstances nor modified the questioned policy. The Court's reticence gave elected leaders time to impose policies that diluted the effect of their ostensibly unconstitutional policies, to offer alternate solutions, or even, in some cases, to issue decrees or laws prohibiting further judicial decisions or the execution of judicial sentences on such cases.[20] Most often, the Court continued holding the rest of the cases, declared them moot, or legitimated the questioned policy in decisions handed down years later. This penchant to challenge and retreat likely suggested to elected leaders that even the most heated interbranch confrontation held a tacit promise of Court submission, and that constitutional limits were, after all, flexible.

To sum up, interbranch interactions over economic governance in the post-authoritarian period in Argentina were unstable. Most often, those interactions were marked by Court submission: The CSJN tended to issue stronger endorsements and weaker challenges to the exercise of government power, and elected leaders tended to comply only partially, but not retaliate. Nonetheless, judicial and political leaders sometimes became embroiled in heated confrontation when the Court's rulings strongly challenged elected leaders and those leaders complied partially or not at all, and/or retaliated against them.

5.3. EXPLAINING INTERBRANCH INTERACTIONS: THE COURT CHARACTER THESIS

Why did high court–elected branch relations in Argentina follow this combined pattern, and why are the patterns in Argentina so different from the more stable pattern of interbranch accommodation that emerged in Brazil? I advance the Court character thesis to account for that variation. An interrelated and fairly stable set of informal high court features – referred to in aggregate as a Court's character – sets incentives that induce Courts and elected leaders

[20] The case studies at the end of this chapter illustrate each of these.

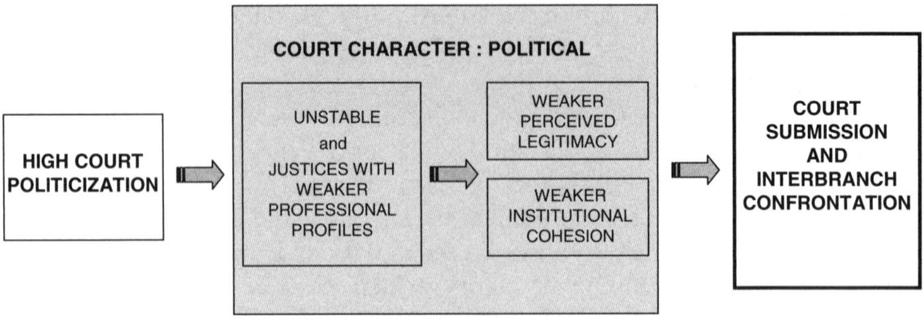

FIGURE 5.1. Explaining patterns of interbranch interaction over economic governance in Argentina: The Court character thesis.

to interact over politically crucial cases in similar ways over time, channeling interbranch struggles into relatively persistent patterns. As earlier chapters outlined, a Court's character comprises its stability, professional profile, legitimacy, and institutional cohesion. Court character tends to remain somewhat stable over time even though the institutional features that compose it are mainly informal (not mandated by or formalized in written rules, laws, or the constitution) because those features are rooted in dynamics that tend to evolve slowly: historically rooted Court-crafting politics, public opinion, and internal Court practices that become part of institutional culture.

Figure 5.1 depicts the Court character thesis as applied to Argentina. As Chapter 3 discussed, politicization was the dominant politics of Court crafting in Argentina from the mid-twentieth century through the postauthoritarian period. That is, leaders repeatedly sought to manipulate the Court's size and composition, and often (although not always) appointed justices with whom they had some connection, even if their qualifications were sometimes dubious. Although it is possible to identify moments of greater and lesser politicization (the two Menem presidencies represent an escalation in the trend), politicization has been the most prevalent politics of Court crafting in Argentina, forming the basis of the CSJN's political character.

The Court's political character shone through more clearly at some moments than others during the postauthoritarian period (e.g., during the Menem and Duhalde presidencies). Nonetheless, throughout the period under study, the CSJN was unstable and insecure due both to institutional threats elected leaders periodically issued and to successful initiatives to manipulate its size and membership. Relatively few of its justices had a background in constitutional law (although certain members were notable jurists), an important minority had not formed part of the federal judiciary or held an important national-level government post prior to appointment, and various justices had partisan and/or personal ties to their appointer. Consequently, the Court had relatively weak perceived legitimacy as measured by its public and professional support. Finally, continual changes in the CSJN's configuration and the weaker qualifications of some justices made it more difficult for the Court to develop institutional cohesion: Compared with the Brazilian STF, there was less consensus among justices on the role the CSJN should play; its leadership was less well-recognized; justices infrequently functioned as a unit (that is, the Court was less collegial); and its operations were marked by procedural inconsistencies.

Precisely how did the CSJN's overall political character contribute to producing the combined pattern of interbranch interaction over economic policy just described – Court submission to elected leaders punctuated by moments of interbranch confrontation? I consider the effect of each aspect of Court character in turn (discussing the first two in tandem).

First, the Court's instability and the weaker professional backgrounds of some of its justices helped to produce the combined pattern of interaction. When the judicial and elected branches were "aligned" (that is, when the current president had appointed a majority of the sitting justices as was the case under Alfonsín and Menem), or when relations were friendly (as occurred under De la Rúa, who neither attacked nor threatened the Court), the CSJN tended to adopt a deferential approach to decision making (that is, tended to take the elected branches' preferences into account) when ruling on cases in the crucial economic realm, and to endorse or only weakly challenge the exercise of government power. In other words, the Court was submissive. In part, the CSJN's instability explains this behavior. So accustomed to institutional attack, the Court sought to avoid a fresh round of politicization (and not antagonize leaders who had not yet threatened it). Yet the Court's professional profile also played a role: With a few very notable exceptions, politicization produced a Court that struggled to deal effectively with complicated cases regarding highly technical economic policy, and it thus tended to defer to policy makers.[21]

However, during moments of interbranch tension or pronounced institutional threat – when elected leaders sought to unsuccessfully modify the CSJN's composition, as in the mid 1980s under Alfonsín and the early 2000s under Duhalde – the Court issued rulings strongly challenging the exercise of government power in the economic realm. Given the Court's history of instability, the justices knew that no threats emanating from the executive could be dismissed as idle (even when they did not immediately result in changes in the Court's membership). They thus issued threats of their own (challenging rulings on economic policy cases) in hopes of dissuading leaders from additional politicization. In other words, initiatives such as Duhalde's plan to encourage the resignation or impeachment of the *entire* CSJN provided the unstable Court with a rallying point. Moreover, the justices may not have been fully attuned to the potential economic or constitutional consequences that striking down key elements of the administration's economic program could engender (or, simply may not have cared). For their part, elected leaders had little incentive to comply with the unstable Court's very challenging decisions, continually confident

[21] One former justice explained to me that in cases regarding economics, the Court generally engaged in more superficial constitutional review, tending to respect government policy (EC-30).

that, like their predecessors, they would eventually find a way to repoliticize the CSJN – that is, create their "own court."

Why did the Court use cases regarding economic policy to initiate (or perpetuate) such battles, in what way were the Court's rulings on such cases a threat to elected leaders, and why did the Court tend to issue an opening salvo but then retreat? On several occasions, the Court received tens of thousands of repeat cases questioning pension or salary policies, or elected leaders' responses to economic crisis (i.e., bank freezes and devaluations). Challenging elected leaders with a decision on *one* such case allowed the Court to confirm very publicly Argentines' belief that the government had acted unconstitutionally *and* to send a powerful message to those leaders that the Court was potentially willing to occasion economic (or, at least, social) turmoil. That is, issuing *one* challenging decision served as a tacit threat that the Court *could* decide *all* of the similar cases it held – often worth millions or billions of *pesos* to the government – in the same direction. Deciding additional cases was unlikely to benefit the political Court, however. Had it done so, elected leaders could have reacted in three ways, only the least likely of which would have been good for the Court: They could have ignored its additional rulings (repeatedly laying bare its weak authority); complied with the rulings (occasioning economic turmoil for which they could blame the Court); or complied without exacerbating crisis (the most difficult option to execute and thus the least likely one – yet the one that Brazilian leaders often chose). Thus the Court issued an initial warning, and then retreated.

Second, the CSJN's low perceived legitimacy also contributed to the tenor of interbranch relations. The Court's poor public image meant that it could not draw on popular support as an exogenous source of authority, making challenging the exercise of government power riskier and encouraging it to submit to elected leaders. Its negative image also meant that it had little to lose when it delayed months and years before handing down crucial decisions for which the populace was waiting, or when it issued pro-government rulings it knew would disappoint or anger the public and engender harsh criticism from the legal community and the press. As discussed previously, the CSJN did not once adopt a support-building approach to decision making when ruling on the cases under study (that is, popular opinion was never one of the most important considerations in its deliberations). By the same token, the Court had little to lose when it strongly challenged the exercise of government power as the elected branches' failure to comply with such decisions could do little to worsen its image. For their part, whereas elected leaders saw some merit in complying with the Court's weaker challenges, the political cost of failing to comply with its very challenging decisions (or complying very slowly and partially) remained relatively low. In this way, the Court's low legitimacy also encouraged periodic interbranch confrontation over economic policy.

Finally, the CSJN's lack of institutional cohesion meant that it had no endogenous sources of authority that might have helped it to stand up to the elected branches when they pressured it to decide cases a certain way, again facilitating

Court submission. In particular, the Court's lack of procedural continuity compromised its ability to push back (and facilitated its cooperation) when the government filed cases with it under aberrant conditions in order to defuse judicial contestation of key policies.[22] Likewise, the justices' lack of a unified notion of the CSJN's mission and weak procedural continuity made it possible for the Court to issue a strong challenge to the exercise of government power but then fade back into the woodwork, issuing no further rulings regarding the government's ostensibly unconstitutional behavior – even when elected leaders failed to comply with its initial decision *and* the Court held thousands or tens of thousands of similar cases. Likewise, the CSJN's lack of institutional cohesion freed elected leaders to comply only partially with its decisions (or in fact to ignore them), considering it unlikely that the justices would be able to coordinate to publicly highlight or retaliate against their lack of compliance. In these ways, the CSJN's instability and the weaker professional experience of some justices, combined with its weak perceived legitimacy and institutional cohesion, encouraged Court submission and interbranch confrontation in the crucial economic policy realm.

As noted previously, the Court character thesis extends existing theoretical approaches to explaining how elected leaders and Courts interact. Most accounts of interbranch relations in polities where judicial power only recently began to expand fall in the strategic camp. Such accounts understand judges and government officials to be goal-driven and ultimately empowered and constrained by the resources, preferences, relative power, and likely actions of other actors. This study certainly considers judicial and political leaders to be motivated by concrete objectives, and does not dispute that influences and limitations deriving from the political context affect their actions. Yet it seeks to offer a more nuanced account of interbranch relations by demonstrating that the strategies that justices and elected authorities adopt when interacting with each other, and the way in which contextual factors influence those strategies, are shaped by the character of the Court. Justices and elected leaders' behavior, I submit, is both strategic *and* informed and influenced by history.

One set of strategic accounts highlights how political divisions affect interbranch interactions. Epstein et al. (2001: 131–2), for instance, suggest that in young democracies with pronounced political divisions, Courts will only rule on cases in policy areas on which there is consensus among all elected leaders, and will generally weakly endorse the exercise of government power. Ginsburg (2003), by contrast, posits that where a dominant party holds the presidency and the legislature, courts are more cautious, whereas in contexts of party system fragmentation (in which it is more difficult for presidents to act in concert with congress), courts issue more important decisions, which are

[22] Previously mentioned examples are *Aerolíneas* (in which the government appealed a case to the CSJN directly from a lower court skipping the appeals court) and *Smith* and various cases concerning pensions (in which leaders employed mechanisms specifically created to expedite the filing of particular kinds of cases with the high court).

obeyed. The Court character thesis also highlights the importance of political divisions – but focuses on how party system fragmentation affects elected leaders' Court-crafting practices, thereby shaping Court character and interbranch interactions, rather than suggesting that fragmentation affects elected leaders' ability to retaliate against judicial rulings.[23]

Indeed, Epstein et al.'s account does not seem to explain interbranch interactions in Argentina as well as it does in Russia. The Radicals and the Peronists had different ideas about how to carry out economic reform (and, indeed, not even all Peronists were in agreement on the matter). Yet at moments when government was the most divided (the later 1980s and 2000–1), the CSJN in fact decided several cases concerning economic policy. Moreover, during periods of ostensibly greater elected-branch agreement on economic policy (the 1990s), the Court weakly endorsed the exercise of government power in only one of the twelve cases it decided. Further, whereas Epstein et al.'s model implies that one government entity alone – the president, or the upper or lower house of parliament – can threaten high courts, that is not the case in Argentina (at least formally): As Chapter 3 discussed, changing the size of the Court and removing justices require action by both houses of congress, and high court appointments require coordination between the president and the senate. There is greater synergy between the Court character thesis and Ginsburg's theory. Political divisions in Argentina prevented certain presidents from politicizing the Court as much as they wished, resulting in "misalignments" between elected leaders and the CSJN and interbranch confrontation. Yet these misalignments engendered interbranch confrontation (rather than accommodation, as in Brazil), I insist, *only* because of the history and anticipated continuation of high court politicization, and the Court's resulting political character.

The second set of strategic accounts emphasizes how societal support for courts or public opinion about court rulings influences interbranch interactions. Vanberg (2001), for instance, posits that high courts are more likely to be assertive, and government authorities more likely to comply with their rulings, when Courts have a loyal constituent base ("support structures") ready to defend them. Staton (2002) suggests that Courts are more likely to challenge elected leaders when they can expect compliance-inducing public support for such rulings. The Court character thesis draws on and extends these accounts.

Vanberg's argument applies somewhat less well to Argentina simply because the country's (admittedly somewhat weak) high court "support structures" – organizations such as the Center for Legal and Social Studies (*Centro de Estudios Legales y Sociales*, CELS) and the Forum for Studies of the Administration of Justice (*Foro de Estudios sobre la Administración de Justicia*, FORES) – have mainly advocated for a stronger, more independent Supreme Court, rather than supporting or protecting the existing political Court. However, in line with

[23] See the account of Court crafting in Argentina in Chapter 3, and data in Web Appendix 3.3.

Staton's account to some degree, the CSJN handed down its most challenging decisions in cases with relatively great social salience. And even though the CSJN never adopted a support-building approach to decision making in the cases under study here (i.e., popular opinion regarding a *case* was never a decisive factor in its decision making), I argue that the Court's weak perceived legitimacy (i.e., public opinion about the Court as an *institution*, a crucial part of its character) contributed to shaping interbranch interactions.[24] To wit, the CSJN's *lack* of legitimacy led it to issue challenging rulings even absent an expectation that elected leaders would comply.

Again, the Court character thesis does not deny that contextual and political factors matter to interbranch interactions. For instance, as just discussed, political fragmentation and public opinion certainly affect the tenor of interbranch relations. Moreover, the various elements of interbranch relations highlighted here (high courts' assertiveness and approach to decision making, and elected branches' compliance and retaliation) are themselves interrelated: The frequency and intensity with which Courts issue challenging decisions affect elected branch compliance and retaliation, just as elected branch adherence and retribution affect high court decision making. What I seek to argue is that the *way* in which contextual factors influence interbranch interactions, and the *way* in which high court behavior affects elected leaders and vice versa, are shaped and mediated by attributes of high courts themselves – by their character. All high courts are not created equal, and that institutional variation matters to their decision making on crucial cases and to elected leaders' reactions to their rulings. At its core, the Court character thesis argues that we should look *around* high courts *but also inside them*, at their historical institutional foundations, to fully explain the ways in which they and elected leaders interact over crucial political issues.

5.4. CASE STUDIES

This book seeks to account for *patterns* of interbranch interaction in Argentina and Brazil. Yet each country's predominant patterns are composed of multiple individual cases embodying the dynamics of those patterns. Analyzing these individual cases helps to illustrate the dominant patterns, and to demonstrate how Court character contributed to producing them. This section offers three case studies of interbranch interaction in posttransition Argentina: one episode of confrontation over pension policy (*Rolón Zappa*, decided in 1986), one episode of Court submission over a freeze on bank accounts (*Peralta*, decided in 1990), and one paired case study in which Court submission gave way to confrontation over public sector salaries (*Guida*, decided in 2000, and *Tobar*, decided in 2002). Any of the eighteen cases under study might have been selected to illustrate the Court character thesis; these cases were chosen

[24] Public support for the judiciary and the CSJN in particular was already quite negative by the late 1980s, and remained weak throughout the time period of interest (see Chapter 3).

with any eye to varying the type of policy questioned, time period, and type of interbranch interaction to help demonstrate the robustness of the thesis.

Confrontation: *Rolón Zappa*[25]

The Argentine pension system entered into a state of crisis (due both to demographic dynamics and mismanagement) in the mid-twentieth century, and that crisis worsened through the 1980s. Rather than adjusting pension payments upwards in response to popular dissatisfaction, the government repeatedly passed laws and emergency decrees empowering the executive to tinker with the pension system – generally lowering payments. In the mid-1980s, the National Social Welfare Commission (*Comisión Nacional de Previsión Social*) issued an administrative resolution establishing an index for pensions. In response, Victor Rolón Zappa filed suit against the state. Rolón Zappa claimed that the indexing violated the Educators' Statute (Law 14.473, published in 1958) and the New System of Retirements and Pensions Law (Law 18.037, published in 1969), which established pension minimums, and demanded that his pension be paid pursuant to the existing legislation.[26] Rolón Zappa's claim was denied in the first instance court. When he appealed, however, the National Labor Appeals Court (*Cámara Nacional de Apelaciones del Trabajo*) deemed that the indexes established in the National Social Welfare Commission's administrative resolution set pensions at an unconstitutionally low ("confiscatory") level and violated property rights (1853 Constitution, Article 17), and called for the revocation of the resolution (and, implicitly, an adjustment of Rolón Zappa's pension).

The National Social Welfare Commission appealed the decision to the Supreme Court, suggesting that if the appeals court continued to impose its "solution" when ruling on the thousands of related cases it could receive, the inevitable result would be the bankruptcy of the national pension system. Indeed, pensioners were turning to the courts in droves to challenge various aspects of the legal framework for pensions by the late 1970s, and by March 1986, 45,000 cases against the state had been filed. Most continued to work their way through the judiciary, as the government persistently appealed cases it lost in lower courts in order to postpone paying pensioners (NP 02–30, NP 02-E-02).[27] *Rolón Zappa* became the test case for how the high court would deal with the crucial issue of pensions in the early postauthoritarian period.

[25] *Rolón Zappa, Victor contra Estado Nacional* (decided September 30, 1986). Unless otherwise indicated, all information about Argentine CSJN and Brazilian STF cases and rulings is drawn from the actual opinions, on file with the author.

[26] Law 14.473 established a pension floor at 82 percent of the inflation adjusted salary of a worker doing the job the pensioner had previously done. Law 18.037 modified the minimum rate for most pensions to 70 percent of the active salary (for men retiring at age 60 and women retiring at age 55), but established that those working beyond the minimum retirement age would receive an additional 1 percent annually for each additional year worked (Miller 2000: 38, fn 59). *La Nación,* October 3, 1986, "Fallo en favor de los jubilados."

[27] In total, pensioners would eventually file 65,000 cases seeking retroactive pension payments (NP 02–29); millions of pensioners could have potentially filed similar cases (EC-07).

The case arrived to the Court at a critical moment. Only two and a half years had passed since Argentina had transitioned from one of the harshest military regimes in South American history, and the shaky government had already weathered three military uprisings. The country continued to experience economic crisis, and it was already clear that the government's most successful attempt at stabilization, the heterodox *Austral* Plan launched in mid-June 1985, would soon need to be reformulated or replaced. Moreover, relations between the high court and elected leaders were tense: President Alfonsín had lost his loyal majority on the Court with the resignation of Justice Carrió in April 1985, and had antagonized the Court through various attempts to shift the balance of power back toward justices aligned with his administration (Pellet Lastra 2001: 449–50).

On September 20, 1986, the CSJN ruled on the *Rolón Zappa* case. The Court dismissed the government's appeal, in effect confirming the National Labor Appeals Court's decision suspending the administrative resolutions and requiring the state to pay the plaintiff the stipends mandated by existing legislation. In its ruling, the Court followed a jurisprudential line that dictated declaring unconstitutional any reduction in pension payments that led those payments to be unreasonably disproportionate to the salaries of active workers doing the job the pensioner had previously held (Bidart Campos 1986: 562). It also emphasized its willingness to strike down any laws that violated the constitutional right to an adjustable pension (Article 14 bis) or property rights (Article 17). And it ruled that restructuring the pension system required congressional action, and that any executive measures regarding pensions issued prior to new legislation must comply with the existing legislation (Miller 2000: 383). The Court also noted that the government's assertion that it lacked the resources to pay legislated pension benefits and its declaration of a state of emergency for social security funds (*Cajas Nacionales de Previsión*) were irrelevant to the judiciary and the legal question at hand. The ruling aimed both to reinforce the separation of powers and demonstrate that the justices' decisions were not dictated by short-term political imperatives (Santiago 1998: 396–400; Oteiza 1994: 158; EC-06; EC-26). Although the decision only applied to Rolón Zappa's case, it offered hope to pensioners nationwide; in fact, the high court ruled in the same direction in another 300 cases before the end of 1986 (NP 02–198).

Even before the Court's ruling, the government had made patently clear its inability to increase pension payments. Accordingly, it failed to comply with the ruling in any meaningful way.[28] Its subsequent actions further inflamed interbranch tensions. Two months after the decision, on November 28, 1986, the Alfonsín government issued Decree of Necessity and Urgency (DNU) 2196, which declared the pension system in a state of emergency, reestablished

[28] While the Alfonsín administration introduced several schemes to pay some of what the state owed pensioners in the late 1980s, the structural nature of the problem made it resistant to such ad hoc measures, which mainly led to continued debt and more court cases (Díaz 2002: 214).

pensions at 27 percent of salary (far below the limit established in existing legislation), and suspended – for two years – both the execution of judicial decisions against the government for failing to adhere to existing pension legislation *and* any further litigation regarding pensions (Santiago 1998: 399–400; Miller 2000: 383–4). There was little precedent and no case law to justify those actions (Miller 2000: 383–4), and the message to the judiciary and thus to the high court was clear: Stay out of the pensions issue. Further, in November 1987, Alfonsín sent a bill to congress proposing various changes in the organization and function of the high court including an increase in the number of justices. Opposition from the Court itself, the bar association (*Colegio Público de Abogados*), and congressmen resulted in the shelving of the plan by April 1988 (Pellet Lastra 2001: 449–50), but the institutional threat had been issued.

The CSJN reacted in a way that would become typical: it backed down. It abided by DNU 2196, delaying decisions on its backlog of pensions cases for almost two years. It took those cases up only after the introduction of a new law (Law 23.568, passed June 1988) reorganizing the pension system (and derogating DNU 2196), and then decided them in a way that did not challenge the government (Miller 2000: 7). In fact, when the government eventually filed a second appeal of the ruling the National Labor Appeals Court had issued on the *Rolón Zappa* case, the Court accepted the appeal and on August 25, 1988, ruled in the government's favor, contradicting its own previous decision. And when it was called upon to decide the constitutionality of the part of DNU 2196 that had suspended the execution of judgments and litigation concerning pensions, the Court ruled that, in light of Law 23.568, the question was moot (Miller 2000: 7). While confrontation marked the first stage of this interbranch interaction over economic policy, in the longer-term, high court–elected branch interactions reverted to Court submission.

How did the Court's political character contribute to interbranch confrontation? First, the episode occurred amidst interbranch tension set off when President Alfonsín lost his loyal majority on the Court and subsequently sought (ultimately unsuccessfully) to bring it back into the fold. Alfonsín's efforts seemed natural given the CSJN's traditional and continuing instability, and given the connections between the administration and an important subset of the sitting justices. Moreover, the fact that the CSJN included no justices with significant political experience made the Court somewhat indifferent to the government's financial predicament (and the possible consequences of its ruling), at least initially. And confrontation was exacerbated when the administration failed to comply with the ruling, likely still confident that it could find a way to regain its loyal majority (as evidenced by Alfonsín's continuing attempts to change the organization and function of the Court).

The Court's lack of legitimacy – and the weak legitimacy of the judiciary more broadly – also contributed to this paradigmatic episode of interbranch confrontation. Elected leaders did not hesitate to announce that they would not abide by the CSJN's ruling, or to suspend the execution of related judicial decisions and further litigation. They likely would not have taken such quick and decisive action had the Court been well-respected, implying higher political costs for defying and undermining it. Finally, the high court's weak institutional cohesion was also a factor. Due to weak consensus on the Court regarding its role as well as its procedural inconsistency, the justices did not feel obligated to continue deciding the thousands of cases related to Rolón Zappa's that the CSJN held or received after its ruling on that test case. Likewise, it was not compelled to decide the related cases it *did* decide in the same direction as it had decided *Rolón Zappa* once the government's moratorium was lifted. Indeed, the Court eventually overruled itself on the *Rolón Zappa* case. Each aspect of the Court's political character, then, contributed significantly to this episode of interbranch confrontation.

What about the broader effects of this interbranch interaction? The Court's initial ruling on *Rolón Zappa* could have helped entrench the rule of law (and almost certainly enhanced the Court's image in society). And its resolution of only a small subset of the cases it held related to the questioned pension policy before retreating effectively signaled to elected leaders – and the country – that it considered the policy unconstitutional, but avoided the risks entailed in repeatedly ruling against the measure (undermining the rule of law if elected leaders ignored its rulings, or engendering financial disaster if leaders respected them). Yet any positive institutional effects were ephemeral, given elected leaders' subsequent behavior. Indeed, ironically, had the Court delayed longer in ruling on the *Rolón Zappa* case, thereby *not* prompting elected leaders to shut the judiciary out of the pensions question, the implications for the rule of law might have been more positive. The Court's 1988 rulings had clearer effects: They not only deprived tens of thousands of pensioners of their constitutionally and legally mandated pension benefits, but also implicitly validated the issuing of economic policy by decree, thus freeing the executive from the need to negotiate with congress (Miller 2000: 7). In all, while these interbranch interactions might have helped Argentina retain an economic foothold by preventing the state from being eviscerated by its pension debt, their broader implications for society and the rule of law were less positive.

Court Submission: *Peralta*[29]

Argentina had been passing through rough economic waters for most of the 1980s, and by 1989 had descended into hyperinflation. The exchange rate (pesos/dollars) was increasing at a shocking rate as the government printed more and more money. Banks had been loaning extraordinary amounts to the government, meaning that depositors essentially held public debt. And simultaneously, in order to attract customers, banks offered extremely high interest rates, encouraging huge speculative deposits. In an attempt to halt the inflationary spiral, restructure public debt, and reduce the excessive monetization

[29] *Peralta, Luis Arcenio y otro contra Nación Argentina (Ministerio de Economía – Banco Central de la República Argentina) s/ amparo* (decided December 27, 1990).

of the economy, the Menem administration imposed the so-called Bonex Plan via DNU 36 in late December 1989. Among other measures, the economic restructuring program froze certain fixed-term private savings accounts above the sum of one million *australes* (the currency at the time) and converted the entrapped funds into ten-year government bonds (*Bonos Externos* or BONEX 1989) in dollars. The "frozen" money was remitted to the Central Bank, which backed the frozen accounts and emitted the bonds that the government would use to temporarily cover the country's internal debt (Carrió 1996: 174).[30] The text of the measure acknowledged that the executive was assuming a legislative function by imposing an economic program by decree, but insisted that the country's dire economic situation required quick, drastic measures.

The constitutionality of the decree was challenged in a spate of court cases brought by individuals whose savings it had frozen.[31] Luis Peralta and Sara Foralledo brought what would become the leading case. The plaintiffs had a fixed-term deposit with the Commercial Finance Bank (*Banco Comercial de Finanzas S.A.*) that expired the very day Plan Bonex came into effect. Consequently, they were only able to withdraw one million *australes* of that deposit in early January 1990; the rest was forcibly converted into government bonds. Peralta filed an *amparo* alleging that the arbitrary and illegal measure violated constitutional rights and guarantees including property rights (Article 17), and demanding the return of his money. The first instance judge dismissed the case on technical grounds (indicating, among other factors, that an *amparo* was not the appropriate legal instrument for the plaintiff to use). Peralta appealed, and the appeals court ruled in his favor, citing DNU 36's lack of required congressional ratification and violation of property rights. The Central Bank and the Solicitor General's office (*Procuración del Tesoro de la Nación*)[32] filed separate appeals. The appeals court (which must approve petitions for appeal to the CSJN, see Web Appendix 2.2) denied the Central Bank's petition but granted the Solicitor General's; the granting of that petition suspended the appeals court's ruling and allowed the case to proceed to the high court, where it arrived in June 1990.

The *Peralta* case was widely considered to be the "most ... politically crucial decision of the Menem Court" (Gargarella 2004: 191; see also Santiago 1998: 274; Miller 2000: 400). Filed in the midst of grave economic crisis, the case gave the Court the opportunity to examine the executive's legislative

[30] The immediate loss for depositors was noteworthy. The government bonds had a weak market value (30 percent of the value of the money frozen) and were not issued until more than four months after bank accounts had been frozen. Further, the bonds only began to pay interest after a year had passed (Carrió 1996: 174). Nonetheless, by the time the bonds came due, they would prove to have been a decent (if compulsory) investment (EC-11).

[31] Despite tens of thousands of depositors being affected, only thirty court cases were initially filed (Verbitsky 1993: 159); the immediate reaction was thus very different from that following the bank freeze imposed in 2001, which quickly generated tens of thousands of court cases, including *Kiper* and *Smith* (see Table 5.2).

[32] This office is charged with offering legal assistance to the president and public functionaries; it represents the nation in certain cases and audits others in which the state is involved.

powers (the constitutional possibility of DNUs) and its emergency powers (the constitutional validity of using national emergency to justify a considerable restriction of property rights). In its landmark December 1990 ruling, the CSJN overturned the appeals court's decision in favor of Peralta, upholding the government's economic stabilization plan.[33] The decisive ruling had four principal points. The Court (1) reaffirmed its authority to evaluate the constitutionality of laws in *amparos* in order to protect a constitutional right;[34] (2) asserted that the historical circumstances warranted a "flexible" interpretation of the division of powers and a dynamic interpretation of the constitution;[35] (3) considered constitutionally admissible the issuing of DNUs by the executive in exceptional circumstances; and (4) indicated that the economic emergency made reasonable the "temporary deferral" of citizens' ability to exercise their property rights.

The questioned decree was almost certainly unconstitutional,[36] but the Court endorsed it nonetheless (without explicitly defending its constitutionality), adopting a deferential approach to decision making primarily motivated by Menem's strong desire to move forward with his broad state restructuring program unimpeded by institutional limitations (Gargarella 1998: 442; Gill Domínguez 2002: 14; EC-13; E-04; E-05; E-07; E-09; E-22). The country's dire economic situation and the potential ramifications of a ruling against the government pushed the justices in the same direction (EC-08; EC-19; EC-20; EC-23; EC-24; EC-33).

Several features of the CSJN's political character encouraged Court submission. First, the Court's instability and professional profile clearly influenced the ruling. Just months before the Court's ruling on *Peralta*, President Menem had expanded the Court from five to nine members (Law 23.744 published April 1990) and packed it with justices with strong ties to the government (some with questionable qualifications). Justices alleged to form part of Menem's "automatic majority" all voted in one direction while each Alfonsín appointee voted in the opposite direction, reflecting the Court's internal divisions and its lack of consensus on its role. Even on a case of such significance, Court

[33] Even the two dissents did not call for the return of the plaintiff's funds: Justice Oyhanarte's vote overturned the appeals court ruling and Justice Belluscio's dismissed the *amparo* (Miller 2000: 400).

[34] The government's appeal had suggested that Law 16.986 (of 1966) denied courts jurisdiction to assess the constitutionality of laws and decrees when deciding *amparos* as such cases must be decided quickly, precluding the thoughtfulness needed to evaluate constitutionality.

[35] The Court was at pains to highlight that congress had previously delegated legislative power to the executive to deal with complex and technical economic issues. Moreover, it debuted its "tacit approval" thesis, suggesting that congress's failure to specifically disallow the decree (and its mentioning of the measure in subsequent legislation) implied legislative acceptance.

[36] The issuance of DNUs was legally questionable prior to their constitutionalization in 1994 (see Chapter 2). Further, while the CSJN had recognized limits to property rights under emergency circumstances in the past, in previous cases, the emergency had been established *by law* or, if established by decree, had been explicitly validated by the legislature (as in *Rolón Zappa*) (Santiago 1994: 77–8; Carrió 1996: 175–6; Miller 2000: 402; E-12; E-15).

leadership was not strong enough to compel a less divided decision. Menem's Court packing, which had been roundly criticized by the legal community, had further compromised the Court's already weak legitimacy, meaning that the "Menem justices" had little to lose by infringing the property rights of, and conferring major financial losses on, many middle-class Argentines (Nino 1993: 328; Santiago 1998: 274; Chavez 2001: 87).

With regard to broader implications, the Court's ruling in *Peralta* caused little social upheaval.[37] However, it effected a dramatic shift in the balance of power between the executive and legislature. By actively authorizing presidents to sidestep congressional debate and confrontation in the formulation of policy, the Court encouraged President Menem to "rule by decree" throughout the 1990s (Gargarella 1998: 442; Pellet Lastra 2001: 26; E-07; E-21; E-08; E-11; E-15);[38] indeed, the *Peralta* ruling may have paved the way for the inclusion of DNUs in the constitutional reform of 1994 (E-21). Without a doubt, the specter of the president decreeing policy hung over the opposition during congressional negotiation of every important policy throughout the decade (Bohmer 2000: 28). Yet the ruling's decisiveness could also be considered in a more positive light. The Court clearly outlined its doctrine regarding emergency, and its clarity – regardless of one's view of the doctrine – may have enhanced governability (EC-30; E-04). The ruling also likely facilitated monetary stability and helped the executive to address Argentina's economic chaos (EC-26) and restructure its internal debt (EC-32). Yet these potential benefits came at a significant cost to the rule of law and the development of constitutionalism. Interbranch interactions around *Peralta*, then, perfectly illustrate the tension between the legal and economic transitions, and the difficult position in which deciding cases in which the two are in conflict places high courts, and responding to their rulings can place elected leaders.

From Court Submission to Confrontation: *Guida* and *Tobar*[39]

Following stabilization of the Argentine economy with the 1991 Convertibility Plan, the country performed well economically through the early 1990s, and was even dubbed one of the IMF's "star pupils."[40] Nonetheless, it was not immune to the effects of its neighbors' economic crises and was quite negatively impacted by the Mexican financial crisis of 1994 (the so-called Tequila effect). In hopes of reinvigorating the economy (and utilizing the emergency powers he was awarded in view of the economic downturn), on March 1, 1995, President

[37] By the time the Court ruled on DNU 36 (about a year after its emission), popular dissatisfaction with the decree had dissipated as Menem's economic measures were generally successful in moving the country in a positive economic direction.

[38] President Menem issued 335 DNUs in his first term (more than 300 of which he emitted prior to the constitutionalization of DNUs in 1994), and 210 in his second (Manzetti 2003: 333).

[39] *Guida, Liliana contra Poder Ejecutivo Nacional* (decided June 2, 2000); and *Tobar, Leonidas contra Ministerio de Defensa – Contaduría General del Ejército – Ley 25.453* (decided August 22, 2002).

[40] *The Guardian*, April 28, 2002, "IMF's 'one size' fits few."

Menem cut public sector wages by between 5 and 15 percent via DNU 290.[41] The DNU was subsequently ratified by the Argentine Congress in the budget law passed at the end of the year (Law 24.624, published December 1995). The decree did not stipulate how long the salary cut would be in effect, but indicated that its duration was *determinable* (i.e., the measure would be revoked when the crisis had abated) (Gelli 2003b: 706–7).

Throngs of public sector employees filed suit, and Liliana Guida, an employee of the National Atomic Energy Commission, was among them. Guida argued that Articles 1 and 2 of DNU 290 violated rights outlined in the constitution (Articles 14 bis, 16, and 17 – that is, the right to a fair salary and to equal pay for equal work, guarantees of the stability of public sector employment, and property rights). Guida was victorious at the trial-court level. When the government appealed, the administrative appeals court (*Cámara Nacional de Apelaciones en lo Contencioso Administrativo Federal*) also found in her favor, ruling that the DNU violated property rights and, in tandem with subsequent DNUs, the constitutional guarantee of equality. The government appealed to the CSJN, and the Court received the case in April 1997. Despite the filing of many more *amparos*, additional rulings in favor of public sector employees in trial and appeals courts, and the state's continued appeal of those rulings, the CSJN did not rule on Guida's case or any other case regarding DNU 290 through the rest of the decade. Meanwhile, the government gradually passed measures canceling the salary reductions.[42]

By 1999 Argentina's economic situation had worsened significantly, and by mid-May 2000, the De la Rúa administration had begun to plan another public sector salary cut. Magically, Guida's case and others in which the constitutionality of DNU 290 was questioned began to circulate through the high court (NP 01–589). The Attorney General (*Procurador General*) handed down an opinion on *Guida* in late May 2000,[43] declaring the decree constitutional. That same day, the government issued DNU 430, which imposed a new salary cut quite similar to the one imposed in DNU 290 (NP 01–589). And four days later on June 2, 2000 – more than five years after the implementation of the policy questioned in the *Guida* case and more than three years after the

[41] The decree affected the salaries of personnel in the legislature, judiciary, state-owned business, official bank entities, and the municipality of the City of Buenos Aires. Only justices of the Supreme Court, judges of lower instance courts, and members of the Public Prosecutor's Office were excluded. Those making less than $2,000 pesos a month would experience no reduction; those making $2,001 to $3,000 pesos a month would experience a reduction of 5 percent; those making $3,001 to $4,000 pesos a month would experience a reduction of 10 percent; and those making more than $4,001 pesos a month would experience a 15 percent cut (http://infoleg.mecon.gov.ar/infoleg Internet/anexos/10000–14999/14684/norma.htm, accessed August 5, 2005).

[42] In particular, Decree 1421 (published December 1997) annulled Articles 1 and 2 of Decree 290 – the exact measures questioned in the *Guida* case.

[43] The *Procurador General* is head of the Public Prosecutor's Office (*Ministerio Público*); Web Appendix 3.5 outlines the conditions under which the person in this post issues opinions on high court cases.

Court had received the case – the CSJN declared DNU 290 constitutional in a practically unanimous ruling. Among other justifications, the Court noted that DNU 290 complied with the requisites of economic emergency the Court had traditionally demanded; that the measure was generalized, proportional, reasonable, temporary, and prospective and that the constitution awarded the president the power to effect public sector salary cuts with these qualities;[44] and that congressional approval of the measure via the 1996 budget law represented recognition of the emergency situation invoked by the executive as well as the oversight of DNUs required of congress (Gelli 2003a: 706–07; Fayt 2004: 423).[45]

The *Guida* case is a quintessential example of the Court submission pattern of interbranch interactions. First, the Court's delay in ruling on the case allowed the Menem government to pass measures that incrementally addressed the unconstitutionality of the decree questioned in the case (DNU 290). Further, as two former government lawyers confirmed in an interview, the CSJN ruled on *Guida* at President De la Rúa's specific request. De la Rúa feared the fiscal implications of a negative ruling, was reluctant to introduce another salary reduction in an atmosphere in which the constitutionality of the previous cut (and the status of the avalanche of *amparos* challenging it) remained in question, and wanted to design his policy knowing whether the Court would enforce constitutional limits on such reductions (EC-11; EC-21). In short, De la Rúa requested that the CSJN clear the way for another salary cut, and it did so in its ruling on *Guida*. How did the CSJN's character encourage this outcome?

De la Rúa had not appointed a single justice who sat on the Court in June 2000 – yet he had sought to give the Court institutional guarantees (explicitly and implicitly). His 1999 presidential campaign had emphasized the importance of strong democratic institutions, and he had made it clear that he would not seek to replace any justices were he to win election (Miller 2000). Moreover, De la Rúa's strongest opponent in the 1999 presidential elections, Eduardo Duhalde, was an arch-rival of the incumbent president (Menem), who had appointed a majority of the Court and to whom that majority was quite loyal. Thus De la Rúa gained the favor of a Court accustomed to manic manipulation simply by not being Eduardo Duhalde (who embodied institutional peril), and by not threatening the Court upon assuming office in December 1999. How did the CSJN's weak legitimacy encourage it to endorse the policy? Given the Court's already tarnished public image, the possibility that confirming the pay cut would engender allegations that it had ruled as it did because high

[44] The constitution does not guarantee salary stability for all public sector workers; only the president and vice-president of the nation, cabinet ministers, judges, and the members of the *Ministerio Público* have a vested right to retain a certain salary level.

[45] The one dissent, that of Justice Petracchi, reflected his perennial posture: that DNUs cannot be issued in the absence of legislative oversight, and thus the salary reduction was only constitutional once Law 24.624 came into effect in 1995 (Bianchi 2002a I: 249, 438).

court justices' salaries were not included in the cut did not dissuade it. And the Court's weak institutional cohesion – in particular its lack of compulsion to establish or follow particular procedures – allowed it to delay significantly in resolving Guida's case (and then do so very suddenly), facilitating Court submission to elected leaders.

The question of public sector salaries soon reappeared on the high court's agenda. This time, however, interbranch interaction would be of a completely different type, due again to the Court's political character. Argentina's economic situation continued to worsen through late 2000 and early 2001. Heartened by the CSJN's ruling in *Guida* and its failure to challenge the salary cut he imposed in May 2000 (via DNU 430),[46] on July 13, 2001, De la Rúa imposed another cut on public sector salaries – of 13 percent – via DNU 896 and Administrative Decision 107 (issued two weeks later).[47] Soon thereafter, in an effort to increase confidence in Argentina's flagging economy, congress passed the far broader Law of Zero Deficit (Law 25.453). The law introduced a new fiscal regime that implied that the state could not spend more than it collected. Among various mechanisms to prevent the state from incurring debts and obligations, the law derogated DNUs 430 and 896 and simultaneously incorporated the regime established by the latter, allowing the government to impose up to a 13 percent reduction in public sector salaries (and pensions) at any point in order to avoid running a deficit.

Despite the government's efforts, by late 2001, Argentina had fallen into one of the worst crises in its history. That crisis eventually entailed the cessation of internal and international debt payments, the freezing of savings accounts, harsh fiscal adjustment measures required by international lenders, corruption scandals, and a generalized panorama of insecurity and social upheaval including street violence and riots (Cavallo 2002: 216). President De la Rúa fled the presidential palace at the end of December 2001 amidst pot-banging demonstrations, and three interim leaders held the reins of power before congress appointed Eduardo Duhalde president for a two-year period on January 1, 2002. From the moment Duhalde assumed power, newspapers began to report that he was considering various schemes to "purify" or "clean out" the Court, either by impeachment or through the forced resignation of justices. In fact, by early 2002, there were already fourteen requests for impeachment of high court justices waiting to be activated in congress (01-R-276).

Elected leaders had chosen an inauspicious moment to antagonize the high court. *Amparos* filed by public sector workers questioning the constitutionality of the salary cut imposed via DNU 896 and Law 24.453 began to pour into the judiciary during the second half of 2001. Among them was an *amparo* filed by Leonidas Tobar, a civilian employee of the Argentine Army. Tobar questioned

[46] The CSJN finally considered (and endorsed) DNU 430 in April 2003 in the *Müller* case (E-03).

[47] DNU 896 modified Article 34 of the Law of Financial Administration (Law 24.156, published October 29, 1992); the administrative decision was emitted according to the delegation established by Decree 934/2001.

the constitutionality of Article 1 of DNU 896 and Article 10 of Law 25.453, claiming that the measures unlawfully altered the conditions of his employment contract and demanding that the state pay him the money that had been discounted from his salary since those laws went into effect in July 2001. A first instance judge ruled in Tobar's favor. When the state appealed, the appeals court confirmed the trial court's ruling. The state appealed again, and the case arrived to the high court in April 2002. When it was sent to the attorney general for consideration, he ruled DNU 896 and Law 24.453 unconstitutional in July 2002 (NP 01–829). Fearing a strong challenge from the CSJN, the government initiated a series of frenetic attempts to convince the justices to postpone or alter their decision. Duhalde even enlisted the aid of former president Menem in reasoning with the Court. Aware that the success of the negotiations rested on the Court's assessment of the likelihood that the government would persevere with its impeachment initiatives (E-04; EC-15; EC-16), the administration promised a rapid end to congressional impeachment attempts (NP 02–53).

The government's overtures proved futile. On August 22, 2002, less than four months after receiving Tobar's case, the CSJN handed down a 7–2 decision declaring unconstitutional the salary cut established via Decree 896 and Law 25.453. The Court ordered the government to discontinue the cut and repay the money that had been discounted from public sector salaries since the implementation of the policies. The justices argued that while the executive was authorized to reduce public sector salaries to address a situation of emergency, the cut imposed by the questioned norms was insufficiently reasonable, predictable, and temporary: It subjected salaries to arbitrary, discretionary executive decisions, thereby converting salaries into a tool of economic policy and violating property rights. Anticipating criticism that its ruling on *Tobar* contradicted its June 2000 ruling on *Guida,* the Court highlighted that the decree questioned in *Guida* in fact *had* set temporal and quantitative limits on the salary reduction it imposed. Moreover, the justices argued that the implosion of Argentina's economy between the introduction of Decree 896 in July 2001 and the Court's August 2002 ruling on *Tobar* – including the *peso's* loss of two-thirds of its value in early 2002 and the return of inflation – meant that the effect on public sector employees and pensioners of the salary cut imposed by the decree had grown more adverse over time: The measures had *become* unreasonable (confiscatory), and thus unconstitutional (Gelli 2003b: 133).

The government's initial reaction – seized upon by the media – was swift and defiant: Whereas it had already planned to deactivate the salary cut and would eventually do so, repaying the withheld monies was out of the question (NP 02-E-18; NP 02–53). A month later, in mid-September 2002, the government issued its formal response to the ruling, in the form of DNU 1819. Per the decree, the salary cut would remain in place through the end of the year. Delayed deactivation would allow elected leaders to keep hitting crucial fiscal targets (thus pleasing the IMF). Yet it also meant that a policy the highest court in the land had unambiguously declared unconstitutional – and which had already been in effect for more than a year – would remain in place for another four months.[48] The decree also indicated that rather than reimbursing public sector workers' and pensioners' withheld funds (estimated at $3.1 billion *pesos*), the state would issue long-term public bonds, beginning in 2003 (NP 02-E-18; NP 02-R-68).[49] Yet the government continued to stall. Finally, almost a year later (September 2003), it emitted Administrative Decision 75, outlining the repayment system. Pensioners over 80 years of age would be repaid directly, and a subset of the other workers and pensioners whose wages and benefits had been affected would receive five-year bonds, which could be cashed in for ten equal biannual payments between March 2004 and September 2008.[50] Despite the government's slow and partial compliance – and newspapers' persistent suggestions that the Court was "debating the big cases" (NP 02-R-79) – the CSJN would not resolve any further cases concerning DNU 896 and Law 24.453. Nonetheless, when it appeared the Court would hand down a significant ruling challenging a key economic policy in late 2002, President Duhalde (2002–3) resurrected calls for the impeachment of several justices.[51] Duhalde's renewed threats against the Court, while ultimately empty, perpetuated both high court politicization and interbranch confrontation.

How did the Court's political character contribute to this bitter bout of interbranch confrontation? First, the CSJN's traditional instability made politicizing the Court, as Duhalde repeatedly sought to do, seem the natural option. Second, the political Court instinctively rejected Duhalde (a rival of their patron, Menem). Further, by the time the Court received the *Tobar* case, it had been working under the shroud of impeachment for more than a year and a half, and its strong ruling in that dispute reflected frustration not only with these renewed attempts at manipulation, but with decades of politicization (Bianchi 2002b: 65). With its decision, the Court sent a strong signal to the executive that it was willing to induce significant economic havoc if the executive and congress continued with their impeachment initiative (NP 01–46; NP 01–47; NP 01–49; NP 01–50; NP 01–51; NP 01–52; NP 01-E-20; NP 01–62; NP 01–65; NP 01-E-33; NP 01-R-171; EC-03; EC-05; EC-07; EC-11; EC-15; EC-16; EC-17; EC-18; EC-19).[52] For his part, even though Duhalde had promised to deactivate impeachment attempts against the Court, his initial public rebuke of its ruling, his month-long delay in developing a policy response, his retention of the salary cut through the end of the year, and his decision to issue bonds rather than reimburse workers and pensioners were predicated on his

[48] Of course, the Court's criticism of the decree concerned its vagueness, not its substance; by specifying the exact date at which the salary cut would be suspended, the government hoped to make more difficult subsequent judicial rulings against the cut (NP 02-E-20).

[49] Note that like all CSJN decisions, the *Tobar* ruling only had *inter partes* effects and thus only formally required repaying Tobar's withheld salary.

[50] http://www.puntoprofesional.com/P/0444/DAM_08–03.HTM, accessed December 3, 2009.

[51] *La Nación*, December 22, 2002, "El plan de Duhalde para frenar la Corte."

[52] While the De la Rúa administration had issued the questioned DNU and law, given the time lapse, it was the Duhalde administration for whom the Court's ruling in *Tobar* created problems.

continued efforts to purge the Court, and his anticipation that they would ultimately prove successful.

The Court's weak legitimacy likewise contributed to interbranch confrontation: It freed the CSJN to issue a challenging decision on *Tobar* without great concern about the effect that weak compliance (which was, given the economic situation, quite likely) would have on its image, and freed elected leaders to respond slowly and partially (as the political cost of such a response was low). Further, even though some constitutional scholars did not consider the CSJN's ruling in *Tobar* a contradiction of its decision in *Guida* (e.g., EC-08; Bianchi 2002: 65), others held that the two rulings *were* contradictory (e.g., E-16) despite the legal scaffolding the Court sought to erect – a contradiction that the Court's lack of role consensus and operational inconsistency allowed. Indeed, the legal viability of asserting that a policy had *become* constitutional due to changing political circumstances was questioned by various legal scholars (e.g., EC-34),[53] and again reflected the justices' weaker professional profiles and the Court's juridical inconsistency.

What broader results did these interbranch interactions have? Given that the CSJN delayed more than half a decade before deciding the *Guida* case, the ruling did not induce public furor. While the decision allowed the government to avoid exacerbating its significant budget deficit, within a month of its issuance, talks with the IMF had frozen due to its concerns about Argentina's political instability (NP 02-R-64). Moreover, the decision reinforced the idea that the executive could, in emergency situations, alter public sector salaries (E-03), further compromising confidence in juridical security and the rule of law and probably discouraging public sector employees from filing cases questioning the new salary cut (NP 01–591; NP 01–593). These negative ramifications notwithstanding, the most dire predictions about the ruling's effects failed to come true. Indeed, one particularly inflammatory newspaper editorial suggested that the CSJN's ruling on *Tobar* produced "problems of unpredictable and devastating dimensions that put the country's immediate future at risk" (NP 02–59), and another opined that the decision jeopardized elected leaders' ability to negotiate a highly sought-after agreement with the IMF (NP 02-E-16).[54] In the event, the government's compliance – slow and partial as it was – did not engender economic devastation. Yet the episode also failed to serve the function of bolstering the rule of law, as the combination of a check on government power and partial compliance might have done in another context with a less-political Court. The CSJN's challenge to elected leaders signaled that the Court was willing to use critical cases as a political tool. Likewise, the government's slow compliance emphasized that it would obey the law and the political court's decisions on its own terms.

[53] Chapter 3 discussed this doctrine and its dubious viability as deployed by the Argentine Court.

[54] The IMF's Western Hemisphere director was extraordinarily critical of the high court's ruling (NP 02-E-23).

5.5. CONCLUSIONS

This chapter explored the combined pattern of high court–elected branch interaction over economic policy that emerged in Argentina in the postauthoritarian era. The comparative judicial politics literature has thoroughly addressed the question of high court decision making; however, fewer studies examine how quickly and completely elected leaders comply with Court rulings that challenge their interests, and even fewer examine these outcomes together (i.e., mutual interbranch relations). Yet without analyzing the two phenomena in tandem, we can misunderstand judicial dynamics. For instance, without examining compliance with high court rulings, we might have mistaken the pattern of interbranch confrontation in Argentina (in which strong Court challenges to elected leaders are partially or fully ignored) for a pattern of Court domination (in which strong Court challenges to elected leaders are obeyed). In short, identifying variation in how high courts and elected leaders interact – and, more broadly, understanding what difference Courts make to politics and policy making – require examining what happens *after* Courts rule.

Analyzing eighteen important cases regarding economic policy decided by the Argentine Supreme Court during the two decades after regime transition reveals that the dominant pattern of high court–elected branch interaction in the economic realm was Court submission. Adopting a deferential approach to decision making, the Court tended to strongly endorse the exercise of government power while only rarely and weakly challenging elected leaders. Elected leaders, for their part, complied partially with the Court's weak challenges but rarely retaliated. Yet Court submission was periodically interrupted by episodes of interbranch confrontation over economic policy – when the CSJN issued challenging rulings (assuming anything *but* a deferential approach to decision making), with which the elected branches complied partially or not at all, while often retaliating against the Court. The chapter sought to account for that combined pattern of interbranch interaction, taking a first step toward advancing an explanation for why the observed patterns are so different in Argentina and Brazil.

I suggest that we look inside Courts – as well as to the political environment – to explain high court–elected branch interactions over politically crucial cases. My institutional explanation, the Court character thesis, argues that a relatively stable congeries of informal high court features shapes the way high courts and elected leaders interact when crucial policy objectives clash with the rule of law, channeling their interactions into persistent patterns. Of course, contextual and political factors – political fragmentation, economic crisis, and many others – also affect the tenor of interbranch relations: Political institutions do not interact in a vacuum, and political (and judicial) actors respond strategically to their surroundings (and each other). Yet the effect such political factors have on interbranch relations, I argue, is mitigated and shaped by institutional history – by the character of the high court.

In Argentina, leaders had long tended to politicize the CSJN, seeking to manipulate its size and composition and appoint justices with whom they had some connection, even if their qualifications were sometimes weak. The result was a political Court: unstable, with a weaker professional profile, lower legitimacy, and weaker institutional cohesion. When the Court and elected branches were aligned or when relations were otherwise friendly, the CSJN tended to submit to elected leaders, endorsing the exercise of government power in the crucial economic realm. This behavior was encouraged by the Court's weak perceived legitimacy and lack of internal cohesion: The CSJN had neither exogenous nor endogenous sources of strength on which it could draw in order to challenge the elected branches (and indeed, no institutional prestige to lose when it issued poorly formulated, deferential rulings). Yet at moments of interbranch tension or misalignment, the Court took advantage of the salience (to government leaders, society, and the international investment community) of crucial cases concerning economic policy to issue decisions that strongly challenged the exercise of government power, as elected leaders' partial compliance (or, indeed, their failure to comply at all) would do little to impoverish the Court's already negative image. And indeed, leaders often only partially obeyed or even ignored such challenging decisions, assuming that the Court could not coordinate to highlight their lack of compliance, that they could easily substitute the Court with one that *would* defer to them, and that the political cost of defying the Court was relatively low. In this way, the Court's political character encouraged interbranch interactions generally marked by Court submission but punctuated by moments of confrontation in the realm of economic governance.

The next chapter examines high court–elected branch interactions over economic policy in postauthoritarian Brazil. Due to the Brazilian Court's very distinct statesman character, interbranch interactions played out quite differently: A pattern of interbranch accommodation over politically crucial cases emerged. These different patterns of interbranch interaction and the legal and political choices they embody have critical implication for economic governance and the rule of law in Latin America. The book's conclusion expands further on this point.

6

The Statesman Court and Interbranch Accommodation in Brazil

> "*Absolutely, a Supreme Court justice must think of the consequences of his decisions.*"[1]
>
> – An STF justice, discussing high court decision-making (CSM-01)

> "*The day that the Supreme Federal Tribunal interprets the constitution according to economic programs and not the opposite, chaos will have been established in the juridical order.*"[2]
>
> – A retired STF justice, discussing high court decision-making (CSM-04)

> "*When the president's chief of staff got news of the STF's ruling, he said 'the government is shocked.' And I said, 'that's their fault, they stuck their finger in the socket.'*"[3]
>
> – An STF justice, referring to a ruling declaring unconstitutional a key aspect of President Cardoso's pension reform initiative (CSM-03)

6.1. INTRODUCTION

How can we characterize and explain the patterns of interaction that emerged as justices and elected leaders tangled over crucial economic policies in postauthoritarian Latin America? Chapter 5 explored these questions in Argentina, and this chapter examines them in Brazil. The 1988 Constitution's statist and nationalist tendencies practically invited constitutional controversy over Brazilian leaders' market-based reforms and efforts to achieve fiscal rectitude. Opposition political parties and other actors repeatedly turned to courts to question the government's economic initiatives through the 1990s, and economic governance was significantly judicialized during the first twenty postauthoritarian years. As lower courts often sided with those questioning

[1] Original quote: "*Um Ministro tem que pensar, sim, nas conseqüências da sua decisão.*"

[2] Original quote: "*No dia que o Supremo interpretar a constituição no rumo de um programa econômico, e não o contrário, então, está estabelecido o caos na ordem jurídica.*"

[3] Original quote: "*O ministro da Casa Civil, quando ele recebeu a noticia, ele disse, 'O governo está chocado'.... E eu falei, 'culpa dele, pôs o dedo na tomada elétrica.'*"

government policy, elected leaders were repeatedly pummeled by judicial challenges as they sought to reform the economy. Inevitably the government appealed these lower court rulings, and Brazil's highest court received hundreds of thousands of cases dealing with countless aspects of economic policy. In particular, tens of thousands of repeat cases regarding salary levels and pension benefits, the introduction of new stabilization programs, and new taxation schemes arrived to the Court. Given the strong constitutional basis for legal challenges, and in view of the Court's historic independence, we might have expected an adversarial high court–elected branch relationship to emerge in the economic realm.

Instead, analyzing interbranch relations around twenty-six important court cases regarding economic policy reveals that high court–elected branch interactions over economic governance followed a stable pattern of *accommodation* during the first two postauthoritarian decades. Table 6.1 outlines the parameters of this pattern of interaction. First, the STF was selectively assertive: it both challenged and endorsed the exercise of government power, and it challenged weakly and strongly (and endorsed weakly and strongly) with similar frequency. Further, it adopted various approaches to decision making when ruling on these politically crucial cases. For their part, elected leaders tended to comply with STF rulings, and never retaliated significantly against them.

This pattern of interbranch interaction over economic policy contrasts significantly with Argentina's more volatile interbranch relations in which the dominant pattern of Court submission was punctuated by moments of interbranch confrontation. What accounts for this variation? This study's institutional account – the Court character thesis – supplements existing explanations of interbranch relations in the strategic vein, showing how informal yet relatively persistent institutional features of Courts themselves help to explain the behavioral patterns that emerge as judicial and elected authorities interact repeatedly over politically crucial cases. In Brazil, the STF's statesman character – its stability, stronger professional profile, and greater legitimacy and cohesion – contributed considerably to the emergence of interbranch accommodation over economic governance. This chapter develops that argument, concluding with case studies of interbranch interplay that bring the pattern of accommodation to life and show how Court character helped to create it.

6.2. INTERBRANCH ACCOMMODATION IN THE ECONOMIC POLICY REALM IN BRAZIL

Pressure to address economic crisis and carry out market-based reform aggressively and quickly during Brazil's first two posttransition decades incentivized elected leaders to push institutional limits on their power when introducing economic measures. In response, the political opposition, civil society actors, and ordinary citizens turned to the courts to challenge certain economic policies, and many cases eventually reached the high court. As high-profile and difficult tests of the STF's authority and the strength of the rule of law, the

TABLE 6.1. *Pattern of High Court–Elected Branch Interaction over Economic Governance in Brazil*

Pattern of Interaction	Tendencies in STF's Behavior				Tendencies in Elected Leaders' Behavior	
	Assertiveness			Approach to Decision Making	Compliance with STF's Rulings	Retaliation against STF's Rulings
	Direction of Rulings	Intensity of Endorsements	Intensity of Challenges			
Accommodation	No clear tendency	No clear tendency	No clear tendency	Various (*not* Deferential)	Partial/Significant	Infrequent

cases were of immense institutional significance to the Court and the country. Given that such cases could impact tens of thousands of Brazilians and be worth millions or billions of dollars to the government, the cases were also of extraordinary political and economic importance. In resolving these cases, the STF found itself between a rock and a hard place – in essence deliberating between measures elected leaders believed would foster economic growth and recovery, and constitutionalism. Likewise, reacting to STF rulings that struck down crucial policies required elected leaders to choose between shelving their key policies, or partially or completely disregarding the decisions of the highest Court in the land (a tempting but problematic option in view of the rule of law rhetoric elected leaders had adopted and the ongoing legal transition). How did the STF and elected leaders interact over these crucial cases – and why did they interact as they did?

To answer these questions, I examined a systematically selected sample of twenty-six of the most important cases concerning economic policy decided by the STF in the first twenty postauthoritarian years.[4] Table 6.2 presents the cases in chronological order.[5] The table describes the direction and intensity of the STF's ruling on each case (column three), the approach to decision making it adopted when deciding each (column four), and the degree to which elected leaders complied with and/or retaliated against the Court's challenging decisions (column five). The final column, aggregating the scores on all of the cases, indicates the overall pattern of high court–elected branch interaction over economic governance in postauthoritarian Brazil: accommodation. This section describes the cases, evaluates each aspect of high court–elected branch interaction in turn, and discusses the overall pattern of interbranch interaction.

The Cases

Appendix 6.1 lists the twenty-six discrete cases under study in chronological order, indicating the case type, number, and topic; the parties to the case; the issue area, policy questioned in the case, and the plaintiff's claim; the timing of the decision-making process; and the STF's ruling. The majority of the cases (nineteen of twenty-six, or 73 percent) are abstract review cases, mainly ADIns; only 15 percent of the cases are REs and none are AGs.[6] These proportions

[4] Appendix 1.1 discusses case selection.

[5] Given the STF's tremendous case load, it often decides hundreds or thousands of cases on the same policy or topic. While employing my case-selection technique generated a sample of twenty-six discrete cases, six pairs of those key cases concerned the same policy (prevention of filing of injunctions against Collor Plan I, Collor Plan I's bank freeze, FINSOCIAL, IPMF, CPMF, and a tax on public sector pensions). For each pair, the STF's rulings on the cases were no more than a year apart, and the elected branches generally reacted to the two decisions in tandem. Consequently, these case pairs are considered together in the analysis (referred to from here forward as "cases" for simplicity), reducing the N from 26 to 20. Carrying out the analysis in this way also facilitates comparison with Argentina, where there was a one-to-one correspondence between questioned economic policies and high court cases.

[6] Web Appendix 2.3 discusses the mechanisms used most frequently to reach the STF.

TABLE 6.2. *Pattern of High Court–Elected Branch Interaction over Economic Governance in Brazil (twenty cases/case pairs decided 1985–2004, in chronological order)*

President	Case (year of decision)[a]	STF Assertiveness: Direction and Intensity of Ruling[b]	STF Approach to Decision Making[c]	Elected Branch Compliance with/ Retaliation against Challenging Decisions[d]	Pattern of Interbranch Interaction
Sarney					
Collor	Collor Plan I (no injunctions) (ADIn 223 & ADIn 295) (I = 1990)	Weaker endorsement (–8)	Pragmatic	(Not applic.)	
	Constitution's capping interest rate at 12 percent (ADIn 04) (FD = 1991)	Stronger endorsement (–12.5)	Pragmatic	(Not applic.)	
	Collor Plan I (bank freeze) (ADIn 259 & ADIn 534) (I = 1991)	Weaker endorsement (–7.75)	Pragmatic	(Not applic.)	
	Adjustment of retirement benefits of 147.06 percent (RE 147864) (FD = 1992)	**Stronger challenge** (10.5)	*Support-building*	Partial compliance/ no retaliation (5)	Accommodation
Franco	Fund for Social Investment (FINSOCIAL) (RE 150755 & RE 150764[e]) (FD = 1992)	Weaker challenge (7.25)	Principled	Significant compliance/ no retaliation (4)	
	Provisional Tax on Financial Transactions (IPMF) (ADIn 926 & ADIn 939) (FD/I = 1993)	**Stronger challenge** (14.25)	Pragmatic	Significant compliance/ some retaliation (8.5)	
	Contribution for Financing Social Security (COFINS) (ADC 01) (FD = 1993)	Stronger endorsement (–10.5)	Pragmatic	(Not applic.)	

(*continued*)

TABLE 6.2. (*Continued*)

President	Case (year of decision)[a]	STF Assertiveness: Direction and Intensity of Ruling[b]	STF Approach to Decision Making[c]	Elected Branch Compliance with/ Retaliation against Challenging Decisions[d]	Pattern of Interbranch Interaction
	Salary retention for public sector workers (10.94 percent) (MS 21969) (I = 1994)	Weaker challenge (9)	*Protective*/ Pragmatic	**Noncompliance/** some retaliation (16)	
Cardoso I	Privatization of the Vale do Rio Doce Company (CVRD) (ADIn 1582) (I = 1997)	Stronger endorsement (−9.5)	Principled	(Not applic.)	
	Salary increase of 28.86 percent (RMS 22307) (FD=1998)	Weaker challenge (8)	*Protective*/ Pragmatic	Partial compliance/ some retaliation (10.5)	
Cardoso II	Maternity leave benefits (ADIn 1946) (I = 1999)	Weaker challenge (9.5)	Principled	Partial compliance/ no retaliation (5)	Accommodation
	Provisional Contribution on Financial Transactions (CPMF) (ADIn 1497 & ADIn 2031[e]) (I = 1996/1999)	Weaker challenge (1.25)	Principled	Partial compliance/ no retaliation (7)	
	Tax on public sector pensions (I) (ADIn 2010) (I = 1999)	**Stronger challenge** (12)	Principled/ *Protective*	Significant compliance/ some retaliation (8.5)	
	Formula for calculating retirement benefits (ADIn 2111) (I = 2000)	Stronger endorsement (−8.5)	Principled/ Pragmatic	(Not applic.)	

	Privatization of the Bank of São Paulo State (BANESPA) (PET 2066) (FD = 2000)	Stronger endorsement (–10)	Principled	(Not applic.)	
	Adjustment of accounts in an employment-security fund (FGTS) (RE 226855) (FD = 2000)	Weaker challenge (8.5)	Pragmatic	Partial compliance/ no retaliation (4.5)	
	Annual salary review for public sector workers (ADIn 2061) (FD = 2001)	**Stronger challenge (11)**	*Protective*/ Pragmatic/ Principled	Partial compliance/ no retaliation (5.5)	Accommodation
	"The black-out" (O "*apagão*") (ADC 09) (FD = 2001)	Stronger endorsement (–9)	Pragmatic	(Not applic.)	
Lula	Tax on public sector pensions (II) (ADIn 3105 & ADIn 3128) (FD = 2004)	Weaker endorsement (–8)	*Deferential*/ Pragmatic/ Principled	Significant compliance/[f] no retaliation (2.5)	
	Law of Fiscal Responsibility (ADIn 2238) (FD = 2007)	Weaker endorsement (–7.5)	Pragmatic	(Not applic.)	

Notes: [a] The ruling referenced is (and year given refers to) the ruling to which the government, public, and press reacted; at times such rulings came in the form of an injunction (I), and at other times in the form of a final decision (FD) on the case.

[b] Numeric scores are based on data in Appendices 6.2 and 6.3: –15.5 (strongest endorsement) to –1 (weakest endorsement) and 1 (weakest challenge) to 18.5 (strongest challenge). Font darkness likewise reflects judicial assertiveness: rulings in grey font are least assertive and rulings in bold font are most assertive.

[c] Approaches in italic font are strategic. See Appendix 6.4 for data supporting these scores.

[d] Numeric scores are the sum of the "compliance" and "retaliation" scores for each case (see data in Appendix 6.5) and indicate the overall degree to which elected leaders' response challenged the Court: 1 to 8.25 (weaker challenge); 8.25 to 15.5 (moderate challenge); 15.5 to 23(stronger challenge). Font darkness likewise reflects how much elected leaders' response challenged the Court: responses in bold font are the most challenging and responses in grey font the least challenging.

[e] The rulings on these two cases went in opposite directions: one was a weak challenge and the other a weak endorsement; together, they challenged the exercise of government power slightly more than they endorsed it.

[f] A small part of the policy was challenged in the ruling and elected leaders followed the Court's dictates.

contrast with those of the Court's overall case load,[7] suggesting that the politically important cases the Court hears are qualitatively different from most of its docket, and that it tends to make its most important rulings in abstract review cases.[8] Nonetheless, more than a quarter of the cases under study are concrete review cases, demonstrating that the STF hands down politically crucial decisions – or decisions that become crucial due to the way in which the elected branches respond to them – in many different types of cases. This is underappreciated in the literature on the Court, which focuses heavily on ADIns (e.g., Werneck Vianna et al. 1999; Moreira Maués and Belém Leitão 2003; Taylor 2008).[9]

Reviewing the main issue areas into which the Court was drawn over time reveals how its involvement in economic governance developed in postauthoritarian Brazil. Tens of thousands of cases contesting various stabilization programs eventually reached the STF, beginning in the early 1990s (for example, regarding Collor Plan I and the bank freeze it imposed – ADIns 223, 295, 259, and 534), and lasting into the 2000s (for example, RE 226855, which dealt with adjustments to accounts in an employment security fund [*Fundo de Garantía do Tempo do Serviço*, FGTS]). Elected leaders' efforts to sell off inefficient state enterprises also generated significant conflict (for instance, in the cases of the privatization of a major mining concern [*Companhia Vale do Rio Doce*, ADIn 1582] and of São Paulo's state bank [BANESPA, PET 2066]). Attempts to spend less on public sector salaries or benefits and decrease pension contributions were questioned repeatedly (e.g., RMS 22307, MS 21969, and ADIn 2061, dealing with salaries; and ADIns 2010, 2111, 3105, and 3108, as well as RE 147684 dealing with pensions). The government's efforts to extract more were also challenged: various tax initiatives generated STF cases (e.g., ADC 01; ADIns 1497, 2238, 926, and 3939; and REs 150755 and 150764). The economic issue areas in which the STF became involved in the postauthoritarian period, then, were quite similar to those in which the Argentine CSJN became involved.

The most frequent filers of the ADIns considered here were opposition political parties (which filed nine)[10] and the Brazilian bar association (which filed

[7] As Web Appendix 2.4 shows, extraordinary appeals and direct appeals (REs and AGs) consistently compose at least 90 percent of the STF's case load whereas ADIns generally account for no more than 2 percent.

[8] Since 1999, all STF decisions on abstract review cases have had *erga omnes* effects and have been binding on all other courts and the public administration.

[9] Indeed, my case-selection technique, which entailed counting mentions of STF cases in (among other sources) interviews with scholars who study the Court and studies of its jurisprudence, may have biased case selection toward ADINs: My sample may contain as many ADIns as it does not only because they are objectively more important, but because they are studied more often.

[10] Opposition parties – that is, those not in the coalition supporting the president – filed far fewer cases concerning economic policy with the STF after the PT's victory in 2003, as filing such cases implied questioning policies that were either their own, or essentially an extension of their own (given the continuity between Cardoso's economic policy and Lula's early economic initiatives).

three). The rest of the cases were filed by the state – appeals of decisions against it on cases questioning a government policy or action, or ADCs (requests by government authorities that the Court declare a policy *constitutional*). This situation contrasts with Argentina, where most cases analyzed were filed with the CSJN by individuals (in part because the Argentine Court cannot carry out abstract review).

In terms of the object of the cases and the claims made, while scholars have emphasized Brazilian executives' overuse or misuse of provisional measures (*medidas provisórias*, MPs),[11] an MP was questioned in only five cases (19 percent of the sample). In another eight cases (31 percent of the sample) however, some other sort of administrative policy or decision issued by the executive was questioned – such that executive action was at the core of half of the twenty-six cases. The constitutionality of a complementary or ordinary law was questioned in eight of the cases (36 percent of the sample), and the constitutionality of a constitutional amendment was challenged in another six cases (or 27 percent of the sample).[12] Legislative and executive actions, then, were questioned at the STF with approximately the same frequency.[13] On a related note, as in Argentina, policy *content* was questioned much more often than the *form* policies took: the former was questioned in seventeen cases (or 65 percent of the sample), whereas both form and content were questioned in four cases (or 15 percent of the sample). Again, one interpretation of this finding is that presidents did not cross the constitutional boundary between executive and legislative power – at least in the area of economic governance – as much as scholars have suggested.

Concerning timing, none of the cases selected for study was decided – or even filed – before 1988. In part, this is because the STF spent much of the period from 1985 (regime transition) to 1988 (constitutional transition) in something of a holding pattern, waiting to determine where it would fit, and what role it would play, in the new democracy's reformed constitutional structure (CSE-06). As in Argentina, the time that it took the STF to hand down final decisions on the cases under study varied dramatically – from a month (MS 21969) to more than eleven years (ADIn 295). But the long wait in Brazil did not necessarily mean that the STF made no ruling on the case in the interim. In fact, particularly with ADIns, the Court was often quick to hand down an injunction,[14] and slow to take the case up again to issue a final decision;[15] when

[11] Chapter 2 describes this decree power; see also Figueiredo and Limongi (2000) and Negretto (2004).

[12] Both executive and legislative actions were questioned in one case.

[13] Of course, several of the laws questioned *originated* as MPs and were converted into law by congress; further, draft constitutional amendments are often submitted to the legislature by the executive and thus also bear the president's fingerprints.

[14] Here and throughout, the term "injunction" refers to what is commonly called a "preliminary injunction" in U.S. law.

[15] While this informal practice likely stemmed from the STF's overwhelming case load, as Faro de Castro (1997b) has asserted, the STF also uses injunctions to signal how it will rule on a

this occurred, the injunction basically stood in for the final decision, which generally either confirmed the injunction or ruled the case moot.[16] Although not reflected in Appendix 6.1, it bears mentioning that it was generally the Court sitting *en banc* (rather than a single STF justice or one of the Court's two chambers) that issued injunctions and handed down final rulings in the cases under study. Further, in eight of the twenty-six cases (31 percent of the sample), the Court's injunction or final ruling was unanimous;[17] the Argentine Court, by contrast, was much more likely to issue divided decisions.

Evaluating Interbranch Interactions

This subsection evaluates each aspect of the interactions between the STF and elected leaders over the cases under study, discussing columns three through five of Table 6.2.

High Court Selective Assertiveness

How willing was the STF to challenge elected leaders in the sensitive realm of economic policy? On the one hand, given the country's precarious economic and fiscal situation, we might have expected that the Court would tread lightly. On the other hand, given the constitutional complications inherent in economic governance, we might have anticipated that the STF would be consistently assertive when ruling on cases regarding economic policy. Indeed, some students of the Court's decision making (e.g., Arantes 1997; Sadek 1999; Werneck Vianna et al. 1999; Santiso 2004; Taylor 2008) posit that the Court is quite assertive with respect to the elected branches. Yet still others assert that the central tendency in the Court's jurisprudence is to issue "*decisões solomónicas*" ("Solomonic decisions") – compromise rulings in which neither side wins or loses completely (CSE-10; CSE-14; CSM-06; EC-12; EC-30; EC-41; EC-42; EC-36; JG-05–02; see also Koerner 2006).

The present analysis suggests that none of these accounts is fully accurate, at least with respect to the Court's most politically important rulings (see column three of Table 6.2).[18] The Court is by no means a timid institution – it issued some blistering rejections of the exercise of government power. Yet concerns (or enthusiasm) about its assertiveness may be misplaced, as it also handed

particular type of case, tentatively indicating to elected leaders that they are about to suffer a significant defeat, for instance.

[16] A procedural change implemented in 2002 made it easier for the Court to issue a final decision immediately in ADIns; see Web Appendix 4.6.

[17] In several other cases, the vote on an injunction or a final decision was a majority vs. a single justice, and that justice was usually Justice Marco Aurelio Mello; indeed, in some circles he bore the nickname "*o ministro vencido*" (the defeated minister) for the frequency with which he formed part of the minority or was the single dissenting vote in STF rulings.

[18] Appendices 6.2 and 6.3 outline how decision direction and intensity were scored. Slight modifications were made to the scoring scheme used in Argentina (outlined in Appendices 5.2 and 5.3) to accommodate differences in the two institutional systems.

down several strong endorsements of elected leaders' power. Indeed, as noted previously and like the Argentine Court, the STF was selectively assertive in the economic realm (although it was somewhat more evenhanded than the CSJN). The STF challenged and endorsed the exercise of government power in ten cases each; six of its ten challenges were weaker while six of its ten endorsements were stronger.[19] The CSJN, by contrast, endorsed more often than it challenged; further, it issued strong challenges (when it was in confrontation with elected leaders) just as frequently as weak challenges (in the Court submission pattern of interbranch interaction), and was much more likely to endorse strongly than to endorse weakly (as reflected in the greater duration of the Court submission pattern of interbranch interaction). While these differences are important, the two Courts contrast even more starkly with regard to the *motivations* behind their rulings, discussed in the subsequent subsection and clearly illustrated in the case studies.

The scoring again differentiates between rulings' letter and spirit, as at times the intensity with which the STF challenged (or endorsed) a particular policy in a ruling differed from the intensity with which it challenged (or endorsed) the broader exercise of government power in that ruling (see again Appendices 6.2 and 6.3). Indeed, particularly at the beginning of the time period under consideration, some challenges and endorsements were coded "stronger" because of the way the STF used cases regarding economic policy to address and reconcile institutional conflicts, and to clarify and define the extent (or limits) of its new powers – and those of elected leaders – in the post 1988 Constitution institutional system. For example, the STF's ruling on the Contribution for Financing Social Security (COFINS) case was a stronger endorsement of the exercise of government power not only because the Court upheld the law imposing the tax, but because it upheld the constitutionality of the ADC abstract review mechanism, which enhanced the government's ability to negotiate the "policy gauntlet" erected by the 1988 constitution.[20] Moreover, in a few cases, the Court challenged a particular policy in its ruling while simultaneously endorsing the broader exercise of government power – and in other cases did the opposite. For example, in its decision on ADIn 223, in which certain aspects of Collor Plan I were questioned, the STF tacitly endorsed the policy (refusing to issue an injunction to suspend it) but practically encouraged pensioners to file claims in lower courts.

[19] Considering the STF's rulings on the twenty-six cases individually rather than pairing cases concerning the same policy illustrates the Court's evenhandedness even more clearly: it challenged the exercise of government power in eleven cases and endorsed it in fifteen (42 percent and 58 percent of the time, respectively); weakly challenged the exercise of government power slightly more often than it strongly challenged (six and five challenges, respectively), and weakly endorsed the exercise of government power slightly more often than it strongly endorsed (eight and seven endorsements, respectively).

[20] Likewise, even though the STF only weakly challenged the IPMF tax in ADIns 926 and 939, it strongly asserted its ability to consider the constitutionality of constitutional amendments (a significant challenge to elected leaders' power).

High Court Approach to Decision Making

As noted in Chapters 1 and 5, this study identifies six approaches a Court might adopt when ruling on politically crucial cases, depending upon what type(s) of considerations dominated in its decision-making process (*principled, preference-driven*, *self-protective*, *support-building*, *deferential*, and *pragmatic*). Column four of Table 6.2 indicates the approaches the STF adopted when deciding the cases under study: pragmatic, principled, and far less often, three strategic approaches (support-building, protective, and deferential, in italics).[21] Patterns in the STF's adoption of these approaches are discussed in the next subsection, but a few points can be highlighted here.

According to expert opinion, the Court adopted a pragmatic approach to decision making – in which the economic or political context or rulings' potential repercussions were paramount to the justices' calculations – more often than any other when deciding the crucial economic policy cases under study (in twelve of the twenty cases or 60 percent of the time). The Court adopted this approach both when it challenged and when it endorsed the exercise of government power. Significantly, pragmatic considerations were more than twice as important in Brazil than in Argentina, where experts considered them to be important to only 28 percent of the rulings under study. This finding suggests that STF justices were more cognizant of or attentive to, and more willing to play an independent role in, economic governance compared with their Argentine counterparts.

The STF adopted a principled approach – in which law or legal considerations impinged heavily on its decision making – when ruling on 45 percent (nine of twenty) of these economically crucial cases. Again, and like the CSJN, the STF adopted this approach both when endorsing and when challenging the exercise of government power. The Argentine Court also adopted a principled approach to decision making second most often but did so less frequently than the STF (in 33 percent of the rulings under study). Further, the STF adopted a *fully* principled approach (i.e., no other consideration impinged significantly on its ruling) a quarter of the time (in five of the twenty cases), more than twice as often as this occurred in Argentina (11 percent of the time). In sum, per expert opinion, the principled approach was more central to the STF's decision making.

Finally, the STF engaged in strategic decision making (adopting a self-protective, support-building, or deferential approach) far less often than the Argentine Court. Although the STF assumed a self-protective approach to

[21] Again, these approaches reflect the considerations that were mentioned in the Court's written decision or in interviews with justices, or that newspaper articles, experts I interviewed, or scholarly sources indicated were important to the Court's decision making on each case. The data supporting the scoring are reported in Appendix 6.4. I interpret the number of times a consideration was mentioned in connection with a case to reflect the likelihood that it weighed heavily in the justices' decision-making calculus (that is, the more often a consideration was mentioned the more likely it was important).

decision making (in which justices' corporate or institutional interests were imputed to have been an important consideration) with approximately the same frequency that the Argentine Court did so – in five of the twenty cases (or 25 percent of the time) – this apparent similarity is misleading. Most of the Argentine CSJN's self-protective rulings aimed to *threaten* the executive out of fear of, or in retaliation against, attacks on the Court. In Brazil's more stable institutional context where elected leaders had professionalized rather than politicized the high court, not once did the STF adopt a self-protective approach in order to threaten elected leaders. Rather, when institutional considerations motivated the STF, they generally related to defending its income,[22] avoiding blame for the failure of a critical policy,[23] or demonstrating its independence from the executive or ability to carry out a particular function (such as declaring unconstitutional constitutional amendments).[24] Thus, even though institutional interests motivated the two Courts with similar frequency, there were important differences between their self-protective approaches to decision making.

According to experts, the STF almost never adopted a deferential approach to decision making (in which the elected branches' preferences are an important consideration) when ruling on the cases under study, doing so in only one case (5 percent of the time). In Argentina, by stark contrast, experts suggested that the high court adopted a deferential approach to decision making more often than any other when deciding the cases under study (in ten out of the eighteen rulings or 56 percent of the time). This finding offers concrete evidence to underpin the conventional wisdom that the Brazilian Court is far more independent from elected leaders than the Argentine. And finally, experts suggested that the STF, like the CSJN, paid little attention to public opinion, adopting a support-building approach (in which popular sentiment about a particular case weighs heavily on the justices' deliberations) in only one of the twenty cases (or 5 percent of the time). Again however, the reasons *why* public opinion was not salient for the two Courts probably differ. Compared with other Latin American high courts, the STF maintained a relatively positive public image during much of the time period of interest. As such, justices likely felt they did not need to respond to what they called "*o clamor da sociedade*" (public pressure) to maintain that image as long as they issued pragmatic, principled decisions (CSM-04, among others). In Argentina, by contrast, the CSJN's image was already sullied by the late 1980s, and justices likely calculated they could gain little by attending to public opinion, and lose little by neglecting it, when ruling on the crucial cases concerning economic policy that came before them.

[22] For instance, in RMS 22307 (concerning a salary increase of 28.86 percent) or ADIn 2010 (the first of two cases concerning a tax on pension benefits).

[23] For instance, in the cases concerning injunctions related to Collor Plan I (ADIns 223 and 295).

[24] Experts suggested both of these as important considerations in the Court's decision making on cases concerning the IPMF tax (ADIns 926 and 939).

Elected Branch Compliance and Retaliation

How did elected leaders respond to the STF's challenging decisions?[25] As column five of Table 6.2 indicates, Brazilian leaders consistently complied partially (on six occasions) or significantly (on four occasions) with the STF's rulings (completely failing to comply only once)[26] – seeking to adhere to its decisions while attenuating their effect on the state's coffers (as illustrated in the case studies at the end of this chapter). Brazilian leaders' compliance tendencies thus certainly differ from those of their Argentine counterparts (where elected leaders never complied significantly with a CSJN ruling and failed to comply at all on two occasions). Yet perhaps even more importantly – as the analysis and case studies illustrate, and, I argue, as a direct result of the Courts' contrasting characters – partial compliance sprung from different impulses in the two contexts. In Argentina, the source was foot-dragging and resistance on the part of elected leaders, while in Brazil partial compliance was the result of constrained efforts at cooperation. Finally, Brazilian leaders retaliated against STF rulings in only four of the twenty cases studied here (one-fifth of the time), whereas Argentine authorities retaliated against fully half of the CSJN's challenging decisions in the economic realm.[27]

Pattern of Interbranch Interaction

Analyzing the scores in Table 6.2 in the aggregate reveals the pattern that interactions between the STF and the elected branches over economic policy tended to follow in postauthoritarian Brazil (indicated in the final column): accommodation.[28] As mentioned previously, the STF challenged and endorsed the exercise of government power equally frequently (ten times each): there was no clear tendency in the direction of its rulings.[29] Likewise, the Court

[25] Appendix 6.5 assesses elected leaders' compliance with and retaliation against STF rulings, employing the same scheme used to evaluate compliance with and retaliation against the CSJN's rulings in Argentina.

[26] The number of compliance events sums to eleven (while the number of challenges, as discussed previously, totals ten) because in one case pair in which the STF mainly endorsed the exercise of government power (ADIns 315 and 3128, decided under President Lula), the Court challenged a small aspect of the policy in question, requiring that compliance with and retaliation against the ruling be considered.

[27] Moreover, threats issued by elected leaders were far more often empty in Brazil. For instance, while Brazilian leaders did sometimes publicly call for judicial reform and or "external control" of the courts after particularly challenging STF decisions, when judicial reform finally materialized in December 2004, it augmented rather than reduced the STF's authority and did not establish an external review organ: the National Justice Council created by reform answers, ultimately, to the high court.

[28] Table 6.1 outlines the tendencies in high court and elected branch behavior that make up this pattern.

[29] As noted in Chapter 1, this study considers a "tendency" to exist when at least two-thirds of a Court's rulings or elected leaders' reactions are in a particular direction, of a particular type, and so on.

issued six strong and four weak endorsements, and six weak and four strong challenges – thus there was no clear tendency in the intensity of its decisions. Whereas the Court adopted a range of approaches to decision making, it very rarely assumed a *deferential* approach. For their part, elected leaders complied partially or significantly (although never fully) with the letter and spirit of each of the STF's challenging decisions save one and retaliated against the Court infrequently. To describe the pattern more intuitively, the high court defended the constitution but allowed elected leaders some leeway, while elected leaders complied as best they could and rarely threatened the Court. As was the case with interbranch confrontation in Argentina, the argument is not that the Court necessarily ruled as it did or that elected leaders responded as they did *in order to* accommodate the other – simply that judicial decisions and politicians' compliance in the end had that effect.

Interactions between the STF and elected leaders exhibited various forms of accommodation. Sometimes accommodation occurred in the context of a single case. For instance, as noted earlier, six of the STF's ten challenging decisions were weaker challenges to the exercise of government power. In some of these cases, the Court attenuated its challenge with the result that the ruling accommodated elected leaders (again, without the ruling being *motivated* by a desire to accommodate them – the FGTS case study at the chapter's end illustrates this dynamic). Elected leaders tended to comply partially with the STF's weak challenges (doing so in four of six cases), thereby accommodating the Court.

On other occasions, accommodation came about as the branches interacted over two or more cases (i.e., "over-time" accommodation). For instance, the Court sometimes issued two rulings on the same policy in tandem – one weakly endorsing the exercise of government power and the other weakly challenging – such that the pair embodied an accommodating compromise. This occurred, for instance, with the rulings on the cases concerning the Fund for Social Investment (FINSOCIAL), and the CPMF tax. Here elected leaders accommodated the Court by complying partially, or more significantly, but not retaliating. At other times, the Court issued a very challenging decision concerning a certain policy, elected leaders reformulated the policy addressing the constitutional flaws the Court had highlighted (thereby accommodating the Court), and the STF, when called on to consider that revised policy, handed down a ruling more favorable to (and that thus accommodated) elected leaders (reminiscent of Fisher's [2007] constitutional dialogues). This occurred, for instance, with the cases concerning the IPMF and CPMF taxes (1993, 1996/1999), analyzed in this chapter's first case study. It also occurred in the two cases regarding the introduction of a tax on public sector retirees' pension benefits (1999 and 2004), engendering an evolution in the government's strategy from taxing benefits via law (under Cardoso) to doing so via constitutional amendment (under Lula). In still other cases, the STF quickly followed up a strong challenge with a strong endorsement; this occurred with the IPMF and COFINS cases in 1993, the Tax on public sector pensions [I] and Formula for calculating retirement benefits cases in 1999/2000, and the Annual salary review for public sector workers and Black-out cases in 2001. Indeed, interview respondents clearly indicated that the STF's ruling on the Black-out case represented "compensation" for its previous strong challenges (e.g., CSE-06).

Interbranch interactions over economic policy in postauthoritarian Brazil were thus marked by accommodation of various types. At times the STF offered middle-of-the-road solutions (weak challenges or endorsements), whereas at other moments it engaged in over-time accommodation involving more than one ruling. The elected branches' actions likewise accommodated the Court: they consistently complied with the STF's weak and strong challenges and addressed their policies' constitutional flaws, but tried to minimize the cost of doing so, sometimes delaying compliance or obeying incompletely. On the whole, judicial and elected authorities worked together in the interest of economic governance.

6.3. AN INSTITUTIONAL ACCOUNT OF INTERBRANCH INTERACTIONS: THE COURT CHARACTER THESIS

Interbranch accommodation over economic governance is a somewhat unexpected outcome in Brazil. Neoliberal reform and reform of the state more generally were controversial, especially in the early 1990s as initial attempts at economic stabilization and adjustment failed repeatedly (see, e.g., Weyland 1996, 2002). Of course, important aspects of the institutional framework for neoliberal reform were established via amendments to the 1988 constitution that served to preauthorize, facilitate, or, indeed, carry out reform (the so-called "economic amendments" introduced under Cardoso, see Chapter 2). Nonetheless, the statist and nationalist bent of some constitutional articles concerning how the economy should be run (and what role government should play therein), as well as the economic rights the charter included, meant that various economic reform initiatives conflicted with constitutional content. As such, the constitution served as the basis for multifaceted well-grounded challenges to elected leaders' neoliberal reform initiatives, creating the potential for significant interbranch confrontation. Why, then, were interbranch relations over economic governance consistently marked by accommodation?

I propose that "opening the black box" of the judiciary helps us to understand the patterns in which interbranch relations over economic governance emerged in postauthoritarian Latin America. The Court character thesis argues that a particular set of interrelated, informal features of high courts themselves – their stability, professional profile, legitimacy, and institutional cohesion – incentivizes justices and elected authorities to interact over politically important cases in similar ways over time, creating persistent patterns in their interactions. These high court features, referred to in the aggregate as Court character, facilitate the emergence of enduring *patterns* of interbranch interaction because they tend to be durable themselves: they have their roots in elected leaders' traditional politics of Court crafting (employed repeatedly over decades and thus entrenched); public opinion (which is often slow to change);

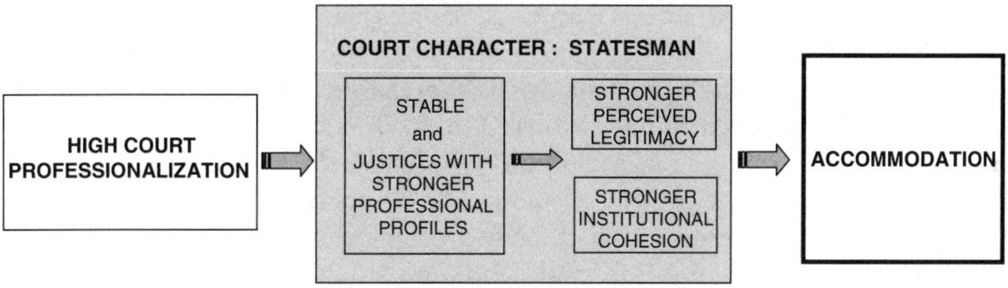

FIGURE 6.1. Explaining patterns of interbranch interaction over economic governance in Brazil: The Court character thesis.

and the informal practices that become an ingrained part of high court culture. Of course, as strategic accounts of interbranch relations rightly emphasize, a range of actors, forces, and pressures in the political environment impinge on high courts and elected leaders and affect their interactions. I build on these accounts to show how Court character conditions the choices that justices and elected leaders make as they respond to their environment and to each other, channeling their interactions into relatively stable patterns.

Figure 6.1 applies the argument to Brazil. Since the mid-twentieth century, Brazilian leaders professionalized the STF, eschewing high court manipulation and appointing well-qualified justices (see Chapter 4). Their perpetuation of that politics into the postauthoritarian period served as the foundation for the STF's statesman character after regime transition. In stark contrast to Argentina, the STF was (and is) a stable institution. Further, most Brazilian justices had prior experience in the prestigious federal judiciary or as public prosecutors and/or had held posts in the federal executive or legislature, many were well-versed in constitutional law, and few had strong ties to their appointers. Those qualities led the Court to enjoy relatively high levels of perceived legitimacy and also helped it to build comparatively strong institutional cohesion. There was consensus among the justices on the role the Court should play (if some disagreement about *how* it should play that role), and two distinct types of recognized leadership on the Court. Moreover, the Court was a relatively collegial and deliberative institution, and a good deal of continuity marked its procedures and operation. But how did the Court's statesman character contribute to producing a pattern of interbranch accommodation in the realm of economic governance over the first twenty postauthoritarian years? I discuss the effect of each aspect of Court character in turn.

First, since the Court had long been a stable institution composed of judicial and political professionals, justices felt relatively secure from individual or institutional attack by elected leaders. The Court could thus hand down very challenging decisions from time to time, confident that those rulings would neither elicit retaliation nor be disregarded. The Court's heterogeneous professional composition also encouraged the overall pattern of high court decision making discussed above – selective assertiveness in service of interbranch accommodation. As noted in Chapter 4, justices with strong backgrounds in the federal judiciary tended to be "legalists" – more oriented to a literal defense of the constitution and to challenging the exercise of government power when political leaders seemed to have violated the charter. The important subset of justices (twice as many as in Argentina) who had held high-ranking positions in the federal government prior to joining the Court tended to be "consequentialists" – more concerned with the effect their decisions could have on the country's complicated political and economic situation, and more likely to endorse the exercise of government power on cases worth millions of dollars to the state. Sometimes the two types of justices compromised (an outcome facilitated by the Court's strong leadership and collegiality): Ten of the rulings studied here can be characterized as "middle-of-the-road" decisions (*decisões solomónicas*) that neither sanctioned significant constitutional violations nor broke the national bank. At other points, the legalists and consequentialists alternated at the Court's helm as it decided different cases, resulting in the back and forth patterns of over-time accommodation noted previously. The strong presence on the Court of consequentialist justices also helps to explain the Court's penchant for adopting a pragmatic approach to decision making.

The Court's stability and professional profile likewise encouraged elected leaders to comply with its decisions and discouraged them from retaliating. Given the ongoing judicialization of economic governance, political authorities could expect judicial challenges to their economic policy initiatives to continue. Moreover, as noted in Chapter 2, the judicial centralization in which leaders engaged dictated appealing cases lost in lower courts to the STF in hopes of a more favorable ruling. Given the long history of high court professionalization and the STF's legitimacy, ignoring its rulings or politicizing it Argentine-style would have antagonized the justices as well as the Court's supporters in the legal and political communities, thus potentially poisoning relations with a Court before which elected leaders anticipated they were bound to appear again and again. Further, the existence of justices with recent experience in the federal executive or legislature facilitated the interbranch negotiations that sometimes occurred around crucial cases, encouraging consensus solutions with which elected leaders complied as they could (Faro de Castro 1997a: 243, 247; EG-04; CSE-23; EC-05; EC-13; EC-31; EC-32; EC-36).[30] In short, the Court's stability and its members' professional profiles encouraged elected branch adherence – albeit often slow or partial – with the STF's challenging decisions.

The Court's multifaceted legitimacy also promoted interbranch accommodation. On the one hand, the STF's legitimacy within the influential legal

[30] Newspaper articles periodically discussed "visits" to the STF by government officials, and interview respondents confirmed that it was not uncommon for the attorney general to converse with some justices to clarify the government's views on a particular case. However, respondents emphasized that such contact had to be handled very delicately: Only on special occasions did other cabinet ministers visit the Court, and deputies and senators would never "dare" to do so (EC-13; EC-28; EC-29). These data suggest that such negotiations neither compromised the STF's independence nor had as their goal pressuring it into deference.

community and among the public raised the political cost of defying or retaliating against it, facilitating its periodic issuance of quite challenging rulings. Yet in order to retain its legitimacy with both of those constituencies, the Court needed elected leaders to *consistently* comply with its challenging decisions, partly motivating some of its weaker challenges.[31] Taking decisions broadly viewed as principled further enhanced the Court's legitimacy in the eyes of the legal community. On the other hand, to retain credibility with politicians,[32] the Court needed to hand down pragmatic rulings and endorse the exercise of government power periodically. These competing pressures and incentives encouraged a pattern of over-time accommodation from the Court's angle. For elected leaders, the significant political costs of defying the legitimate Court edged them toward accommodating its challenging rulings – while trying to control the economic and fiscal drain that obeying those decisions sometimes implied.

Finally, the Court's institutional cohesion also encouraged a pattern of interbranch accommodation in the realm of economic policy. As suggested previously, the STF's overall collegial and deliberative nature and the existence of strong leadership led it to hand down compromise rulings even when (indeed, especially when) consequentialist and legalist justices were at odds. Compromise and negotiation – often led and guided by the Court's intellectual leader (*decano*) – is evident from the transcripts of the STF's deliberations on several cases under study here (e.g., the FGTS case, discussed later).[33] Also, the STF's tradition of procedural continuity helped it to stave off any pressures that elected leaders might have placed on it to cut procedural corners in order to issue fewer or weaker challenges.

The STF's institutional cohesion – in particular its operational and jurisprudential consistency – also affected the elected branches' behavior toward the Court. For instance, as mentioned previously, on several occasions just in connection with the cases under study, elected leaders methodically corrected flaws the Court had highlighted when it declared one of their policies unconstitutional. This would have made little sense unless those leaders were confident that doing so would make it more likely the Court would uphold the revised policy if it were challenged in the judiciary – confidence the Court's consistency generated. Similarly, the elected branches occasionally extended

[31] The general *impression* of elected-branch compliance with STF decisions was at least as important for the Court's legitimacy as the actual level of compliance. Most expert interview respondents assured me that the STF's rulings were consistently followed (for instance, EC-03; EC-13; EG-06, CSE-09, CSE-10), although some acknowledged that the government often appealed or otherwise resisted, delayed, or negotiated compliance (e.g., EC-28; EC-31; EC-36).

[32] Thirteen of the twenty-three entries in Web Appendix 4.5 that reflect politicians' views (generally statements to the press) were wholly supportive of the high court and judiciary (with the most positive assessments articulated at the beginning of the time period); the views of the Court held by politicians and government personnel interviewed in connection with this project were also generally positive (e.g., EC-02; EC-13; EC-26; EC-28) or neutral (EC-05).

[33] These transcripts include all conversation that occurs when the STF deliberates *en banc* as well as the justices' actual votes on cases.

an award the STF had stipulated for plaintiffs in a particular concrete review case to *everyone* in a similar situation, expecting the consistent Court would continue to issue the same decision on all like cases.[34] More generally, elected leaders could expect that the STF's institutional cohesion would make it a formidable enemy if they confronted it with noncompliance on a case of crucial political importance, given the damage that such noncompliance would do to the Court's carefully maintained image (EC-32). The Court certainly possessed sufficient ammunition to retaliate strongly. At practically any point throughout the posttransition period, the STF held an immense range of cases worth billions of *reais* (or the currency of the day) to the government. Moreover, an important subset of these were "macro-cases" involving thousands or tens of thousands of identical individual cases, on which the consistent Court could be expected to quickly hand down the same ruling.[35] Thus for elected leaders, the most prudent course of action was to comply with the Court's rulings on politically crucial cases – albeit slowly or incompletely in view of their economic and fiscal constraints. In this way the STF's statesman character encouraged a steady pattern of high court–elected branch accommodation in the economic policy realm.

As discussed in the previous chapters, the Court character thesis builds on strategic accounts of interbranch relations, the main strands of which focus on the effects that political divisions, and support structures for courts or public opinion about their rulings, have on interactions between justices and elected leaders. As Chapter 5 suggested, Epstein et al.'s (2001) examination of the Russian Constitutional Court is a good example of the first strand. They posit that a Constitutional Court can identify the degree of consensus that exists among elected leaders in particular issue areas and will only decide cases (weakly endorsing policy) concerning issues on which there is consensus among the president, the upper house, and the lower house of congress. One observable implication of this theory is that Courts should decide few politically salient cases (and should weakly endorse the exercise of government authority when they do so) under conditions of divided government. Epstein et al. also predict that Courts will issue increasingly challenging rulings in a growing range of policy arenas over time, with consistent compliance. By contrast, Ginsburg (2003) argues that courts issue more important decisions (with which elected branches comply) in countries with fragmented party systems because it is more difficult for politicians in such fragmented regimes to coordinate action against the Court.

As in Argentina, political divisions do not seem to matter to interbranch relations in Brazil in the ways scholars have suggested. The STF challenged

[34] This occurred in the case concerning a 147.06 percent pension benefits adjustment (decided in 1992), the case about a 28.86 percent salary increase (decided in 1998), and the *FGTS* case (decided in 2000) discussed later.

[35] To name one beyond those mentioned in the present study, the STF received thousands of repeat cases regarding inflation readjustment of home mortgages under the 1990 Collor Plan, with an estimated potential cost to the state of 87 billion *reais* (Taylor 2004a: 132).

just as often as it endorsed the exercise of government power when deciding the twenty cases under study,[36] achieving partial or significant compliance despite indisputably divided government and the perpetually fragmented nature of Brazil's party system.[37] Instead, the Court character thesis suggests that political divisions affect *previous* choices – elected leaders' politics of Court crafting – thereby shaping Court character and, through it, interbranch relations.[38] The extraordinary fragmentation of Brazil's party system meant that every postauthoritarian president who had the opportunity to appoint STF justices needed to cobble together senate majorities to confirm them, complicating the appointment of justices with weak qualifications or strong ties to their appointer – that is – encouraging the professionalization (and thereby the statesman character) of the Court.

As Chapter 5 also discussed, other strategic accounts argue that Court-*society* relations – rather than simply intragovernment dynamics – affect interactions between justices and elected leaders. Some analysts point to the importance of public support for particular court decisions, suggesting that Courts will challenge the exercise of government power, and elected leaders will feel compelled to comply, when justices anticipate public support for a challenging decision (e.g., Staton 2004). Other scholars assert that courts with a loyal constituent base are more likely to challenge elected leaders more vigorously and to have their rulings obeyed (e.g., Vanberg 1998, 2001; Carrubba and Van Winkle 2000). As in Argentina, public support for particular judicial rulings does not seem to drive interbranch relations in Brazil. As column four of Table 6.2 demonstrates, the STF assumed a support-building approach to decision making (that is, public opinion about a case was a primary consideration in its decision-making calculus) when ruling on only one case under study.

The presence of a loyal constituent base for the high court, by contrast, *is* important to interbranch interactions in Brazil – though in a different way than posited in existing strategic accounts. As discussed in Chapter 4 (and Web Appendix 4.5), public support for the STF or the judiciary was positive prior to 1995 and slightly weaker in the next decade, and the views of the legal community reflected those of the public. In other words, the Court had a loyal constituent base among the population and legal community that grew a bit less loyal over time. On that basis, existing strategic accounts would predict

36 As suggested previously, given the case selection technique employed here (see Appendix 1.1), there is reason to believe that the sample of cases under study is representative of the broader population of politically important cases the STF received during the time period of interest.

37 The STF's treatment of constitutional amendments in particular runs counter to Epstein et al.'s (2001) account. Often initiated by the president, amendments must be passed by 60 percent of each house of congress in two rounds of voting, suggesting considerable governmental consensus around such amendments. Yet the STF declared constitutional amendments *unconstitutional* on several occasions during the first twenty posttransition years (including on a case analyzed here, ADIn 1946 decided in 1999).

38 Chapter 4 (together with Web Appendix 4.4) describe Court crafting in Brazil.

more challenging rulings and stronger compliance in the late 1980s and early 1990s, and fewer challenging rulings and weaker compliance in the second postauthoritarian decade. The data only partially bear out this prediction: The STF was no more assertive during the first postauthoritarian decade than during the second, although elected leaders did tend to comply somewhat more completely in the first period.

Yet the Court character thesis posits that the STF's legitimacy (an important element of its character) affected the direction and intensity of its rulings, and the *approaches* to decision making it adopted, as well as elected leaders' responses to its challenging rulings, in a different way. The STF's multifaceted legitimacy with the public, the legal community, and politicians (and its desire to maintain legitimacy with each) not only encouraged it to alternate between endorsing and challenging the exercise of government power throughout the postauthoritarian period, but also to vary its approach to decision making (see again column four of Table 6.2), adopting a principled approach at some points in a nod to the legal community, and a pragmatic approach at other points in solidarity with politicians. Indeed, in only one ruling under study did the STF *not* adopt one or both of these approaches to decision making. Moreover, we see the Court adopting a principled approach five times as often in the second postauthoritarian decade compared with the first, likely at least in part in a bid to shore up flagging support from the legal community. And to recapitulate the discussion at the beginning of this section, the Court's legitimacy both encouraged elected branch compliance with its rulings and discouraged retaliation. In sum, the Court character thesis integrates and extends strategic accounts of interbranch relations, showing how Court character conditions the way in which justices and elected leaders respond to political impulses as they interact with each other.

6.4. CASE STUDIES

This section presents case studies of two episodes of STF-elected branch interaction during Brazil's first twenty postauthoritarian years, one concerning the imposition of a tax on financial transactions (the IPMF and CPMF cases), and the second concerning adjustments made to accounts in an employment security fund through the introduction of several economic stabilization programs (the FGTS case). The cases were chosen from among the twenty considered here because they clearly show how the STF's statesman character contributed to different types of interbranch accommodation (over-time accommodation in the first case study and accommodation in the context of a single case in the second) throughout the time period under study (the cases were decided in 1993, 1996, and 2000), and across different types of economic policy. Further, the STF challenged (rather than endorsed) the exercise of government power in each case, making accommodation less likely by definition, and making these cases a harder test of the Court character thesis.

Over-Time Accommodation: The IPMF and CPMF Tax Cases[39]

In December 1992, Brazil's first directly elected president in more than twenty-five years, Fernando Collor, became the first president in the country's history to be impeached by congress on charges of corruption. His embattled vice-president Itamar Franco, who assumed the reins of power when Collor resigned, inherited a country on the verge of economic collapse: hyperinflation loomed and fiscal crisis swirled. Even though leaders had attempted to enhance the country's capacity to collect taxes repeatedly since 1988, efforts at large-scale tax reform had been frustrated by politicians' inability to agree on the mechanics of reform (EC-45).

On March 17, 1993, Congress finally passed Constitutional Amendment No. 3, a "mini fiscal reform" that included thirty-three alterations to the tax system (Favetti 2003: 134). In particular, the amendment called for the creation of a Provisional Tax on Financial Transactions (*Imposto Provisório sobre Movimentação Financeira*, IPMF), which Congress implemented via the Rita Camata Law (Complementary Law 77) on July 13, 1993. A broad-based tax to be levied on individuals, private entities, as well as states and municipalities, the IPMF imposed a charge of 0.25 percent on all financial transactions (above a certain minimum) involving debits on bank accounts. Financial institutions were to collect the tax and remit lump sums to the government without detailing the individual transactions that together produced those sums (EC-46, EC-47). The tax began to be collected on August 26, 1993, and was to extend through December 31, 1994 (Vilhena Vieira 2002: 145; Favetti 2003: 118).

Even though Brazil's tax burden remained relatively low in 1993, the IPMF tax was quite unpopular. Companies complained that its cumulative nature would raise the prices of their products and make them uncompetitive (CSE-10), and financial institutions predicted that the tax would lead individuals and businesses to stop depositing money in banks. Moreover, even though Complementary Law 77 stipulated that the tax authorities *would not* have access to individualized information, many (especially those in Brazil's immense informal sector) worried that the IPMF tax was a government strategy to uncover tax evasion (EC-11; EC-45; EC-46; EC-47).[40] Consequently, thousands filed suits questioning the constitutionality of the tax (Favetti 2003: 119).

[39] ADIn 926, *Governors of the states of Paraná, Santa Catarina, Mato Grosso do Sul, Tocantins, and Mato Grosso v. President of the Republic and Congress*, distributed August 25, 1993, injunction September 1, 1993, decided March 2, 1994; ADIn 939, *National Confederation of Commerce Workers (CNTC) v. President of the Republic and Congress*, distributed September 8, 1993, injunction September 15, 1993, final decision December 15, 1993; ADIn 1947, *National Confederation of Health Workers (CNTS) v. Congress*, distributed September 2, 1996, injunction September 9, 1996, decision December 20, 2003.

[40] Brazilians feared that if authorities knew how much money people and companies were moving, they could estimate how much they should be paying in taxes and compare that figure with actual tax receipts. A former government official confirmed in an interview that evaluating tax evasion was, in fact, one motivation for imposing the IPMF tax (EC-47).

In August 1993 – just as Brazil was gearing up for a broad process of constitutional reform (the *Congresso Revisor*)[41] and the very month in which the IPMF began to be collected – the governors of five states jointly filed the first ADIn questioning the tax (ADIn 926, with an injunction request). The states alleged that Article 2, clause 2 of the amendment, which stated that several articles of the 1988 Constitution would not apply to the amendment,[42] violated those very articles (including Article 150, part III, letter "b," which establishes that taxes cannot be collected in the same fiscal year in which they are legislated ["anteriority"], and Article 150, part VI, which establishes that the union, states, and municipalities cannot tax each other ["reciprocal immunity"]), as well as Articles 1, 28, and 60, concerning federalism.

The STF wasted no time, issuing a unanimous injunction a week after the case was filed (September 1, 1993) suspending the questioned paragraph of the amendment – and the levying of the tax on states and municipalities – until the Court could make a final ruling on the tax's constitutionality. In the injunction, the STF adopted part of the states' reasoning: by authorizing violation of the constitutional principle of "reciprocal taxation immunity" among federal, state, and municipal government, the amendment had undermined an essential element of Brazilian federalism, which the constitution establishes as an unamendable principle. The injunction was significant both because it partially suspended the imposition of a critical tax,[43] and because it represented the first time the STF ruled on the constitutionality of a constitutional amendment.[44] In the context of a high-profile constitutional amendment process, the STF took pains to emphasize and justify its ability to evaluate the constitutionality of constitutional amendments, and to declare them unconstitutional in an injunction.

A week later (September 8, 1993), the National Confederation of Business Workers (*Confederação Nacional dos Trabalhadores do Comércio*, CNTC) filed ADIn 939 (again with an injunction petition) questioning the constitutionality of both Constitutional Amendment No. 3 and Complementary Law 77.

[41] The 1988 Constitution called on congress to convene a special unicameral session in 1993 during which the constitution could be amended by an absolute majority of the full congress (a lower threshold than amendment normally requires). The *Congresso Revisor* was installed in October 1993, officially convened in March 1994, and completed in May 1994 (Power 2000: 21). While some 30,000 amendments were proposed, only six were adopted.

[42] Indeed, Congress imposed the reform by constitutional amendment in part in hopes of circumventing particular constitutional prohibitions (Arantes and Kerche 2003: 212); the inclusion of Article 2, clause 2 in the amendment made transparent precisely which constitutional clauses it violated (Vilhena Vieira 2002: 144).

[43] The tax authorities (*Receita Federal*) suggested that the exemption of states and municipalities from paying the tax would imply a loss of US$ 160 million to 180 million out of the US$ 7.4 billion in tax revenues the IPMF would generate annually (*O Estado de São Paulo*, August 26, 1993, "Estados vão ao Supremo contra o IPMF; Ações não reduzem tributo, diz Receita"; NP 02-E-76).

[44] The STF can declare a constitutional amendment unconstitutional only if it violates a fundamental constitutional principle understood not to be amendable (*cláusula pétrea*).

As in the ADIn filed by the states, the CNTC alleged that the amendment and law violated the constitutional principle of anteriority in taxes (i.e., freedom from paying taxes in the same year they were imposed), which it suggested was a fundamental constitutional principle not open to amendment. The CNTC also alleged that the amendment violated the principle of reciprocal immunity in taxation, constitutional prohibitions against taxes being cumulative, and double taxation (Article 154, part I). On September 15, the STF issued another injunction, this time suspending Article 2 of the amendment *and* all of Complementary Law 77, mandating a complete halt to the tax pending a decision on the merits. The STF dismissed the CNTC's request that it order the government to return the IPMF taxes that it had paid, indicating that the issue of a tax refund would have to be raised in a separate case.

The government immediately complied with the letter of the ruling, suspending the IPMF tax until January 1994.[45] Compliance was clearly expensive: Newspaper headlines over the next few days quoted government officials' allusions to the budget cuts that would be necessary to compensate for the lost revenue, which they estimated at between US$ 1.6 billion and 2.4 billion.[46] Further, the government's compliance clearly did not spring from a lack of commitment to levying the tax. Indeed, over the next months, as the Franco administration developed and presented to congress a new stabilization plan (the *Real* plan, brainchild of finance minister and future president Fernando Henrique Cardoso), it repeatedly insisted that its ability to levy a tax on financial transactions was crucial to the plan's success (NP 02–507).

The STF considered the merits of ADIn 939 (filed by the CNTC) three months after receiving it, on December 15, 1993.[47] In a badly divided (six-five) decision, the Court ruled that the IPMF *could* be imposed in 1994, but that collection of the tax in 1993 had been unconstitutional as Constitutional Amendment No. 3 violated the constitutional principle prohibiting anteriority of taxation. It also indicated that states and municipalities – as well as temples, political parties, unions, and nonprofit educational and social assistance organizations (explicitly listed in Article 150, part VI) – were exempt from the tax (as the amendment violated the constitutional principle of reciprocal immunity) (Vilhena Vieira 2002: 183; Sepúlveda Pertence 2001).[48]

In line with the spirit of the ruling – although, importantly, not required by it – the government announced that it would emit a tax refund to all who

[45] Central Bank Circular 2.363 (September 22, 1993) suspended Complementary Law 77.

[46] *O Estado de São Paulo,* September 16, 1993, "Itamar manda cortar orçamento;" NP 02-E-80.

[47] This ruling resolved the IPMF question; the STF issued its final ruling on the states' ADIn (ADIn 926) on March 2, 1994, dismissing it as moot.

[48] Likewise, the justices declared unconstitutional Articles 3, 4, and 8 of Complementary Law 77 (for failing to exclude from the application of the IPMF tax the entities and issues that the 1988 Constitution, Article 150, part VI identified as exempt from taxation), as well as Article 28 (which permitted the application of the IPMF tax in the same year that it was legislated, 1993).

had paid the IPMF tax in 1993 (NP 02-E-80).[49] Yet logistical obstacles soon appeared. As noted previously, congress was able to pass the IPMF tax only after the tax authorities had agreed that banks would collect the tax revenues and remit them in lump sums each month. As such, the banks did not report, and thus state authorities could not ascertain, which clients had moved what sums of money. Consequently, the tax authorities did not know to whom they owed a refund, nor what size refunds they owed.[50] In order to calculate and award refunds, the tax authorities asked banks to provide them with lists of their customers and details of their financial transactions. Some banks insisted on obtaining the permission of their clients before submitting that information to the government, and some clients were unwilling to divulge it; other banks were completely unwilling to submit the information considering doing so an illegal breach of bank secrecy (*sigilio bancário*) (EC-46). Nonetheless, most banks eventually submitted lists containing information provided by their willing clients, and within the first few months of 1994, the government had returned US$ 70 million of the US$ 270 million wrongly collected in 1993.

This episode would not mark the end of interbranch interactions over the tax on financial transactions, however. The tax was collected in 1994 and 1995. Given the problems it created in the judiciary (and more generally), the tax was reestablished as a "contribution" (the *Contribuição Provisória sobre Movimentação Financeira*, CPMF) in 1996 (via Constitutional Amendment No. 12, promulgated August 18, 1996). Contributions are guided by different (and in some ways less strict) constitutional rules than those regulating taxes:[51] They can begin to be collected just ninety days after their legislation,[52] and can be levied on states and municipalities (whereas revenues do not have to be shared with them). Moreover, Congress clearly stipulated in the amendment that information regarding individual transactions *could* be released to the tax authorities.[53]

The STF's rulings on the IPMF cases offered significant guidance for how to establish the tax in a way that would minimize collisions with the constitution

[49] An *Instrução Normativa* of the tax authorities (IN/SRF n° 99, issued December 20, 1993) regulated the tax refund.

[50] Further, the government could not use the banks as an intermediary for the refund. According to the process for tax refunds outlined in the tax code, while the responsible entity is the bank, monies can only be refunded directly to the people and entities from whom they were collected (EC-46).

[51] Money collected via contributions must be earmarked for a certain purpose, however; the CPMF was the brainchild of then Minister of Health Adib Jatene, who wished the revenues collected to be applied to the health budget (EC-11); it is unclear whether this occurred (EC-46).

[52] In fact, the government overcompensated when designing the CPMF, stipulating that it would not begin to be collected until January 1997 – the year after it was introduced.

[53] A former head of the tax office explained to me that one of the laws regulating the CPMF indicated that even though the tax office could *collect* financial information at the individual/entity level, that information could not be used to impose other taxes or initiate an investigation. Nonetheless, having the information allowed the office to begin to evaluate informally the degree to which individuals and entities were engaging in tax evasion (EC-47).

and the courts – guidance leaders took into account as they reformulated the revenue source as a contribution (Teixeira 1997: 110, 116; Favetti 2003: 119). Nonetheless, the CPMF tax was questioned before the STF shortly after its passage. On August 30, 1996, the National Confederation of Health Workers (*Confederação Nacional dos Trabalhadores da Saude,* CNTS) filed ADIn 1497, contending that the new contribution violated individual rights, and since it had the same base as another tax, violated constitutional prohibitions against cumulative taxation (1988 Constitution, Articles 60 and 154). The Court ruled on the case just ten days later, dismissing the CNTS's request for an injunction and thus tacitly endorsing the policy.[54]

The STF and elected leaders' interactions over taxing financial transactions demonstrated over-time accommodation. By declaring only certain parts of the IPMF tax unconstitutional and ultimately approving its imposition in 1994, the STF's rulings served to accommodate elected leaders' interests. Yet importantly, the rulings were not a "victory" for the government as some at the time suggested (e.g., NP 02–513): The STF notified elected authorities that not even by constitutional amendment (which requires congressional supermajorities) could they collect a tax in the same year it was legislated or levy taxes on states and municipalities. Moreover, the STF established that *it* would be the institution with the final say over constitutional amendments (NP 02–432). The government's response – suspending the tax immediately after the Court's injunction in September 1993 and refunding as much of the erroneously collected revenue as it could following the Court's December ruling (NP 01–301) – accommodated the Court. And in the last round, the STF accommodated elected leaders by finally providing a tacit endorsement of the tax on financial transactions.[55]

How did the STF's statesman character contribute to interbranch accommodation? Given the justices' strong professional profiles (their knowledge of both politics and constitutional law), they recognized that the breadth and depth of the 1988 Constitution meant that major policy changes often had to be effected via constitutional amendment, and realized that the impending process of constitutional reform (the *Congresso Revisor*) could have profound implications.[56] In short, the Court understood the power to review amendments as crucial to its ability to safeguard the core of the constitution and facilitate governability (CSM-05; EC-50; Souza Cruz 2003). This conviction, combined with the relative consensus among the justices concerning the Court's central role (constitutional protection), spurred the image-conscious STF to use the IPMF cases as a vehicle to clarify that evaluating the constitutionality

[54] The Court issued a final decision on the case on October 30, 2003, ruling it moot.

[55] The STF would be called upon to rule on the CPMF yet again after Constitutional Amendment No. 21 of March 1999 increased the rate at which the tax was charged and extended it for an additional 36 months. In ADIn 2031, the Worker's Party alleged that several procedural and substantive aspects of the amendment were unconstitutional; while the STF suspended a small part of the amendment, it allowed the lion's share to stand.

[56] As one justice commented concerning the *Congresso Revisor* and the probability of future constitutional amendments, "Congress is capable of doing truly dangerous things" (CSM-01).

of constitutional amendments fell within its purview (Teixeira 1997; CSE-14; NP 02–432).[57] Likewise, the Court's desire to retain its multifaceted legitimacy – and consequentialist justices' concern with the government's ability to combat ongoing economic crisis (EC-45; NP 02–432) – encouraged accommodation. Moreover, elected leaders had corrected the problems the Court had indicated the IMPF suffered (CSE-18; EC-19), facilitating the tacit endorsement of the policy by the procedurally consistent Court.

For their part, elected leaders could be sure they would soon find themselves before the same Court again (given the institution's stability), recommending that they not antagonize it with noncompliance or institutional attack. Further, the Court's multifaceted legitimacy made noncompliance with its dictates politically costly, motivating elected leaders to suspend the tax after the Court's initial challenging injunction. Also, given the justices' strong professional backgrounds and the Court's procedural continuity, governing authorities could anticipate that its rulings on follow-up cases filed by those wishing to retrieve funds erroneously paid when the tax was unconstitutionally imposed in 1993 would be consonant with its ruling on the constitutionality of the IPMF itself (that is, they would likely require elected leaders to refund the taxes). Given that assurance, elected leaders simply preempted the process, accommodating the Court ex ante by offering to refund taxes paid – doing so to the best of their ability given the information they had. Their expectation of procedural continuity likewise led them to correct the IPMF's constitutional flaws (per the Court) when they levied its successor (the CPMF). In sum, the Court's statesman character contributed significantly to producing interbranch accommodation over the multiyear history of the tax on financial transactions.

What broader results did these interbranch interactions have? The STF cemented its power to review the constitutionality of constitutional amendments, reinforcing its role as constitutional guardian. Further, the Court's measured challenges to elected leaders' fiscal policy – which notified both the government and Brazilians that the Court was monitoring government behavior – and the government's strong efforts at compliance likely helped to entrench constitutionalism. Importantly, interbranch interactions over these cases did *not* seem to destabilize the economy or hamper economic reform. In other words, interbranch accommodation produced a balance between strengthening the rule of law and stabilizing the economy, two crucial imperatives of the posttransition era.

Accommodation in a Single Case: The FGTS Case[58]

In the 1980s and early 1990s, Brazil's leaders implemented a series of economic stabilization programs in an effort to address crisis and reduce inflation. Most

[57] In fact, the Court may have gone too far. Some experts questioned whether the IPMF tax really violated the fundamental constitutional principle of federalism as the Court said it did – and even suggested that the ruling itself might have violated fundamental principles (such as the separation of powers) (Vilhena Vieira 1999: 182; Arantes and Kerche 2003: 213; EC-46).

[58] RE 22855, *Caixa Econômica Federal (CEF) v. Ademar Gomes Mota and others*, distributed April 16, 1998, decision October 26, 2000.

of the plans prior to the *Real* Plan (which was implemented in a series of steps in 1994 and ultimately stabilized the economy) imposed wage and price freezes, and introduced a new inflation index and a new currency (among other measures). These new indices were problematic because they interrupted the periodic and automatic adjustments which had been written into many existing contracts in an effort to guard against the corrosive effects of inflation, and dictated incremental increases that were noticeably smaller than those stipulated in those contracts.[59] From an economic standpoint, interrupting these adjustments made sense as they perpetuated and in fact accelerated inflation (generating "inertial inflation"). From the standpoint of contract holders and workers in particular, however, interrupting the adjustments seemed to deprive them of the clearly stipulated percentage increase they should have received in the month a plan was imposed. Indeed, the transparency of automatic indexation made immediately evident and documentable the amount of money people had "lost" when prices and wages were frozen and a new index was imposed, encouraging many Brazilians to turn to the courts to claim those "lost" adjustments.

One set of cases concerned adjustments to individual accounts within an employment security fund known as the Length of Service Guarantee Fund (*Fundo de Garantía do Tempo do Serviço*, FGTS). Each month, certain employers deposited an amount equal to 8 percent of each of their employee's pay in a restricted bank account attached to the Fund (administered by the *Caixa Econômica Federal*, CEF, a large federal bank).[60] Workers could only access their accounts under exceptional circumstances (for instance, if they were fired without cause, retired, or were terminally ill). In the mid 1990s, workers who believed their FGTS accounts had been compromised by the stabilization programs of the 1980s and 1990s in the way just described began to file court cases claiming their right to a (re)adjustment of their accounts. Rulings issued in first and second instance courts were mixed in terms of whom they favored, but all were appealed, ultimately arriving to the STF. The high court dismissed thousands of these cases, indicating they did not involve a constitutional issue (EC-12; NP 04–38). However, in view of its repeated losses in lower-level courts and the ever-growing number of cases, the government eventually convinced the Court to begin to consider the cases (CSE-13).

The first case the STF decided on the issue was RE 226855, filed by ten workers against the CEF (although the national government included itself as a defendant) (NP 04–37). The plaintiffs, asserting that their relationship with the CEF was contractual, claimed that the adjustments made to their accounts via the application of indices associated with five economic plans were illegal (as they violated existing contracts) and unconstitutional (as they violated

[59] This mechanism of automatic indexation or "monetary adjustment" (*correção monetária*) was created in the 1960s as a palliative for (or insurance against) inflation (EC-06). For example, an employment contract might indicate that a worker would receive X *cruzeiros* (or the currency of the day) in the first month of employment, X + the percentage of X stipulated in the relevant inflation index (many indices existed simultaneously) in the second month, and so on.

[60] All private sector workers and civil servants involved in labor relationships regulated by Brazil's main labor law had interest-bearing (3 percent) accounts in the fund.

property rights and other constitutional guarantees).[61] The plaintiffs demanded (1) that the adjustments made to their accounts when the plans were introduced be recalculated according to the index originally stipulated in their FGTS contract (the IPC [*Índice precios consumidor*], akin to the Consumer Price Index), and (2) that they be paid the difference between the adjustment made on the basis of the new index introduced with each economic plan, and the adjustment that applying the IPC would have awarded them. The first instance court ruled *against* the workers on all counts, finding that the plans had not violated their vested rights. The appeals court (Federal Regional Tribunal of the Fourth Region, *Tribunal Regional Federal*, TRF), however, ruled that FGTS accounts active at the time of the introduction of all five economic plans should be adjusted according to the IPC announced just following their introduction.[62] The CEF appealed the TRF's ruling to the STF, and the case reached the high court in February 1998.

By early 1998, the high court had accrued thousands of cases addressing the extraordinarily controversial issue (beyond those it had already dismissed), and continued to receive more cases – literally by the truck-load – on a daily basis (CSM-02). Those cases were distributed to all of the justices, making each acutely aware of the magnitude of the problem.[63] In order to develop a solution, Justices Galvão and Moreira Alves (the latter being the Court's senior member or *decano*) made a deal. Separately and without consultation, each would write an opinion on one of the FGTS cases the Court had received (ultimately settling on RE 226855, just described). Then, they would present the two opinions to the full Court, asking the rest of the justices to decide which of the two solutions should be the model for all of the other cases regarding FGTS accounts (CSM-02).

As the two justices studied the test case, pressure on the Court rose to a fever pitch.[64] Government spokespersons and newspaper editorials repeatedly warned of the dire economic consequences of rulings in favor of workers on all such cases. Referring to the cases as the "largest of all time" in aggregate financial terms, the government suggested that adjusting all accounts for all of the economic plans questioned in the cases would cost the state between

[61] The five economic plans were the Funaro Plan (March 1986), the Bresser Plan (July 1987), the *Verão* (Summer) Plan (February 1989), Collor Plan I (May 1990), and Collor Plan II (March 1991). A justice suggested that the FGTS case was chosen as the lead case in part because it included almost all of the economic plans being questioned in these types of cases, giving the Court the opportunity to set its jurisprudence with regard to each plan in one ruling (CSM-02).

[62] Specifically, the TRF called for accounts active in March 1986 to be readjusted according the April 1986 IPC; for accounts active in July 1987 to be adjusted by 8.04 percent; for accounts active in January 1989 to be adjusted 20.37 percent; for accounts active in April 1990 to be adjusted by 44.8 percent; and for accounts active in March 1991 to be adjusted by 7 percent.

[63] As one justice joked, "I returned to my chambers at one point and found them crammed with cases, stacked from floor to ceiling, and I asked, 'has someone converted my chambers into a depository?'" (CSM-02).

[64] The large daily newspaper O *Estado de São Paulo* ran more than 100 articles on the STF's consideration of the case.

R$ 50 billion and R$ 70 billion (NP 04–37; NP 04-E-49).[65] Further, certain cabinet ministers paid visits to the high court (NP 04–97) to "educate" the justices about the economic havoc a decision in favor of the workers would wreak (EC-16; CSE-05).[66] Judicial and economic experts of all stripes filed briefs with the Court, and workers mobilized to pressure for a positive ruling, filling the plaza in front of the STF on more than one occasion.[67]

By the time the STF initiated deliberations on RE 226855 on April 12, 2000, some 600,000 cases regarding FGTS accounts involving millions of workers (many of the cases were collective) were being heard at various levels of the judiciary, and the STF had before it 10,000 such cases (NP-04–36; NP 04–38; NP 04–97).[68] Given the Court's procedural continuity, the first item of business was whether it should consider the case at all, given that it had already dismissed without consideration thousands of similar cases. After an extended discussion the justices voted 7–4 to rule on the case (EC-12). Just over three months later, on August 31, 2000, the STF issued its landmark decision, in line with Justice Moreira Alves's compromise vote. The Court dismissed without consideration the portion of the state's appeal having to do with adjustments made in January 1989 (following the introduction of the *Verão* Plan) and April 1990 (following the introduction of Collor Plan I) – meaning that the TRF's decision *awarding* adjustments to FGTS accounts active in those months would stand.[69] With regard to the three other economic plans in question, the Court adopted the CEF's argumentation. Understanding FGTS accounts to result from and be regulated by law (rather than being contractual in nature), the Court applied its settled jurisprudence, which holds that there are no vested rights to particular legal regimes (as such regimes can be modified at the will of the legislature).[70] In sum, the Court called on elected leaders to adjust the workers' FGTS accounts to compensate for losses generated by the imposition of two of the five economic stabilization plans involved in the case.

[65] In response to this "media terrorism," attorneys representing workers repeatedly questioned the government's estimations of the potential monetary damage of decisions against the state on the FGTS cases. Experts suggested that it was extremely difficult to calculate how much the various decisions the Court might issue would cost the government (EC-12, EC-16).

[66] The Brazilian Bar Association eventually strongly denounced the attorney general for repeatedly escorting the ministers of economy and treasury to speak with the justices (EC-16).

[67] In stark contrast to the protests in the plaza in front of the Argentine CSJN in 2001 and 2002, however, these demonstrations were not *against* the high court, but rather *for* workers' rights.

[68] The number of FGTS accounts involved in judicial challenges would eventually reach 15 million (EC-06; EC-12; EC-18; CSE-24).

[69] The exact percentage adjustments to be applied were eventually determined by the Supreme Tribunal of Justice: Accounts active in January 1989 would be adjusted by 16.64 percent; accounts active in April 1990 would be adjusted by 44.8 percent (NP 04-E-57).

[70] The Bresser, Collor I, and Collor II plans had all been announced in the middle of a month before account holders had "earned" the entire adjustment for that month; without a vested right to the inflation index stipulated in their FGTS contract, they had no right to an adjustment beyond the one stipulated by the plans (CSE-05).

The STF's ruling held only for the ten workers who had filed the case. Nonetheless, in view of the Court's general procedural and juridical consistency (and particularly given that it had already engaged in uncharacteristic wavering with respect to these cases), it was clear that the same ruling would ultimately, and potentially quite quickly, be handed down on every similar case.[71] Further, the STF's ruling on RE 226855 was likely to encourage workers to file cases and, if they lost in lower courts, to appeal. Yet if the owners of the 20 million to 30 million FGTS accounts eligible for the same adjustments rushed to file cases, the judiciary would be paralyzed (implying yet another expense for the government – hiring additional judges and government functionaries) (EC-18; EC-25; NP 04-E-73). Consequently, on September 22, 2000, the Cardoso administration announced that adjustments for losses FGTS accounts incurred when the *Verão* and Collor I Plans were introduced would be extended to *everyone* who had possessed an FGTS account on the relevant dates, irrespective of whether they had filed a case claiming the payment and despite estimates that adjusting all FGTS accounts per the STF's ruling would cost the state R$ 38.9 billion (approximately 4 percent of GDP) (Furtado ND; NP 04-E-49).[72]

Yet obstacles quickly appeared. The most immediate was that it was not financially feasible for the money for the adjustments to be drawn from the fund itself as it contained only between R$ 7 billion and R$ 9 billion in liquid resources (NP 04-E-52; NP 04-E-130).[73] In early November 2000, then, the government initiated negotiations with key unions and business representatives to develop a strategy for paying account holders while keeping the fund active and liquid. Negotiations moved slowly, however, and the chasm between the intentions of the government (that the unions propose a solution and that the fund be recapitalized with as little government involvement as possible) and the pretensions of the unions (that the government foot the entire bill immediately) was evident from the beginning (NP 04-E-130; NP 04–155; NP 04–159). Nonetheless, after nine months – considered by some the most extensive government-union negotiations in Brazilian history (EC-25) – an agreement, codified in Complementary Law 110 of June 29, 2001, was reached.

[71] Per the STF's internal rules, the thousands of like cases the Court held could be decided by individual justices (as long as their rulings aligned with the Court's jurisprudence); in the event, many of those additional cases were quickly resolved with the same formula applied to each.

[72] Estimating the economic consequences of the ruling was complicated in part because there were 200 million active and inactive FGTS accounts between 1989 and 1990, making identifying which were to be adjusted difficult (NP 04-E-131). Some experts believed the adjustments the Court required implied a smaller financial burden on the state than those it had denied (EC-12; EC-37; EC-41; CSE-05); in contrast, the lawyer for the workers who filed the test case estimated that his clients won 69 percent of the total money they hoped to be awarded (EC-16).

[73] Since workers could only access their FGTS accounts under emergency conditions, only a small part of the fund was kept liquid at any point in time. The government invested the balance of the monies, generally in infrastructure and social works projects (EC-03; EC-06). Further, adjusting individual accounts without adjusting the terms of the contracts of those projects would place the fund in disequilibrium (NP 04–36).

The law stipulated several schemes for crediting those who held FGTS accounts in 1989 and 1990. The general logic was that those who were owed comparatively more money would have their reimbursement discounted and would be reimbursed over a longer period of time, whereas those who were owed the least would receive full payment immediately.[74] Account holders had a choice between taking the government's deal or continuing with their judicial suits (or initiating a suit),[75] and the government encouraged them to take the deal (CSE-23). Shifting the resolution of the cases out of the judicial arena reduced the amount the state would have to reimburse and allowed it to avoid paying the legal fees associated with losing cases in court (EC-12). Nonetheless, the holders of approximately 1.5 million accounts (in particular, larger accounts) continued to pursue their court cases (EC-37).[76] In the end, the government fully complied with the law (EC-05; EC-06; EC-11; EC-16; CSE-05) and paid when it lost the remaining judicial disputes (EC-12; EC-16), ultimately withdrawing from many such cases so as not to drag out the appeals process (NP 04-E-229).[77] In sum, the high court's "split-the-difference" ruling accommodated the elected branches, and the state negotiated a compliance scheme that accommodated the Court (while maintaining fiscal discipline).

How did the high court's statesman character contribute to this outcome? First, the ruling reflected the justices' strong professional backgrounds, and the Court's legalist/consequentialist divide in particular. Legalist justices (who often had the strongest judicial backgrounds) saw a clear constitutional violation to be redressed; indeed, all four dissenting justices had extensive experience in the judiciary or the Office of the Public Prosecutor. Yet in the wake of the late 1990s Russian and Asian financial crises and after seven hard-fought years of fiscal discipline by elected leaders, consequentialists were reluctant to issue a decision that would impose a significant fiscal burden on the state (particularly since the case resulted from poor decisions made by *previous* leaders) (CSM-02; CSM-03; EC-09; EC-12; EC-16; EC-30; EC-42; CSE-14); accordingly, justices with the most experience in government formed part of the six-justice majority.

Further, the Court's strong institutional cohesion – its essentially collegial nature and, very importantly, the leadership of *decano* Moreira Alves – allowed

[74] Estimates suggested that 80 percent of account holders held only 23 percent of the resources, meaning that the vast majority of account holders were owed less money (NP 04-E-152).

[75] In late September 2000 the government issued MP 1984–22, which changed the statute of limitations for filing cases regarding adjustments to FGTS accounts from 30 years to five, in hopes of preventing the filing of additional cases, but additional cases continued to be filed.

[76] Holders of large FGTS accounts knew they would ultimately win their court cases, and preferred to thereby be awarded the full adjustment (at least with respect to the *Verão* and Collor I Plans) rather than receiving the discounted adjustment contemplated in the agreement. Moreover, those who signed the agreement lost the interest on the adjustments, which was awarded to account holders in judicial rulings.

[77] To keep the fund afloat while FGTS accounts were being credited, all companies that contributed to the fund were required to contribute an additional 0.5 percent monthly (over the total wage bill) and to contribute 10 percent of the salary of each worker they fired (NP 04-E-190).

the Court to overcome internal disagreement and arrive at its compromise solution. The presence of consequentialist justices also facilitated the interbranch negotiation that, according to one well-connected legal scholar, was crucial to the Court resisting pressure from opposition parties and workers and issuing its compromise solution (EC-37). The Court's interest in maintaining legitimacy with both the legal and political communities also encouraged a middle-of-the-road ruling (EC-30).

The STF's character likewise shaped the way elected leaders interacted with the Court. Given that they were knee-deep in the intricate process of state reform (and given the leanings of some clauses of the 1988 Constitution), leaders knew the FGTS case would not be the last constitutional controversy that would bring them before the high court. Given the STF's stability, it was likely they would face the same eleven justices in their next meeting. In view of the STF's procedural and jurisprudential continuity, elected authorities could anticipate that the Court would continue to issue the same compromise ruling on the tens of thousands of cases concerning the FGTS that were making their way through the judiciary. And given the STF's legitimacy, the political cost of failing to comply would be significant. Consequently, it was in their interest to follow the Court's mandate as best they could by devising a compromise plan that attenuated the fiscal impact of compliance.

The Court's compromise ruling likely produced both relief and consternation among the tens of thousands of FGTS account holders who felt the Brazilian state had defrauded them. Yet it was precisely such accommodation – equally reflected in elected leaders' response to the Court's ruling – that allowed interbranch interactions in Brazil to produce more positive effects than they generated in Argentina. The episode left little doubt that judicial and political leaders took seriously the Court and the constitutional guardian role it played, as well as the fiscal constraints under which the government was operating. As with interbranch interactions around the IPMF/CPMF cases then – and in large part due to the character of the Court – justices' and elected leaders' mutually accommodating actions kept the rule of law and economic stability in balance.

6.5. CONCLUSIONS AND COMPARISONS

Understanding the ways in which high courts and elected leaders interact over politically crucial cases offers a window on the roles that Courts play as judicial power expands and courts become more important political actors. Chapters 5 and 6 deployed an integrated analytic framework combining study of high-court decision making and elected branch behavior to identify and account for the patterns of interbranch interaction over economic governance that emerged in Argentina and Brazil during the first twenty years after the transition to democracy. The structured qualitative analysis of an intermediate-N set of cases in each context (concerning monetary policy, taxes, privatizations, salaries, and pensions) found that the trajectory of interbranch interactions in Argentina was very different from that in Brazil.

Interbranch interactions were more erratic in Argentina: a combined pattern emerged in which Court submission to elected leaders was periodically interrupted by episodes of interbranch confrontation. In Brazil, by contrast, interbranch interactions followed a more stable pattern of accommodation. The STF was selectively assertive, like its Argentine counterpart, but somewhat more centrist and evenhanded – less cautious than the Argentine CSJN in the Court submission pattern and more cautious than the CSJN in a confrontation pattern. The STF challenged the exercise of government power with the same frequency as it endorsed it, and most often adopted a *pragmatic* approach to decision making (in which the potential political and economic consequences of its rulings weighed heavily). The Court's middle-of-the-road weaker endorsements and challenges, as well as its alternation between strong challenges and strong endorsements (or strong challenges of particular policies followed by weaker challenges or endorsements of similar policies), served to accommodate elected leaders. And those leaders consistently complied with the Court's challenging rulings (thereby accommodating the Court), but did so slowly and at times incompletely, given the economic and fiscal constraints under which they operated.

Brazil and Argentina are certainly not unique with regard to the increasing frequency and importance of interactions between high courts and elected leaders. Since the mid-1980s, postauthoritarian leaders high Courts in many Latin American polities have increasingly tangled over critical political issues, interacting in different ways. What causes high courts' and elected leaders' interactions over such conflicts to follow particular patterns? The institutional account advanced here, the Court character thesis, extends strategic accounts that can overlook the historical institutional foundations of interbranch relations. I argue that a high court's character shapes the way that it decides cases of crucial political significance and the way that elected leaders respond to its rulings. Put another way, the comparatively stable informal institutional features that compose a Court's character condition the choices justices and elected leaders make as they react to their environment and each other when politics are judicialized, channeling their interactions into relatively enduring patterns. Court character is relatively persistent despite being composed of *informal* features because it has its roots in a country's traditional politics of Court crafting (informal practices themselves that are shaped by partisan politics and formal rules), in inertial public and professional opinion (i.e., a Court's perceived legitimacy), and in entrenched internal Court practices (related to its institutional cohesion). Of course, Court character does not completely explain the nature of interbranch interactions: contextual factors – economic crisis, societal upheaval, and political divisions – all matter to the way elected leaders and Courts interact. But the *way* such factors affect those interactions, I argue, is mediated by Court character.

The very different nature of the Argentine and Brazilian high courts, then, played an important role in producing the contrasting patterns of interbranch interaction over politically crucial cases in the two countries. Argentine leaders' politicization of the CSJN produced a political Court in the postauthoritarian period, leading to interbranch interactions marked by Court submission and confrontation. Brazilian authorities, by contrast, professionalized the STF (as they had traditionally done), shying away from manipulating its size or composition and appointing justices with strong, varied professional backgrounds. This politics of Court crafting produced a statesman Court – a stable, professional institution with stronger perceived legitimacy and institutional cohesion. As this chapter has shown, the Court's statesman character, in turn, contributed to generating a stable pattern of interbranch accommodation around judicialized economic conflicts.

The STF's mix of consequentialist justices (most often those with recent experience in government) and legalist justices (those with more experience in the judiciary), in combination with its generally collegial character, led it to issue middle-of-the-road rulings (of weaker intensity) that neither sanctioned significant constitutional violations nor exacerbated crisis. The presence of the consequentialist justices also led the Court to hand down pragmatic rulings (often endorsements), and facilitated interbranch negotiation around crucial cases, both of which served to accommodate elected leaders. The strong presence of legalist justices plus the Court's legitimacy with the influential legal community (and its desire to retain that legitimacy) led it to issue strong challenges to the exercise of government power in some cases, however. Yet such challenges were often followed by less-challenging rulings (sponsored by consequentialists and designed at least in part to retain the Court's legitimacy with politicians). The result was over-time accommodation. With regard to elected leaders, it was clear that they would continue to appeal judicial challenges to their economic policies to the high court – *and* that defying the Court would be politically costly given its multifaceted support. It was also evident that completely failing to comply with its rulings – or even more dramatically, strongly retaliating against them it – would antagonize the statesman STF (rather than compelling it to back down, as strategic approaches often suggest and the effect noncompliance or manipulation might have had on a Court of a different character). And it was likewise apparent, given the Court's institutional coherence, that it could be a formidable enemy. Brazilian leaders thus sought to cooperate with the Court, obeying its rulings as they could.

In countries undergoing simultaneous legal and economic transformation, legal and economic imperatives can be at odds. Policies aimed at reforming the economy or addressing crisis may appear to violate the constitution, just as strict adhesion to constitutional limitations may seem to inhibit the implementation of key solutions to economic problems. Developing economic policy, then, requires elected leaders to balance legality and constitutionalism against economic stability and development. When their policies are challenged before high courts, justices engage in the same balancing act. And when Courts prioritize legality and constitutionalism over economic governance and strike down key policies, elected leaders must decide whether to comply with their dictates, thus reexperiencing their original quandary. The way in which justices and elected leaders resolve these interactive dilemmas over time – reflected in the patterns of interbranch interaction under study here – has important implications for the entrenchment of constitutionalism and for economic reform and governance. The present study suggests that in the postauthoritarian era, interbranch interactions in Argentina facilitated economic stabilization and reform but likely stunted the entrenchment of constitutionalism, while in Brazil high courts and elected leaders more effectively balanced the two imperatives. This book's conclusion explores these ideas in more detail.

7

Conclusions and Implications

7.1. INTRODUCTION

In September 1997 the Constitutional Chamber of the Costa Rican Supreme Court mandated the provision of free antiretroviral drugs to all AIDS patients in Costa Rica. By December 1998 over 400 AIDS patients had achieved free access to the medicines, and following the filing of additional law suits, access eventually became automatic (Wilson and Rodríguez-Cordero 2006: 339). In August 2000, the Mexican Supreme Court awarded congress the right to examine a government-controlled trust account from which it was alleged that President Zedillo (1994–2000) had illegally siphoned campaign funds. Zedillo immediately directed his secretary of finance and public credit to release the information (Staton 2002: 1, 2010: 1). And in Colombia in 2003, the Constitutional Court refused to act as a rubber stamp for President Alvaro Uribe's (2002–10) multifaceted political reform initiative, striking down several of its important aspects and fundamentally altering its contours.

As these examples and those discussed in this book suggest, in some Latin American countries today, high courts are more assertive with respect to elected leaders, and elected leaders are more willing to obey challenging high court rulings, than at any point in the region's history. Yet those polities continue to constitute a minority. In many other countries of the region – for instance, Peru, Venezuela, and Paraguay – high courts do not challenge the elected branches, or if they do, leaders do not consistently obey their dictates. Of course, these phenomena – and this variation – are part of a broader trend. Courts have become more involved in politics – if haltingly and unevenly – in many parts of the world in a "global expansion of judicial power" (Tate and Vallinder 1995) that has fostered the judicialization of politics. Courts have begun to make a difference to politics and society in contexts as diverse as India, Italy, South Africa, and Hungary, for instance, while remaining largely nonfunctioning or irrelevant in large swaths of Africa and Southeast Asia.

As Courts have emerged as politically relevant actors in some countries, the field of comparative judicial politics has blossomed.[1] Since the 1990s, students of comparative politics and public law have developed diverse theories addressing the fundamental questions that underlie these compelling dynamics: When and why do leaders empower courts? Under what conditions do courts challenge the exercise of government power? How do elected leaders react when courts challenge them – in the short and longer term? More broadly, what new roles are courts playing in politics and policy making, and what larger impact does the way in which high courts and elected leaders interact over crucial political issues have on democratic quality and stability, governance, and the rule of law?

This book contributes to the debates around these questions, advancing a new explanation for the patterns of interaction that emerge between Courts and elected leaders over critical political conflicts: the Court character thesis. Drawing on both rational choice and historical institutionalism, I argue that a high court's character – a set of relatively stable informal institutional features – shapes the way that it decides cases of crucial political significance and conditions the way elected leaders respond to its challenging decisions, leading to identifiable patterns of interbranch interaction. Court character contributes to producing comparatively enduring patterns of interaction between high courts and elected leaders because it is relatively stable itself, rooted in the politics of Court crafting that political authorities have traditionally employed, in slow-changing popular opinion, and in the Court's own institutional culture. Of course, many factors in the political context – constitutional reform, economic turmoil, regime instability – also affect interbranch interactions. But their effect on those interactions, I submit, is mediated by the character of the high court.

The book illustrated this account through an examination of interbranch struggles over economic governance in postauthoritarian Argentina and Brazil. Since the 1990s, many Latin American democracies – like developing democracies in other world regions – have been struggling to stabilize their economies and to introduce market-based policies. Simultaneously, efforts have been afoot to entrench the rule of law. Given the complexity and long-term importance of these processes, understanding how interactions between high courts and elected leaders contribute to or undermine them is crucial. This final chapter

[1] To name just a small subset of the comparative judicial politics literature, see Arantes (1997); Slaughter, Stone Sweet, and Weiler (1998); Larkins (1998); Klug (2000); Prillaman (2000); Schwartz (2000); Stone Sweet (2000); Couso (2002); Peerenboom (2002); Sadurski (2002); Shapiro and Stone Sweet (2002); Ginsburg (2003); Chavez (2004a): Hirschl (2004); Lasser (2004; 2009), Scribner (2004); Helmke (2005): Sieder, Schjolden, and Angell (2005); Vanberg (2005); Huneeus (2006); Rios-Figueroa (2006); Brinks (2007); Hilbink (2007); Moustafa (2007); Finkel (2008); Taylor (2008); Trochev (2008); Mate (2009); Simmons (2009); Staton (2010); Popova (2012).

reviews the book's main findings and lessons and explores how it speaks to broader debates in public law and comparative politics.

7.2. FINDINGS AND LESSONS

Argentina and Brazil, like many developing democracies, have been experiencing a dual transition *since* regime change in the mid-1980s. First, a halting and uneven legal transition has been in progress, entailing greater salience of rule of law issues, constitutional revision, increased rights consciousness among citizens and within civil society, the empowerment of courts, and the judicialization of politics. Second and more familiar to scholars of politics in developing democracies, these countries have also been undergoing an economic transition involving the abandonment of inward-looking state-led development models and the adoption of neoliberal economics. Sometimes these new market-oriented policies (or the way in which they were introduced) were legally or constitutionally questionable; often they were unpopular. In many contexts, due to the simultaneity of the legal and economic transitions, citizens, civil society, and the political opposition turned to courts to contest economic reform and crisis management policies. The interaction of the legal and economic transitions thereby induced a judicialization of economic governance.

When courts in certain Latin American contexts began to challenge elected leaders' crucial political projects, including their economic reform initiatives, those challenges could not be blithely dismissed (as they might have been in the past) as those same leaders had often promoted constitutional renewal, advocated rule of law entrenchment, and implemented judicial reform. Elected authorities in some polities thus developed a two-pronged approach to the courts that would help to address the judicialization of politics, and the judicialization of economic governance in particular. On the one hand, they centralized judicial power in the highest court (increasing its control over the judiciary, and using various means to move cases up the judicial hierarchy to the Court); on the other hand, they sought to craft a Court that would facilitate governance. Argentine and Brazilian leaders employed somewhat similar methods to centralize judicial power in their high courts. However, their Court crafting practices were quite different – despite their being equally motivated to craft cooperative Courts and despite formal appointment procedures in both countries delegating responsibility for appointments entirely to elected leaders. What influenced leaders' choices?

In both countries, a particular politics of Court crafting had emerged in the mid-twentieth century and become locked-in through repetition over the ensuing decades. In Argentina, executives had often proactively *politicized* the high court, particularly during the country's democratic moments, manipulating its size and composition repeatedly, and appointing justices with whom they had personal or political connections, even if some had weaker qualifications. While formal rules of judicial appointment and removal, in interaction with partisan politics, sometimes limited and sometimes facilitated elected leaders' ability to perpetuate politicization in the postauthoritarian period, politicization was the dominant practice. That politicization produced a *political* Court – a less stable, less professional institution with weaker legitimacy among citizens and within the legal community and weaker institutional cohesion. Brazilian leaders, by contrast, had generally engaged in high court *professionalization* in the latter half of the twentieth century, keeping the size of the Court steady, waiting for vacancies to appear before appointing new members, and appointing justices with stronger legal or political backgrounds. Contemporary institutional and political dynamics (formal judicial selection rules, dramatic party system fragmentation, and weak party loyalty) reinforced those practices in the postauthoritarian period, and they served as the foundation for the Brazilian Court's *statesman* character. The STF was more stable, had a stronger and more heterogeneous professional profile, enjoyed greater perceived legitimacy, and had stronger institutional cohesion than its Argentine counterpart. In short, Court crafting – and thus Court character – are rooted in history, but shaped by formal institutions and political contingencies.

Courts of very different characters were thus propelled into the political arena in postauthoritarian Argentina and Brazil. Understanding the impact the judicialization of economic governance had on politics, policy making, and the rule of law in the two contexts required analyzing the behavior of the two Courts (studying their decision making on critical cases concerning economic policy) *as well as* analyzing how quickly and how completely elected leaders complied with their challenging decisions and to what degree they retaliated against them. Specifically, I examined how the high court and elected leaders in each polity interacted over forty-four systematically selected high court cases concerning significant economic policies. I identified strikingly different patterns of interbranch interaction in the sensitive and critical realm of economic governance in the two countries, and argued that the character of the two high courts shaped those patterns.

In Argentina, a combined pattern emerged. The high court often adopted a *deferential* approach to decision making – prioritizing elected leaders' preferences in their decision-making calculus and endorsing their policies or challenging them only weakly – producing a pattern of *Court submission*. Yet that pattern was punctuated at particular moments by tense interbranch *confrontation*. When under institutional attack, the Court adopted a *self-protective* approach to decision making, handing down strongly challenging rulings that elected leaders complied with very partially or practically ignored. The Court's political character contributed to this pattern. The political Court was often practically ill-equipped (given its lack of institutional cohesion) and politically indisposed to challenge the exercise of government power when elected officials had enacted constitutionally questionable laws and decrees. Yet when elected branch threats provided a rallying point, the Court had little to lose by capitalizing on the unique threat potential of critical cases concerning economic governance to challenge the exercise of government power. Its historic instability suggested that it would at some point be disbanded anyway, and elected leaders' failure to comply with its dictates would do little to damage its poor image. Confident of their ability to replace the Court with one that would defer to them (given the success of high court politicization in the past), and doubting that their defiance of the unpopular Court would generate much political fallout – or that the weakly cohesive Court would retaliate strongly – elected leaders had little incentive to obey its challenging decisions.

In Brazil by contrast, a more stable pattern of interbranch *accommodation* emerged. The statesman high court was selectively assertive (like its Argentine counterpart), but in a very different way. Given the mix of justices with strong judicial and political backgrounds (and the collegial Court's penchant for compromise), it sometimes issued "middle-of-the-road" rulings that neither endorsed significant constitutional transgressions nor induced economic chaos (thus accommodating elected leaders). Yet it also engaged in over-time accommodation, alternating between adopting a *principled* approach to decision making and issuing strong challenges to the exercise of government power (helping to retain legitimacy with the legal community, and with little fear of reprisal given Brazil's history of high court professionalization), and adopting a *pragmatic* approach and strongly endorsing the exercise of government power (helping to maintain its legitimacy with politicians). For their part, Brazil's leaders were destined – by the judicialization of economic governance and by the locked-in politics of Court crafting (professionalization) – to continue appealing judicial challenges to the same justices. Noncompliance would antagonize the statesman Court – and given its institutional cohesion and the hundreds of thousands of cases against the state it held, it would be a formidable enemy. Moreover, defying the Court would be politically costly given its multifaceted legitimacy. Elected leaders thus consistently complied with the high court's rulings (if slowly and often incompletely, within their economic and fiscal constraints), thus accommodating the Court.

The Court character account pairs rational choice and historical institutionalism to highlight how history and institutions structure and condition the strategic context in which justices and elected leaders interact. Interbranch relations over politically crucial court cases can be thought of as a repeated – and linked – series of interactive dilemmas. Factors in the political setting certainly guide justices' and elected authorities' strategic calculations about how to interface with each other. Indeed, as I demonstrate, elected leaders' Court-crafting practices are influenced by partisan politics; moreover, economic conditions, popular pressures, and political power configurations, among other political dynamics, all impinge on justices, presidents, and legislators as they interact. Yet in contrast to some strategic accounts that make universalizing assumptions about political actors' preferences and goals and emphasize the contingent nature of their strategizing, I trace persistent patterns in the way elected and judicial leaders interact and show how history and institutions – embodied in the notion of Court character – contribute to producing those patterns. High court character can help to produce such patterns because the institutional features that compose it are relatively enduring despite being informal – rooted in elected leaders' informal politics of Court crafting (which have become ingrained over time), public opinion, and the high court's internal culture. In short, even in politically unstable contexts, institutions can have (informal) historical trajectories that structure and condition law and politics.

The analysis contributes to several conversations in comparative judicial politics. First, the study integrates various accounts of judicial behavior to argue that high courts employ multiple approaches to decision making as they rule on politically critical cases over time. Some scholars of judicial behavior have posited that justices are primarily motivated by one stimulus – be it their policy preferences (the attitudinal model, e.g., Segal and Spaeth 1993), the configuration and power of their political counterparts (the strategic model, e.g., Chavez 2004a; Helmke 2005; Vanberg 2005; Moustafa 2007) or law and institutions (the legal and new institutional models, e.g., Clayton and Gillman 1999; Lasser 2004). I offer empirical evidence to support the idea – now being advocated by a growing number of scholars – that these models best explain variation in judicial behavior when deployed *together*: Judicial decision making comprises a *set of* varied- and differently motivated-behaviors.

Second, through identifying the approaches to decision making that Courts adopt and favor, the study demonstrates that Courts do not necessarily seek to rule as assertively as they can, as often as they can. Some comparative judicial studies suggest that Courts' main goal is constructing their authority through issuing decisions that challenge powerful actors (e.g., Dodson and Jackson 2003; Gloppen, Gargarella, and Skaar 2004), or that Courts are motivated to rule within elected leaders' "tolerance intervals" as doing so can eventually lead to the weakening of those constraints, allowing courts to be more assertive (Epstein et al. 2001; see also Cooter and Ginsburg 1996). Yet the present analysis, and the Brazilian experience in particular, show that some Courts are perfectly willing and able to self-restrain.[2] For instance, when justices envisage a governing role for Courts – and when they anticipate that challenging elected leaders' policies might negatively affect governability – they may adopt a *pragmatic* approach to decision making, endorsing or only weakly challenging arguably unconstitutional exercises of government power. Alternatively, Courts might self-restrain in order to demarcate the boundaries of their jurisdiction.[3] This finding recommends simultaneously examining a Court's assertiveness *and* the approach to decision making it adopts in order to gauge its power: Weaker assertiveness is not necessarily an indicator of less power.

Third, identifying the approaches to decision making that high courts adopt also helps to elucidate the normatively and theoretically important relationship

[2] Indeed, Supreme Courts as mighty as that of the United States have done so, endorsing the exercise of government power under precarious conditions, for example, in *Korematsu v. United States* (1944) or *Dennis v. United States* (1951).

[3] Within Latin America, the Chilean high courts are additional examples: They are not blindly power-hungry, although they self-restrain for different reasons than does the Brazilian high court. See Couso (2002); Scribner (2004); Huneeus (2006); and Hilbink (2007) for full analyses.

between judicial assertiveness (a behavior) and judicial independence (a condition).[4] On the one hand, Courts that are not consistently assertive toward (that is, do not consistently challenge) powerful actors do not necessarily lack independence from them. Many of the Brazilian high court's endorsements of the exercise of government power in the economic realm were motivated by a concern for the potentially negative political or economic consequences that more challenging decisions might have had, not pressure from elected leaders. Moreover, where politics have been judicialized, political actors often file cases questioning the constitutionality of government policy *not* because (they believe) elected leaders have acted unconstitutionally, but rather on ideological grounds or for purely political purposes (to place obstacles in the government's way or to attract attention to their cause, for instance).[5] Endorsing the exercise of government power in such cases in no way reflects judicial dependence on elected leaders.

On the other hand, whereas judicial assertiveness toward a particular actor *may* indicate independence from that actor in institutionally unstable contexts, it does not necessarily do so. As this analysis showed, the Argentine Court sometimes handed down decisions that strongly challenged the exercise of government power. Yet when doing so, it generally assumed a self-protective approach to decision making, issuing those decisions in hopes of threatening elected leaders. Like the Court's endorsements of the exercise of government power (which often reflected a deferential approach to decision making), its challenging rulings were a reaction to elected leaders rather than dispassionate decisions based on law and legal merits. As such, they reflected the Court's *dependence* on elected leaders rather than its independence from them. In sum, identifying the multiple approaches to decision making that Courts adopt and detecting those they tend to favor offers considerable insight into judicial independence from elected leaders, and thus interbranch relations.

Finally, the book illustrates the utility (if not the necessity), for fully understanding judicial dynamics, of examining judicial decision making and compliance with judicial rulings in tandem. Examining high courts' assertiveness vis-à-vis elected leaders *and* those leaders' compliance with judicial decisions is obviously indispensable for understanding the nature of interbranch relations. Doing so is also important for evaluating judicial power. After all, both the Argentine and Brazilian high courts were selectively assertive vis-à-vis elected leaders. If we were to evaluate their power solely on the basis of their assertiveness, we might rank the Brazilian Court as just somewhat more powerful

[4] As understood here, judicial independence refers to whether a court is able to issue rulings on the basis of the merits of the cases before it, within the constraints imposed by its jurisdiction and existing law, without being influenced by other actors or fearing pressure or reprisal. This definition (adapted from Kapiszewski and Taylor 2008) brackets the issue of ex ante institutional influence via what this study refers to as Court crafting.

[5] Experts whom I interviewed in both countries emphasized that court cases questioning privatizations were often filed by political actors with an ideological or political, rather than juridical or constitutional, axe to grind (e.g., in Brazil, JG-07; in Argentina, EC-07 and EC-14).

because it challenged only slightly more often. Yet examining elected leaders' compliance with and retaliation against those rulings reveals that Brazilian leaders obeyed high court dictates to a greater degree and retaliated far less often than their Argentine counterparts, suggesting that the Brazilian Court is a *good deal* more powerful than the Argentine. In short, analyzing the actions of Courts *and* elected leaders and studying the over-time trajectories in their behavior aids us in identifying and explaining patterns in their interactions and helps us to more accurately gauge judicial power.

7.3. BROADER DEBATES AND IMPLICATIONS

The analysis and findings presented here also have implications for broader debates in public law and comparative politics. One debate relates to the institutional approach to accounting for political phenomena. The second concerns the law-economics nexus – the relationship between the processes of entrenching the rule of law, and economic reform and development.

The New Institutionalism

Institutionalism has become a central theoretical paradigm in political science since the 1990s. While the approach is internally heterogeneous,[6] its fundamental claim is that the establishment of particular institutional arrangements results in inducements and constraints that lead political actors in particular directions (Collier and Collier 1979; Parsons 2007: 67). Even though the approach has mainly been used to explain outcomes related to political and economic development, students of U.S. and comparative public law are increasingly examining the effects of formal institutions. For instance, the approach is in ascendance in the public law literature addressing the U.S. Supreme Court (e.g., Clayton and Gillman 1999; Gillman and Clayton 1999), and courts in Latin America (e.g., Arantes 2005; Cepeda Espinosa 2005; Wilson 2005; Ríos-Figueroa and Taylor 2006). Public law scholars' adoption of institutionalism represents an effort to expand the field's focus from judicial decision making (the trademark of the behavioralist "revolution" in political science in the 1950s) to broader judicial outcomes, revealing how those outcomes are shaped by courts' "persistent and distinctive" rules, norms, and procedures, and by their position as one institution within a larger political and social context (Whittington 2000: 608, 617).

This book provides further evidence that institutionalist approaches offer significant inferential leverage on judicial politics and interbranch interactions in developing democracies. First, it shows that even in politically (and thus institutionally) unstable settings, path-dependent frameworks may be

[6] New institutionalism is generally understood to comprise historical institutionalism, rational choice institutionalism, and sociological institutionalism (Hall and Taylor 1996; DiMaggio 1998; Immergut 1998; but see also March and Olsen 1984).

fruitfully employed to study Courts' historical trajectories. Path dependence, which scholars of comparative politics have applied to a wide range of empirical phenomena since the 1980s,[7] refers to the notion that the course of action taken at a particular choice point or critical juncture sets in motion a self-sustaining historical trajectory from which exit becomes increasingly less likely over time.[8] This book suggests that at a critical point in the past,[9] leaders in Argentina and Brazil adopted a particular politics of Court crafting that eventually became locked in as expectations formed about high court appointment practices and as leaders needed – or desired – to recreate their Courts. In other words, it became increasingly difficult (or decreasingly desirable) for leaders to deviate from established Court-crafting practices. Further application of path-dependent analysis, or even recasting existing explanations in path-dependent terms,[10] would help to open a broader dialogue between students of comparative law and comparative judicial politics on the one hand, and students of comparative politics on the other, perhaps preventing the development of a divide between comparative scholarship on law and courts and scholarship on comparative politics more generally reminiscent of the one that exists between public law and American politics.

Second and relatedly, the analysis identifies, typologizes, and highlights the importance of *informal* (yet routinized and entrenched) institutional *practices* and *features*. Particularly (but not exclusively) in developing democracies, many of the rules and procedures that structure and regulate the "political game" are "created, communicated, and enforced outside the officially sanctioned channels" (Helmke and Levitsky 2006: 1) – that is, they are "informal institutions." Accordingly, scholars of comparative politics have begun to point to informal institutions to explain diverse political dynamics.[11] Scholars of Latin American courts have likewise begun to consider how informal judicial institutions affect judicial dynamics (e.g., Brinks 2003; Chavez 2004a; Couso 2005; Hilbink 2007). This study highlights the theoretical importance of two closely related phenomena – informal institutional practices and informal institutional features. The high court appointment and removal practices that

[7] Examples include "third-wave" transitions to democracy in Latin America (Karl 1990; Hartlyn 1998) and Eastern Europe (Stark 1994; Stark and Bruszt 1998; Kitschelt et al. 1999), and patterns of regional and local government (Putnam 1993).

[8] See Mahoney (2000), Pierson (2000), and Boas (2007) for nuanced treatments of path dependence.

[9] The particular politics of Court crafting that have dominated in Argentina and Brazil were adopted at a time of major state transition: politicization began in Argentina with Juan Perón's rise to power in the 1940s, and professionalization in Brazil has its roots in the 1930 revolution and the rise of Getúlio Vargas.

[10] Hilbink's (2007) account of the Chilean judiciary, for instance, and certain accounts of the Japanese and some European courts might be good candidates for this type of reconsideration.

[11] Examples include popular attachment to democracy (e.g., Bratton 2007), the organization of parties and the party system (e.g., Levitsky 2003; Smyth, Lowry, and Wilkening 2007), legislative processes (Hansen 1986; Farrell and Heritier 2003), regime change and performance (e.g., Lauth 2005; Eisenstadt 2003; Llamazares 2005), and state building in various developing regions.

together constitute leaders' politics of Court crafting, as well as the resulting institutional features that comprise Court character, are on the whole informal. That is, they are not mandated by or formalized in written rules, laws, or the constitution but rather become entrenched through their own repetition (in the case of Court crafting practices) or through the repetition of related practices (in the case of the high court features that compose Court character). This study suggests that those informal practices and features are of central importance to shaping the way high courts and elected leaders interact over politically crucial conflicts.

If the present account is correct, two implications follow. First, categorizing Courts by their character (that is, by the four informal institutional features that compose it – stability, justices' professional backgrounds, perceived legitimacy, and cohesiveness) may represent an important analytic complement to standard taxonomies that classify Courts by their formal characteristics. The current study identified two types of Court character – *political* (the Argentine Supreme Court) and *statesman* (the Brazilian Supreme Federal Tribunal); the Indian Supreme Court and South African Constitutional Court may likewise be statesman Courts. But other Court characters certainly exist. For instance, Hilbink's (2007) description of the Chilean Supreme Court's political aloofness suggests a "professional" character, but one that is quite distinct from what we observe in Brazil. Likewise, the Constitutional Chamber of the Costa Rican Supreme Court's or the Colombian Constitutional Court's interactions with elected leaders – crusading decision making eliciting significant compliance – suggest that some elements of their characters may be similar to the Brazilian Court's, although the professional profiles of their justices are likely different. Analyzing other Courts in these terms will elucidate where and how Court character shapes the way Courts and elected leader interact – and, indeed, the way Courts and other powerful actors interact. More broadly, examining the inner workings of high courts more carefully, as this study has sought to do, will allow us to bring Courts alive in comparative judicial studies as the distinctive and complicated actors they are.

A second implication of this study's argument that Court character shapes interbranch relations is that it is important to understand how different politics of Court crafting emerge. As Chapter 1 highlighted, scholars have paid some attention to the *effects* of formal judicial selection mechanisms and informal Court crafting practices, but are just beginning to develop theoretical accounts of why certain selection mechanisms are chosen and why certain informal Court-crafting practices emerge. I suggest that contemporary Court-crafting practices are often based on a longer Court-crafting tradition – but that following that tradition is facilitated and constrained by contemporary formal institutions (rules regulating the sizing and composition of Courts) and partisan politics. Pinpointing how formal institutional arrangements and contemporary politics encourage or obstruct the deployment of historical Court-crafting practices in additional country cases would constitute further steps toward developing a theory of Court crafting.

Latin American countries boast a diverse range of formal selection mechanisms. Whereas high court selection procedures in various countries involve the president, few systems are as president-centered as Argentina's and Brazil's. In Mexico, for example, the president submits a list of three candidates for Supreme Court justice to the senate, which then holds hearings to consider each nominee; two-thirds of the senate must vote in favor to appoint justices (who hold their positions for fifteen years).[12] This selection mechanism opens the door to high court personalization if the president's party has sufficient representation in the senate (for instance, in one-party-dominant systems of the type Mexico used to be), yet has encouraged professionalization in Mexico as a multiparty system has emerged (personal communication, Jeffrey K. Staton, July 18, 2011). When a vacancy arises on the Chilean Supreme Court, the justices themselves (who serve terms of unlimited length through the age of 75) provide the president a list of five names; the president then nominates one individual from the list who must be confirmed by a two-thirds vote of the senate.[13] Here elected leaders' Court crafting is more constrained by formal rules (which also include specific requisites for justices' professional backgrounds), and the preferences of Supreme Court justices, encouraging the ideological recycling that Hilbink (2007) highlights.

In other cases, nonelected state powers participate in a more meaningful way in Court crafting. In Colombia, for instance, when Constitutional Court vacancies arise (which they often do in triplicate – justices hold staggered nonrenewable eight-year terms), the Supreme Court, the Council of State, and the president each nominate a group of three candidates, and the senate appoints one candidate from each group. This system prevents any particular state power from dominating the Court-crafting process but establishes the senate as a veto player. The system appears to have engendered fractured politicization of the Court as it encourages each power to nominate candidates who are aligned (or at least ideologically compatible) with the political party that dominates that body at the moment (and who have sufficient political clout to be confirmed by the senate). It has also helped to guarantee that candidates have strong professional and/or academic qualifications (personal correspondence, Pablo Rueda, July 17, 2011). Concerning Chile's Constitutional Tribunal, justices (who sit for one nine-year term) are appointed directly by various state powers: Three are appointed unilaterally by the president, four are elected by congress (two appointed by the senate and two proposed by the chamber of deputies for approval or rejection by the senate), and three are elected by the Supreme Court (2005 reform to the 1980 constitution, Article 92). In this arrangement, again, no particular body can craft the Court it wishes, though negotiation and logrolling among the groups is certainly possible. The system could also engender

[12] http://www.scjn.gob.mx/2010/conoce/Paginas/conformadaSCJN.aspx#dos, accessed July 19, 2011.

[13] http://www.poderjudicial.cl/PDF/InfoInstitucional/corte_suprema.pdf?opc_menu=1&opc_item=3, accessed July 19, 2011.

fractured politicization if each appointing body sought to get "its representative" on the Court, however. And without a final institutional check, candidates may not need the political clout that Colombian Constitutional Court justices likely have, for instance, or equally strong professional backgrounds.

Finally, high court appointments are handled by one branch of government alone in some polities, offering that branch significant Court-crafting latitude. For instance, when an opening arises on the Costa Rican Supreme Court (to which justices are elected for renewable eight-year terms), a legislative commission organizes a public competition, formally interviews applicants, and makes a recommendation to the full National Assembly, which then votes (with a two-thirds vote necessary for appointment).[14] Here legislative and party politics play a direct and undiluted role in Court crafting. For instance, even though historically appointments to the Court's constitutional chamber (Sala IV) alternated (with regard to their political predilections) based on an agreement between the two major parties, since the dissolution of the traditional party system, appointment battles occur in congress to secure the necessary two-thirds majority, leading to the exclusion of well-qualified candidates based on the perception that they were or are too close to one of the parties (personal correspondence, Bruce Wilson, July 21, 2011).

In still other cases, high courts are completely insulated from crafting by politicians. When a justice retires from the Colombian Supreme Court (on which justices have life tenure to the age of 65), the Judicial Council (an organ of the judiciary) administers a public contest, ranks applicants, and then the Court itself appoints its new member from among the highest-ranking applicants. Here Court-crafting politics are all internal to the judiciary – negotiated between the Judicial Council and the Supreme Court.

Of course, this book argues that historical trajectories of Court crafting play at least as crucial a role as do formal institutions in shaping contemporary Court-crafting practices – setting baselines, expectations, and preferences. To develop a complete account of Court crafting in other Latin American polities those trajectories would need to be investigated.[15] Nonetheless, as these examples suggest, formal institutions can both limit and expand political and judicial actors' Court-crafting latitude. When, where, how, and why those limits bind, and how they interact with history and politics to structure the crafting of high courts, seem important questions for the comparative judicial politics research program to address.

The Rule of Law and Economic Governance

Finally, in assessing how Courts interact with elected leaders over cases concerning economic policy, this research also contributes to fundamental debates

[14] http://www.poder-judicial.go.cr/generalidadespj/historia.html, accessed July 19, 2011.

[15] This is the case when Courts have an institutional history; the Colombian Constitutional Court, for example, was created by the 1991 Colombian Constitution.

regarding the relationship between law and economic development. An important theoretical referent for these debates is the law and development movement of the 1960s.[16] That movement proposed that the adoption of U.S.-based ideas about the law in developing countries would facilitate the emergence of U.S.-style capitalist development, producing "modernization," and a concomitant strengthening of the rule of law. This proved not to be the case (in Latin America at least) engendering the movement's decline by the 1970s. However, the core notion experienced a "revival" (Carothers 1998) during the latest wave of democracy, though not an uncontroversial one. Although some scholars (and many members of the international financial community) currently argue that the rule of law, and market-led reform and development, are reciprocally reinforcing, critics contend that the two are not necessarily mutually supporting.[17]

Some sanguine accounts posit an overall elective affinity between constitutionalism and economic liberalization (Farber 2002). Other scholars suggest a conditional connection, asserting that the desire to attract foreign investment will lead to the establishment of the rule of law and effective courts in some contexts but not in others (Silverstein 2003). Still others are less tentative, asserting a much stronger relationship. One strand of argumentation suggests that adherence to the rule of law is necessary for market-led reform to succeed, as the former enhances the appearance of certainty and predictability, reduces transaction costs, eases access to capital, and generally levels the playing field (North and Weingast 1989). Some political economists assert that potential investors may seek evidence that property rights are secure before investing, recommending that political leaders strengthen their states' public commitment to protecting those rights and/or abiding by legal strictures more generally (e.g., Olson 1993; Weingast 1993; Borner, Brunetti, and Weder 1995; Farber 2002). Dezalay and Garth (2010) trace the increasing importance of law and lawyers to governance of the economy in postcolonial South and Southeast Asia. And many scholars and countless World Bank publications have insisted that effective courts are essential for economic development in the long run (North 1990; Williamson 1994; La Porta 1997; Castelar Pinheiro 2000), and judicial reform consequently has been touted as a prerequisite thereof.

Other scholars downplay the importance of law to economic development, and some directly challenge the proposition that rule of law entrenchment and economic development naturally reinforce each other. Posner (1998), for instance, questions how crucial an independent judiciary is to development. Ginsburg (2000: 830), reviewing scholarship on the role of law in economic development in East Asia, suggests that "by most accounts, law has not played a major role in Asian economic growth" (see in particular Davis 1998 – although he emphasizes that the question is by no means resolved). Perry (2000: 779)

[16] The work of social theorists such as Marx and Weber are of course fundamental theoretical referents as well (Ginsburg 2000: 829).

[17] The following synopsis of the debate is brief and schematic. For an in-depth appraisal of the evolution in thinking on the law-economic development nexus, see Trubek and Santos (2006).

asserts that there is scant evidence that effective legal systems are a prerequisite for foreign direct investment and growth in most developing contexts given investors' limited ability to make rational decisions, and the importance of parallel informal mechanisms structuring business relationships in such contexts. Still other analysts suggest that legal entrenchment and economic development can actively conflict. Rulings by United States federal courts – including the Supreme Court – on cases regarding economic policy from the late 1800s through the late 1930s illustrate the obstacles courts can place in the way of economic governance and the conflicts that can result when economic change is judicialized (Landes and Posner 1975: 876). Ballard (1999) likewise shows how the transition to open-market economies can produce potentially justiciable conflicts and a concomitant increase in litigation that disrupts and distracts from economic reform. And legal scholarship and political analysis have suggested that judicial enforcement of social rights (arguably a facet of rule of law entrenchment in countries where such rights are constitutionalized) has negative fiscal implications and can lead to or exacerbate economic disarray (for instance, Cass Sunstein's earlier writings [e.g., 1993] and Monahan 1987, among many others).

This book straddles the two camps. It highlights the fundamental tensions and trade-offs that can arise when developing democracies attempt to restructure their economies in a context of legal transformation in which the economic status quo is constitutionally protected, new policies impinge on constitutional rights, or both. When broad policies designed to address economic crisis (such as bank freezes or devaluations) impinge on property rights, or when initiatives to address fiscal imbalance violate constitutional guarantees – and when such conflicts are captured in an accelerating judicialization of politics – significant interbranch turmoil can result. Yet the study also suggests two ways to reconcile the debate surrounding the relationship between law, and economic reform and development. First, how economic and legal change interact and progress in different contexts, and the academic discord over their relationship, may hinge on their sequencing. Second, the roles courts play in prioritizing the economic and legal transitions' competing imperatives can exacerbate or temper the conflict their simultaneity produces.

First, drawing on arguments advanced by Marshall (1950), O'Donnell (2001), Zakaria (2003), and others, it seems plausible that the conflict between entrenching the rule of law and fomenting economic development emerged in Latin America (and in Central and Eastern Europe, for instance, but not in other contexts) due to the sequencing – that is, the simultaneity – of legal and economic change. As Zakaria (2003: 29–53) has suggested, in the West's constitutional democracies, the rule of law led to capitalism, which together with power struggles led to liberalism, which *then* led to democracy. As suggested earlier, strengthening the trappings of legal systems – adopting a rule of law discourse, reformulating constitutions, and formally empowering courts – may serve as an effective "signal" (Farber 2002) of a regime's commitment to property rights and legal rules in general, encouraging growth-enhancing investment that can in turn facilitate (or dull the pain of) subsequent economic reform.[18] In regions such as Africa, by contrast, aggressive economic reform programs were implemented in the absence of much attention to rule of law and judicial reforms, and economic reform soon faltered. And to repeat, many new, crisis-prone democracies such as those of Latin America followed a third path, attempting to liberalize the economy and entrench the rule of law *simultaneously* (even in a halting and uneven fashion), producing significant constitutional controversies over economic change. This conflict created the perception, at least in the short term, that the transitions are fundamentally at odds, and complicated both consolidation of the rule of law and economic reform. Adapting Sartori's famous reflection on the route from constitutional liberalism to democracy, traveling in the opposite direction may be much more difficult.[19]

Nonetheless, even in developing democracies, once the rule of law has consolidated and the most wrenching phases of economic reform have passed, law and economic development almost certainly become mutually reinforcing. This book's second contribution to this theoretical debate, then, concerns the role of Courts in facilitating that reconciliation. Whether the tensions engendered by the simultaneity of the two transitions are defused or inflamed in the medium term and how quickly the two processes start to reinforce one another, I suggest, depends in part on what sorts of controversies are ushered to high courts, how they face the conundrum of adjudicating between the rule of law and economic solutions, and how leaders react to their challenging decisions. In other words, when economic governance is judicialized, judicial institutions are positioned to address the tensions between the legal and economic transitions, with important implications for both. To articulate the idea methodologically, courts may be an important missing variable in discussions of how the two transitions interact. Reconsidering interbranch interactions over the *Guida* and *Tobar* cases in Argentina (discussed in Chapter 5) and the *FGTS* case in Brazil (described in Chapter 6) reinforces this point.

As readers will recall, the Argentine high court's endorsement of a constitutionally questionable public sector salary cut in *Guida* allowed elected leaders to avoid worsening the budget deficit but implied that they could lower public sector salaries under emergency conditions. Even though interbranch interactions over this ruling likely facilitated economic governance, they weakened confidence in juridical security and undermined the rule of law. In the *Tobar* case, the Court challenged a similar wage policy. Yet many interpreted the ruling as a signal that the CSJN was willing to use critical cases as a political tool, whereas elected leaders' desire to avoid economic fallout meant that they

[18] O'Donnell (2001) suggests something similar: In the "Northwest quadrant" (i.e., established democracies such as those of Western Europe, the United States, and Canada), the rule of law was entrenched prior to economic liberalization, and the positive synergies between the two processes emerged relatively quickly, allowing each to progress more rapidly.

[19] The original quote is less optimistic: "the itinerary is not reversible" (Zakaria 2003: 58).

complied only slowly and grudgingly with the decision. Ultimately, then, the first interaction may have eased economic governance and the second done little to destabilize it – but both had unfortunate implications for the rule of law. In the Brazilian *FGTS* case (concerning an employment security fund), by contrast, the Court handed down a typically middle-of-the-road ruling with which elected leaders complied – in fact extending compensation beyond those who won the case – while retaining fiscal discipline. Interbranch interaction over the case made clear that justices and elected officials alike took fiscal responsibility *and* the constitution seriously. Very different from its Argentine counterpart, by holding elected leaders to constitutional standards without placing insurmountable obstacles in the way of economic policy making (thus encouraging compliance), the STF played a positive role in balancing the economic and legal transitions, guiding economic reform *without* forfeiting the rule of law.

The analysis further suggests that whether Courts are willing and able to take on the role of balancing macropolitical imperatives has much to do with their character. Both the Argentine and Brazilian high courts tended to shepherd economic reform and crisis management, facilitating economic governance. The difference between the two countries' experiences lay in the constitutional damage done in the process. Over most of the postauthoritarian period, Argentina's *political* Court virtually resigned its role as constitutional guardian: It repeatedly submitted to the elected branches, and when it failed to submit (using its privileged position to threaten elected leaders, issuing decisions to thwart their economic policy initiatives), confrontation and noncompliance resulted. Here the conflict between constitutionalism and economic governance was maximized and the trade-off stark, with elected leaders' preferences generally carrying the day. In Brazil by contrast, the *statesman* Court upheld elected leaders' economic policies as often as it struck them down but never fully forsook the constitution in its decisions – just as elected leaders sought to comply as best they could with the Court's challenges. Emphasizing pragmatism, the Court worked to attenuate the law-economic tension, guiding economic reform through the constitutional gauntlet created by Brazil's 1988 charter. It defended the constitution but avoided extended and dramatic periods of constitutional strife.

In sum, even in weakly institutionalized contexts (and perhaps particularly there), whether and how Courts and elected leaders balance legal and economic imperatives has critical implications for the entrenchment of the rule of law, for economic governance, and for how citizens experience the state. Of course, the suggestion that Courts can help to balance the economic and legal transitions may immediately raise empirical and normative objections. Courts in Latin America – and many developing democracies – have historically been unwilling or unable to compel elected leaders to abide by the constitution, allowing the scale to tilt precipitously toward political imperatives when policy clashed with the charter. Expecting courts to tilt the scale in the opposite direction and balance it – particularly when deciding cases in the controversial realm of economic policy – may be unrealistic. Further, closer adherence to the constitution – particularly social constitutions such as Mexico's, Colombia's, or Brazil's – can seem a luxury that developing democracies can ill afford. And political actors, judicial actors, and scholars alike will protest that reconciling the two transitions is not the proper role for courts. Justices like Brazil's "legalists" will argue that courts should steadfastly defend the constitution, while government officials will suggest that at critical moments courts should throw constitutional caution to the wind and support their crucial economic projects.

As additional evidence and analysis about the contours and consequences of judicial involvement in economic governance emerge, empirical correctives can be applied to normative assertions. To offer just one observation, however, the more accommodating interbranch interactions over economic governance in Brazil do not appear to have impeded macroeconomic progress in that country: Indeed, Brazil is in a far stronger economic situation today than is Argentina (although a host of factors have obviously contributed to that outcome). The critical imperative is to continue to examine the broader impact of interactions between high courts and elected leaders over politically crucial court cases, as interbranch relations around such disputes can affect myriad actors in addition to the parties involved, and induce dynamics that ripple far beyond the political battleground on which such struggles occur.[20]

I conclude with a broad observation about the judicial politics enterprise. This book implicitly and explicitly suggests that the empowerment of high courts, the formal rules that guide the appointment and removal of justices and attendant informal Court-crafting practices, high court decision making, and compliance with and retaliation against high court rulings are parts of a larger whole or grander cycle: They are facets of an interacting *system*. Certainly I am not the first person to suggest the cyclical nature of judicial politics. Gauri and Brinks (2008) posit a four-stage "life cycle of public policy litigation" (the filing of a case, a judicial ruling, a response, and additional litigation), the product of which is the legalization of policy in a particular area. And Gloppen (2006: 43) depicts what she refers to as the "anatomy of the social rights litigation process," highlighting four facets (the filing of a case, court responsiveness, judges' capability, and public authorities' compliance and implementation). These are important formulations. Yet I submit that judicial-political cycles or systems with an even broader range of interacting parts (those mentioned above) exist in many countries – systems our piecemeal study of judicial dynamics (that is, the focus of most studies on judicial empowerment *or* judicial decision making *or* compliance with judicial decisions) has prevented us from seeing.

A fruitful next step in the comparative judicial politics research program, then, would be to explore how the constitutive parts of these systems interact – how they work together *as a system* – a subsystem of the broader institutional

[20] Scholars of comparative judicial politics have begun to examine the broader impact of courts and their rulings (see, e.g., Epp 1998; Hertogh and Halliday, 2004; Santiso 2004; Sieder et al. 2005; Wilson 2005; Gauri and Brinks 2008; Kapiszewski, Silverstein, and Kagan forthcoming).

system.[21] This study, for instance, suggests that Court-crafting practices affect both high court decision making and compliance with high court rulings (interbranch interactions). Certainly other parts of these larger systems interact as well. Tracing these interactions over time and identifying patterns therein will reveal the variety of relationships that can obtain between the different elements of the system, helping us to move beyond some of the assumptions on which the judicial politics enterprise tacitly rests. This book has called into question the notion that high court–elected branch relationships are necessarily adversarial, for example, showing that interbranch dialogue and cooperation are empirical possibilities (following on ideas posited by scholars such as Fisher 2007 and Gargarella 2011). Elucidating the particular configurations in which the elements of the system tend to appear will help us to determine what accounts for the emergence of those configurations – and what difference they make to politics and governance.

Thinking of judicial politics in this more holistic way dovetails with the notion – clearly demonstrated in this study – that in many contexts, courts are a critical aspect of the political process and a crucial part of the political regime. Courts cogovern. Their rulings can and do have formative effects on macrodynamics such as regime transition and consolidation, the development of the state, and economic transformation. Understanding courts as one cog in the larger governing wheel will help us to generate better theory to address the questions that animate the judicial politics research program: what roles courts play in politics and governance, and why they play the roles that they do.

[21] Stone Sweet 1999 encourages something similar.

Appendices

APPENDIX 1.1. CASE-SELECTION METHODOLOGY, ARGENTINA AND BRAZIL

I. Selecting the Sample

The sample of high court cases (N = 122) includes the most politically important cases to come before the Argentine Supreme Court (CSJN) between 1984 and 2003 (N = 67), or before the Brazilian Supreme Federal Tribunal (STF) between 1985 and 2004 (N = 55). Politically important cases are those in which a high court had the opportunity to: set boundaries on the exercise of government power (for instance, by reinforcing the separation of powers, enforcing limits on state interference in society, or reviewing the constitutionality of central government policy); prioritize competing rights; or rationalize the institutional system.

To obtain the sample, I developed a systematic, replicable case-selection technique that triangulated data from three sources. I initiated the first two aspects of case selection simultaneously, and carried out the third after the first was completed.[1]

Step A, Mentions of Cases in Articles and Books

I assembled a bibliography of books and articles addressing the jurisprudence of each high court since each country's transition to democracy.

- In order to facilitate the selection of relevant books and articles in Argentina, I conducted fifteen introductory interviews with constitutional scholars and leaders of nongovernmental organizations (NGOs) that deal with judicial themes to solicit their opinions, and consulted with Research Assistant (RA)

[1] I used mentions of legal, ideological, strategic, and pragmatic considerations in the sources I used to carry out case selection to identify the approaches to decision making the Courts adopted. Consequently, it was important that my sources, in aggregate, not overrepresent any particular type of case or consideration. Accordingly, the source-types had different biases in terms of what sorts of cases (and considerations) were likely to appear in them: newspapers and expert respondents were more likely to discuss cases that were politically controversial (for instance, in which the Court strategically challenged or endorsed) or in which particular justices' ideologies played an important role, while case descriptions in legal journals and books were more likely to emphasize legal reasoning. The multifaceted case-selection technique also helped to ensure that the sample in each country contained cases that were politically, rather than just juridically, important.

Lucas Arrimada, who had recently completed a law degree at the Universidad de Buenos Aires. The first-level bibliography included twenty-six books and articles written by Argentine constitutional scholars and lawyers, four dissertations written by U.S. graduate students (all in political science), and one article by a U.S. law professor; in these works, high court cases were discussed in some detail. A second-level bibliography included four Argentine constitutional law texts that each mentioned hundreds of Supreme Court decisions and rarely discussed their details.
- In Brazil, I conducted introductory interviews with professors of law to solicit their opinions. The first-level bibliography included forty-two books and articles written by Brazilian constitutional scholars and lawyers, five articles by U.S. political science and/or law professors, and one dissertation written by a U.S. political science graduate student; in these works, high court cases were discussed in some detail. A second-level bibliography included two Brazilian constitutional law texts that each mentioned hundreds of STF decisions and rarely discussed their details.

I then skimmed all of the books and articles and made a list that included every CSJN (STF) case that they mentioned. I divided the list by topic (cases having to do with politics, with economic policy, and with rights), and noted the number of times each case was mentioned in works from both the first-level and second-level bibliographies. I then made a separate "list of politically important cases" containing just the cases that had been mentioned three or more times in the first-level bibliography.

Step B, Mentions of Cases in Newspapers

- In Argentina, I hired two RAs to read every issue of *La Nación* (a prominent daily newspaper) from December 1983 (Argentina's transition to democracy) through December 2003 searching for articles that **focused on** a case of the Argentine CSJN. Over a month of full-time work, these two RAs and I developed a systematic methodology for assessing and selecting articles. We also developed three types of forms for the RAs to record the bibliographic material and information regarding the case discussed in each selected article. As the RAs read *La Nación,* they selected articles that coincided with our article selection criteria, took a digital picture of each article selected, and filled out the appropriate form. Simultaneously, we created a running list (in chronological order) of all the cases mentioned in *La Nación* and the articles associated with each case.
- In Brazil, I hired four RAs to read every issue of *O Estado de São Paulo* (an important Brazilian daily newspaper) from March 1985 (Brazil's transition to democracy) through December 2004 searching for articles that **focused on** a case of the Brazilian STF. For six weeks, I trained these RAs on the systematic methodology for assessing, selecting, and chronicling articles that my Argentine RAs and I had developed, and we adapted the three types of forms used in Argentina for employment in Brazil. The RAs did not begin work

until all four of them and I could read through one month of *O Estado de São Paulo* and choose and categorize the same articles 80 percent of the time.

Step C, Mentions of Cases in "Case Selection Interviews"

Following completion of Step 1, in each country, I carried out twenty-five interviews with experts (including justices, retired justices, lawyers, constitutional scholars, members of NGOs dealing with judicial themes, and government officials) to solicit their opinions regarding which were the most politically important *cases* to come before the CSJN between 1984 and 2003 (and, in Brazil, to come before the STF between 1985 and 2004).[2]

To emphasize, I tried to reduce selection effects and maximize variation on the high court assertiveness aspect of the dependent variable by asking respondents to identify *cases* (rather than decisions) in which the high court *had the opportunity* to affect (rather than did affect) the political system, the conduct or policies of the central government, or national laws.

The structured questionnaire I developed in Argentina (and translated for use in Brazil) clearly indicated my specific definition of "politically important" and requested that respondents indicate cases by time period (an effort to ensure that the sample would include politically important cases from the whole period under study, not just recent years).

- In Argentina, respondents were asked to name *three* politically important cases from the period during which Alfonsín was president (1984 to 1989), *three* politically important cases from the period during which Menem was president (1989 to 1999), and *three* politically important cases from the "post-Menem" period (2000 to 2003).
- In Brazil, respondents indicated *two* politically important cases from the period during which Sarney was president (1985 to 1990), *two* politically important cases from the period during which Collor and Franco were president (1990 to 1994), *four* politically important cases from the time period during which Cardoso was president (1995 to 2002), and *one* from the first two years of the Lula presidency (2003 to 2004).

Two days before each interview, I sent the questionnaire to each respondent to emphasize that my questions required respondents to think of specific CSJN (STF) cases (which I had already mentioned in my initial communication). Upon arriving at the interviews, I reinforced my definition of "politically important." This methodology worked well; often respondents had created a list of politically important cases in advance of the interview.[3]

[2] In Brazil I conducted thirty-three interviews to obtain twenty-five valid case-selection interviews (interviews in which respondents successfully named cases in the way that I requested); in Argentina, my first twenty-five interviews were successful.

[3] In both countries, respondents took great pride in identifying cases that previous respondents had not mentioned. Respondents often looked at me expectantly after mentioning a case that they found particularly noteworthy and asked, "Did others mention that case yet?"

After completing the portion of the interview in which respondents were requested to name the cases they considered to be the most politically important, I presented respondents with the "list of politically important cases" created through Step A above and asked them to indicate which cases on that list they considered to be politically important. (I included this step in the interest of having some standard data across all interviews, and because the cases on that list were mainly found in legal articles and texts, and thus I was sure that they all had *juridical* importance, but was less sure of their *political* importance.)

In each country, after completing all of these steps, I created a table that included (a) the cases from the original list from Step A *and* (b) all of the cases that had been mentioned in the spontaneous portion of my case-selection interviews. There were 136 case candidates in Argentina and 113 case candidates in Brazil.

Case	Year	(i) # of mentions in literature (first level)	(ii) # of mentions in literature (second level)	(iii) # of mentions in case-selection interviews	(iv) # of times checked on list in case-selection interviews	(v) # of mentions in newspaper	Score

I then established strict decision rules to determine which of these cases would constitute my sample of cases. Specifically, I set a number of mentions "bar" for each category ([i] through [v]), and included a case in my sample if the number of times it was mentioned met or exceeded that bar in three categories; an additional requirement for a case to enter the sample was that it be mentioned in the spontaneous portion of at least one case-selection interview.

The bars set for categories (i) and (iv) varied slightly among the three time periods in Argentina (and the four time periods in Brazil) for two reasons. First, the bibliographies mentioned in Step A contained many more sources analyzing the initial time periods (1984–1989 and 1989–1999 in Argentina;[4] 1985–1990, 1990–1994, and the beginning of 1995–2002 in Brazil) than the later ones. Second, the coverage of the CSJN increased dramatically in *La Nación* between 1984 and 2003 (as did the coverage of the STF in *O Estado de São Paulo* between 1985 and 2004) not strictly because cases became more important, but rather because the media began to focus much more heavily on the high courts.

Further, in Brazil, I raised the bar for "number of mentions in case-selection interviews" slightly for the final period (2000–2003) because it was shorter than the other two, and respondents found it much easier to name three (or more) cases for that period.

[4] However, the second-level sources were all very recent in Argentina.

II. Selecting the Subsample

Carrying out the close qualitative analysis required to trace and measure compliance with judicial rulings and to show how Court character influences cross-national variation in patterns of interbranch interaction required studying fewer cases. The cases used to illustrate the book's argument are a subset of the sample: those in which central government economic policy was questioned (18 cases in Argentina and 26 cases in Brazil, for a total of 44 cases). This choice, easily justifiable empirically, also has several methodological advantages.

Cases concerning economic policy represented the largest issue-specific subset of cases in each country's sample. Further, studying cases regarding economic policy facilitated tracing and quantifying the difficulty of complying with high court rulings (the amount of money that compliance requires is often publicly discussed when it is quite large) and how much compliance actually occurred (since compliance often entailed payments, refunds, tax credits, etc.). Moreover, limiting the scope of the study to one policy area eliminated "policy domain" as an explanation for over time and cross-national differences in interbranch interactions. Focusing on a single policy realm also lent coherence to the analysis and allowed greater analytic depth.

APPENDIX 5.1. *Eighteen Crucial Economic Policy Cases Decided by the Argentine CSJN (1984–2003) (in chronological order by year of ruling)*

Case Name *Type of Case*	Parties	Issue Area Target Decree/Law/Constitutional Amendment/ Other Norm or Action (all federal-level) Claim against the Target	Date Entered CSJN/ Date of Final Ruling * Time Elapsed	Ruling
Rolón Zappa *Recurso extraordinario*	Rolón Zappa v. Argentina	**Issue area:** Pensions **Target:** Law 21.864 (Articles 1, 4) (September 1978); administrative decision restructuring the pension system and applying new indexes to pensions **Claim:** Plaintiff claimed constitutional right to adjustable pension	March 11, 1986/ September 30, 1986 * 6 months; 19 days	Insisted administrative changes to pension system had to comply with existing legislation
Soengas *Recurso de queja*	Soengas and others v. Argentine Railways (Ferrocarriles Argentinos)	**Issue area:** Labor relations **Target:** Law 21.476 (December 1976) (Art. 2, Inc. D) which denied Soengas automatic indexation of his salary (awarded via a previous labor agreement) **Claim:** Plaintiff argued that de facto Law 21.476 was unconstitutional as it violated vested rights	April 24, 1988/ August 7, 1990 * 2 years; 3 months; 14 days	Law 21.476 upheld
Dromi/Aerolíneas *Recurso extraordinario per saltum s/amparo*	Fontela v. Argentina (filed directly before the CSJN by Minister of Public Works and Services Dromi)	**Issue area:** Privatization **Target:** Decree 1024 (May 1990) which privatized Aerolíneas Argentinas **Claim:** Opposition congressman Fontela alleged that the form of the privatized entity was not included in Law 23.696 (Law of State Reform) which outlined the acceptable forms	July 11, 1990/ September 6, 1990 * 1 month; 26 days	Case dismissed on grounds Fontela lacked standing

Peralta *Recurso extraordinario s/amparo*	Peralta and another v. Argentina (Ministry of Economy/Central Bank)	**Issue area:** Monetary policy **Target:** DNU 36 (January 1990) which launched a dramatic economic program ("Plan Bonex") including a bank freeze **Claim:** Plaintiff alleged that the bank freeze violated his constitutional property rights	June 21, 1990/ December 27, 1990 * 6 months; 6 days	Plan Bonex upheld
Arenera *Recurso extraordinario*	Argentina v. Arenera el Libertador (a shipping company)	**Issue area:** Taxation/tolls **Target:** Law 22.424 and Resolutions 53 (1982) (Annex I and Article 4) of the Ministry of Economy and 55 (1983) (Annex I and Article 6) of the Secretary of Interests **Claim:** Shipping company alleged that a toll imposed by the cited legislation (which two of its ships had passed through the Mitre Canal without paying) violated several articles of the Constitution	April 25, 1988/ June 18, 1991 * 3 years; 1 month; 21 days	Upheld state's ability to charge tolls as constitutional
Cocchia *Recurso extraordinario s/amparo*	Cocchia v. Argentina (and others)	**Issue area:** Labor relations **Target:** Decree 817 (May 1992) (Articles 34–37) which abrogated a wide variety of clauses in several collective bargaining agreements **Claim:** Plaintiff alleged that the decree violated rights established in Article 14bis of the Constitution	January 29, 1993/ December 2, 1993 * 10 months, 3 days	Small part of the decree declared unconstitutional
Cafés la Virginia *Recurso extraordinario*	Cafés la Virginia v. Argentina	**Issue area:** Fiscal **Target:** Resolution 174 (1986) and Law 23.101 (November 1984) establishing taxes on coffee imports **Claim:** Plaintiff claimed that taxes violated international treaties to which Argentina is signatory	July 13, 1992/ October 13, 1994 * 2 years; 3 months	Government required to refund taxes paid by Cafés la Virginia

(*continued*)

APPENDIX 5.1. (*Continued*)

Case Name *Type of Case*	**Parties**	**Issue Area** **Target Decree/Law/Constitutional Amendment/ Other Norm or Action (all federal-level)** **Claim against the Target**	**Date Entered CSJN/ Date of Final Ruling** * **Time Elapsed**	**Ruling**
Benito *Recurso de queja*	Benito v. National Industrial, Commercial and Civil Pensions Bank	**Issue area:** Pensions **Target:** Various norms regulating Law 18.037 (1969) **Claim:** Plaintiff alleged that the updating of pension payments via unrepresentative indexes, the establishing of caps, and the reduction of pension scales violated his right to an adjustable pension; Article 14bis of the Constitution	March 19, 1993 / October 27, 1994 * 1 year; 7 months; 12 days (N.B. Court did not rule on the merits until July 1997)	Preliminary decision (CSJN indicated it would consider the case) suspended the ruling a lower instance court had issued in favor of Benito
Video Club Dreams *Recurso extraordinario s/amparo*	Video Club Dreams v. the National Institute of Cinematography	**Issue area:** Fiscal **Target:** DNU 2736/91 (January 1992) and DNU 949/92 (June 1992) which extended the tax on theater tickets to video showings/sales **Claim:** Plaintiff questions constitutionality of establishing a tax by decree	June 3, 1993/ June 6, 1995 * 2 years; 3 days	Ruled that the president cannot impose taxes by decree
Chocobar *Recurso extraordinario*	Chocobar v. the National Pensions Bank for Personnel of the State and Public Services	**Issue area:** Pensions **Target:** Government's failure to pay adjustable pension; Law 23.298 (implicitly considered) (October 1985); Law 24.463 (implicitly considered) (March 1995) dealing with pension adjustments **Claim:** Plaintiff claimed government's failure to adjust pension payments over time violated his right to an adjustable pension	20 May 1994/ December 27, 1996 * 2 years; 7 months; 7 days	Declared part of Law 24.463 unconstitutional and established pension rate

Rodríguez *Direct presentation by cabinet minister before high court*	Ten deputies and the Ombudsman v. the National Executive (Menem's chief of staff filed case directly before the CSJN)	**Issue area:** Privatization **Target:** DNU 842 (August 1997) privatizing airports **Claim:** Plaintiffs alleged decree was unconstitutional because its content violated the Constitution's restrictions on the subject matter of DNUs and because there was a law pending in congress on the issue of airport privatization	October 17, 1997/ December 17, 1997 * 2 months	Found the judiciary has no competence to rule in the case, and plaintiffs lacked standing
Prodelco *Recurso extraordinario s/amparo*	PRODELCO v. National Executive	**Issue area:** Privatization/regulation **Target:** Decree 92 (February 1997), which approved significant modifications to the General Structure of Telephone Service Tariffs **Claim:** Plaintiffs alleged that the new telephone rate structure violated the bid terms and conditions, various agreements, and Constitutional Articles 17, 31 and 42	October 3, 1997/ May 7, 1998 * 7 months, 4 days	Dismissed the case on basis that it was a political question and plaintiffs lacked standing
Verrocchi *Recurso extraordinario s/amparo*	Verrocchi v. Argentina (National Executive)	**Issue area:** Salaries/benefits **Target:** DNU 770 (July 1996); DNU 771 (July 1996), which excluded workers earning more than a minimum from receiving a certain additional payment **Claim:** Plaintiff claimed that suspension of family subsidy violated his constitutional right to "family protection" (Art. 14bis) and the International Pact of Economic, Social, and Cultural Rights	December 11, 1996/ August 19, 1999 * 2 years; 8 months; 8 days	Declared the DNUs unconstitutional

(*continued*)

APPENDIX 5.1. *(Continued)*

Case Name *Type of Case*	**Parties**	**Issue Area** **Target Decree/Law/Constitutional Amendment/ Other Norm or Action (all federal-level)** **Claim against the Target**	**Date Entered CSJN/ Date of Final Ruling** * **Time Elapsed**	**Ruling**
Guida *Recurso extraordinario*	Guida v. National Executive	**Issue area:** Salaries/income **Target:** DNU 290 (March 1995), which reduced public sector salaries **Claim:** Plaintiff alleged that DNU 290 violated her right to a fair salary and to equal pay for equal work; the guarantee of the stability of public sector employment; and property rights	April 22, 1997/ June 2, 2000 * 3 years; 1 month; 11 days	Decree upheld
Kiper *Recurso de apelación por salto de instancia*	Kiper v. Argentina (lower court ruling appealed to CSJN by Bank of the City of Buenos Aires)	**Issue area:** Monetary **Target:** Decree 1570 (December 2001), which imposed a freeze on bank accounts **Claim:** Plaintiff alleged that the bank freeze violated his constitutional rights; bank claimed that it did not have the money to return and should not be forced to comply with a ruling on a case to which it was not a party and in which it could not defend itself	December 27, 2001/ December 28, 2001 * 1 day	Struck lower court ruling on technical grounds
Smith *Recurso de apelación por salto de instancia*	Smith v. National Executive (appealed to CSJN by Banks of Galicia and Buenos Aires)	**Issue area:** Monetary **Target:** Decree 1570 (December 2001), which established a freeze on bank accounts **Claim:** Plaintiff alleged that bank freeze violated Article 17 of the Constitution and contradicted Law 25.466; bank claimed that it did not have the money to return and did not have to comply with a ruling on a case to which it was not a party and in which it could not defend itself	January 2, 2002/ February 1, 2002 * 30 days	Declared the questioned decree unconstitutional

Tobar *Recurso extraordinario s/amparo*	Tobar v. Ministry of Defense	**Issue area:** Salaries/benefits **Target:** DNU 896 (July 2001) calling for public sector salary cuts; Law 24.453 (July 2001) (Law of Zero Deficit) **Claim:** Plaintiff claimed that policies that altered the conditions of his public employment contract violated his constitutional rights	April 26, 2002/ August 22, 2002 * 3 months; 27 days	Declared the questioned norms unconstitutional
San Luis *Acción originaria (amparo)*	Province of San Luis v. Argentina	**Issue area:** Monetary **Target:** Decree 1570 (December 2001); DNU 214 (February 2002), Articles 2 and 12; DNU 320 (February 2002) regarding a bank freeze and forced conversion of dollars to *pesos* **Claim:** Plaintiff claimed questioned norms violated property rights guaranteed in Article 17 of the Constitution and the Pact of San José de Costa Rica	February 20, 2002/ March 5, 2003 * 1 year; 13 days	Declared the questioned norm unconstitutional

APPENDIX 5.2. *Intensity of Argentine CSJN Rulings Endorsing the Exercise of Government Power on Crucial Economic Policy Cases (strongest to weakest)*

Case (year decided)	Type of Policy	Text of Decision[a]	Timing of Decision[b]	Relationship of Decision to Decision of Next Lowest Court[c]	Form of Decision[d]	Procedure[e]	Vote[f]	TOTAL 12 – 7.5 = Stronger Endorsement 7 – 2 = Weaker Endorsement	Conversion –11 = Strongest Endorsement –1 = Weakest Endorsement
Peralta (1990)	Monetary	4	0	2	2	0	2	10 (Stronger)	–9
Aerolíneas (1990)	Privatization	3	1	2	1	1	1	9 (Stronger)	–8
Soengas (1990)	Salaries	4	0	2	2	0	1	9 (Stronger)	–8
Arenera (1991)	Fiscal	4	0	1	2	0	2	9 (Stronger)	–8
Cocchia (1993)	Labor relations	3.5	0	2	2	0	1	8.5 (Stronger)	–7.5
Guida (2000)	Salaries	2.5	1	2	2	0	1	8.5 (Stronger)	–7.5
Rodríguez (1997)	Privatization	3	0	2	1	1	1	8 (Stronger)	–7
Prodelco (1998)	Privatization	1.5	1	2	1	0	2	7.5 (Stronger)	–6.5
Benito (1994)	Pensions	0	0	2	1	1	2	6 (Weaker)	–5
Kiper (2001)	Monetary	0	0	2	1	0	2	5 (Weaker)	–4

[a] *Scoring*: 0 (Decision silent on policy; silent on government power); 0.5 (Decision partially endorses policy; silent on government power); 1 (Decision endorses policy; silent on government power); 1.5 (Decision silent on policy; partially/weakly endorses government power); 2 (Decision partially endorses policy; partially/weakly endorses government power); 2.5 (Decision endorses policy; partially/weakly endorses government power); 3 (Decision silent on policy; endorses government power); 3.5 (Decision partially endorses policy; endorses government power); 4 (Decision endorses policy; endorses government power)

[b] *Scoring*: –1 (Delayed ruling to withhold endorsement); 0 (No strategic importance attached); 1 (Quick ruling *or* delayed ruling to allow endorsement or stronger endorsement)

[c] *Scoring*: 1 (Confirmed); 2 (Suspended or overturned)

[d] *Scoring*: 1 (Did not decide on merits [batted away; preliminary ruling, etc.]); 2 (Decided on merits)

[e] *Scoring*: 0 (No procedural irregularities); 1 (Procedurally irregular – constitutionally questionable acceptance or consideration)

[f] *Scoring*: 1 (Divided); 2 (Unanimous)

APPENDIX 5.3. *Intensity of Argentine CSJN Rulings Challenging the Exercise of Government Power on Crucial Economic Policy Cases (weakest to strongest)*

Case (year decided)	Type of Policy	Policy's Importance to Government[a]	Government that Issued Policy Still in Power at Time of Decision[b]	Text of Decision[c]	Timing of Decision[d]	Relationship of Decision to Decision of Next Lowest Court[e]	Form of Decision[f]	Procedure[g]	Vote[h]	TOTAL 3–11 = Weaker Challenge 11.5–19.5 = Stronger Challenge	Conversion 1 = Weakest Challenge 17.5 = Strongest Challenge
Cafés la Virginia (1994)	Fiscal	0	1	4	0	1.5	2	0	1	9.5 (Weaker)	7.5
Chocobar (1996)	Pensions	4	1.5	0.5	−1	2	2	0	1	10 (Weaker)	8
Verrocchi (1999)	Salaries	0	2	4	0	1	2	0	1	10 (Weaker)	8
Video Club Dreams (1995)	Fiscal	0	2	3.5	0	1	1.5	1	1.5	10.5 (Weaker)	8.5
Tobar (2002)	Salaries	4	1	4	1	1	2	0	1	14 (Stronger)	12
San Luis (2003)[i]	Monetary	4	2	2.5	−1	N.A.	2	0.5	1	11 (Stronger)	13
Rolón Zappa (1986)	Pensions	4	2	5.5	0	1	1	0	2	15.5 (Stronger)	13.5
Smith (2002)	Monetary	4	1	4	1	1	2	1	2	16 (Stronger)	14

[a] *Scoring*: 0 (Policy no longer in place at time of decision); 2 (Low); 4(High).
[b] *Scoring*: 1 (No); 2 (Yes).
[c] *Scoring*: 0 (Decision silent on policy; endorses government power); 0.5 (Decision partially challenges policy; endorses government power); 1 (Decision challenges policy; endorses government power); 1.5 (Decision silent on policy; silent on government power); 2 (Decision partially challenges policy; silent on government power); 2.5 (Decision challenges policy; silent on government power); 3 (Decision silent on policy; partially/weakly challenges government power); 3.5 (Decision partially challenges policy, partially/weakly challenges government power); 4 (Decision challenges policy; partially/weakly challenges government power); 4.5 (Decision silent on policy; challenges government power); 5 (Decision partially challenges policy; challenges government power); 5.5 (Decision challenges policy; challenges government power).
[d] *Scoring*: −1 (Delayed ruling to allow weaker challenge); 0 (No strategic importance attached to timing); 1 (Quick ruling *or* delayed ruling to allow challenge or stronger challenge).
[e] *Scoring*: 1 (Confirmed); 2 (Suspended or overturned).
[f] *Scoring*: 1 (Did not decide on merits [batted away; preliminary ruling, etc.]); 2 (Decided on merits).
[g] *Scoring*: 0 (No procedural irregularities); 1 (Procedurally irregular acceptance or consideration).
[h] *Scoring*: 1 (Divided); 2 (Unanimous [of those voting]).
[i] Scoring range for San Luis: 2–9.5 = weaker challenge; 9.5–17 = stronger challenge.

APPENDIX 5.4. *Considerations Imputed to be Important to Argentine CSJN Rulings on Eighteen Crucial Economic Policy Cases and Approach to Decision Making (ordered by ruling assertiveness – from strongest to weakest endorsement; from weakest to strongest challenge)*

Consideration and Approach Key:[a]

(JI) Justices' ideology (Approach = preference-driven)
(JCI) Justices' corporatist interests (Approach = self-protective)
(PO) Public opinion (Approach = support-building)
(EBP) Elected branches' preferences (Approach = deferential)
(PR) Potential repercussions of decision (for economy; governance; institutional system) (Approach = pragmatic)
(L) Legal merits (constitutional procedure; constitutional substance; strength of legal reasoning) (Approach = principled)

Case (year decided)	Scores for Considerations Mentioned by CSJN in Opinion and by Justices in Interviews	Scores for Considerations Mentioned in Newspapers	Scores for Considerations Mentioned in Expert Interviews	Scores for Considerations Mentioned in Scholarly Sources Used to Choose Cases	Consideration Totals and Corresponding Approaches to Decision Making[b]
STRONGER ENDORSEMENT					
Peralta (1990)	• PR • L		• EC-08: PR • EC-11: EBP • EC-11: PR • EC-13: EBP • EC-19: PR • EC-20: PR • EC-23: PR • EC-24: PR • EC-26 : L • EC-26: PR • EC-26: EBP • EC-33: PR	• Miller 2000: EBP • Miller 2000: PR • Gargarella 1998: EBP • Bohmer 2000: EBP • Gil Domínguez 2002: EBP • Santiago 1998: EBP • Bianchi 1998: EBP	• **EBP: 54%** (15/28 mentions) • **PR: 39%** (11/28 mentions) • L: 7% (2/28 mentions) • **Approach: Deferential & Pragmatic**

			• E-02: PR • E-02: EBP • E-04: EBP • E-05: EBP • E-07: EBP • E-09: EBP • E-22: EBP		
Aerolíneas (1990)	• PR • L	• NP 01–36: EBP	• EC-07: L • EC-11: L • EC-13: EBP • EC-14: L • EC-15: L • EC-20: L • EC-22: EBP • EC-24: EBP • EC-26: JCI • EC-26: L • EC-26: EBP • EC-28: L • EC-33: L • EC-33: EBP • E-02: EBP • E-08: EBP • E-10: EBP • E-21: EBP • E-22: EBP	• Miller 2000: JCI • Miller 2000: EBP • Santiago 1998: EBP • Gargarella 1998: EBP • Gil Domínguez 2002: EBP • Verbitsky 1993: EBP • Bianchi 2002a: L • Bianchi 2002a: JCI • Bianchi 2002a: PR • Bianchi 2002a: EBP	• JCI: 9% (3/32 mentions) • **EBP: 53%** (17/32 mentions) • PR: 6% (2/32 mentions) • L: 31% (10/32 mentions) • **Approach: Deferential**
Soengas (1990)	• PR • L		• E-18: EBP	• Gargarella 1998: EBP • Verbitsky 1993: EBP • Bianchi 2002: EBP	• **EBP: 67%** (4/6 mentions) • PR: 17% (1/6 mentions) • L: 17% (1/6 mentions) • **Approach: Deferential**

(*continued*)

APPENDIX 5.4. (*Continued*)

Case (year decided)	Scores for Considerations Mentioned by CSJN in Opinion and by Justices in Interviews	Scores for Considerations Mentioned in Newspapers	Scores for Considerations Mentioned in Expert Interviews	Scores for Considerations Mentioned in Scholarly Sources Used to Choose Cases	Consideration Totals and Corresponding Approaches to Decision Making[b]
Arenera (1991)	• PR • L		• EC-15: PR • EC-21–01: L • EC-26: PR	• Santiago 1994: PR • Verbitsky 1993: EBP	• EBP: 14% (1/7 mentions) • **PR: 57%** (4/7 mentions) • L: 29% (2/7 mentions) • **Approach: Pragmatic**
Cocchia (1993)	• PR • L • EBP		• EC-0: EBP • EC-05: EBP • EC-06: EBP • EC-10: EBP • EC-15: EBP • EC-26: EBP	• Santiago 1998: EBP • Santiago 1998: PR • Bianchi 2002a: EBP	• **EBP: 75%** (9/12 mentions) • PR: 17% (2/12 mentions) • L: 8% (1/12 mentions) • **Approach: Deferential**
Guida (2000)	• L • PR	• NP 01–589: EBP • NP 01–589: JI	• EC-05: EBP • EC-11: EBP • EC-11: PO • EC-13: EBP • EC-24: EBP • EC-26: EBP • E-03: EBP • EC-03: L	• Bianchi 2002a: EBP • Gelli 2003b: L	• JI: 7% (1/14 mentions) • PO: 7% (1/14 mentions) • **EBP: 57%** (8/14 mentions) • PR: 7% (1/14 mentions) • L: 21% (3/14 mentions) • **Approach: Deferential**
Rodríguez (1997)	• L • PR	• NP 02–658: EBP • NP 02–659: EBP • NP 02-E-183: EBP • NP 02–663: EBP • NP 02–664: EBP	• EC-08: L • EC-15: L • EC-21: EBP • EC-23: EBP • E-07: EBP • E-12: EBP	• Santiago 1998: EBP • Bianchi 2002a: EBP • Miller 2000: L • Gelli 2003b: PO	• PO: 5% (1/20 mentions) • **EBP: 65%** (13/20 mentions) • PR: 5% (1/20 mentions) • L: 25% (5/20 mentions) • **Approach: Deferential**

			• E-15: EBP • E-21: EBP • E-21: L		
Prodelco (1998)	• L	• NP 02–701: EBP • NP 02-E-199: EBP	• EC-10: L • EC-11–03: L • EC-15: L • EC-15: EBP • EC-21: L • E-07: EBP • E-12: L • E-15: L • E-15: EBP • E-19: L	• Santiago 1998: L	• **EBP: 36%** (5/14 mentions) • **L: 64%** (9/14 mentions) • **Approach: Principled & Deferential**
WEAKER ENDORSEMENT					
Benito (1994)	• EBP • L	• NP 02–341: EBP • NP 02–343: JCI	• EC-06: EBP • EC-06: L	• Pellet Lastra 2003b: EBP	• JCI: 14% (1/7 mentions) • **EBP: 57%** (4/7 mentions) • L: 29% (2/7 mentions) • **Approach: Deferential**
Kiper (2001)	• L		• EC-02: EBP • EC-05: EBP • EC-05: PR • EC-10: L • EC-11: L • EC-15: L • EC-21: L • EC-22: L • EC-24: PR • EC-25: L • EC-26: L • EC-26: EBP • E-22: EBP		• EBP: 29% (4/14 mentions) • PR: 14% (2/14 mentions) • **L: 57%** (8/14 mentions) • **Approach: Principled**

(continued)

Case (year decided)	Scores for Considerations Mentioned by CSJN in Opinion and by Justices in Interviews	Scores for Considerations Mentioned in Newspapers	Scores for Considerations Mentioned in Expert Interviews	Scores for Considerations Mentioned in Scholarly Sources Used to Choose Cases	Consideration Totals and Corresponding Approaches to Decision Making[b]
WEAKER CHALLENGE					
Cafés la Virginia (1994)	• PR • L		• EC-05: L • EC-05: PR • EC-05: EBP • EC-13: EBP • E-17: EBP	• Santiago 1998: PR	• **EBP:** 38% (3/8 mentions) • **PR:** 38% (3/8 mentions) • L: 25% (2/8 mentions) • **Approach: Deferential & Pragmatic**
Chocobar (1996)	• L •PR •EBP	• NP 02-E-139: PR • NP 02–46: EBP	• EC-06: EBP • EC-06: JCI • EC-07: EBP • EC-23: PR • EC-24: PR • EC-24: JCI • EC-26: PR • E-17: EBP • E-04–02: EBP • E-21: EBP	• Santiago 1998: PR	• JCI: 13% (2/16 mentions) • **EBP:** 44% (7/16 mentions) • **PR:** 38% (6/16 mentions) • L: 6% (1/16 mentions) • **Approach: Deferential & Pragmatic**
Verrocchi (1999)	• JCI • L		• EC-05: L • EC-10: L • EC-13: L • EC-13: JCI • EC-15: L • EC-26: L • EC-32: L		• **JCI:** 36% (5/14 mentions) • PO: 7% (1/14 mentions) • **L:** 57% (8/14 mentions) • **Approach: Principled & Protective**

			• E-06: L • EC-06: JCI • E-15: JCI • EC-15: PO • E-18: JCI		
Video Club Dreams (1995)	• L		• EC-04: L • EC-05: L • EC-10: L • EC-11: L • EC-21: L • EC-26: L	• Santiago 1998: L	• **L: 100%** (8/8 mentions) • **Approach: Principled**
STRONGER CHALLENGE					
Tobar (2002)	•PR • L	• NP 02–54: JCI • NP 02-E-15: JCI • NP 02-E-23: JCI • NP 02–59: JCI	• EC-04: JCI • EC-07: PO • EC-10: L • EC-10: JCI • EC-20: PO • EC-26: PO • EC-26: JCI • E-03: JCI • E-15: JCI • E-16: JCI • EC-16: PO • E-18: PO	• Bianchi 2002b: L • Bianchi 2002b: JCI • Bianchi 2002b: PR • Gelli 2003b: L • Gelli 2003b: PO • Gelli 2003b: JCI	• **JCI: 50%** (12/24 mentions) • PO: 25% (6/24 mentions) • PR: 8% (2/24 mentions) • L: 17% (4/24 mentions) • **Approach: Protective**
San Luis (2003)	• L • PR	• NP 02-E-40: L • NP 02-E-40: EBP • NP 02-E-84: L • NP 02-E-86: PR • NP 02–89: L • NP 02–89: PR • NP 02–93a: L	• EC-08: PO • EC-08: JCI • EC-15: PR • EC-15: L • EC-20: L • EC-21: PR • EC-21: PO		• JCI: 14% (5/36 mentions) • PO: 11% (4/36 mentions) • EBP: 22% (8/36 mentions) • **PR: 25%** (9/36 mentions) • **L: 28%** (10/36 mentions) • **Approach: Principled & Pragmatic**[c]

(continued)

APPENDIX 5.4. (*Continued*)

Case (year decided)	Scores for Considerations Mentioned by CSJN in Opinion and by Justices in Interviews	Scores for Considerations Mentioned in Newspapers	Scores for Considerations Mentioned in Expert Interviews	Scores for Considerations Mentioned in Scholarly Sources Used to Choose Cases	Consideration Totals and Corresponding Approaches to Decision Making[b]
		• NP 02–93b: PR • NP 02–93c: PR • NP 02–94: L • NP 02–86: EBP • NP 02–87: EBP	• EC-21: EBP • EC-23: PR • EC-24: JCI • EC-26; JCI • EC-26: L • EC-26: PR • EC-26: PO • EC-28: EBP • EC-28: PO • EC-32: EBP • E-10: L • E-14: JCI • E-19: JCI • EC-10: EBP • E-07: EBP		
Rolón Zappa (1986)	• L		• EC-06: JCI • EC-26: L • E-19: PO	• Santiago 1998: L • Oteiza 1994: JCI	• **JCI:** 33% (2/6 mentions) • PO: 17% (1/6 mentions) • **L:** 50% (3/6 mentions) • **Approach: Principled & Protective**
Smith (2002)	• PR • L • JCI	• NP 01–46: JCI • NP 01–47: L • NP 01–47: JCI	• CC-05: PO • CC-05: JCI • EC-03: JCI	• Gargarella 2003: JCI • Gelli 2003b: L	• **JCI:** 67% (33/49 mentions) • PO: 10% (5/49 mentions) • EBP: 2% (1/49 mentions)

- NP 01–49: JCI
- NP 01–50: JCI
- NP 01–51: PO
- NP 01–51: JCI
- NP 01–52: L
- NP 01–52: JCI
- NP 01-E-20: JCI
- NP 01-E-23: PO
- NP 01–62: JCI
- NP 01–65: JCI
- NP 01-E-33: JCI

- EC-05: L
- EC-05: JCI
- EC-05: PO
- EC-07: JCI
- EC-11: JCI
- EC-15: L
- EC-15: JCI
- EC-16: JCI
- EC-17: JCI
- EC-18: L
- EC-18: JCI
- EC-19: JCI
- EC-22: JCI
- EC-24: JCI
- EC-26: PO
- EC-26: JCI
- EC-28: EBP
- EC-33: JCI
- E-03: JCI
- E-11: JCI
- E-14: JCI
- E-15: L
- E-15: JCI
- E-16: L
- E-16: JCI
- E-20: JCI
- E-22: JCI

- PR: 2% (1/49 mentions)
- L: 18% (9/49 mentions)
- **Approach: Protective**

[a] Each consideration mentioned in each CSJN opinion, by each expert respondent, in each newspaper article, and in each academic source, was counted separately.

[b] Approach to decision making corresponds to considerations that constituted 33% or more of mentions.

[c] As no consideration constituted 33% or more of mentions, the limit was lowered to 25%. An alternative would have been for approach to decision making to correspond to the consideration that was most-often mentioned, yet the fact that no consideration was mentioned in more than 28% of the sources suggests that multiple considerations motivated the ruling; lowering the limit to 25% captures that logic.

APPENDIX 5.5. *Elected Branches' Compliance with and Retaliation against CSJN Rulings Challenging the Exercise of Government Power (in order of degree of compliance)*

Case (year decided)	Type of Policy	Extent to which Ruling Obeyed[a]	Difficulty/ Speed of Compliance – Letter[b]	Difficulty/ Speed of Compliance – Spirit[c]
Smith (2002)	Monetary	0	0.5	1.5
Rolón Zappa (1986)	Pensions	0	0.5	1.5
Cafés la Virginia (1994)	Fiscal	2	0.5	0
Verrocchi (1999)	Salaries	2	0.5	0
Video Club Dreams (1995)	Fiscal	2	1	0
San Luis (2003)	Monetary	2	0.5	1.5
Chocobar (1996)	Pensions	2.5	0.5	1.5
Tobar (2002)	Salaries	3.5	0.5	1.75

[a] *Scoring*: –1 (Letter not obeyed; spirit ignored); –0.5 (Letter not obeyed; no relationship between ruling and compliance with spirit); 0 (No connection between obeying letter and ruling; no relationship between ruling and compliance with spirit); 0.5 (Letter partially obeyed; spirit ignored); 1 (Letter obeyed; spirit ignored); 1.5 (Letter partially obeyed; no relationship between ruling and compliance with spirit); 2 (Letter obeyed; no relationship between ruling and compliance with spirit); 2.5 (Letter not obeyed; spirit partially obeyed); 3 (Letter partially obeyed; spirit partially obeyed); 3.5 (Letter obeyed; spirit partially obeyed); 4 (Letter not obeyed; spirit obeyed); 4.5 (Letter partially obeyed; spirit obeyed); 5 (Letter obeyed; spirit obeyed).

[b] *Scoring*: 0 (Not obeyed); 0.5 (Easy/Slow [more than 6 months]); 1 (Easy/Quick [less than 6 months]); 1.5 (Difficult/Slow [more than 6 months]); 2 (Difficult/Quick [less than 6 months]).

[c] *Scoring*: 0 (Not obeyed or policy no longer in place once ruling made); 0.5 (Easy/Slow [more than 1 year]); 1 (Easy/Quick [less than 1 year]); 1.5 (Difficult/Slow [more than 1 year]); 2 (Difficult/Quick [less than 1 year]).

[d] *Scoring*: If the government passed a decree or law that undermined the Court's decision, the degree to which it did so: –1 (significant); –0.5 (some); 0 (none).

[e] *Scoring*: Degree to which government threatened the Court as an institution: –1 (significant); –0.5 (some); 0 (none).

Degree of Compliance −1 to 2 = Noncompliance 2.5–5.5 = Partial 6–9 = Significant	Conversion 11 = Least Compliance 1 = Most Compliance	Degree of Retaliation – Policy[d]	Degree of Retaliation – Institutional[e]	Degree of Retaliation −2 = Significant −1 = Some 0 = None	Conversion 12 = Most Significant 0 = None
2 (Noncompliance)	8	−1	−1	−2 (Significant)	12
2 (Noncompliance)	8	−1	0	−1 (Some)	6
2.5 (Partial)	7.5	0	0	0 (None)	0
2.5 (Partial)	7.5	0	0	0 (None)	0
3 (Partial)	7	0	0	0 (None)	0
4 (Partial)	6	0	−1	−1 (Some)	6
4.5 (Partial)	5.5	0	0	0 (None)	0
5.75 (Partial)	4.25	−0.75	−0.5	−1.25 (Some)	7.5

APPENDIX 6.1. *Twenty-Six Crucial Economic Policy Cases Decided by the Brazilian STF (1985–2004) (in chronological order by year of ruling)*

Case Type and Number **Case Topic**	**Parties**	**Issue Area** **Target Decree/Law/Constitutional Amendment/Other Norm or Action (all federal-level)** **Claim against the Target**	**Date Distributed / Date of Final Ruling** * **Time Elapsed**	**Ruling**[a]
ADIn 04 Capping of interest rate in Constitution at 12%	Democratic Workers Party (PDT) v. President	**Issue area:** Monetary policy **Target:** *Parecer* of the *Consultor Geral* (SR no. 70, published October 1988) and Central Bank *Circular* 1365 based on that *parecer* **Claim:** Plaintiff claimed that policies violated Constitutional Article 192 (which established the interest rate at 12%)	October 12, 1988/ March 7, 1991 * 2 years, 4 months, 26 days	Upheld constitutionality of the government policies
ADIn 259 & ADIn 534 Collor Plan I – freezing of savings accounts	Workers Party (PT) v. President & Brazilian Socialist Party (PSB) v. Congress	**Issue area:** Monetary policy **Target:** 18 MPs composing Collor Plan I including MP 168 (March 1990) which instituted a new currency and blocked savings accounts in excess of 50,000 *cruzados novos* (US$ 1,300) for 18 months **Claim:** Plaintiff alleged that 18 MPs were unconstitutional but did not stipulate basis for each allegation & **Target:** Law 8024 (April 1990) into which MP 168 (March 1990) had been converted, (specifically Articles 5–10, 19, and 20 and others connected to them)	April 6, 1990/ March 11, 1991 * 11 months, 5 days & 20 June 1991/ 26 August 1992 * 1 year, 2, months, 6 days	Dismissed without consideration citing technical flaws & Ruled that it could not suspend the law in abstract review, emphasized that decision did not suspend either cases in course or decisions already taken at other levels of the judiciary

		Claim: Plaintiff alleged that the policy represented a "compulsory loan" and its establishment via an MP (and other procedural aspects of its emission) violated Article 148 of the Constitution (which delineates the rules by which compulsory loans can be imposed)		
RE 147684 Readjustment of retirement benefits of 147.06%	The Public Ministry and Brazil v. Union of Workers in the Metallurgic, Mechanical, and Electrical Industries of São Paulo	**Issue area:** Pensions **Target:** A government policy (*Portaria* 3485 of September 1991) that established that certain retirees would not receive a 147.06% adjustment in their benefits **Claim:** Collective plaintiff alleged that their union's retirees had a right to the 147.06% increase in benefits (since those benefits were linked to the minimum wage, which had been increased by 147.06%), and that the questioned *Portaria* (which set the adjustment at a lower level) violated Transitory Articles 58 and 59 of the Constitution and Laws 8.212, 8.213, and 8.222 of 1991	April 23, 1992/ June 26, 1992 * 2 months, 3 days	Directed the government to adjust certain pensioners' benefits by 147.06%
RE 150755 & RE 150764 Fund for Social Investment (FINSOCIAL)	Brazil v. Nordeste Segurança de Valores, Ltda. & Brazil v. Empresa Distribuidora Vivacqua de Bebidas, Ltda.	**Issue area:** Fiscal policy **Target:** Article 28 of Law 7.738 (March 1989), which established a 0.5% FINSOCIAL tax on public and private service-providers; FINSOCIAL, created by Decree-Law 1940 (May 1982), taxed gross earnings of firms selling merchandise or merchandise and services, financial institutions, and insurance companies	July 1, 1992/ November 18, 1992 * 4 months, 17 days & August 4, 1992/ December 16, 1992 * 5 months, 12 days	Upheld one of the articles that had been declared unconstitutional by the lower court & Declared unconstitutional several incremental increases in the FINSOCIAL tax

(*continued*)

APPENDIX 6.1. (*Continued*)

Case Type and Number Case Topic	Parties	Issue Area Target Decree/Law/Constitutional Amendment/Other Norm or Action (all federal-level) Claim against the Target	Date Distributed / Date of Final Ruling * Time Elapsed	Ruling[a]
		Claim: A company dedicated to service-provision petitioned to be exempt from the FINSOCIAL tax & **Target:** Article 9 of Law 7.689 (December 1988); Article 7 of Law 7.787 (June 1989); Article 1 of Law 7.894 (November 1989), and Article 1 of Law 8.147 (December 1990), which incrementally increased the FINSOCIAL tax to be paid by companies selling merchandise, and mixed companies (engaged in selling merchandise and providing services) **Claim:** A mixed company questioned whether the FINSOCIAL tax was constitutional after Law 7.689		
ADC 01 Contribution for Financing Social Security (COFINS)	President, leaders of the Senate and Chamber of Deputies (*all plaintiffs*)	**Issue area:** Fiscal policy **Target:** Complementary Law 70 (December 1991), which instituted the Contribution for Financing Social Security (COFINS) (among other stipulations) **Claim:** Claimants petitioned to have the policy declared *constitutional* in its entirety	August 3, 1993/ December 1, 1993 * 3 months, 29 days	Declared certain articles of law constitutional; declared constitutionality of ADC mechanism

ADIn 926 & ADIn 939 Provisional Tax on Financial Transactions (IPMF)	Governors of five states v. President/ Congress & National Confederation of Commerce Workers (CNTC) v. President/ Congress	**Issue area:** Fiscal policy **Target:** Constitutional Amendment No. 3 (March 1993), which established the IPMF, specifically Article 2, clause 2, which asserted the inapplicability to the amendment of Article 150, part III, letter "b"; of Article 150 part VI; and of Article 153, clause 5 of the Constitution **Claim:** Plaintiff claimed that the amendment violated the constitutional principle of reciprocal immunity in taxation (Constitutional Article 150, part VI, letter "a") & **Target:** Constitutional Amendment No. 3 (March 1993), which established the IPMF (several aspects) and Complementary Law 77 (July 1993) **Claim:** Plaintiff claimed that the amendment and the law violated the constitutional principle of anteriority in taxes (Constitutional Article 150, part III, letter "b"); the principle of reciprocal immunity in taxation (Constitutional Article 150, part VI, letter "a"); and guarantees prohibiting taxes from being cumulative, and prohibiting bi-taxation (Constitutional Article 154, part I)	August 25, 1993/ March 2, 1994 * 6 months, 5 days & September 8, 1993/ December 15, 1993 * 3 months, 7 days	Suspended the questioned paragraph of Constitutional Amendment No. 3 and the levying of the IPMF tax on the states, federal district, and municipalities until it could make a final ruling on the tax's constitutionality & Suspended Constitutional Amendment No. 3 (Article 2) and Complementary Law 77 – thereby preventing the IPMF from being imposed in 1993, but deeming constitutional its imposition in 1994

(continued)

APPENDIX 6.1. (*Continued*)

Case Type and Number Case Topic	Parties	Issue Area Target Decree/Law/Constitutional Amendment/Other Norm or Action (all federal-level) Claim against the Target	Date Distributed / Date of Final Ruling * Time Elapsed	Ruling[a]
MS 21969 Salary retention for certain public sector workers (10.94%)	Union of Congressional Workers and Workers of the Tribunal de Contas (SINDILEGIS) v. President	**Issue area:** Salaries **Target:** Minister of the Treasury's removal (via Aviso 336) of 10.94% of the March 1994 salary from the bank account of some employees of the legislature and Tribunal de Contas **Claim:** Plaintiff alleged that the executive's action violated the independence of the legislature (guaranteed in Article 2 of the Constitution) as well as Article 52 (part XIII), which awards the legislature the power to set its employees' salaries	March 24, 1994/ May 5, 1994 * 1 month, 11 days	Ordered that the disputed funds be placed in an escrow account until the case could be decided in full; eventually ruled moot
ADIn 223 & ADIn 295 Collor Plan I – no injunctions in cases related to the Plan	Democratic Workers Party (PDT) v. President & Federal Council of the Brazilian Bar Association v. President	**Issue area:** Monetary policy **Target:** MP 173 (March 1990), which prohibited courts from issuing injunctions in cases resulting from MPs and other norms associated with Collor Plan I **Claim:** Plaintiff alleged that MP violated Constitutional Article 5, item 35 (which prohibits excluding norms from review by the judiciary) and item 49 (which provides for the specific judicial mechanism that MP 173 prohibited), and item 65 (which prohibits preventing people's access to their goods) &	March 28, 1990/ February 26, 1996 * 6 years, 10 months, 29 days & June 4, 1990/ November 9, 2001 * 11 years, 5 months, 5 days	Found that MP 173 did not contravene the constitutional guarantee of access to the judiciary & Refused to issue an injunction, arguing that the MP did not imply the risk the plaintiff suggested

		Claim: Plaintiff argued that MP 173 violated Constitutional Article 2 (which establishes the independence of the branches of government) and Article 5, item 35 (which prohibits excluding norms from review by the judiciary)		
RMS 22307 Salary increase of 28.86%	Janete Balzani Marques and others v. Brazil	**Issue area:** Salaries **Target:** The inequity generated by the awarding of a larger salary adjustment to military employees of the executive than to civil employees via Laws 8.622 and 8.627 (of January 1993 and February 1993, respectively) **Claim:** Plaintiffs alleged that their failure to receive a 28.86% salary increase violated Article 37 (paragraph X) of the Constitution, which guarantees salary equality between military and civilian public sector workers	June 1, 1995/ March 11, 1998 * 2 years, 9 months, 10 days	Awarded plaintiff a salary adjustment (though allowed government to take into account previous salary adjustments she had received)
PET 2066 Privatization of the Bank of the State of São Paulo (BANESPA)	Brazil v. Third Regional Federal Tribunal (TRF)	**Issue area:** Privatizations **Target:** Injunction issued by Regional Federal Tribunal (TRF) of the Third Region suspending the sale of BANESPA (declaring unconstitutional the headnote of the opening of the sale process, the government's encouragement of foreign entities to bid on the bank, and the timeline for the sale) **Claim:** Plaintiffs argued that the suspension of the sale would result in a risk to public order and national economic stability	July 11, 2000/ August 29, 2000 * 1 month, 18 days	Allowed the sale to go through

(*continued*)

APPENDIX 6.1. (*Continued*)

Case Type and Number Case Topic	Parties	Issue Area Target Decree/Law/Constitutional Amendment/Other Norm or Action (all federal-level) Claim against the Target	Date Distributed / Date of Final Ruling * Time Elapsed	Ruling[a]
RE 226855 Adjustment of accounts in an employment security fund (the Length of Service Guarantee Fund, FGTS)	Caixa Econômica Federal (CEF) v. Ademar Gomes Mota and others	**Issue area:** Monetary policy **Target:** Constitutionality of adjusting accounts in employment security fund (FGTS), managed by the Caixa Económica Federal (CEF) according to indices associated with five economic stabilization plans imposed between 1986 and 1991 **Claim:** Plaintiffs claimed that the alterations to the indices applied to their FGTS accounts via laws associated with the economic plans were illegal (as they violated the contract they had with the FGTS) and unconstitutional (as they violated property rights and guarantees of equity in the Constitution)	April 16,1998/ October 26, 2000 * 2 years, 8 months, 10 days	Ruled that plaintiffs' FGTS accounts should be readjusted due to losses imposed by the imposition of two of the economic plans
ADIn 2061 Annual salary review for public sector workers	Democratic Workers Party (PDT) and Workers Party (PT) v. President	**Issue area:** Salaries **Target:** President's failure to send to congress an annual bill including a revision of public sector salaries	September 16, 1999/ April 25, 2001 * 1 year, 7 months, 9 days	Declared unconstitutional the president's failure to send congress a bill reviewing public sector salaries in 1999 (per Article 37 of the Constitution) and indicating that the executive should do so

		Claim: Plaintiffs argued that Constitutional Article 37 (as amended by Constitutional Amendment No. 19) required the president to send a bill to congress each year reviewing the remuneration of federal public sector workers; the president had failed to do so by June 5, 1999, one year after the article had been amended. They requested that the STF stipulate a period within which the president must send the bill to congress and remind him of his duty to send such proposals at least every 12 months.		
ADC 09 "The black-out"	President and Attorney General (*both plaintiffs*)	**Issue area:** Public services **Target:** Articles 14 through 18 of MP 2.152–2 (originally of June 2001, and reedited as MP 2.198–5 in August 2001), which revoked MP 2148–1 (May 2001) and established policies to address an energy crisis including consumption goals and a tariff regime **Claim:** Plaintiff (the president) petitioned the STF to declare Articles 14 through 18 of MP 2.152 constitutional, given judicial controversy over policy	June 11, 2001/ December 13, 2001 * 6 months, 2 days	Declared policy constitutional
ADIn 1582 Privatization of the Vale do Rio Doce Company (CVRD)	Federal Council of the Brazilian Bar Association v. President/ Congress	**Issue area:** Privatizations **Target:** Law 9074 (Article 27 and paragraphs I and II) (July 1995) which established procedure for privatizing public services (including the CVRD)	April 15, 1997/ August 7, 2002 * 5 years, 3 months, 23 days	Allowed the sale to go through

(*continued*)

APPENDIX 6.1. (*Continued*)

Case Type and Number Case Topic	Parties	Issue Area Target Decree/Law/Constitutional Amendment/Other Norm or Action (all federal-level) Claim against the Target	Date Distributed / Date of Final Ruling * Time Elapsed	Ruling[a]
		Claim: Plaintiff alleged that the procedures for privatization outlined in the law violated Constitutional Article 175, regarding the government's responsibility to provide public utility services		
ADIn 1497 & ADIn 2031 Provisional Contribution on Financial Transactions (CPMF)	National Confederation of Health Workers (CNTS) v. Congress & Workers Party (PT) v. Congress	**Issue area:** Fiscal policy **Target:** Constitutional Amendment No. 12 (August 1996), which established Transitory Article 74 which stipulated the ability to impose the CPMF tax **Claim:** Plaintiff alleged that the amendment violated Constitutional Articles 60 (§ 4°, paragraph IV) and 154 (paragraph I) (i.e., violated individual rights, and was cumulative) & **Target:** Constitutional Amendment No. 21 (March 1999), which established Transitory Article 75, which extended the CPMF for 36 months, changed its rate, and extended the implementing legislation	September 2, 1996/ October 30, 2003 * 7 years, 1 month, 28 days & August 2, 1999/ October 3, 2002 * 3 years, 2 months*, 1 day	Endorsed the exercise of government power, upholding the state's ability to impose the CPMF tax & Struck down §3 of Article 75 in the Act of Transitory Constitutional Clauses, which authorized the national state to emit bonds

		Claim: Plaintiff alleged that the procedure through which the amendment was approved did not follow the procedure outlined in Constitutional Article 60, § 2 and was thus void; further, the laws that the amendment extended were, at the time of extension, no longer in force; further, the tax was confiscatory, thus violating Constitutional Articles 150 and 7; the tax also violated Constitutional Articles 154 and 5		
ADIn 1946 Maternity leave salary	Brazilian Socialist Party (PSB) v. Leadership of the Chamber of Deputies & Senate, and the Minister of Pensions and Social Assistance	**Issue area:** Salaries **Target:** Article 14 of Constitutional Amendment No. 20 (December 1998), which established a maximum limit (R$ 1,200/month) for the value of benefits of the retirement system for private sector workers stipulated in Article 201 of the Constitution (as well as Article 6 of *Portaria* 4883 [1988] which implemented that constitutional article) **Claim:** Plaintiff alleged that Article 14 of Constitutional Amendment No. 20 (which capped maternity leave benefits) violated Constitutional Article 3 (paragraph IV) and Article 5 (headnote and paragraph I) which prohibit gender discrimination, and Article 7 (paragraph XVIII) which guarantees that women will earn their full salary during maternity leave – and therefore, Article 60 (§4°, paragraph IV) which outlines the constitutional principles that cannot be violated or amended	January 21, 1999/ April 3, 2003 * 4 years, 2 months, 13 days	Ruled that the amendment had to be understood in a way such that it did not cap maternity leave benefits at R$1,200 monthly

(*continued*)

APPENDIX 6.1. (*Continued*)

Case Type and Number Case Topic	Parties	Issue Area Target Decree/Law/Constitutional Amendment/Other Norm or Action (all federal-level) Claim against the Target	Date Distributed / Date of Final Ruling * Time Elapsed	Ruling[a]
ADIn 2010 Public sector workers' and retirees' retirement contributions (I)	Federal Council of the Brazilian Bar Association v. President/ Congress	**Issue area:** Pensions **Target:** Law 9.783 (January 1999), which regulated the contribution of public sector pensioners to the public sector retirement fund, specifically, Article 1, Article 2 and its only paragraph, and Article 3 and its only paragraph **Claim:** Plaintiff argued that laws that institute or raise pensions should be complementary laws; that Congress had violated congressional procedures outlined in Constitutional Article 67; that the tax was confiscatory and violated Constitutional Article 150 (paragraph IV); that the law violated the principle of actuarial balance outlined in Constitutional Article 195 (§ 5) and Article 37 (paragraph XV) and Article 194 (paragraph IV) regarding the irreducibility of salaries and benefits; that the progressive structure of social security contributions violated Article 5 (headnote) and Article 150; that taxing pension benefits violated Article 40 (§ 12) and Article 195 (paragraph II); and that the law violated vested rights (Article 5, paragraph XXXVI)	June 7, 1999/ March 15, 2004 * 4 years, 8 months, 6 days	Suspended several aspects of Law 9.783: Article 1 (which called for contributions by retirees); Article 2 (which established a temporary sliding-scale increase in pension contributions for those with a monthly salary in excess of R$ 1,200); and Article 3 (which set a threshold below which retirees' pension benefits would not be taxed)

ADIn 3105 & ADIn 3128 Tax on public sector pensions (II)	National Association of Public Ministry (CONAMP) v. Congress & National Association of Federal Prosecutors (ANPR) v. Congress	**Issue area:** Fiscal policy **Target:** Article 4 of Constitutional Amendment No. 41 (December 2003) which established a tax on retired state and local public sector workers' retirement benefits equal to the retirement contributions paid by active workers (11%) **Claim:** Plaintiffs alleged that the benefits of those who were already in retirement when the amendment was passed should continue to be regulated by the norms of the retirement system in place when they retired, and as such, that Constitutional Amendment No. 41 (Article 4) violated their individual vested rights per Constitutional Article 5 (a fundamental constitutional clauses that cannot be amended or violated)	December 31, 2003/ August 18, 2004 * 7 months, 19 days & February 5, 2004/ August 18, 2004 * 6 months, 13 days	Upheld the amendment; but adjusted the amount of tax retirees would have to pay
ADIn 2111 Formula for calculating retirement benefits ("fator previdenciário")	National Metalworkers Confederation v. President/ Congress	**Issue area:** Pensions **Target:** Law 9.876 (November 1999), which set the formula for calculating pension contributions and benefits, in particular, Article 2 (which revised Article 29 of Law 8.213 of July 1991), and Article 3 **Claim:** Plaintiff alleged that Congress had violated procedures established in Constitutional Article 65 when passing the law, and that Articles 2 and 3 of the law violated Constitutional Article 5 (Paragraph XXXVI) and Article 201 (§1° E 7°), as well as Constitutional Amendment No. 20 (Article 3)	December 1, 1999/ No final decision	Upheld the law

(*continued*)

APPENDIX 6.1. (*Continued*)

Case Type and Number Case Topic	Parties	Issue Area Target Decree/Law/Constitutional Amendment/Other Norm or Action (all federal-level) Claim against the Target	Date Distributed / Date of Final Ruling * Time Elapsed	Ruling[a]
ADIn 2238 Law of Fiscal Responsibility	Communist Party of Brazil (PCdoB), Workers Party (PT), Brazilian Socialist Party (PSB) v. President/ Congress	**Issue area:** Fiscal policy **Target:** Complementary Law 101 (May 2004) – in its entirety and various parts – and two articles of MP 1980–18 (May 2000) **Claim:** Plaintiffs alleged that the promulgation of Law 101 had not followed the rules stipulated in Article 64 of the constitution, and that more than 20 aspects of the law's content violated innumerable constitutional principles including the separation of powers and federalism	July 4, 2000/ No final decision	Upheld most of the law

[a] The ruling discussed in this column is the ruling to which the government, public, and press reacted. On some occasions, and in particular with cases of the type "ADIn," the ruling that mattered was an injunction, with the final decision on the case only following years later.

APPENDIX 6.2. *Intensity of Brazilian STF Rulings Endorsing the Exercise of Government Power on Crucial Economic Policy Cases (strongest to weakest)*

Case	Case Type and Number (year decided) I = Injunction FD = Final Decision	Type of Policy	Text of Decision[a]	Timing of Decision[b]	Relationship of Decision to Decision of Next Lowest Court[c]	Form and Type of Decision that Gained Importance[d]	Procedure[e]	Vote in Decision that Gained Importance[f]	TOTAL 14.5–7.5 = Stronger Endorsement 7–0 = Weaker Endorsement	Conversion −15.5 = Strongest Endorsement −1 = Weakest Endorsement
Constitutional capping of interest rate at 12%	ADIn 04 (I = 1988; FD = 1991)	Monetary	4	0	2.5	2.5	0.5	1	11.5 (Stronger)	−12.5
Contribution for Financing Social Security (COFINS)	ADC 01 (FD = 1993)	Tax/fiscal	3.5	−1	2.5	2.5	0	2	9.5 (Stronger)	−10.5
Privatization of the Bank of the State of São Paulo (BANESPA)	PET 2066 (FD = 2000)	Privatizations	4	0.5	1.5	2.5	0.5	0	9 (Stronger)	−10
Privatization of the Vale do Rio Doce Company (CVRD)	ADIn 1582 (FD = 2002)	Privatizations	2.5	0	2.5	1.5	0	2	8.5 (Stronger)	−9.5
"The black-out" (O "*apagão*")	ADC 09 (FD = 2001)	Public services	2.5	0.5	2.5	1.5	0	1	8 (Stronger)	−9
Formula for calculating retirement benefits ("factor previdenciário")	ADIn 2111 (No FD)	Pensions/ benefits	2.5	0	2.5	1.5	0	1	7.5 (Stronger)	−8.5
Public sector pensioners' retirement contributions (II)	ADIn 3105 (FD = 2004) ADIn 3128 (FD = 2004)	Pensions/ benefits	1	0	2.5	2.5	0	1	7 (Weaker)	−8

(*continued*)

APPENDIX 6.2. *(Continued)*

Case	Case Type and Number (year decided) I = Injunction FD = Final Decision	Type of Policy	Text of Decision[a]	Timing of Decision[b]	Relationship of Decision to Decision of Next Lowest Court[c]	Form and Type of Decision that Gained Importance[d]	Procedure[e]	Vote in Decision that Gained Importance[f]	TOTAL 14.5–7.5 = Stronger Endorsement 7–0 = Weaker Endorsement	Conversion −15.5 = Strongest Endorsement −1 = Weakest Endorsement
Provisional Contribution on Financial Transactions (CPMF)	ADIn 1497 (FD = 2003)	Tax/fiscal	2	0	2.5	1.5	0	1	7 (Weaker)	−8
Collor Plan I – no injunctions in cases related to Plan	ADIn 223 (I = 1990; FD = 1996)	Monetary	0.5	0	2.5	1.5	0	1	ADIn 223: 5.5 (Weaker)	−8
	ADIn 295 (I = 1990; FD = 2001)	Monetary	3.5	0	2.5	1.5	0	1	ADIn 295: 8.5 (Stronger) Average: 7 (Weaker)	
Collor Plan I – freezing of savings accounts	ADIn 259 (FD = 1991)	Monetary	1.5	0	2.5	2	0	1	ADIn 259: 7 (Weaker)	−7.75
	ADIn 534 (I = 1991; FD = 1992)	Monetary	0.5	1	2.5	1.5	0	1	ADIn 534: 6.5 (Weaker) Average: 6.75 (Weaker)	
Law of Fiscal Responsibility	ADIn 2238 (No FD)	Tax/fiscal	2	0	2.5	1.5	−0.5	1	6.5 (Weaker)	−7.5
Fund for Social Investment (FINSOCIAL)	RE 150755 (FD = 1992)	Tax/fiscal	1	0.5	1.5	2.5	0	1	6.5 (Weaker)	−7.5

[a] *Scoring*: 0 (Decision silent on policy; challenges government power); 0.5 (Decision weakly endorses policy; challenges government power); 1 (Decision endorses policy; challenges government power); 1.5 (Decision silent on policy; silent on government power); 2 (Decision weakly endorses policy; silent on government power); 2.5 (Decision endorses policy; silent on government power); 3 (Decision silent on policy; partially/weakly endorses government power); 3.5 (Decision weakly endorses policy; weakly endorses government power); 4 (Decision endorses policy; partially/weakly endorses government power); 4.5 (Decision silent on policy; endorses government power); 5 (Decision partially endorses policy; endorses government power); 5.5 (Decision endorses policy; endorses exercise of government power)

[b] *Scoring*: −1 (Delayed ruling to withhold endorsement); 0 (No strategic importance attached); 1 (Quick ruling *or* delayed ruling to allow endorsement or stronger endorsement)

[c] *Scoring*: 1 (Confirmed); 1.5 (Suspended or overturned/concrete case filed directly with STF); 2.5 (ADIn, ADC, or ADPF)

[d] *Scoring*: 1 (Injunction – batted away on technicality); 1.5 (Injunction – considered the matter); 2 (Final decision – Technical [i.e. batted away on technicality or related to form of policy or petition]); 2.5 (Final decision – On the merits [i.e. addressed content of policy])

[e] *Scoring*: −1 (To weaken endorsement); 0 (No procedural irregularities); 1 (Procedurally irregular – constitutionally questionable acceptance or consideration)

[f] *Scoring*: 0 (Single justice or one chamber); 1 (Full Court – divided); 2 (Full Court – unanimous)

APPENDIX 6.3. *Intensity of Brazilian STF Rulings Challenging the Exercise of Government Power on Crucial Economic Policy Cases (weakest to strongest)*

Case	Case Type and Number (year decided) I = Injunction FD = Final Decision	Type of Policy	Policy's Importance to Government[a]	Government that Issued Policy Still in Power at Time of Decision[b]	Text of Decision[c]	Timing of Decision[d]	Relationship of Decision to Decision of Next Lowest Court Ruling[e]	Form and Type of Decision that Gained Importance[f]	Procedure[g]	Vote in Decision that Gained Importance[h]	TOTAL 1–9.5 = Weaker Challenge 10–18.5 = Stronger Challenge
Fund for Social Investment (FINSOCIAL)	RE 150764 (FD = 1992)	Tax/ fiscal	1	1	0.5	0	1.25	2.5	0	1	7.25 (Weaker)
Salary increase of 28.86%	RMS 22307 (FD = 1998)	Salaries	1.5	1	2	−0.5	1.5	2.5	−1	1	8 (Weaker)
Adjustment of accounts in employment security fund (FGTS)	RE 226855 (FD = 2000)	Pensions/ benefits	2	1	2	−1	1.5	2.5	−0.5	1	8.5 (Weaker)
Salary retention for certain public sector workers (10.94%)	MS 21969 (I = 1994)	Salaries	1	2	2	0	1.5	1.5	0	1	9 (Weaker)
Maternity leave benefits	ADIn 1946 (FD = 2003)	Pensions/ benefits	1	2	0.5	0	2.5	1.5	0	2	9.5 (Weaker)
Provisional Contribution on Financial Transactions (CPMF)	ADIn 2031 (FD = 2002)	Tax/ fiscal	0.5	2	2	0	2.5	1.5	0	1	9.5 (Weaker)
Adjustment retirement benefits of 147.06%	RE 147864 (FD = 1992)	Pensions/ Benefits	1.5	2	4	−1	1	2	0	1	10.5 (Stronger)

(continued)

APPENDIX 6.3. *(Continued)*

Case	Case Type and Number (year decided) I = Injunction FD = Final Decision	Type of Policy	Policy's Importance to Government[a]	Government that Issued Policy Still in Power at Time of Decision[b]	Text of Decision[c]	Timing of Decision[d]	Relationship of Decision to Decision of Next Lowest Court Ruling[e]	Form and Type of Decision that Gained Importance[f]	Procedure[g]	Vote in Decision that Gained Importance[h]	TOTAL 1–9.5 = Weaker Challenge 10–18.5 = Stronger Challenge
Annual salary review for public sector workers	ADIn 2061 (FD = 2001)	Salaries	1.5	2	0.5	0	2.5	2.5	0	2	11 (Stronger)
Public sector workers' and retirees' retirement contributions (I)	ADIn 2010 (FD = 2004)	Pensions/ benefits	2	2	2.5	0	2.5	1.5	0	1.5	12 (Stronger)
Provisional Tax on Financial Transactions (IPMF)	ADIn 926 (I = 1993; FD = 1994)	Tax/ fiscal	1	2	5	0	2.5	1.5	0	2	ADIn 926: 14 (Stronger)
	ADIn 939 (I = 1993; FD = 1993)		1.5	2	5	0	2.5	2.5	0	1	ADIn 939: 14.5 (Stronger) Average: 14.25 (Stronger)

[a] *Scoring*: 0 (Policy no longer in place at time of decision); 1 (Low); 2 (High).

[b] *Scoring*: 1 (No); 2 (Yes).

[c] *Scoring*: 0 (Decision silent on policy; endorses government power); 0.5 (Decision partially challenges policy; endorses government power); 1 (Decision challenges policy; endorses government power); 1.5 (Decision silent on policy; silent on government power); 2 (Decision partially challenges policy; silent on government power); 2.5 (Decision challenges policy; silent on government power); 3 (Decision silent on policy; partially/weakly challenges government power); 3.5 (Decision partially challenges policy; partially/weakly challenges government power); 4 (Decision challenges policy; partially/weakly challenges government power); 4.5 (Decision silent on policy; challenges government power); 5 (Decision partially challenges policy; challenges government power); 5.5 (Decision challenges policy; challenges government power).

[d] *Scoring*: – 1 (Delayed ruling to allow weaker challenge); 0 (No strategic importance attached to timing); 1 (Quick ruling *or* delayed ruling to allow challenge or stronger challenge).

[e] *Scoring*: 1 (Confirmed); 1.5 (Suspended or overturned / concrete case filed directly with STF); 2.5 (ADIn, ADC, or ADPF).

[f] *Scoring*: 1 (Injunction – batted away on technicality); 1.5 (Injunction – considered the matter); 2 (Final decision – Technical [i.e., batted away on technicality or related to form of policy or petition]); 2.5 (Final decision – on the merits [i.e., addressed content of policy]).

[g] *Scoring*: –1 (To decrease challenge); 0 (No procedural irregularities); 1 (Procedurally irregular – constitutionally questionable acceptance or consideration to increase challenge).

[h] *Scoring*: 0 (Single justice or chamber); 1 (Full Court – divided); 2 (Full Court – unanimous).

APPENDIX 6.4. *Considerations Imputed to be Important to Brazilian STF Rulings on Twenty Crucial Economic Policy Cases/Case Pairs and Approach to Decision Making (ordered by ruling assertiveness – from strongest to weakest endorsement; from weakest to strongest challenge)*

Consideration and Approach Key:[a]

(JI) Justices' ideology (Approach = preference-driven)
(JCI) Justices' corporatist interests (Approach = self-protective)
(PO) Public opinion (Approach = support-building)
(EBP) Elected branches' preferences (Approach = deferential)
(PR) Potential repercussions of decision (for economy; governance; institutional system) (Approach = pragmatic)
(L) Legal merits (constitutional procedure; constitutional substance; strength of legal reasoning) (Approach = principled)

Case (year decided)	Scores for Considerations Mentioned by STF in Opinion and by Justices in Interviews	Scores for Considerations Mentioned in Newspapers	Scores for Considerations Mentioned in Expert Interviews	Scores for Considerations Mentioned in Scholarly Sources Used to Choose Cases	Consideration Totals, and Corresponding Approaches to Decision Making[b]
STRONGER ENDORSEMENT					
Constitutional capping of interest rate at 12% (I = 1988; FD = 1991)	• Dec/inj: PR • Dec/inj: L • CSM-01–01: PR • CSM-03: PR	• NP 01–217: EBP • NP 01–217: PR	• CSE-11: PR • CSE-11: L • CSE-17: PR • EC-07: PR • EC-11: PR • EC-21–03: JCI • EC-21–03: PR • EC-23: PO • EC-26: PR • EC-30: PR • EC-31: PR	• Rocha 2004: PR	• JI: 4% (1/24) • JCI: 4% (1/24) • PO: 4% (1/24) • EBP: 4% (1/24) • **PR: 75% (18/24)** • L: 8% (2/24) • **Approach: Pragmatic**

(continued)

APPENDIX 6.4. (*Continued*)

Case (year decided)	Scores for Considerations Mentioned by STF in Opinion and by Justices in Interviews	Scores for Considerations Mentioned in Newspapers	Scores for Considerations Mentioned in Expert Interviews	Scores for Considerations Mentioned in Scholarly Sources Used to Choose Cases	Consideration Totals, and Corresponding Approaches to Decision Making[b]
			• EC-40: PR • EC-42: PR • EC-42: JI • EC-45: PR • EC-50: PR • EC-51: PR		
Contribution for Financing Social Security (COFINS) (FD = 1993)	• Dec/inj: L • Dec/inj: PR • Dec/inj: JCI • CSM-06: PR	• NP 02–472: PR • NP 02–473: PR	• CSE-22: PR • EC-11: PR • EC-20: PR • EC-31: PR • EC-46: EBP	• Ribeiro de Oliveira 2003: PR • Favetti 2003: EBP • Favetti 2003: PR	• JCI: 7% (1/14) • EBP: 14% (2/1) • **PR:** 71% (10/14) • L: 7% (1/14) • **Approach: Pragmatic**
Privatization of the Bank of the State of São Paulo (BANESPA) (FD = 2000)	• I: L • I: PR • CSM-03: L	• NP 04–110: L	• EC-15: L • EC-19: L • EC-03: PR • EC-31: L		• PR: 25% (2/8) • **L:** 75% (6/8) • **Approach: Principled**
Privatization of the Vale do Rio Doce Company (CVRD) (FD = 2002)	• Dec/inj.: L • CSM-02: L • CSM-02: JCI • CSM-03: L	• NP 03–366: EBP	• CSE-13: JI • CSE-13: EBP • CSE-13: PR • CSE-13: JCI • CSE-13: L • EC-15: L • EC-19: L • EC-29: JI		• JI: 11% (2/19) • JCI: 21% (4/19) • EBP: 16% (3/19) • PR: 11% (2/19) • **L:** 42% (8/19) • **Approach: Principled**

			• EC-30: PR • EC-31: JCI • EC-31: L • EC-34: JCI • EC-37: L • EC-37: EBP		
"The black-out" (O "*apagão*") (FD = 2001)	• Dec: L • Dec: PR • AS-02: JCI • AS-02: PR • CSM-01: PR • CSM-03: PR	• NP 04-E-165: EBP • NP 04–204: PO • NP 04–204: PR	• EC-03: PO • EC-09: L • EC-21: PO • EC-21: PR • CSE-06: PR • CSE-06: L • CSE-10: JCI • CSE-15: EBP	• Vilhena Vieira 2002: PR	• JCI: 11% (2/18) • PO: 17% (3/18) • EBP: 11% (2/18) • **PR: 44%** (8/18) • L: 17% (3/18) • **Approach: Pragmatic**
Formula for calculating retirement benefits ("factor previdenciário") (No FD)	• Inj: L • Inj: PR		• CSE-02: PR • CSE-06: L • EC-01: L • EC-11: PR • EC-14: L • EC-17: L • EC-22: L		• **PR: 33% (3/9)** • **L: 67%** (6/9) • **Approach: Principled/ Pragmatic**
WEAKER ENDORSEMENT					
Public sector pensioners' payment of retirement contributions (II) (FD = 2004)	• Dec/inj: L • JG-02: L • JG-03: L • JG-03: PR • CSM-03: PR	• NP 04-E-289: PR • NP 04-E-289: EBP • NP 04-E-295: PR • NP 04-E-298: EBP • NP 04-E-301: EBP	• EC-04: L • EC-01: PO • EC-02: PO • EC-02: L • EC-07: EBP • EC-08: EBP • EC-08: PO • EC-14: L		• JCI: 10% (4/42) • PO: 10% (4/42) • **EBP: 29%** (12/42) • **PR: 26%** (11/42) • **L: 26%** (11/42) • **Approach: Deferential/ Pragmatic/Principled**[c]

(*continued*)

APPENDIX 6.4. (*Continued*)

Case (year decided)	Scores for Considerations Mentioned by STF in Opinion and by Justices in Interviews	Scores for Considerations Mentioned in Newspapers	Scores for Considerations Mentioned in Expert Interviews	Scores for Considerations Mentioned in Scholarly Sources Used to Choose Cases	Consideration Totals, and Corresponding Approaches to Decision Making[b]
			• EC-14: EBP • EC-14: JCI • EC-07: JCI • EC-22: L • EC-29: PO • EC-29: L • EC-34: L • EC-37: PR • EC-37: EBP • EC-42: L • EC-42: PR • EC-48: EBP • EC-49: PR • EC-51: PR • CSE-02: EBP • CSE-10: EBP • CSE-10: JCI • CSE-13: JCI • CSE-18: PR • CSE-21: EBP • CSE-22: PR • CSE-25: PR • CSM-01: EBP • CSM-02: L		

No injunctions in cases related to Collor Plan I (I = 1990; FDs = 1996, 2001)	• Dec/inj (ADIn 223): PR • Dec/inj (ADIn 223): L • Dec/inj (ADIn 295): PR • Dec/inj (ADIn 295): L • CSM-06: PR		• CSE-03: PR • CSE-14: JCI • CSE-14: PR	• Ballard 1999: JCI • Rosenn 2000: JCI • Teixeira 1997: JCI • Teixeira 1997: EBP • Souza Júnior 2004: PR	• JCI: 31% (4/13) • EBP: 8% (1/13) • **PR: 46%** (6/13) • L: 15% (2/13) • **Approach: Pragmatic**
Collor Plan I – freezing of savings accounts (I = 1991; FDs = 1991, 1992)	• JG-01: PR • JG-06: EBP • CSM-03: JCI • CSM-03: PR • CSM-03: L • Dec/inj: L • Dec/inj: L • Dec/inj: PR • CSM-06: PR • JG-02: PR • CSM-01: JCI • CSM-01: PR	• NP 02–153: PR • NP 02–143: PR • NP 02–149: PR • NP 02–149: JCI • NP 02–149: PO • NP 02–149: EBP • NP 02-E-38: PR	• CSE-01: PR • CSE-02: PR • CSE-11: JI • CSE-12: PR • CSE-13: EBP • CSE-13: JCI • CSE-17: PR • CSE-21: PR • EC-04: PR • EC-11: EBP • EC-11: PR • EC-13: PR • EC-19: PR • EC-19: PO • EC-30: PR • EC-31: PR • EC-35: JCI • EC-36: JCI • EC-40: PR • EC-41: PR • EC-42: PR	• Ballard 1999: JCI • Fonseca de Araújo Faria 1998: PR • Teixeira 1997: PR • Teixeira 1997: L • Teixeira 1997: JCI • Marques de Lima 2001: PR • Fonseca de Araújo Faria 1998: L • Fonseca de Araújo Faria 1998: PR • Fonseca de Araújo Faria 1998: EBP	• JI: 2% (1/55) • JCI: 16% (9/55) • PO: 4% (2/55) • EBP: 11% (6/55) • **PR: 56%** (31/55) • L: 11% (6/55) • **Approach: Pragmatic**

(continued)

Case (year decided)	Scores for Considerations Mentioned by STF in Opinion and by Justices in Interviews	Scores for Considerations Mentioned in Newspapers	Scores for Considerations Mentioned in Expert Interviews	Scores for Considerations Mentioned in Scholarly Sources Used to Choose Cases	Consideration Totals, and Corresponding Approaches to Decision Making[b]
			• EC-50: EBP • CSE-03: PR • CSE-03: L • CSE-05: JCI • CSE-05: PR • CSE-06: PR		
Law of Fiscal Responsibility (No FD)	• Dec: L • Dec: PR • CSM-03: PR	• NP 04-E-93: JCI • NP 04-E-87: JCI • NP 04–143: L • NP 04-E-97: PR • NP 04–296: PR • NP 04-E-213: PR • NP 04–334: PR • NP 04–140: PR	• EC-03: PR • EC-11: PR • EC-41: PO • EC-52: PO • CSE-17: L • CSE-17: EBP	• Souza Cruz 2004: EBP	• JCI: 11% (2/18) • PO: 11% (2/18) • EBP: 11% (2/18) • **PR:** **50%** (9/18) • L: 17% (3/18) • **Approach: Pragmatic**
WEAKER CHALLENGE					
Fund for Social Investment (FINSOCIAL) (FD = 1992)	• Dec: L • CSM-06: L • Dec: L • CSM-06: L	• NP 02–290: EBP • NP 02-E-71: PR	• CSE-19: PR		• EBP: 14% (1/7) • PR: 14% (1/7) • **L:** **57%** (4/7) • **Approach: Principled**
Provisional Contribution on Financial Transactions (CPMF) (FDs = 2002, 2003)	• Dec/inj: L • Dec/inj: L		• CSE-18: EBP • CSE-19: PR • EC-19: EBP • EC-28: EBP • EC-31: PR		• JCI: 10% (1/10) • EBP: 30% (3/10) • PR: 20% (2/10) • **L:** **40%** (4/10) • **Approach: Principled**

			• EC-46: L • EC-46: JCI • EC-47: L		
Salary increase of 28.86% (FD = 1998)	• Dec: L • CSM-03: PR	• NP 03–283: JCI • NP 03–416: PR • NP 03–417: JCI	• CSE-10: JCI • EC-11: JCI • EC-12: PR	• Fonseca de Araújo Faria 1998: PR • Faro de Castro1997b: JCI • Gomes de Mattos 2003: L	• **JCI: 45%** (5/11) • **PR: 36%** (4/11) • L: 18% (2/11) • **Approach: Protective/ Pragmatic**
Adjustment of accounts in employment security fund (FGTS) (FD = 2000)	• Dec: L • Dec: PR • CSM-02: PR • CSM-03: PR	• NP 04–38: PR	• EC-09: PR • EC-11: L • EC-12: EBP • EC-12: JI • EC-12: PR • EC-16: PR • EC-16: EBP • EC-16: PO • EC-25: PO • EC-30: PR • EC-30: JCI • EC-37: EBP • EC-42: PR • EC-24: JCI • EG-08: PO • CSE-04: L • CSE-13: EBP • CSE-14: EBP • CSE-14: PR • CSE-14: JI • CSE-24: L		• JI: 8% (2/26) • JCI: 8% (2/26) • PO: 12% (3/26) • EBP: 19% (5/26) • **PR: 38%** (10/26) • L: 15% (4/26) • **Approach: Pragmatic**

(continued)

APPENDIX 6.4. (*Continued*)

Case (year decided)	Scores for Considerations Mentioned by STF in Opinion and by Justices in Interviews	Scores for Considerations Mentioned in Newspapers	Scores for Considerations Mentioned in Expert Interviews	Scores for Considerations Mentioned in Scholarly Sources Used to Choose Cases	Consideration Totals, and Corresponding Approaches to Decision Making[b]
Salary retention for certain public sector workers (10.94%) (I = 1994)	• Lim: L • Lim: PR	• NP-01-E-83: PR • NP-01-E-04: PR • NP-01–304: JCI	• CSE-09: JCI • CSE-13: JCI • EC-45: JCI		• **JCI: 50%** (4//8) • **PR: 38%** (3/8) • L: 13% (1/8) • **Approach: Protective/ Pragmatic**
Maternity leave benefits (FD = 2003)	• Dec: L		• EC-01: L • EC-02: L • EC-14: JCI • EC-22: PO	• Werneck Vianna et al. 1999: L	• JCI: 17% (1/6) • PO: 17% (1/6) • **L: 50%** (3/6) • **Approach: Principled**
STRONGER CHALLENGE					
Readjustment of retirement benefits of 147.06% (FD = 1992)	• Dec/inj: L • JG-01: PR		• EC-14: L • EC-14: PO • EC-22: PO • EC-22: PR • EC-48: JCI • EC-01: JI • EC-02: PO • EC-02: L • EC-05: PO • EC-12: PR		• JI: 8% (1/12) • JCI: 8% (1/12) • **PO: 33%** (4/12) • PR: 25% (3/12) • L: 25% (3/12) • **Approach: Support-building**
Annual salary review for public sector workers (FD = 2001)	• Dec: L • Dec: PR • CSM-02: PR		• EC-11: JCI • EC-25: JCI • CSE-04: L		• **JCI: 33%** (2/6) • **PR: 33%** (2/6) • **L: 33%** (2/6) • **Approach: Protective/ Pragmatic/Principled**

Public sector workers and retirees retirement contributions (I) (FD = 2004)	• Dec: L • CSM-02: L • CSM-03: JCI • CSM-04: L	• NP 03–603: L • NP 03–610: L • NP 03–568: JCI • NP 03–601: JCI • NP 03–604: JCI • NP 03–605: JCI • NP 03–607: L • NP 03–609: JCI • NP 03–613: JCI • NP 03-E-88: L • NP 03-E-90: L • NP 03–616: L • NP 03–617: L • NP 03–621: JCI	• CSE-04: JCI • CSE-12: L • CSE-13: JCI • CSE-23: JCI • EC-01: JI • EC-01: L • EC-01: JCI • EC-10: JCI • EC-11: L • EC-02: L • EC-08: JCI • EC-14: JCI • EC-31: JCI • EC-37: JCI • EC-49: JCI	• Taylor 2004a: JCI • Taylor 2004a: JCI • Barbalho Leite 2004: JCI	• JI: 3% (1/36) • **JCI: 58%** (21/36) • **L: 39%** (14/36) • **Approach: Protective/ Principled**
Provisional Tax on Financial Transactions (IPMF) (I = 1993; FDs = 1993, 1994)	• Dec/inj: L • Dec/lim: L • CSM-01: JCI • CSM-01: PR • CSM-05: JCI	• NP 02–423: PR • NP 02-e-79: PO • NP 02–432: L • NP 02–432: PR • NP 02–432: JCI	• EC-50: JCI • EC-45: JCI • EC-45: PR • CSE-14: JCI • CSE-14: PR • EC-42: L • CSE-24: JCI • EC-47: JCI	• Néri da Silveira 1996: JCI • Souza Cruz 2004: JCI • Werneck Vianna et al. 1999: PR • Werneck Vianna et al. 1999: PR • Marques de Lima 2001: PO	• **JCI: 43%** (10/23) • PO: 9% (2/23) • PR: 30% (7/23) • L: 17% (4/23) • **Approach: Protective**

[a] Each consideration mentioned in each STF opinion, by each expert respondent, in each newspaper article, and in each academic source, was counted separately.
[b] Approach to decision making corresponds to considerations that constituted 33% or more of mentions.
[c] As no consideration constituted 33% or more of mentions, the limit was lowered to 25%. An alternative would have been for mode of decision making to correspond to the consideration that was most-often mentioned, yet the fact that no consideration was mentioned in at least a third of the sources suggests that multiple considerations motivated the ruling; lowering the limit to 25% captures that logic.

APPENDIX 6.5. *Elected Branches' Compliance with and Retaliation against STF Rulings Challenging the Exercise of Government Power (in order of degree of compliance)*

Case (case number) (year decided)[a]	Type of Policy	Extent to which Ruling Obeyed[b]	Difficulty/ Speed of Compliance – Letter[c]	Difficulty/ Speed of Compliance – Spirit[d]
Salary retention for certain public sector workers (10.94%) (MS 21969) (I = 1994)	Salaries	0	0	0
Provisional Contribution on Financial Transactions (CPMF) (ADIn 2031) (I = 1999)	Fiscal/tax	2	1	0
Annual salary review for public sector workers (ADIn 2061) (FD = 2001)	Salaries	2.25	1.5	.75
Maternity leave benefits (ADIn 1946) (I = 1999)	Pensions/ benefits	3.5	1	0.5
Readjustment of retirement benefits of 147.06% (RE 147864) (FD = 1992)	Pensions/ benefits	3	0.5	1.5
Salary increase of 28.86% (RMS 22307) (FD = 1998)	Salaries	3.5	0.5	1.5
Adjustment of accounts in employment security fund (FGTS) (RE 226855) (FD = 2000)	Pensions/ benefits	3.5	0.5	1.5
Provisional Tax on Financial Transactions (IPMF)				
(ADIn 926) (I = 1993; FD = 1994)	Fiscal/tax	3.5	1	1
~				
(ADIn 939) (I = 1993; FD=1993)	Fiscal/tax	3.5	1	2
Fund for Social Investment (FINSOCIAL) (RE 150764) (FD = 1992)	Tax/ fiscal	3.5	1	1.5
Public sector pensioners' payment of retirement contributions (I) (ADIn 2010) (I = 1999)	Pensions/ benefits	5	2	0.5
Public sector pensioners' payment of retirement contributions (II) (ADIn 3105 & ADIn 3128) (FD = 2004)	Pensions/ benefits	5	1	1.5

[a] *Scoring*: I (Injunction); FD (Final decision).

[b] *Scoring*: –1 (Letter not obeyed; spirit ignored); –0.5 (Letter not obeyed; no relationship between ruling and compliance with spirit); 0 (No connection between obeying letter and ruling; no relationship between ruling and compliance with spirit); 0.5 (Letter partially obeyed; spirit ignored); 1 (Letter obeyed; spirit ignored); 1.5 (Letter partially obeyed; no relationship between ruling and compliance with spirit); 2 (Letter obeyed; no relationship between ruling and compliance with spirit); 2.5 (Letter not obeyed; spirit partially obeyed); 3 (Letter partially obeyed; spirit partially obeyed); 3.5 (Letter obeyed; spirit partially obeyed); 4 (Letter not obeyed; spirit obeyed); 4.5 (Letter partially obeyed; spirit obeyed); 5 (Letter obeyed; spirit obeyed).

[c] *Scoring*: 0 (Not obeyed); 0.5 (Easy/Slow [more than 6 months]); 1 (Easy/Quick [less than 6 months]); 1.5 (Difficult/Slow [more than 6 months]); 2 (Difficult/Quick [less than 6 months]).

[d] *Scoring*: 0 (Not obeyed or policy no longer in place once ruling made); 0.5 (Easy/Slow [more than 1 year]); 1 (Easy/Quick [less than 1 year]); 1.5 (Difficult/Slow [more than 1 year]); 2 (Difficult/Quick [less than 1 year]).

[e] *Scoring*: If the government passed a decree or law that undermined the Court's decision, the degree to which it did so: –1 (significant); –0.5 (some); 0 (none).

[f] *Scoring*: Degree to which government threatened the Court as an institution: –1 (significant); –0.5 (some); 0 (none).

Degree of Compliance −1 to 2 = Noncompliance 2.5–5.5 = Partial 6–9 = Significant	Conversion 11 = Least Compliance 1 = Most Compliance	Degree of Retaliation – Policy[e]	Degree of Retaliation – Institutional[f]	Degree of Retaliation −2 = Significant −1 = Some 0 = None	Conversion 12 = Most Significant 0 = None
0 (Noncompliance)	10	−1	0	−1 (Some)	6
3 (Partial)	7	0	0	0 (None)	0
4.5 (Partial)	5.5	0	0	0 (None)	0
5 (Partial)	5	0	0	0 (None)	0
5 (Partial)	5	0	0	0 (None)	0
5.5 (Partial)	4.5	−1	0	−1 (Some)	6
5.5 (Partial)	4.5	0	0	0 (None)	0
5.5 (Partial)	4.5	−0.5	0	−0.5 (Some)	3
6.5 (Significant)	3.5	−0.5	−0.5	−1 (Some)	6
6 (Significant)	4	0	0	0 (None)	0
7.5 (Significant)	2.5	−0.5	−0.5	−1 (Some)	6
7.5 (Significant)	2.5	0	0	0 (None)	0

Notes Concerning Citations to Interviews and Newspaper Articles

- Citations of the form "LetterLetter(Letter)-Number" – are references to interviews carried out in association with this project. Respondents' names are not mentioned to protect confidentiality.
  - For Argentina: citations with the prefix "II" were early informational interviews; the prefix "E" designates case selection interviews; the prefix "J" or "JG" designates interviews with justices; the prefix "EC" or "CC" designates expert interviews regarding economic policy cases; the prefix "SC" designates interviews with Supreme Court clerks.
  - For Brazil: citations with the prefix "I" were early informational interviews; the prefix "EG" designates general expert interviews; the prefix "CSE" designates case selection interviews; the prefix "CSM" or "JG" designates interviews with justices; the prefix "EC" designates expert interviews regarding economic policy cases; the prefix "AS" designates interviews with Supreme Court clerks.
- Citations of the form NP oX-Number; NP oX-C-Number; NP oX-E-Number; NP OX-R-Number, are references to newspaper articles published between 1984 and 2003 in the Argentine newspaper, *La Nación* or between 1985 and 2004 in the Brazilian newspaper, *O Estado de São Paulo*. All articles are on file with the author.

References

Acuña, Carlos. 1994. "Politics and Economics in the Argentina of the Nineties (Or Why the Future No Longer Is What It Used to Be)." In William C. Smith, Carlos Acuña, and Eduardo A. Gamarra, eds. *Latin American Political Economy in the Age of Neoliberal Reform: Theoretical and Comparative Perspectives*. Coral Gables: North-South Center.

1995. "Introduction." In Carlos Acuña, ed., *La nueva matriz política argentina*. Buenos Aires: Ediciones Nueva Visión.

Alarie, Benjamin R. D., and Andrew Green. 2007. "The Reasonable Justice: An Empirical Analysis of Frank Iacobucci's Career on the Supreme Court of Canada." *University of Toronto Law Journal* 57: 195–226.

Amann, Edmund, and Werner Baer. 2002. "Neoliberalism and Its Consequences in Brazil." *Journal of Latin American Studies* 34: 945–59.

2005. "From the Developmental to the Regulatory State: The Transformation of the Government's Impact on the Brazilian Economy." *The Quarterly Review of Economics and Finance* 45: 421–31.

Amorim Neto, Octavio, Gary W. Cox, and Matthew D. McCubbins. 2003. "Agenda Power in Brazil's Cámara dos Deputados 1989–98." *World Politics* 55(4): 550–78.

Arantes, Rogério Bastos. 1997. *Judiciário e Política No Brasil*. São Paulo: IDESP.

2005. "Constitutionalism, the Expansion of Justice and the Judicialization of Politics in Brazil." In Rachel Sieder, Line Schjolden, and Alan Angell, eds., *The Judicialization of Politics in Latin America*. New York: Palgrave Macmillan.

Arantes, Rogerio Bastos, and Fábio Kerche. 2003. "Poder Judicial y Democracia en Brasil." In Vicente Palermo, ed., *Política Brasileña Contemporánea*. Buenos Aires: Siglo XXI / Instituto di Tella.

Arenas de Mesa, Alberto, and Fábio M. Bertranou 1997. "Learning from Social Security Reforms: Two Different Cases, Chile and Argentina." *World Development* 25(3): 329–48.

Ballard, Megan J. 1999. "The Clash Between Local Courts and Global Economics: The Politics of Judicial Reform in Brazil." *Berkeley Journal of International Law* 17: 230–76.

Barbalho Leite, Fábio. 2004. "O Supremo Tribunal Federal e a Contribuição de Servidores Inativos e Pensionistas (EC no. 41/03): Lineamentos para o Reconhecimento de sua Constitucionalidade." *Revista Brasileira de Direito Público (RBDP)* 2(5): 43–72.

Barnes, Jeb. 2007. "Bringing the Courts Back in: Interbranch Perspectives on the Role of Courts in American Politics and Policy Making." *Annual Review of Political Science* 10: 25–43.

Barros, Sérgio Resende de. 2000. "Controle De Constitucionalidade: Proposta De Simplificação." *Revista Da Procuradoria Geral Do Estado De São Paulo* 54: 21–43.

Barros, Robert. 2003. "Dictatorship and the Rule of Law: Rules and Military Power in Pinochet's Chile." In José María Maravall and Adam Przeworski, eds., *Democracy and the Rule of Law*. Cambridge: Cambridge University Press.

Baum, Lawrence. 1976. "Implementation of Judicial Decisions." *American Politics Quarterly* 4: 86–114.

1993. "Making Judicial Policies in the Political Arena." In Carl Van Horn, ed., *The State of the States*, 2nd ed. Washington DC: CQ Press.

2006. *Judges and Their Audiences: A Perspective on Judicial Behavior*. Princeton: Princeton University Press.

Bergman, Marcelo. 2009. *Tax Evasion and the Rule of Law in Latin America: The Political Culture of Cheating and Compliance in Argentina and Chile*. State College: Penn State University Press.

Bianchi, Alberto. 2002a. *Control de constitucionalidad, Tomo I y II*. Buenos Aires: Abaco.

2002b. "De Guida a Tobar (La sinuosa ruta de los salarios de los agentes públicos)." *Jurisprudencia Argentina* 2002-III, suplemento del fascículo no. 11.

ND. ¿Ha llegado la Corte Suprema al final de su lucha por una jurisdicción discrecional? Perspectivas actuales y futuras del Recurso Ordinario." *El Derecho*.

Bidart Campos, German J. 1986. "La Corte Suprema no achica ni agranda su función (un caso más de jubilaciones)." *El Derecho* 120: 562–3.

Boas, Taylor. 2007. "Conceptualizing Continuity and Change: The Composite-Standard Model of Path Dependence." *Journal of Theoretical Politics* 19(1): 33–54.

Bohmer, Martin. 2000. "La Corte de los '80 y la Corte de los '90, Un diálogo sobre el Rule of Law Argentino." Trabajo preparado para el SELA 2000.

Borner, Silvio, Aymo Brunetti, and Beatrice Weder. 1995. *Political Credibility and Economic Development*. London: St. Martin's Press.

Bratton, Michael. 2007. "Formal versus Informal Institutions in Africa." *Journal of Democracy* 18(3): 96–110.

Brinks, Daniel M. 2003. "Informal Institutions and the Rule of Law: The Judicial Response to State Killings in Buenos Aires and São Paulo in the 1990s." *Comparative Politics* 36(1): 1–19.

2005. "Judicial Reform and Independence in Brazil and Argentina: The Beginning of a New Millennium?" *Texas International Law Journal* 40(30): 595.

2007. *The Judicial Response to Police Killings in Latin America: Inequality and the Rule of Law*. New York and Cambridge: Cambridge University Press.

Brinks, Daniel M. and Sandra Botero. 2010. "Inequality and the Rule of Law: Ineffective Rights in Latin American Democracies." Paper presented at the American Political Science Association Annual Meeting, Washington, DC, September 2–5, 2010.

Burley, Anne-Marie, and Walter Mattli. 1993. "Europe before the Court: A Political Theory of Legal Integration." *International Organization* 47(1): 41–76.

Caldeira, Gregory A., and James L. Gibson. 1995. "The Legitimacy of the Court of Justice in the European Union: Models of Institutional Support." *American Political Science Review* 89: 356–76.

Canon, Bradley C., and Charles A. Johnson. 1999. *Judicial Policies: Implementation and Impact*. Washington, DC: Congressional Quarterly Press.

Carothers, Thomas. 1998. "The Rule of Law Revival." *Foreign Affairs* 77(1): 95–106.

Carrió, Alejandro. 1996. *La Corte Suprema y su independencia*. Buenos Aires: Abeledo Perrot.

Carrubba, Clifford J. 2003. "The European Court of Justice, Democracy, and Enlargement." *European Union Politics* 4(1): 75–100.

Carrubba, Clifford J., and Steven Van Winkle. 2000. "An Analysis of Monitoring Systems." Paper presented at the American Political Science Association Annual Meeting, Washington, DC, August 31–September 3.

Castagnola, Andrea, and Aníbal Pérez-Liñán. 2011. "Bolivia: The Rise (and Fall) of Judicial Review." In Gretchen Helmke and Julio Ríos-Figueroa, eds., *Courts in Latin America*. Cambridge and New York: Cambridge University Press.

Castelar Pinheiro, Armando, ed. 2000. *Judiciário e Economia No Brasil*. São Paulo: Editora Sumare.

Cavallo, Claudio. 2002. "Esto… ¿Será Justicia? Una visión sobre la decisión de la Corte acerca del recorte de haberes del sector público y jubilados." *La Ley*, Nota a fallo, 2002-F.

Cepeda Espinosa, Manuel J. 2005. "The Judicialization of Politics in Colombia: The Old and the New." In Rachel Sieder, Line Schjolden, and Alan Angell, eds., *The Judicialization of Politics in Latin America*. New York: Palgrave.

Chavez, Rebecca B. 2001. "The Construction of the Rule of Law in Nascent Democracies: Judicial Autonomy in Latin America." Doctoral Dissertation, Political Science, Stanford University.

2004a. *Rule of Law in Nascent Democracies: Judicial Politics in Argentina*. Stanford: Stanford University Press.

2004b. "The Evolution of Judicial Autonomy in Argentina: Establishing the Rule of Law in an Ultrapresidential System." *Journal of Latin American Studies* 36: 451–78.

Clayton, Cornell, and Howard Gillman, eds. 1999. *Supreme Court Decision-Making: New Institutionalist Approaches*. Chicago: University of Chicago Press.

Collier, David, and James Mahoney. 1996. "Insights and Pitfalls: Selection Bias in Qualitative Research." *World Politics* 49(1): 56–91.

Collier, Ruth Berins. 1999. *Paths toward Democracy: The Working Class and Elites in Western Europe and South America*. Cambridge: Cambridge University Press.

Collier, Ruth Berins, and David Collier. 1979. "Inducements vs. Constraints: Disaggregating Corporatism." *American Political Science Review* 73(4): 967–86.

1991. *Shaping the Political Arena: Critical Junctures, the Labor Movement, and Regime Dynamics in Latin America*. Princeton: Princeton University Press.

Cooter, Robert, and Tom Ginsburg. 1996. "Comparative Judicial Discretion: An Empirical Test of Economic Models." *International Review of Law and Economics* 16: 295–313.

Costin, Claudia. 2006. "State Reform in Brazil (1995–2005)." Unpublished manuscript.

Couso, Javier A. 2002. "The Politics of Judicial Review in Latin America: Chile in Comparative Perspective." Ph.D. Dissertation, Jurisprudence and Social Policy Program, University of California, Berkeley.

2005. "Judicial Independence in Latin America: the Lessons of History in the Search for an Always Elusive Ideal." In Tom Ginsburg and Robert A. Kagan eds., *Institutions and Public Law: Comparative Approaches*. New York: Peter Lang.

Couso, Javier, Alexandra Huneeus, and Rachel Sieder, eds. 2010. *Cultures of Legality: Judicialization and Political Activism in Contemporary Latin America*. New York: Cambridge University Press.

Couto, Cláudio G., and Rogério Bastos Arantes. 2003. "Constitución o políticas públicas? Una evaluación de los años FHC." In Vicente Palermo, ed., *Política Brasileña Contemporánea: de Collor a Lula en Años de Transformación*. Buenos Aires: Instituto Di Tella/Siglo Veintiuno.

2008. "Constitution, Government, and Democracy in Brazil." *World Political Science Review* 4(2): 1–33.

Dahl, Robert A. 1957a. "The Concept of Power." *Behavioural Science* 2: 202–10.

1957b. "Decision Making in a Democracy: The Supreme Court as a National Policy Maker." *Journal of Public Law* 6: 279–95.

Davis, Michael C. 1998. "The Price of Rights: Constitutionalism and East Asian Economic Development." *Human Rights Quarterly* 20: 303–37.

Davis, Richard. 2005. *Electing Justice: Fixing the Supreme Court Nomination Process*. Oxford University Press.

Desposato, Scott W. 2004. "The Impact of Party Switching on Legislative Behavior in Brazil." Unpublished manuscript.

2006. "Parties for Rent? Ambition, Ideology, and Party Switching in Brazil's Chamber of Deputies." *American Journal of Political Science* 50(1): 62–80.

Dezalay, Yves, and Bryant G. Garth. 2002. *The Internationalization of Palace Wars: Lawyers, Economists, and the Contest to Transform Latin American States*. Chicago: University of Chicago Press.

2010. *Asian Legal Revivals: Lawyers in the Shadow of Empire*. Chicago: University of Chicago Press.

Díaz, Rodolfo. 2002. *¿Prosperidad o Ilusión? Las reformas de los 90 en la Argentina*. Buenos Aires: Abaco.

DiMaggio, P. J. 1998. "The New Institutionalisms: Avenues of Collaboration." *Journal of Institutional and Theoretical Economics* 154(4): 696–705.

Dixon, Rosalind. 2007. "Creating Dialogue about Socioeconomic Rights: Strong-Form versus Weak-Form Judicial Review Revisited." *International Journal of Constitutional Law* 5(3): 391–418.

Dodson, Michael, and Donald W. Jackson. 2003. "Horizontal Accountability and the Rule of Law in Latin America." In Scott Mainwaring and Christopher Welna, eds., *Democratic Accountability in Latin America*. Oxford: Oxford University Press.

Dolbeare, Kenneth M., and Phillip E. Hammond. 1971. *The School Prayer Decisions*. Chicago: University of Chicago Press.

Dolinger, Jacob. 1990. "The Influence of American Constitutional Law on the Brazilian Legal System." *The American Journal of Comparative Law* 38(4): 803–37.

Domingo, Pilar. 2004. "Judicialization of Politics or Politicization of the Judiciary: Recent Trends in Latin America." *Democratization* 11(1): 104–26.

2005. "Judicialization of Politics: The Changing Political Role of the Judiciary in Mexico." In Rachel Sieder, Line Schjolden, and Alan Angell, eds., *The Judicialization of Politics in Latin America*. New York: Palgrave.

Druker, Jeremy. 2008. "Czech Republic." In Jeannette Goehring, ed., *Nations in Transit 2008: Democratization from Central Europe to Eurasia*. New York: Freedom House.

Eisenstadt, Todd. 2003. "Thinking Outside the (Ballot) Box: Informal Electoral Institutions and Mexico's Political Opening." *Latin American Politics and Society* 45(1): 25–54.

Epp, Charles C. 1998. *The Rights Revolution: Lawyers, Activists, and Supreme Courts in Comparative Perspective*. Chicago: University of Chicago Press.

Epstein, Lee, and Jack Knight. 2000. "Toward a Strategic Revolution in Judicial Politics: A Look Back, A Look Ahead." *Political Research Quarterly* 53(3): 625–61.

Epstein, Lee, Jack Knight, and Olga Shvetsova. 2001. "The Role of Constitutional Courts in the Establishment and Maintenance of Democratic Systems of Government." *Law and Society Review* 35(1): 117–64.

2002. "Selecting Selection Systems." In Stephen Burbank and Barry Friedman, eds., *Judicial Independence at the Crossroads: An Interdisciplinary Approach*.

Epstein, Lee, and Jeffrey A. Segal. 2005. *Advice and Consent: The Politics of Judicial Appointments*. New York: Oxford University Press.

Fallos de la Corte Suprema de Justicia de la Nación. Buenos Ares. Various years.

Farber, Daniel A. 2002. "Rights as Signals." *Journal of Legal Studies* XXXI: 83–98.

Faro de Castro, Marcus. 1997a. "The Courts, Law, and Democracy in Brazil." *International Social Science Journal* 49(152): 241–52.

1997b. "O Supremo Tribunal Federal e a Judicialização Da Política." *Revista Brasileira De Ciências Sociais* 12(34): 147–56.

Farrell, H., and A. Heritier. 2003. "Formal and Informal Institutions under Co-Decision: Continuous Constitution-Building in Europe." *Governance* 16(4): 577–600.

Faundez, Julio. 2005. "The Rule of Law Enterprise: Promoting a Dialogue Between Practitioners and Academics." *Democratization* 12(4): 567–86.

Favetti, Rafael Thomaz. 2003. *Controle de Constitucionalidade e Política Fiscal*. Porto Alegre: Sergio Antonio Fabris Editor.

Fayt, Carlos. 2004. *La Corte Suprema y la Evolución de su Jurisprudencia Leading Cases y Holdings Casos Trascendentes*. Buenos Aires: La Ley.

Ferejohn, John. 2002. "Judicializing Politics, Politicizing Law." *Law and Contemporary Problems* 65: 41–69.

Ferejohn, John, Frances Rosenbluth, and Charles Shipan. 2007. "Comparative Judicial Politics." In Carles Boix and Susan Stokes, eds., *The Oxford Handbook of Comparative Politics*. New York: Oxford.

Ferreyra, Raul Gustavo. 2004. "Corte Suprema de Justicia Argentina y Control de Constitucionalidad: Vicsitudes y retos del papel institucional del tribunal." Presentado como ponencia en el Congreso Internacional de Culturas y Sistemas Jurídicos Comparados, UNAM, Instituto de Investigaciones Jurídicas, México, febrero de 2004.

Figueiredo, Argelina, and Fernando Limongi. 2000. "Presidential Power, Legislative Organization and Party Behavior in the Legislature." *Comparative Politics* 32: 151–70.

Finkel, Jodi. 2001. "Judicial Reform in Latin America: Market Economies, Self-Interested Politicians, and Judicial Independence." Ph.D. Dissertation, Department of Political Science, University of California, Los Angeles.

2003. "Supreme Court Decisions on Electoral Rules After Mexico's 1994 Judicial Reform: An Empowered Court." *Journal of Latin American Studies* 35: 777–99.

2004. "Judicial Reform in Argentina in the 1990s: How Electoral Incentives Shape Institutional Change." *Latin American Research Review* 39(3): 56–80.

2005. "Judicial Reform As an 'Insurance Policy' in Mexico in the 1990s: A Supreme Court Willing and Able to Enter the Political Fray." *Latin American Politics and Society* 47(1): 87–113.

2008. *Judicial Reform as Political Insurance: Argentina, Peru and Mexico in the 1990s*. Notre Dame: University of Notre Dame Press.

Fisher, Louis. 2007. *Constitutional Dialogues: Interpretation as Political Process*. Princeton: Princeton University Press.

Fishlow, Albert. 2000. "Brazil and Economic Realities." *Daedalus* 129(2): 339–57.

Fonseca de Araújo Faria, Lilian. 1998. "The Role of the Judicial Branch in Managing the Brazilian Government's Economic Policy." Instituto Cultural Minerva, Institute of Brazilian Issues, The George Washington University.

Freedom House. 2006. "Freedom in the World – Argentina (2006)." Available at www.freedomhouse.org, accessed 27 May 2007.

French, John D. 2004. *Drowning in Laws: Labor Law and Brazilian Political Culture*. Chapel Hill: University of North Carolina Press.

Friedman, Barry. 2006. "Taking Law Seriously." *Perspectives on Politics* 4(2): 261–76.

2009. *The Will of the People: How Public Opinion Has Influenced the Supreme Court and Shaped the Meaning of the Constitution*. New York: Farrar, Straus and Giroux.

Frühling, Hugo. 1984. "Law in Society: Social Transformation and the Crisis of Law in Chile, 1830–1970." Doctoral Dissertation, Harvard University School of Law.

Furtado, Adolfo. ND. "Correção das contas do FGTS: um dilema distributivo." *Cadernos Aslegis* 13.

Gandhi, Jennifer. 2008. *Political Institutions Under Dictatorship*. Cambridge and New York: Cambridge University Press.

Gargarella, Roberto. 1998. "Después del diluvio. El perfeccionismo conservador en la nueva jurisprudencia de la Corte Suprema (1990–1997)." *Desarrollo Económico Revista de Ciencias Sociales*. 38(149): 439–56.

2003. "Inconsistencia y parcialidad. Un examen histórico de la jurisprudencia de la Corte Suprema Argentina." *Lexis Nexis Jurisprudencia Argentina* (Número especial, "140 anos de la Corte Suprema de Justicia de la Nación"), JA 2003-IV, fascículo n. 9: 19–35.

2004. "In Search of Democratic Justice – What Courts Should Not Do: Argentina, 1983–2002." In Siri Gloppen, Robert Gargarella, and Elin Skaar, eds., *Democratization and the Judiciary: The Accountability Function of Courts in New Democracies*. London: Frank Cass.

2011. "Dialogic Justice in the Enforcement of Social Rights." In Siri Gloppen and Alicia Yamin, eds., *Litigating Health Rights: Can Courts Bring More Justice to Health?* Cambridge, MA: Harvard University Press.

Gauri, Varun and Daniel M. Brinks. 2008. "Introduction: The Elements of Legalization and the Triangular Shape of Social and Economic Rights." In Varun Gauri and Daniel M. Brinks, eds., *Courting Social Justice: Judicial Enforcement of Social and Economic Rights in the Developing World*. New York: Cambridge University Press.

Gauri, Varun, and Daniel M. Brinks, eds. 2008. *Courting Social Justice: Judicial Enforcement of Social and Economic Rights in the Developing World*. New York: Cambridge University Press.

Gelli, María Angélica. 2003a. *Constitución de la Nación Comentada y Concordada*. Buenos Aires: La Ley.

2003b. "El mundo jurídico y los dilemas del poder de la Corte Suprema." *Especial para La Ley*. T.2003-E, Sec. Doctrina, 986–89.

2003c. "El caso 'Provincia de San Luis v. Estado Nacional', entre el debido proceso adjetivo y el control de razonabilidad." *Jurisprudencia Argentina*, 2003-II-1294.

Gerchunoff, Pablo and Lucas Llach. 2003. *El ciclo de la ilusión y el desencanto: un siglo de políticas económicas argentinas*. Buenos Aires: Ariel.

Gerhardt, Michael. 2000. *The Federal Appointments Process: A Constitutional and Historical Analysis*. Durham: Duke University Press.

Geyh, Charles Gardner. 2010. "Judicial Politics, the Rule of Law, and the Future of an Ermine Myth." Indiana University Maurer School of Law, Research Paper Number 165.

Gibson, James L., Gregory A. Caldeira, and Vanessa A. Baird. 1998. "On the Legitimacy of National High Courts." *American Political Science Review* 92: 343–58.

Gil Domínguez, Andrés. 2002. "La Corte Suprema: Poder Cuestionado." *Todo es Historia* 418(Mayo): 6–17.

Gillman, Howard. 2001. "What's Law Got to Do with It? Judicial Behavioralists Test the 'Legal Model' of Judicial Decision-Making." *Law and Social Inquiry* 26(2): 465–504.

Gillman, Howard, and Cornell Clayton, eds. 1999. *The Supreme Court in American Politics: New Institutionalist Interpretations*. Lawrence: University of Kansas Press.

Ginsburg, Tom. 2000. "Review: Does Law Matter for Economic Development? Evidence from East Asia." *Law and Society Review* 34(3): 829–56.

2002. "Economic Analysis and the Design of Constitutional Courts." *Theoretical Inquires in Law* 3(1): 49–85.

2003. *Judicial Review in New Democracies: Constitutional Courts in Asian Cases*. New York: Cambridge University Press.

Gloppen, Siri. 2006. "Courts and Social Transformation: An Analytical Framework." In Roberto Gargarella, Pilar Domingo, and Theunis Roux, eds., *Courts and Social Transformation in New Democracies: An Institutional Voice for the Poor?* Aldershot: Ashgate.

Gloppen, Siri, Roberto Gargarella, and Elin Skaar, eds. 2004. *Democratization and the Judiciary: The Accountability Function of Courts in New Democracies*. London: Frank Cass.

Gomes de Mattos, Mauro Roberto. 2003. "O Controle dos Poderes Executivo e Legislativo Pelo Supremo Tribunal Federal." *Seleções Jurídicas*. Outubro.

Greenburg, Jan Crawford. 2007. *Supreme Conflict: The Inside Story of the Struggle for Control of the United States*. New York: The Penguin Press.

Grondona, Mariano. 1994. "La justicia y los políticos." In Francisco Diez, ed., *La justicia en crisis*. Buenos Aires: Poder Ciudadano.

Guest, Ian. 1990. *Behind the Disappearances: Argentina's Dirty War Against Human Rights and the United Nations*. Philadelphia: University of Pennsylvania Press.

Haggard, Stephen, and Robert R. Kaufman, eds. 1992. *The Politics of Economic Adjustment*. Princeton: Princeton University Press.

Haggard, Stephen, and Robert R. Kaufman. 1995. *The Political Economy of Democratic Transitions*. Princeton: Princeton University Press.

Hagopian, Frances. 1996. *Traditional Politics and Regime Change in Brazil*. Cambridge: Cambridge University Press.

Hall, Peter A., and Rosemary C. R. Taylor. 1996. "Political Science and the Three New Institutionalisms." *Political Studies* 44(5): 936–57.

Hansen, J. M. 1986. "Detecting and Explaining the Structure of Informal Institutions – Agricultural Policy Networks in the United States Congress." *Legislative Studies Quarterly* 11(1): 131.

Hart, L. A. 1961. *The Concept of Law*. Oxford and New York: Oxford University Press.

Hartlyn, Jonathan. 1998. "Political Continuities, Missed Opportunities, and Institutional Rigidities: Another Look at Democratic Transitions in Latin America." In Scott Mainwaring and Arturo Valenzuela, eds., *Politics, Society, and Democracy: Latin America*. Boulder: Westview Press.

Helmke, Gretchen. 2000. "Ruling Against the Rulers: Court-Executive Relations in Argentina Under Dictatorship and Democracy." Doctoral Dissertation, Department of Political Science, University of Chicago.

2002. "The Logic of Strategic Defection: Court-Executive Relations in Argentina Under Dictatorship and Democracy." *American Political Science Review* 96(2): 291–303.

2005. *Courts Under Constraints: Judges, Generals, and Presidents in Argentina*. Cambridge: Cambridge University Press.

Helmke, Gretchen, and Steven Levitsky. 2004. "Informal Institutions and Comparative Politics: A Research Agenda." *Perspectives on Politics* 2(4): 725–40.

2006. *Informal Institutions and Democracy: Lessons from Latin America*. Baltimore: Johns Hopkins University Press.

Hertogh, Marc and Simon Halliday, eds. 2004. *Judicial Review and Bureaucratic Impact: International and Interdisciplinary Perspectives*. Cambridge: Cambridge University Press.

Hilbink, Elisabeth. 2007. *The Politics of Judicial Apoliticism: Chile in Comparative Perspective*. Cambridge: Cambridge University Press.

Hilbink, Lisa and Elizabeth Woods, eds. 2009. "MiniSymposium: Comparative Sources of Judicial Empowerment: Ideas and Interests." *Political Research Quarterly* 62(4): 745–839.

Hirschl, Ran. 2004. *Towards Juristocracy: The Origins and Consequences of the New Constitutionalism*. Cambridge: Harvard University Press.

2008. "Constitutionalism vs. Theocracy: Constitutional Courts and the Containment of Sacred Law." Presented at the Plenary Session of the U.C. Berkeley Sawyer Seminar on Comparative Judicial Power, Berkeley, CA, November 8, 2008.

Hoekstra, Valerie. 2003. *Public Reaction to Supreme Court Decisions*. New York: Cambridge University Press.

Hoffmann, Florian F. and Fernando R. N. M. Bentes. 2008. "Accountability for Social and Economic Rights in Brazil." In Varun Gauri and Daniel M. Brinks, eds., *Courting Social Justice: Judicial Enforcement of Social and Economic Rights in the Developing World*. New York: Cambridge University Press.

Huneeus, Alexandra. 2006. "The Dynamics of Judicial Transition: Judges, Pinochet-Era Claims, and the Question of Judicial Legitimacy in Chile (1998–2005)." PhD Dissertation, Jurisprudence and Social Policy Program, University of California, Berkeley.

2010. "Judging with a Guilty Conscience: The Chilean Judiciary's Human Rights Turn." *Law and Social Inquiry*, 35(1): 99–135.

Hunter, Wendy. 1997. *Eroding Military Influence in Brazil: Politicians Against Soldiers*. Chapel Hill: University of North Carolina Press.

Hunter, Wendy and Timothy J. Power. 2005. "Lula's Brazil at Midterm." *Journal of Democracy* 16(3): 127–39.

Huntington, Samuel. 1991. *The Third Wave: Democratization in the Late 20th Century*. Norman: University of Oklahoma Press.

Iaryczower, Matías, Pablo T. Spiller, and Mariano Tommasi. 2000. "Un Enfoque Estratégico para Entender el Comportamiento de la Corte Suprema de Justicia de la Nación." Paper presented at the "Conference to Honor Guillermo Molinelli," Centro de Estudio para el Desarrollo Institucional, Buenos Aires, Argentina, November 27.

2002. "Judicial Independence in Unstable Environments, Argentina 1935–1998." *American Journal of Political Science* 46(4): 699–716.

Immergut, Ellen. 1998. "The Theoretical Core of the New Institutionalism." *Politics and Society* 25(4): 5–34.

Ingram, Matthew C. 2009. "Not All Courts Are Created Equal(ly): A Causal Logics Approach to Clarifying Causation in Judicial Politics." Paper presented at the American Political Science Association Annual Meeting, Toronto, Ontario, Canada, September 3–6.

Kagan, Robert, Bliss Cartwright, Lawrence M. Friedman, and Stanton Wheeler. 1978. "The Evolution of State Supreme Courts." *Michigan Law Review* 76: 961–1005.

Kapiszewski, Diana. 2011a. "Power Broker, Policymaker, or Rights Adjudicator? The Brazilian *Supremo Tribunal Federal* in Transition." In Gretchen Helmke and Julio Ríos-Figueroa, eds., *Courts in Latin America*. New York: Cambridge University Press.

2011b. "Tactical Balancing: High Court Decision-Making on Politically Crucial Cases." *Law and Society Review* 45(2): 471–506.

Kapiszewski, Diana and Matthew M. Taylor. 2008. "Doing Courts Justice? Studying Judicial Politics in Latin America." *Perspectives on Politics* 6(4): 741–67.

Forthcoming. "Compliance: Conceptualizing, Measuring, and Explaining Adherence to Judicial Rulings." *Law and Social Inquiry*.

Kapiszewski, Diana, Gordon Silverstein, and Robert A. Kagan, eds. Forthcoming. *Consequential Courts: Judicial Roles in Global Perspective*. New york: Cambridge University Press.

Karl, Terry Lynn. 1990. "Dilemmas of Democratization in Latin America." *Comparative Politics* 23: 1–23.

Karst, Kenneth L. and Keith S. Rosenn. 1975. *Law and Development in Latin America*. Berkeley: University of California Press.

Kerche, Fábio. 1999. "O Ministério Público e a Constituinte de 1987/88." In Maria Teresa Sadek, ed. *O Sistema de Justiça*. São Paulo: IDESP.

Khair, Amir Antonio. 2004. *Diagnóstico do Poder Judiciário Brasileiro: Relatório de Pesquisa*. Unpublished manuscript.

Kingstone, Peter R. 2000. "Muddling Through Gridlock: Economic Policy Performance, Business Responses, and Democratic Sustainability." In Peter R. Kingstone and Timothy J. Power, eds. *Democratic Brazil: Actors, Institutions, and Processes*. Pittsburgh: University of Pittsburgh Press.

2006. "After the Washington Consensus: The Limits to Democratization and Development in Latin America." *Latin American Research Review* 41(1): 153–64.

Kitschelt, Herbert, Zdenka Mansfeldova, Radoslaw Markowski, and Gabor Toka. 1999. *Post-communist Party Systems: Competition, Representation, and Inter-Party Cooperation*. Cambridge: Cambridge University Press.

Klein, David, and Gregory Mitchell, eds. 2010. *The Psychology of Judicial Decision Making*. New York and Oxford: Oxford University Press.

Klug, Heinz. 2000. *Constituting Democracy: Law, Globalism, and South Africa's Political Reconstruction*. New York: Cambridge University Press.

Knight, Jack, and Lee Epstein. 1996. "The Norm of Stare Decisis." *American Journal of Political Science* 40(4): 1018–35.

Koerner, Andrei. 2006. "Decisão judicial, instituições e estrutura socioeconômica por uma análise política do pensamento jurídico brasileiro." In Andrei Koerner, ed., *História da Justiça Penal no Brasil: Pesquisas e Análises*. São Paulo: IBCCRIM.

Kommers, Donald P., John E. Finn, and Gary J. Jacobsohn. 2004. *American Constitutional Law: Essays, Cases, and Comparative Notes, Second edition*. Lanham, MD: Rowman & Littlefield Publishers.

Konder Comparato, Fabio. 1990. "The Economic Order in the Brazilian Constitution of 1988." *The American Journal of Comparative Law* 38(4): 753–71.

Kritzer, Herbert M. and Mark J. Richards. 2010. "Taking and Testing Jurisprudential Regimes Seriously: A Response to Lax and Rader." *Journal of Politics* 72 (April): 285–8.

Kuzio, Taras. 2001. "Transition in Post-Communist States: Triple or Quadruple?" *Politics* 21(3): 168–77.

La Porta, Rafael. 1997. "Legal Determinants of External Finance." *Journal of Finance* 52: 1131–50.

Lamounier, Bolivar. 1999. "Brazil: Inequality Against Democracy." In Larry Diamond, Jonathan Hartlyn, Juan Linz, and Seymour Martin Lipset, eds., *Democracy in Developing Countries: Latin America*. Boulder: Lynne Rienner.

Landes, William M. and Richard A. Posner. 1975. "The Independent Judiciary in an Interest-Group Perspective." *Journal of Law and Economics* 18(3): 875–901.

Larkins, Christopher. 1996. "Judicial Independence and Democratization: A Theoretical and Conceptual Analysis." *The American Journal of Comparative Law* 44 (4): 605–26.

1998. "The Legacies of Hyper-Presidentialism: Executive-Judicial Relations, Constitutional Cultures, and The Future of Democratic Governance in Argentina and Peru." Ph.D. dissertation, University of Southern California.

Lasser, Mitchel de S. O. l'E. 2004. *Judicial Deliberations: A Comparative Analysis of Judicial Transparency and Legitimacy*. Cambridge: Cambridge University Press.

2009. *Judicial Transformations: The Rights Revolution in the Courts of Europe*. Oxford: Oxford University Press.

Lauth, Han-Joachim. 2005. "The Impact of Informal Institutions on Democratic Performance: Theoretical Reflections and Empirical Findings." Paper presented at the American Political Science Association Annual Meeting, Washington, DC, September 1–4.

Lax, Jeffrey R. and Kelly T. Rader. 2010a. "Legal Constraints on Supreme Court Decision Making: Do Jurisprudential Regimes Exist?" *Journal of Politics* 72 (April): 273–84.

2010b. "The Three Prongs of a Jurisprudential Regimes Test: A Response to Kritzer and Richards." *Journal of Politics* 72 (April): 289–91.

Legarre, Santiago. 2004. "Una puesta al día en materia de 'certiorari'." *La Ley* 2004-A: 1267–74.

Levitsky, Steven. 2001. "Organization and Labor-Based Party Adaptation: The Transformation of Argentine Peronism in Comparative Perspective." *World Politics* 54(1): 27–56.

2003. *Transforming Labor-Based Parties in Latin America: Argentine Peronism in Comparative Perspective*. New York: Cambridge University Press.

Lieberson, Stanley. 1991. "Small N's and Big Conclusions: An Examination of the Reasoning in Comparative Studies Based on a Small Number of Cases." *Social Forces* 70(2): 307–20.

Linares, Sebastián. 2010. "Evaluando el gobierno judicial en América Latina: el caso de El Salvador." *Revista Latinoamericana de Política Comparada* 3: 69–98.

Linz, Juan J., and Alfred Stepan. 1996. *Problems of Democratic Transition and Consolidation: Southern Europe, South America and Post-Communist Europe*. Baltimore: Johns Hopkins University Press.

Llamazares, Iván. 2005. "Patterns in Contingencies: The Interlocking of Formal and Informal Political Institutions in Contemporary Argentina." *Social Forces* 83(4): 1671–96.

Llanos, Mariana, and Constanza Figueroa-Schibber. 2007. "Prestando acuerdo: El Senado frente a los nombramientos del Poder Judicial en la Argentina democrática (1983–2006). German Institute of Global and Area Studies Working Paper No. 54.

López-Ayllón, Sergio and Hector F. Fix-Fierro. 2003. ""Faraway, So Close!" The Rule of Law and Legal Change in Mexico 1970–2000." In Lawrence Friedman and Rogelio Pérez-Perdomo, eds., *Legal Culture in the Age of Globalization: Latin America and Latin Europe*. Stanford: Stanford University Press.

Luhmann, Niklas. 1988. "The Unity of the Legal System." In Gunther Tuebner, ed., *Autopoietic Law: A New Approach to Law and Society*. Berlin: Walter de Gruyter.

Magalhães, Pedro C. 1999. "The Politics of Judicial Reform in Eastern Europe." *Comparative Politics* 31(4): 43–62.

Magaloni, Beatriz. 2008. "Enforcing the Autocratic Political Order and the Role of Courts: The Case of Mexico." In Tom Ginsburg and Tamir Moustafa, eds., *Rule by Law: The Politics of Courts in Authoritarian Regimes*. Cambridge: Cambridge University Press.

Mahoney, James. 2000. "Path Dependence in Historical Sociology." *Theory and Society* 29(4): 507–48.

Mainwaring, Scott. 1999. *Rethinking Party Systems in the Third Wave of Democratization*. Stanford: Stanford University Press

Malleson, Kate. 2007. "Introduction." In Kate Malleson and Peter H. Russell, eds., *Appointing Judges in an Age of Judicial Power: Critical Perspectives from around the World*. Toronto: University of Toronto Press.

Malleson, Kate, and Peter H. Russell, eds. 2007. *Appointing Judges in an Age of Judicial Power: Critical Perspectives from around the World*. Toronto: University of Toronto Press.

Manzetti, Luigio. 2003. "Political Manipulations and Market Reforms Failures." *World Politics* 55: 315–60.

March, James G. and Johan P. Olsen. 1984. "The New Institutionalism: Organizational Factors in Political Life." *The American Political Science Review* 78(3): 734–49.

Marques de Lima, Francisco Gerson. 2001. *O Supremo Tribunal Federal – Na Crise Institucional Brasileira: Estudo de Casos*. Fortaleza: ABC Editora.

Marshall, T. H. 1950. *Citizenship and Social Class, and Other Essays*. Cambridge: Cambridge University Press.

Martínez-Lara, Javier. 1996. *Building Democracy in Brazil: The Politics of Constitutional Change 1985–1995*. New York: St. Martin's Press.

Mate, Manoj. 2009. "The Variable Power of Courts: Rights, Governance, and the Indian Supreme Court." Ph.D. Dissertation, Department of Political Science, University of California, Berkeley.

Mattes, Robert, and Michael Bratton. 2001. "Africa's Triple Transition: Popular Perspectives." *African Security Review* 10(1): 48–59.

Mattli, Walter and Anne-Marie Slaughter. 1995. "Law and Politics in the European Union: A Reply to Garrett." *International Organization* 49(1): 183–90.

1998. "Revisiting the European Court of Justice." *International Organization* 52(1): 177–209.

McAllister, Lesley. 2008. *Making Law Matter: Environmental Protection and Legal Institutions in Brazil*. Stanford: Stanford University Press.

McCubbins, Mathew D., Roger G. Noll, and Barry R. Weingast. 1987. "Administrative Procedures as Instruments of Political Control." *Journal of Law, Economics, & Organization* 3(2): 243–77.

Miller, Jonathan. 2000. "Evaluating the Argentine Supreme Court under Presidents Alfonsín and Menem (1983–1999)." *Southwestern Journal of Law and Trade in the Americas* 7: 369–433.

Miller, Mark C., and Jeb Barnes. 2004. *Making Policy, Making Law: An Interbranch Perspective*. Washington, DC: Georgetown University Press.

Molinelli, N. Guillermo, M. Valeria Palanza, and Gisela Sin. 1999. *Congreso, Presidencia y Justicia en Argentina*. Buenos Aires: Temas Grupo Editorial SRL.

Monahan, Patrick. 1987. *Politics and the Constitution: The Charter, Federalism, and the Supreme Court of Canada*. Toronto: Carswell Legal Publications.

Montero, Alfred P. 2000. "Devolving Democracy? Political Decentralization and the New Brazilian Federalism." In Peter R. Kingstone and Timothy J. Power, eds., *Democratic Brazil: Actors, Institutions, and Processes*. Pittsburgh: University of Pittsburgh Press.

2005. *Brazilian Politics*. Cambridge: Polity Press.

Moreira Maués, Antonio G., and Anelice F. Belém Leitão. 2003. "Dimensões da judicialização da política no Brasil: as ADIns dos partidos políticos." In Fernando Facury Scarr, organizador. *Constitucionalizando Direitos: 15 anos da Constituição Brasileira de 1988*. Rio de Janeiro: Renovar.

Moustafa, Tamir. 2003. "Law versus the State: The Judicialization of Politics in Egypt." *Law and Social Inquiry* 28(4): 883–930.

2007. *The Struggle for Constitutional Power: Law, Politics, and Economic Development in Egypt*. New York: Cambridge University Press.

Negretto, Gabriel L. 2004. "Government Capacities and Policy Making by Decree in Latin America." *Comparative Political Studies* 37(5): 531–62.

Néri da Silveira, José. 1996. "O Supremo Tribunal Federal como Guardião dos Direitos Fundamentais." (STF Folheto).

Nino, Carlos Santiago. 1993. "On the Exercise of Judicial Review in Argentina." In Irwin P. Stotzky, ed., *Transition to Democracy in Latin America: The Role of the Judiciary*. Boulder: Westview Press.

1996. *Radical Evil on Trial*. New Haven: Yale University Press.

No Hay Derecho, Año 2, No. 5 (1991); Año 2, No. 6 (1992); Año 3, No. 7 (1992); Año 3, No. 8 (1992); Año 6, No. 10 (1993).

North, Douglass C. 1990. *Institutions, Institutional Change and Economic Performance*. New York: Cambridge University Press.

North, Douglass C., and Barry Weingast. 1989. "Constitutions and Commitment: The Evolution of Institutions Governing Public Choice in Seventeenth-Century England." *Journal of Economic History* 49: 803–32.

Nunes, Rodrigo. 2010. "Politics Without Insurance: Democratic Competition and Judicial Reform in Brazil." *Comparative Politics* 42(3): 313–31.

O'Brien, David M. 2007. "The Politics of Judicial Selection and Appointments in Japan and Ten South and Southeast Asian Countries." In Kate Malleson and Peter H. Russell, eds., *Appointing Judges in an Age of Judicial Power: Critical Perspectives from around the World*. Toronto: University of Toronto Press.

O'Donnell, Guillermo. 1994. "Delegative Democracy." *Journal of Democracy* 5(1): 55–68.

2001. "Democracy, Law, and Comparative Politics." *Studies in Comparative International Development* 36(1): 7–36.

2006. "On Informal Institutions, Once Again." In Gretchen Helmke and Steven Levitsky, eds., *Informal Institutions and Democracy: Lessons from Latin America*. Baltimore: Johns Hopkins University Press.

O'Donnell, Guillermo and Philippe C. Schmitter. 1986. *Transitions from Authoritarian Rule: Tentative Conclusions about Uncertain Democracies*. Baltimore: Johns Hopkins University Press.

O'Donnell, Guillermo, Philippe C. Schmitter, and Laurence Whitehead. 1986. *Transitions from Authoritarian Rule, Volume 2: Latin America*. Baltimore: Johns Hopkins University Press.

Olson, Mancur. 1993. "Dictatorship, Democracy, and Development." *American Political Science Review* 87: 567–76.

Ostberg, C. L. and Matthew E. Wetstein. 1998. "Dimensions of Attitudes Underlying Search and Seizure Decisions of the Supreme Court of Canada." *Canadian Journal of Political Science* 31: 767–87.

2002. "Attitudinal Dimensions of Supreme Court Decision Making in Canada: The Lamer Court, 1991–1995." *Political Research Quarterly* 55: 237–58.

2007. *Attitudinal Decision Making in the Supreme Court of Canada*. Vancouver: UCB Press.

Ostberg, C. L., Matthew E. Wetstein, Donald R. Songer, and Susan W. Johnson. 2009. "Ideological Consistency and Attitudinal Conflict: A Comparative Analysis of the U.S. and Canadian Supreme Courts." *Comparative Political Studies* 42 (6): 763–92.

Oteiza, Eduardo. 1994. *La Corte Suprema: Entre la Justicia sin Política y la Política sin Justicia*. Buenos Aires: Editora Platense/La Plata.

Oxhorn, Philip D. and Graciela Ducatenzeiler, eds. 1998. *What Kind of Democracy? What Kind of Market? Latin America in the Age of Neoliberalism*. State College: Pennsylvania State University Press.

Panizza, Francisco. 2003. "Política y Economía de Brasil Contemporáneo." In Vicente Palermo, ed., *Política Brasileña Contemporánea: de Collor a Lula en Años de Transformación*. Buenos Aires: Institute Di Tella/Siglo Veintiuno.

Parsons, Craig. 2007. *How to Map Arguments in Political Science*. New York: Oxford University Press.

Passos, Edilenice. 2002. *Doing Legal Research in Brazil*. Available on www.LLRX.com.

Peerenboom, Randall. 2002. *China's Long March toward Rule of Law*. New York: Cambridge University Press.

Pellet Lastra, Arturo. 2001. *Historia Política de la Corte 1930–1990*. Buenos Aires: Editorial Ad-Hoc S. R. L. Villela Editora.

2003b. "140 años en los laberintos de la historia de la Cote. Una historia complicada por la falta de conocimiento del rol político del alto tribunal y la tendencia de nombrar jueces 'adictos'." *Lexis Nexis Jurisprudencia Argentina*, 26 de noviembre (Número especial, "140 años de la Corte Suprema de Justicia de la Nación"), JA 2003-IV, fascículo n. 9: 43–8.

Pereira, Anthony W. 2000. "An Ugly Democracy: State Violence and the Rule of Law in Postauthoritarian Brazil." In Peter Kingstone and Timothy J. Power, eds., *Democratic Brazil: Actors, Institutions and Processes*. Pittsburgh: University of Pittsburgh Press.

2005. *Political (In)Justice, Authoritarianism and the Rule of Law in Brazil, Chile, and Argentina*. Pittsburgh: University of Pittsburgh Press.

Pérez-Liñán, Aníbal. 2011. "The Conditions for Effective Constitutional Adjudication: Lessons from Latin America." *Duquesne Law Review* 49(Spring): 133–44.

Pérez-Liñán, Aníbal, and Andrea Castagnola. 2009. "Presidential Control of High Courts in Latin America: A Long-term View (1904–2006)." *Journal of Politics in Latin America* 2: 87–114.

Pérez Perdomo, Rogelio. 2005. "Judicialization and Regime Transformation: The Venezuelan Supreme Court." In Rachel Sieder, Line Schjolden, and Alan Angell, eds., *The Judicialization of Politics in Latin America*. New York: Palgrave MacMillan.

Perry, Amanda. 2000. "Effective Legal Systems and Foreign Direct Investment: In Search of the Evidence." *International and Comparative Law Quarterly* 49(4): 779–99.

Pierson, Paul. 2000. "Increasing Returns, Path Dependence, and the Study of Politics." *American Political Science Review*. 94(2): 251–67.

Pollack, Mark A. 1997. "Delegation, Agency, and Agenda Setting in the European Community." *International Organization* 51(1): 99–134.

Popova, Maria. 2012. *Politicized Justice in Emerging Democracies: A Study of the Courts in Russia and Ukraine*. New York: Cambridge University Press.

Posner, Richard A. 1998. "Creating a Legal Framework for Economic Development." *World Bank Research Observer* 13: 1–11.

Porto Macedo Junior, Ronaldo. 1995. "A evolução institucional do Ministério Público." In Maria Teresa Sadek, ed., *Uma introdução ao Estudo da Justiça*. São Paulo: Editora Sumaré.

Power, Timothy J. 2000. "Political Institutions in Democratic Brazil: Politics as a Permanent Constitutional Convention." In Peter R. Kingstone and Timothy J.

Power, eds., *Democratic Brazil: Actors, Institutions, and Processes*. Pittsburgh: University of Pittsburgh Press.

Prillaman, William C. 2000. *The Judiciary and Democratic Decay in Latin America: Declining Confidence in the Rule of Law*. Westport: Praeger.

Pritchett, C. Herman. 1948. *The Roosevelt Court*. New York: Macmillan.

Putnam, Robert. 1993. *Making Democracy Work: Civic Traditions in Modern Italy*. Princeton: Princeton University Press.

Ramseyer, Mark. 1994. "The Puzzling (In)Dependence of Courts: A Comparative Approach." *Journal of Legal Studies* 23: 721–47.

Rebolledo, Juan and Frances McCall Rosenbluth. 2010. "Political Competition and Judicial Integrity: The Case of Mexico." Paper presented at the American Political Science Association Annual Meeting, Washington, DC, September 2–5.

Reich, Gary M. 1998. "The 1988 Constitution a Decade Later: Ugly Compromises Reconsidered." *Journal of Interamerican Studies and World Affairs* 40(4): 5–24.

Reinhart, Carmen M., and Miguel Savastano. 2003. "The Realities of Modern Hyperinflation." *Finance and Development* 40(2): 20–23.

Ribeiro de Oliveira, Marcelo. 2003. "A fiscalização abstrata da constitucionalidade de normas e o processo objetivo no STF: Uma análise da evolução do controle de constitucionalidade no Brasil e de sua atual estrutura processual." Dissertação de Mestrado na Área de Direito e Estado, Universidade de Brasília.

Richards, Mark J. and Herbert M. Kritzer. 2002. "Jurisprudential Regimes in Supreme Court Decision Making." *American Political Science Review* 96 (June): 305–20.

Ríos-Figueroa, Julio. 2003. "A Minimum Condition for the Judiciary to Become an Effective Power: The Mexican Supreme Court, 1994–2002." Paper presented at the Congress of the Latin American Studies Association, Dallas, TX, March 27–29.

2006. "Institutional Models of Judicial Independence and Corruption in Latin America." Ph.D. Dissertation, Department of Political Science, New York University.

Ríos-Figueroa, Julio and Matthew M. Taylor. 2006. "Institutional determinants of the judicialization of policy in Brazil and Mexico." *Journal of Latin American Studies* 38(4): 739–66.

Rocha, Jean Paul Veiga da. 2004. "A Capacidade Normativa de Conjuntura no Direito Econômico: O Déficit Democrático da Regulação Financeira." Tese da Faculdade de Direito da Universidade de São Paulo.

Rocha, Zélio Maia da and Vicente Paulo. 2003. *O Controle de Constitucionalidade nos Concursos Públicos*. Brasília: Vestcon.

Rodríguez-Garavito, César. 2011. "Beyond the Courtroom: The Impact of Judicial Activism on Social and Economic Rights in Latin America." *Texas Law Review* 89(7): 1669–98.

Rohde, David W. and Harold J. Spaeth. 1976. *Supreme Court Decision Making*. San Francisco: W. H. Freeman.

Rosenn, Keith S. 1984. "Brazil's Legal Culture: The Jeito Revisited." *Florida International Law Journal* I(1): 1–43.

1990a. "Brazil's New Constitution: An Exercise in Transient Constitutionalism for a Transitional Society." *The American Journal of Comparative Law* 38(4): 773–802.

1990b. "The Success of Constitutionalism in the United States and its Failure in Latin America: An Explanation." *University of Miami Inter-American Law Review* 22(1): 1–39.

2000. "Judicial Review in Brazil: Developments under the 1988 Constitution." *Southwestern Journal of Law and Trade in the Americas* 7(2): 291–319.

Russell, Peter H. 2007. "Conclusion." In Kate Malleson and Peter H. Russell, eds., *Appointing Judges in an Age of Judicial Power: Critical Perspectives from around the World*. Toronto: University of Toronto Press.

Sadek, Maria Teresa. 1995. "A Crise do Judiciário Vista pelos Juízes: Resultados da Pesquisa Quantitativa," in Maria Teresa Sadek, ed., *Uma introdução ao Estudo da Justiça*. São Paulo: Editora Sumaré.

1999. "O Poder Judiciário na Reforma do Estado." In Luiz Carlos Bresser Pereira, Jorge Wilheim, and Lourdes Sola, eds., *Sociedade e Estado em Transformação*. São Paulo: Editora UNESP.

Sadurski, Wojciech, ed. 2002. *Constitutional Justice, East and West: Democratic Legitimacy and Constitutional Courts in Post-Communist Europe in a Comparative Perspective*. The Hague: Kluwer Law International.

Sadurski, Wojciech. 2010. "Constitutional Courts and Constitutional Culture in Central and Eastern European Countries." In Alberto Febbrajo and Wojciech Sadurski, eds., *Central and Eastern Europe After Transition: Towards a New Socio-Legal Semantics*. Aldershot: Ashgate.

Samuels, David. 2003. "Fiscal Straitjacket: The Politics of Macroeconomic Reform in Brazil, 1995–2002." *Journal of Latin American Studies* 35: 545–69.

Santiago, Alfonso. 1994. "La Corte de los nueve (Principales fallos institucionales 1990–93)." *Anuario de Derecho de la Universidad Austral*.

1998. *La Corte Suprema y el control político*. Buenos Aires: Abaco.

Santiso, Carlos. 2001. "Democratic Governance and Insulated Economic Policy: The Challenges of Divided Governance in Argentina and Brazil." Paper presented at the VIth International Congress of CLAD on State and Local Administration Reform, Buenos Aires, November 5–9.

2004. "Economic Reform and Judicial Governance in Brazil: Balancing Independence with Accountability." In Siri Gloppen, Robert Gargarella, and Elin Skaar, eds., *Democratization and the Judiciary*. London: Frank Cass.

Savolainen, Jukka. 1994. "The Rationality of Drawing Big Conclusions Based on Small Samples: In Defense of Mill's Methods." *Social Forces* 72(4): 1217–24.

Scheppele, Kim Lane. 2003. "Constitutional Negotiations: Political Contexts of Judicial Activism in Post-Soviet Europe." *International Sociology* 18(1): 219–38.

Schiemann, John. 2001. "Explaining Hungary's Powerful Constitutional Court: A Bargaining Approach." *European Journal of Sociology* 42(2): 357–90.

Schubert, Glendon. 1965. *The Judicial Mind*. Evanston: Northwestern University Press.

Schwartz, Herman. 2002. "Path Dependence and Collective Action; or, the Long Road to Find Mechanisms." Paper presented at the UC Berkeley Center for German and European Studies, April 15.

2000. *The Struggle for Constitutional Justice in Post-Communist Europe*. Chicago: University of Chicago Press.

Scribner, Druscilla L. 2004. "Limiting Presidential Power: Supreme Court – Executive Relations in Argentina and Chile." Ph.D. Dissertation, Department of Political Science, University of California, San Diego.

Seawright, Jason. Forthcoming. *Party-System Collapse: The Roots of Crisis in Peru and Venezuela*. Palo Alto: Stanford University Press.

Segal, Jeffrey A., and Harold J. Spaeth. 1993. *The Supreme Court and the Attitudinal Model*. New York: Cambridge University Press.

1999. *Majority Rule or Minority Will: Adherence to Precedent on the U.S. Supreme Court*. New York: Cambridge University Press.

Sepúlveda Pertence, José Paulo. 2001. "O Controle de Constitucionalidade das Emendas Constitucionais pelo Supremo Tribunal Federal: Crônica de Jurisprudência." São Paulo: Max Limonad.

Shapiro, Martin M. 1981. *Courts: A Comparative and Political Analysis*. Chicago: University of Chicago Press.

Shapiro, Martin M., and Alec Stone Sweet. 1994. "The New Constitutional Politics of Europe." *Comparative Political Studies* 26(4): 397–421.

2002. *On Law, Politics, and Judicialization*. Oxford: Oxford University Press.

Sieder, Rachel, Line Schjolden, and Alan Angell, eds. 2005. *The Judicialization of Politics in Latin America*. New York: Palgrave.

Sikkink, Kathryn. 2005. "The Transnational Dimension of the Judicialization of Politics in Latin America." In Rachel Sieder, Line Schjolden, and Alan Angell, eds. 2005. *The Judicialization of Politics in Latin America*. New York: Palgrave.

Silverstein, Gordon. 2003. "Globalization and the Rule of Law: 'A Machine That Runs of Itself'?" *International Journal of Constitutional Law* 1(3): 427–45.

Simmons, Beth. 2009. *Mobilizing for Human Rights: International Law in Domestic Politics*. Cambridge: Cambridge University Press.

Skidmore, Thomas E. 1988. *The Politics of Military Rule in Brazil, 1964–85*. New York: Oxford University Press.

2000. "Forward: A New Test for Brazilian Democracy." In Peter R. Kingstone and Timothy J. Power, eds. 2000. *Democratic Brazil: Actors, Institutions, and Processes*. Pittsburgh: University of Pittsburgh Press.

Slaughter, Anne-Marie, Alec Stone Sweet, and Joseph Weiler. 1998. *The European Courts and National Courts: Doctrine and Jurisprudence*. Oxford: Hart Publishing.

Smith, Peter H. 1991. "Crisis and Democracy in Latin America." *World Politics* 43 (July): 608–34.

Smithey, Shannon I. and John Ishiyama. 2000. "Judicious Choices: Designing Courts in Post-Communist Politics." *Communist and Post-Communist Studies* 33(2): 163–82.

Smulovitz, Catalina. 1997. "The Discovery of Law: Political Consequences in the Argentine Case." Paper presented at the Conference, "New Challenges for the Rule of Law: Lawyers, Internationalization, and the Social Construction of Legal Rules," organized by the American Bar Foundation, Santa Barbara, CA, November 7–9, 1997.

2005. "Petitioning and Creating Rights: Judicialization in Argentina." In Rachel Sieder, Line Schjolden, and Alan Angell, eds., *The Judicialization of Politics in Latin America*. New York: Palgrave.

Smulovitz, Catalina and Enrique Peruzzotti. 2003. "Societal and Horizontal Controls: Two Cases of a Fruitful Relationship." In Scott Mainwaring and Christopher Welna, eds., *Democratic Accountability in Latin America*. Oxford: Oxford University Press.

Smyth, Regina, Anna Lowry, and Brandon Wilkening. 2007. "Engineering Victory: Institutional Reform, Informal Institutions, and the Formation of a Hegemonic Party in the Russian Federation." *Post-Soviet Affairs* 23(2): 118–37.

Souza, Celina. 1997. *Constitutional Engineering in Brazil: The Politics of Federalism and Decentralization*. New York: St. Martin's Press.

Souza Cruz, Álvaro Ricardo de, ed. 2003. *O Supremo Tribunal Federal Revisitado*. Belo Horizonte: Mandamentos Editora.

Souza Cruz, Álvaro Ricardo de. 2004. "Breve Histórico do Supremo Tribunal Federal e do Controle de Constitucionalidade Brasileiro." In José Adércio Leite Sampaio, ed., *Crises e Desafios da Constituição: Perspectivas Críticas da Teoria e das Prácticas Constitucionais Brasileiras*. Belo Horizonte: Del Rey.

Souza Júnior, Antonio Umberto de. 2004. *O Supremo Tribunal Federal e as Questões Políticas*. São Paulo: Sintese.

Spriggs II, James F. 1997. "Explaining Federal Bureaucratic Compliance with Supreme Court Opinions." *Political Research Quarterly* 50: 567–93.

Stark, David. 1994. "Path Dependence and Privatization Strategies in East Central Europe." In János Mátyás Kovács, ed., *Transition to Capitalism?: The Communist Legacy in Eastern Europe*. Edison, NJ: Transaction Publishers.

Stark, David, and Laszlo Bruszt. 1998. *Postsocialist Pathways: Transforming Politics and Property in East Central Europe*. New York: Cambridge University Press.

Staton, Jeffrey. 2002. "Judicial Activism and Public Authority Compliance: The Role of Public Support in the Mexican Separation-of-Powers System." Ph.D. Dissertation, Department of Political Science, Washington University.

2004. "Judicial Policy Implementation in Mexico City and Mérida." *Comparative Politics* 37(1): 41–60.

2006. "Constitutional Review and the Selective Promotion of Case Results." *American Journal of Political Science* 50(1): 98–112.

2010. *Judicial Power and Strategic Communication in Mexico*. New York: Cambridge University Press.

Staton, Jeffrey and Georg Vanberg. 2008. "The Value of Vagueness: Delegation, Defiance, and Judicial Opinions." *American Journal of Political Science* 52(3): 504–19.

Stepan, Alfred. 1989. *Democratizing Brazil: Problems of Transition and Consolidation*. New York: Oxford University Press.

Stokes, Susan C. 2001. *Mandates and Democracy: Neoliberalism by Surprise in Latin America*. New York: Cambridge University Press.

Stone, Geoffrey R. 2010. "Understanding Supreme Court Confirmations." In Dennis J. Hutchinson, David A. Strauss, and Geoffrey R. Stone, eds., *The Supreme Court Review*. Chicago: University of Chicago Press.

Stone Sweet, Alec. 1999. "Judicialization and the Construction of Governance." *Comparative Political Studies* 32(2): 147–184.

2000. *Governing with Judges: Constitutional Politics in Europe*. Oxford: Oxford University Press.

2002. "Constitutional Courts and Parliamentary Democracy." *Western European Politics* 25(1): 77–100.

Stras, David R. 2008. "Understanding the New Politics of Judicial Appointments." *Texas Law Review* 86: 1033–78.

Sunstein, Cass. 1993. "Against Positive Rights." *East European Constitutional Review* 2: 35–8.

Tamanaha, Brian. 1996. "The Internal/External Distinction and the Notion of a 'Practice' in Legal Theory and Sociolegal Studies." *Law and Society Review* 30(1): 163–204.

Tate, C. Neal, and Torbjörn Vallinder, eds. 1995. *The Global Expansion of Judicial Power*. New York: New York University Press.

Taylor, Matthew. 2004a. "Activating Judges: Courts, Institutional Structure, and the Judicialization of Policy Reform in Brazil, 1988–2002." Doctoral Dissertation, Department of Government, Georgetown University.

2004b. Veto and Voice in the Brazilian Judiciary: Strong Courts, Institutional Frameworks, and Policy Change. Paper presented at the Southern Political Science Association Annual Meeting, New Orleans, LA, January 8–10.

2006. "Courts, Policy Contestation and the Legitimation of Economic Reform under Cardoso." In Lourdes Sola and Laurence Whitehead, eds., *Statecraft and Monetary Authority: Democracy and Financial Order in Brazil*. Oxford: Centre for Brazilian Studies.

2008. *Judging Policy: Courts and Policy Reform in Democratic Brazil*. Stanford: Stanford University Press.

Teixeira, Ariosto Alberto Paz. 1997. "A Judicialização da Política no Brasil (1990–1996)." Tese do Mestrado em Ciência Política, Universidade de Brasília.

Thelen, Kathleen. 1999. "Historical Institutionalism in Comparative Politics." *American Review of Political Science* 2: 369–404.

Trochev, Alexei. 2004. "Less Democracy, More Courts: A Puzzle of Judicial Review in Russia." *Law and Society Review* 38(3): 513–38.

2008. *Judging Russia: Constitutional Court in Russian Politics 1990–2006*. New York: Cambridge University Press.

Trubeck, David, and Alvaro Santos, eds. 2006. *The New Law and Economic Development*. New York and Cambridge: Cambridge University Press.

Ungar, Mark. 2002. *Elusive Reform: Democracy and the Rule of Law in Latin America*. Boulder: Lynne Rienner Publishers.

Uprimny, Rodrigo. 2004. "The Constitutional Court and Control of Presidential Extraordinary Powers in Colombia." In Siri Gloppen, Roberto Gargarella, and Elin Skaar, eds., *Democratization and the Judiciary: The Accountability Function of Courts in New Democracies*. London: Frank Cass Publishers.

Vanberg, Georg. 1998. "Abstract Judicial Review: Legislative Bargaining and Policy Compromise." *Journal of Theoretical Politics* 10: 299–346.

2001. "Legislative-Judicial Relations: A Game Theoretic Approach to Constitutional Review." *American Journal of Political Science* 45: 346–61.

2005. *The Politics of Constitutional Review in Germany*. Cambridge: Cambridge University Press.

Verbitsky, Horacio. 1993. *Hacer la Corte*. Buenos Aires: Planeta.

Vidal Luna, Francisco, and Herbert S. Klein. 2006. *Brazil Since 1980*. Cambridge: Cambridge University Press.

Vilhena Vieira, Oscar. 1999. *A Constituição e Sua Reserva de Justiça*. São Paulo: Malheiros Editores.

2002. *Supremo Tribunal Federal: Jurisprudência Política*. São Paulo: Malheiros Editores.

Viotti da Costa, Emilia. 2001. *O Supremo Tribunal Federal e a Construção da Cidadania*. São Paulo: IEJE (Instituto de Estudos Jurídicos e Econômicos).

Voeten, Eric. 2007. "The Politics of International Judicial Appointments: Evidence from the European Court of Human Rights." *International Organization* 61: 669–701.

VonDoepp, Peter, and Rachel Ellett. 2011. "Reworking Strategic Models of Executive-Judicial Relations: Insights from New African Democracies." *Comparative Politics* 43(2): 147–65.

Wasby, Stephen L. 1970. *The Impact of the United States Supreme Court: Some Perspectives*. Homewood: The Dorsey Press.

Weber, Max (Guenther Roth and Claus Wittich, eds). 1978. *Economy and Society: An Outline of Interpretive Sociology*. Berkeley: University of California Press.

Wechsler, Herbert. 1959. "Toward Neutral Principles of Constitutional Law." *Harvard Law Review* 73(1): 1–35.

Weingast, Barry. 1993. "Constitutions as Governance Structures: The Political Foundations of Secure Markets." *Journal of Institutional and Theoretical Economics* 149: 286–311.

Werneck Vianna, Luiz, et al. 1999. *A Judicialização Da Política e Das Relações Sociais No Brasil*. Rio de Janeiro: Editora Revan.

Weyland, Kurt. 1996. *Democracy Without Equity: Failures of Reform in Brazil*. Pittsburgh: University of Pittsburgh Press.

2000. "The Brazilian State in the New Democracy." In Peter R. Kingstone and Timothy J. Power, eds., *Democratic Brazil: Actors, Institutions, and Processes*. Pittsburgh: University of Pittsburgh Press.

2002. *The Politics of Market Reform in Fragile Democracies: Argentina, Brazil, Peru, and Venezuela*. Princeton: Princeton University Press.

Whittington, Keith. 2000. "Once More Unto the Breach: Post-Behavioral Approaches to Judicial Politics." *Law and Social Inquiry* 25: 601–32.

2005. "Interpose Your Friendly Hand: Political Supports for the Exercise of Judicial Review by the United States Supreme Court." *American Political Science Review*. 99(4): 583–96.

Williamson, Oliver E. 1994. *The Institutions and Governance of Economic Development and Reform*. Working Paper, University of California at Berkeley.

Wilson, Bruce M. 2005. "Changing Dynamics: The Political Impact of Costa Rica's Constitutional Court." In Rachel Sieder, Line Schjolden, and Alan Angell, eds., *The Judicialization of Politics in Latin America*. New York: Palgrave.

Wilson, Bruce M., and Juan C. Rodríguez Cordero. 2006. "Legal Opportunity Structures and Social Movements: The Effects of Institutional Change on Costa Rican Politics." *Comparative Political Studies* 39(3): 325–51.

Wittes, Benjamin. 2006. *Confirmation Wars: Preserving Independent Courts in Angry Times*. Lanham, MD: Rowman and Littlefield.

Zakaria, Fareed. 1997. "The Rise of Illiberal Democracy." *Foreign Affairs* 76(6): 22–43.

2003. *The Future of Freedom: Illiberal Democracy at Home and Abroad*. New York: W. W. Norton.

Zaverucha, Jorge. 1998. "1988 Brazilian Constitution and Its Authoritarian Legacy: Formalizing Democracy While Gutting its Essence." *The Journal of Third World Studies* 15(1): 105–24.

Index